D1356435

# DEATH IN WAR AND PEACE

# DEATH IN WAR AND PEACE

## LOSS AND GRIEF IN ENGLAND, 1914–1970

PAT JALLAND

OXFORD
UNIVERSITY PRESS

# OXFORD
**UNIVERSITY PRESS**

Great Clarendon Street, Oxford OX2 6DP

Oxford University Press is a department of the University of Oxford.
It furthers the University's objective of excellence in research, scholarship,
and education by publishing worldwide in

Oxford New York

Auckland Cape Town Dar es Salaam Hong Kong Karachi
Kuala Lumpur Madrid Melbourne Mexico City Nairobi
New Delhi Shanghai Taipei Toronto

With offices in

Argentina Austria Brazil Chile Czech Republic France Greece
Guatemala Hungary Italy Japan Poland Portugal Singapore
South Korea Switzerland Thailand Turkey Ukraine Vietnam

Oxford is a registered trade mark of Oxford University Press
in the UK and in certain other countries

Published in the United States
by Oxford University Press Inc., New York

British Library Cataloguing in Publication Data

Data available

Library of Congress Control Number.

Data available

Typeset by SPI Publisher Services, Pondicherry, India
Printed in Great Britain
on acid-free paper by
MPG Books Group, Bodmin and King's Lynn

ISBN 978-0-19-926551-0

1 3 5 7 9 10 8 6 4 2

# In Memoriam

In memory of Harry Darbyshire, RN, my uncle lost at sea in 1942 when his ship the *Matabele* was torpedoed on the Russian convoy route. In later years, our mother, Esther, never spoke of Harry's death to my sister Alison and I, though she loved him dearly. There was no body to bury or grave to visit—only silence.

# Acknowledgements

I am grateful to the Australian Research Council for a three-year Discovery Grant which provided funding for this project, including my three essential research visits to British libraries. I am deeply indebted to my two research assistants in England, Geraint Hughes and Jo Workman, for their outstanding contribution. My thanks go also to Laurie Dennett, Russell Doust, and Karen Fox for their valuable assistance in later stages of the project. Karen Smith did a wonderful job in converting my manuscript drafts into electronic form, with remarkable speed and accuracy.

I owe a particular debt of gratitude to generous friends and colleagues who read chapters of my book and offered wise advice and encouragement: Graeme Davison, John Hooper, Ken Inglis, and Di Langmore. Barry Smith again deserves a special word of thanks for helpful comments on the entire book. Many other friends, colleagues and students have also provided valuable suggestions and ideas: Geoffrey Bolton, Mac Boot, Barbara Caine, Joy Damousi, Ingereth Macfarlane, Melanie Nolan, Peter Read, Pat Thane, Jay Winter, and my colleagues in History, RSSS.

I am most grateful to Colin Harris, Superintendant, Special Collections Reading Rooms at the Bodleian Library and Roderick Suddaby, Keeper of the Department of Documents at the Imperial War Museum, for their generous advice and practical assistance in contacting copyright holders, and to the staff of all the libraries and archives who facilitated my research. I also warmly thank the helpful staff at Oxford University Press: Christopher Wheeler, Stephanie Ireland, Seth Cayley, Matthew Cotton, Kate Hind, Rowena Anketell, and also Ruth Parr for her encouragement at an earlier stage of the project.

Permissions for quotations from their manuscript collections have been kindly granted by the Bodleian Library, the University of Oxford (Bickersteth and Violet Milner Papers); the Imperial War Museum (Papers of Miss M. E. Allan, Capt. W. H. Bloor, Mrs A. D. Deacon, the Furniaux family, Mrs B. M. Holbrook, Capt. H. J. C. Leland, Ft. Lieut C. Mitchell); the British

Library (Papers of Sir Sydney Cockerell and Phyllis Bottome). I thank the following copyright owners for permission to publish: Mr David Allan (Miss M. E. Allan); the Rt Revd John Bickersteth KCVO (Bickersteth Papers); Mrs A. D. Deacon MBE; Mr John Bailey (the Furniaux family papers); Mrs B. M. Holbrook; Mr Tom Leland (Capt. H. J. C. Leland); Lord Hardinge of Penshurst (Violet Lady Milner); the Warwickshire County Record Office and the Feilding family (Feilding of Newnham Paddox Correspondence). I offer my apologies to any copyright owners I have been unable to contact.

# Contents

# List of Plates

# Introduction

Death and bereavement come to us all, and the loss of those we love is often the most challenging experience of our lives. The meanings of our mortality are culturally conditioned, determined by a highly complex and changing social history. Cultural norms relating to death and bereavement in England have shifted dramatically over the past hundred years, shaped powerfully by the decline of religion, the major impact of the two world wars, and the medical revolution since the 1930s. There was a gradual change from a dominant Christian culture of acceptance of death and more open expression of grief in the mid-nineteenth century to a culture of avoidance and reticence a century later, when fear of death and divine judgement no longer dominated people's thoughts. In the twentieth century hell had effectively been banished by the churches, people were likely to live to old age and their babies were expected to survive. The fall in mortality from infectious diseases and the rise in life expectancy marked a sharp divide between the two centuries. Understanding death and bereavement in England is further complicated because it must always be mediated by the variables of class, gender, and region.

Historian Julie Rugg has recently observed that the experience of death in England in the twentieth century appears to be a historical record of silence, with 'a taboo on the subject of mortality'. Rugg and sociologist Tony Walter have called for a detailed history of death in England since 1914.[1] My book responds to this challenge by exploring the ways in which these silences surrounding death were created and reinforced in England from the Great War to the 1960s, looking closely at the complex interactions between the experiences of war and peace. After the Great War there was a half-century of relative silence about death both in cultural terms and in the historiography of death itself. By contrast, there has been a plethora of scholarly work by social scientists on death and bereavement over the last thirty years, as illustrated by the wealth of valuable contributions to the journal *Mortality*. This introduction will provide the historical context and an exploration of the major forces of change driving the twentieth-century transformation in ways of death and grieving.

## Victorian Ways of Death: Religion, Class, and Gender

To understand the history of death and bereavement in England in the half-century or so since 1914 its development in the previous century must first be explored, especially given the powerful reaction against Victorian ways of death after the Great War. There was a deep chasm between the cultural norms relating to death and loss in 1851 and in 1951. My earlier book, *Death in the Victorian Family*, argued that religion still played a powerful part in the lives and deaths of most middle- and upper-class Victorians, as well as many respectable working-class people. Half the population of England and Wales still attended church in 1851. From the late eighteenth century the Evangelical movement, with its ideals of piety, discipline, and duty, had strengthened Protestantism in England, reaching the peak of its influence by the 1860s. Evangelicalism revived the medieval ideal of the 'good Christian death' which required piety, spiritual preparation, and fortitude in the face of suffering. But the good death also demanded a Christian home and supportive family, as well as the advantages of wealth, space, and time. The Romantic movement in literature and art partly coincided with the Evangelical revival, and reinforced its appeal to the emotions.[2]

In the nineteenth century Christian faith influenced attitudes to dying and the rituals and consolations available in mourning. Christianity gave families a model of acceptance of death as the will of God and offered some hope of immortality, even family reunions in heaven. It allowed individuals to express sorrow in overtly emotional terms, using the familiar language of the Bible, the prayer book, and popular hymns, which permeated the vernacular in ways unimaginable today. Children learned to regard death as an inevitable part of life, often conditioned to do so by the deaths of siblings and by family discussions of Bible stories.

The Victorian way of death was also characterized by a significant gendered division of labour which operated in death as in life, for all classes. Women have traditionally been more active than men in the care of the dying and in performing the rituals which facilitated the process of grieving. Nurses at the deathbed were usually women because the care of the sick and dying was perceived as a natural part of women's nurturing role. Women also attended to the vital rituals following a death, including the laying-out of the corpse and the viewing of the body which permitted family, friends, and neighbours to farewell the loved one. A common thread across the classes in Victorian culture was the assumption that women experienced the emotions of loss more acutely and would demonstrate those feelings more openly, while observing the social constraints of customary rituals. Women would also take a larger role in remembering the dead: they often reminisced about their lost loved one with other women, kept precious mementoes such as hair and mourning jewellery, and communed with their dead at the cemetery and at home. Such rituals could cross class boundaries and need not be expensive.

The men organized the funeral, a vitally important ritual, especially for the comfortable classes who could afford more elaborate ceremonies and memorials. Women were often excluded from funerals on the assumption that men could better control their emotions, with few words and no tears. The extravagance of Victorian funerals has been overstated by later commentators; indeed the Victorians themselves began to reform excesses and simplify funerals in the second half of the century. While widows dressed in black and followed ritualized etiquette in secluded mourning for many months, widowers were encouraged to seek distraction in employment. Second marriages for widowers were common, whereas the prospects of remarriage for widows were almost negligible, especially after 40.

Expression of grief was powerfully mediated by culture, varying according to class as well as gender, region, and religion. In a fine book, *Death, Grief and Poverty in Britain, 1870–1914*, Julie-Marie Strange has reconstructed a diverse working-class culture of grief, often expressed through silences and symbolic rituals rather than overt emotion and formal language. Poverty, high mortality rates, and overcrowded living conditions did not foster indifference and insensitivity to loss so much as a necessary resignation and pragmatism in managing their emotions. Grief might be inarticulate but it was nonetheless usually genuine. The working classes were familiar with death, encountering it too often. On the deaths of children, distraught mothers might conceal intense grief, showing little 'open, verbal, physical and sentimental affection'. Families shared their living spaces with the dying and the dead; and they needed to keep corpses in their homes for days in order to perform the last rites, which were essential to show their affection and respect. Care of the corpse, viewing the dead, dignified funerals, and communal wakes were part of a vital working-class culture which lasted until the 1940s in some communities in the north and Celtic fringe and in rural areas.[3]

By its very nature the good Christian death was denied to unbelievers. Their numbers increased from the mid-nineteenth century, influenced by the challenges of Darwinian evolutionary theory, biblical criticism, and geological discoveries. There was also a shift in sensibilities amongst advanced thinkers by the late nineteenth century. Thomas Huxley recognized in 1893 that, as an agnostic, his unusual views on religion and death separated him from many of his peers when facing bereavement, 'for me there is neither certainty of faith nor any consolation'.[4] Unbelievers lost the use of the Christian language of consolation which drew on the words of the Bible and well-known hymns: their condolence letters tended to be short and terse, focusing on sympathy, the virtues of time, and praise of the deceased.

From the 1870s there was a decline in Evangelical fervour, and church attendance ceased to keep pace with population growth, though religion remained powerful among the respectable classes. Jose Harris suggests that 'the predominant religion of the late nineteenth century was an undogmatic "social" Christianity, which probably embraced more people and certainly was more publicly influential than the intense private conviction of the evangelical age'.[5] The doctrines of hell and judgement were slowly eroded from the 1850s; the popular view of heaven became increasingly a happy home where earthly families would be reunited. Boyd Hilton notes that 'As Hell ceased to be a fiery furnace, Heaven became a cosy fireside where long-lost loved ones congregated'.[6] The slow process of secularization, far from complete even today, inevitably altered the meanings and significance of death.

Whereas religious faith was a dominant force in the history of death and loss in the nineteenth century, after 1914 it became instead one of several important variables, which also included class and region. Religious influence continues today, albeit in a minor key, despite warnings that Christianity would collapse in the face of secularization. The Christian religion played a diffuse but pervasive role in responses to death and

bereavement up to the 1960s. Though most people were indifferent to
institutionalized religion in England by 1950, most continued to believe in
God and about half had faith in some kind of afterlife. Medical sociologist
David Clark argues that folk religion which draws on a rich mixture of
unofficial beliefs, orthodox church faith, superstition, and magic has
survived well into the twentieth century. Even institutional religion held
its own more powerfully than critics suggest until the 1960s, particularly
the Church of England.[7]

# Mortality and Medicine:
# The Demography of Death

Demographic change played a fundamental role in the twentieth-century
history of death and bereavement—a role as significant as that of religion
in the nineteenth century, and of war and the medical revolution in the
twentieth century. English people living in the twentieth century could
choose to try to ignore death, on the assumption that they would survive
to old age. In the previous century, by contrast, death was omnipresent
because life was often short and tough, and deaths of babies and children
were all too common. The nineteenth-century demographic pattern was
characterized by a short life expectancy and by high mortality, especially
of infants and young children. Preoccupation with the manner and
meaning of death was understandable in those sad circumstances, and
even necessary for social cohesion and some peace of mind. From the
sixteenth century to 1871, English life expectancy at birth varied between
about 30 and 40 years; this increased from 41 years to over 60 years between
1871 and 1930.[8]

The population of Great Britain almost doubled from 20.8 million in
1851 to 40.8 million in 1911; it then rose more slowly to 54 million by 1971,
but increased little thereafter. Up to about 1920 the chief explanation for
rapid population growth was a sharp decline in mortality. Thereafter the
fall in birth rates was the major determinant: the average number of live
births fell from 4.3 in the 1890s to 2 in the 1930s, with families of more
than six increasingly rare.[9] Thus a dramatic new demographic pattern,
starting about 1870, had a powerful impact on the history of death and loss
in the century which followed. It was marked by a continuous decline in
mortality and increased life expectancy. The death rate in England and

Wales fell from 21.8 per thousand per year in 1868 to 14.8 in 1908 and 11.7
in 1928. This decline affected different age cohorts in stages. Mortality of
children aged between 1 and 15 fell steadily from the 1870s, followed by
that of younger adults a decade or so later. Babies and children in their
first year, and adults over 45, only benefited after 1900 from a continuous
decline in their death rates. Infant mortality in England and Wales fell
from 154 per thousand live births in 1900 to 75 in 1925, 30 in 1950, and 8
by 1990.[10]

Experts in demography and epidemiology have hotly contested the
causes of the steep decline in the death rate from the 1870s, especially the
reasons for the fall in intestinal diseases and infectious diseases such as
tuberculosis, whooping cough, and scarlet fever. Thomas McKeown and
Jay Winter have argued that medical advances were not primarily responsible, emphasizing instead improvements in nutrition, sanitation, and
rising standards of living.[11] Roy Porter stressed the value of the public
health movement in changing the urban environment, especially water
supplies and sewage systems. Most historians agree that a complex inter-
play of forces contributed in varying degrees to the decline in mortality;
and that the role of medical therapy was restricted before the 1930s, with
notable exceptions such as the introduction of immunization against
typhoid in 1897.[12]

Medical therapy began to have a direct impact on the decline in
mortality with the introduction of the sulphonamide drugs in 1935 and the
more important development of the 'miracle drug', penicillin, during the
Second World War. As Anne Hardy observes, penicillin 'opened a new
era in modern medicine in which the power of the doctor to cure reached
previously undreamed of heights'. It was highly effective against a broad
spectrum of bacterial infections, including pneumonia, meningitis, diphtheria, and syphilis, and was mass-produced from 1943. It also ensured that
the rates of maternal mortality continued to fall after 1945. The therapeutic revolution of the 1950s brought a range of new drugs, including
cortisone, valuable for allergies, meningitis, and multiple sclerosis; and
vaccines for diseases such as mumps, polio, and measles. New therapies
became more widely accessible in England through the newly established
National Health Service.[13]

Once doctors came to believe that they could cure most diseases, the
loss of a patient represented failure, and death became a topic to be avoided
or evaded. Moreover, as medical science and modern technology progressed,

terminal illnesses and death increasingly moved from home to hospitals, where intervention was possible to prolong life. Thus death was removed from the control of the family at home to that of doctors in sterile institutions concerned with technical efficiency to maximize life. Inevitably the medicalization and hospitalization of death reinforced the growing culture of death avoidance.

Popular expectations of modern medicine may have been raised too high in the 1950s and 1960s. The pace of innovation slowed thereafter.[14] It became clear in the later twentieth century that several major killers continued to be largely incurable, notably cancer, heart disease, and the chronic degenerative diseases. From the 1950s, infectious diseases were increasingly displaced by degenerative diseases as the major causes of death. By the late 1980s, nine out of ten deaths in England were caused by cancer, heart disease, and stroke, as many more people survived to suffer the diseases of old age.[15] Death is increasingly concentrated among the elderly; life expectancy at birth in 2005 was 75 for men and 80 for women, compared with 44 and 47 respectively in 1900. People are prone to suffer longer periods of disability, senility, and frailty in the final months or years before death.[16]

Modern biomedicine and advanced medical technology carried rich rewards, but their limitations were revealed as time passed: public confidence declined and criticism increased. Prolonging life artificially could threaten the dignity of the dying and raised new ethical questions. Doctors were sometimes accused of unwanted interventions to keep people alive, placing their urge to maintain life over the needs of terminal patients for dignified deaths. Chapters 9 and 12 address some of these issues, exploring also the contrasting responses of the palliative care movement and the euthanasia campaign to the advances of modern medicine.

## The Two World Wars and Their Effects

The two world wars had a profound and cumulative impact on the prolonged process of change in death attitudes and practices in England in the fifty years from 1914. The numbers of war dead and the nature of their deaths were horrific and the communal grief overwhelming. The patterns of change from 1918 were very complex, even aside from the two world wars, because of significant variations in attitudes, customs, and behaviour relating to death across class, region, gender, and religion. But the two world wars seriously complicated an already changing history of civilian deaths in peacetime. As the Great War commenced in 1914, the decline in Christian faith and the fall in mortality from infectious diseases were already generating changes in responses to death. But the war forced another major shift. Just as people were becoming accustomed to the survival of babies to adulthood, they suddenly had to face the mass deaths by violence of young adults, whereby children died before their parents, a complete reversal of the natural order.

In a brilliant essay published nearly thirty years ago, David Cannadine argued that death was not privatized and denied in the 1920s, but was all-pervasive. Indeed, interwar England was so obsessed by death and the cult of the dead, 'in the face of bereavement at once so harrowing, so unnatural and so widespread', that the churches and conventional mourning rituals were unable to cope. Victorian death practices seemed both inadequate and inappropriate, especially in the absence of bodies to bury. Instead, collective sorrow was directed during the 1920s towards new, inventive national memorials to commemorate the dead heroes who sacrificed their lives for their country.[17]

While this remarkable national project of commemoration held huge popular appeal and comforted many, it came at some private cost. Traditional mourning rituals for civilians had declined during the war, and became more attenuated thereafter. The national commemoration of heroic young soldiers on such a grand scale overshadowed and limited public compassion for the ordinary deaths of individual civilians in peacetime. Even the 200,000 victims of the influenza pandemic of 1918–19 received little of the attention reserved for the war heroes, partly because emotions were already blunted by the war: this foreshadowed the silences surrounding individual peacetime deaths. In the interwar years there were no more prolonged and ritualized deathbed scenes—care of the dying slowly began to move from the home to the hospital, undertakers started to displace female family members in managing the corpse and the funeral, and bereavement rituals declined in length, fervour, and consolation.

The landscape of civilian deaths was confused and fragmented in the interwar years, with different regions and classes changing their ways of death and grieving at widely varying rates, as we shall see in Chapter 4. In the north of England, the midlands, and the Celtic fringe, and in rural areas, there were strong continuities with the working-class culture of death and loss described by Julie-Marie Strange for the period before 1914. Older traditions were often surprisingly resilient, particularly among female mourners, though they were on a slow path of retreat by 1939. Working-class resistance to the modern concept of cremation continued until the 1950s and beyond. Moreover, throughout the twentieth century the economically depressed areas had far higher death rates than the more prosperous regions. The north-west, even by 1961, still suffered an infant mortality rate 37 per cent higher than in East Anglia; and even by 1998 the north and its cities still had death rates far higher than the rural areas and the south.[18]

Ruth Richardson has suggested the value of interpreting the changing ways of death 'in a loose generational context', despite the difficulty for historians in documenting the concept of 'generation change' in detail. She suggests that 'social, geographical and generational factors operate culturally upon children's early understanding of death and grief, effecting long-term generational changes in society's attitudes towards death'.[19] This is a helpful insight into the complexity of the changing responses to death and loss caused by the two world wars. The interwar generation grew up in a bleak atmosphere of economic depression and mass mourning for the soldiers of the Great War, whose photographs on mantelpieces were reminders of the often silent suffering of bereaved relatives. Sociologist Tony Walter adds that ex-servicemen themselves often chose to forget the horrors of the Great War, if they could, and preferred not to tell their families about them:

This sets up a pattern in families in which stress by women as well as by men, is coped with by not talking about it...Children in the inter-war period typically had parents who chose to remain silent about wartime experience and who bore the depression of the 1930s with quiet stoicism; these children were then required to fight in the Second World War, confirming the necessity for courageous silence. They brought up their own children, my generation, with little reference to the past and with few stories of deceased family members, least of all stories of those who died traumatically.[20]

During the Second World War the defence forces again provided the stoical model for the country to follow, as they had in the earlier war. As George MacDonald Fraser noted after fighting in the war in Burma, 'The celebrated stiff upper lip, the resolve to conceal emotion which is not only embarrassing and useless, but harmful, is just plain common sense'.[21]

Civilians showed their willingness to follow the example of the armed forces in their responses to Churchill's call for courage and stoicism during the German air blitz on British cities. The dark side of the Blitz story was suppressed or sanitized to sustain morale in the interests of survival. The government encouraged civilians not to dwell on the fatalities and the intense distress of individual bereaved people in wartime. The *Manchester Guardian* in 1945 regretted the massive price paid for victory, in 'the suffering of those who bear these losses silently within their families'.[22] Indeed, mass bereavement in one sense devalued the grief of individuals.

The Second World War marked a deeper break with the past than the Great War. The change in cultural norms affecting death and grief was more intense, widespread, and long-lasting from the 1940s. Open and expressive sorrow was more strongly discouraged in favour of a pervasive model of suppressed privatized grieving which became deeply entrenched in the nation's social psychology. The cultural prescription which privileged stoicism in the face of loss had long affected upper-middle-class men, soldiers in wartime, the unskilled working classes, and the poor. But in the twenty years after 1945 it spread more broadly, as it was internalized across much of the English community.

After 1945 suppressed grieving became a cultural norm. The Second World War, even more than the first, had reduced the gendered differences in response to grief, so marked in the nineteenth century, whereby men were more inclined to contain feelings and women to express them. The wars made emotional restraint the customary code for all, regardless of gender, and thus affected women more deeply than men. The gender gap was reduced as women internalized their sorrow, and moved closer to a traditionally male pattern of grieving. They understood during the war that it was self-indulgent 'to spread one's own sorrows' when thousands of others were suffering in silence. Many women had internalized wartime prescriptions about the appropriate way to deal with grief: 'you must hide your feelings: you do your mourning quietly, alone. The same as you might do praying'.[23] This shift in female patterns of grieving made a major contribution to the culture of silence about death and loss that was so pervasive after 1945: it helps to explain why the silence and embarrassment about death and loss was so prolonged and deep-rooted.

As late as 1963 social anthropologist Geoffrey Gorer was so concerned about the community's wish to avoid the subjects of death and loss that he undertook an extensive social investigation, published two years later as

*Death, Grief and Mourning in Contemporary Britain.* Gorer stated that half the deaths in his sample of 359 bereaved people took place in hospital, and out of these three-quarters died alone, instead of at home with their families. Traditional funeral and mourning rituals had been attenuated or abandoned since 1918, depriving the bereaved of vital support and encouraging them to hide their sorrow. Gorer argued that many people internalized society's stoical prescription of acceptable behaviour, 'and deny their feelings of mourning to themselves, as well as in public, and fight against giving them any expression'. Gorer concluded that this situation could be costly in 'misery, loneliness, despair and maladaptive behaviour'.[24] I will evaluate Gorer's important survey and its conclusions, and place it in its historical context, in Chapter 11.

Many social analysts have recognized the culture of avoidance of death in England and in western society, from the 1940s. English writer Philip Toynbee was convinced in the mid-1960s that there was a fundamental refusal in English society 'to face the fact of death at all'. Psychiatrist John Hinton regretted in 1967 that since the 1940s people had not been prepared to face their own death, so they avoided dying people and the subject of mortality. German philosopher Norbert Elias argued in 1982 that advanced western societies tended to conceal the 'unwelcome' idea of death: he saw this as one aspect of a broader shift in emotional history whereby many people repressed strong emotions like grief in public and sometimes in private.[25] My book provides a detailed historical study of English experiences of these profound social and cultural changes relating to death and bereavement in the fifty years after 1914. These silences linger still in this twenty-first century, despite a cultural shift since the 1970s which has placed new emphasis on emotional expressiveness amongst some segments of English society.

# PART
# I

# War and Peace
## 1914–1939

# I

# Death, the Great War, and the Influenza Pandemic

This book begins with the First World War—with soldiers' experiences and responses to mass deaths by violence, to the individual brutal deaths of countless comrades, and to the imminent prospect of their own deaths. This war created the context for death for the next half-century. Psychiatrists such as Beverley Raphael have written of the 'macho' warrior identity of western men who experienced two world wars: the military culture and the cult of manliness required that soldiers behave 'like a man', however terrible their wartime experiences, repressing emotions and coping in silence.[1] However, their instinctive responses to the hideous deaths of comrades and the ever-present fear of being blown to bits were also to some extent culturally prescribed, conditioned by their class, education, upbringing, religion, and personality. The war was seen by most soldiers as a necessary war to save Britain from domination by an autocratic Germany. The war also shaped perspectives on civilian deaths, as seen in British responses to the 1918–19 influenza pandemic. Despite a death toll of over two hundred thousand in England and Wales, the memory of the killer epidemic was almost totally eclipsed by that of the war.

## Death and the Loss of Friends, 1914–1916

Most men joined up for military service and did their duty out of a mixture of motives: these included patriotism, honour, and deference to authority, which all had more influence then than now. Honour and duty were words used frequently in correspondence and diaries across all classes.

The strong recruitment response from the working classes in the early years of the war was also explained by the appeal of steady paid work over a tough life at home. Patriotism and loyalty to their own town or region were also powerful forces in recruiting the so-called 'Pals battalions' of men who knew each other at home or were closely linked. Many were working-class 'pals' from the cotton factories of Manchester or the mines of the north or the midlands: indeed, a quarter of all miners enlisted.[2] For many in the Pals battalions patriotism merged with loyalty to comrades, which sustained morale through group solidarity and shared identity.

There was an added element for the upper-middle-class boys from the English public schools who formed the backbone of the officer class in the early years of the war. These boys imbibed public school traditions of self-sacrifice and chivalry as well as loyalty, courage, and selfless patriotism. The public schools taught a 'muscular Christianity' which sought to mould a boy's character through 'godliness and good learning'. They drew upon the medieval code of chivalry reinforced by nineteenth-century Romanticism, elevating a combination of honour, duty, robust masculinity, and manly games. Such ideals reached a far wider audience than the privileged elite, through the popularity of novels and boys' magazines about the public schools, reinforced by boy's clubs and the Boy Scouts.[3]

This public school ethos promoted war as a way to express the essence of masculinity: Charles Carrington was one of many eager to volunteer in 1914 'to demonstrate my manliness'. Self-sacrifice in war was likewise valorized as a necessary expression of duty, honour, masculinity, and patriotism. Heroic death in battle was glorified as a form of knightly valour—an integral part of the Edwardian public school code. Death in a just war was grim but it was also magnificent—and patriotic. It was easier to conceptualize war in such terms after nearly a century of peace.[4] The influential aristocratic group known as the Souls wrote fervently about the beauty of death, but several of their children were killed in the war in horrific ways that fell far short of the pre-war ideal. One of them, Julian Grenfell, died from wounds at the disastrous second battle of Ypres in April 1915. He described the battle in a deathbed letter to his mother as 'wonderful and glorious', though his men were almost wiped out and his skull was cracked: 'but I'm getting on splendidly. I did awfully well'. He died a hero, following two operations.[5] Such chivalric beliefs encouraged men to 'do one's bit' but ill-prepared them for the savage reality of death in the Great War, which destroyed many boyhood illusions.

Jay Winter has estimated the total number of British servicemen killed in the Great War at 722,785 or close to three-quarters of a million; Gary Sheffield puts it at 744,702. The middle and upper classes took a disproportionate share of the casualties, in part because a higher proportion were junior officers who enlisted early in the war. Time served, as well as rank, influenced casualty rates. Most working-class men served as privates, whereas the majority of the middle and upper classes were officers. Winter also observes that British servicemen only had a one in two chance of surviving the war without being killed, wounded, or taken prisoner: one in eight was killed. Thus many of Kitchener's army of 1914 were wiped out by 1916, including numerous Pals, so that officers were increasingly recruited from the ranks.[6]

For most soldiers the idealized public school view of death in war as 'wonderful and glorious' could not survive the terrible reality of artillery bombardments beyond 1915. The elevated rhetoric continued in use at home, however, especially in commemorating the dead, consoling the bereaved, and softening the horror. Almost three-quarters of wounds in the Great War were shell wounds, which often turned septic. Lord Moran described how artillery shelling induced numbing fear: men were usually prepared for a quick, clean death 'but that shattering, crudely bloody end by a big shell was too much for them. All their plans for meeting death with decency and credit were suddenly battered down. Self-respect had gone out of their hands'.[7] The *Manchester Guardian* brought this reality home to its readers in March 1915 with a detailed report of a wounded officer's experiences at the battle of Neuve Chapelle. The officer described vividly the intoxication of the charge which wounded him and killed many others, as he took his men out of their trenches and over the top:

Thank goodness, in an action like this, you kind of lose your senses. You cease to be your normal self. A kind of elevation above all ordinary feelings comes over you; you feel you are rushing through the air; you become intoxicated with fear and excitement. There is so much to frighten you that you cease to be afraid. There is no time to think of anything, except when you halt under cover—then your senses gradually come back. That is why all infantry attacks should be carried through with one over-whelming rush.[8]

The small British offensive at Neuve Chapelle in 1915 was one of many failed attempts to achieve an early breakthrough on the Western Front, which had degenerated into a prolonged war of attrition. By this time it was clear that artillery bombardment in trench warfare resulted in many more severe wounds and far higher mortality from shell and shrapnel than open fighting.[9]

The military culture and the demands of war assumed that soldiers would not be affected by the constant threat of their own deaths, the shocking deaths of their comrades, and by orders to kill other men. Joanna Bourke's 1999 book, *An Intimate History of Killing*, suggests that fear of dying, not fear of killing, was the most debilitating emotion for soldiers, sustained by warrior myths and the need to do their job of killing on the battlefield.[10] For many soldiers the only way to cope was by suppressing their emotions of grief or terror, allowing them to behave 'like a man', coping in silence and shutting out gruesome memories. Those soldiers whose work was affected by ongoing distress, fear, or depression were likely to be viewed as personally inadequate, not 'man enough'.[11]

Soldiers rapidly became aware of their own mortality with the growing death toll, as at the second battle of Ypres in April 1915 and at Loos in September 1915. Bursting shells and overwhelming noise brought mental as well as physical anguish. Many men lost control as the vibrations of explosions and the dreadful noise affected their nerves, leaving them feeling powerless and utterly exhausted. Some whimpered and others collapsed. When soldiers went over the top in 1915 and 1916, enemy machine guns didn't have to aim, merely to fire into the advancing men to cause horrific casualties.[12] Fear of being killed must often have been agonizing as men waited to go over the top, knowing they were totally exposed and vulnerable. Each man fought his terror alone, but for most, fear of cowardice and betraying comrades triumphed over the selfish dread of personal death. Sergeant Major P. B. Roderick of the Royal Welsh Fusiliers wrote on 20 July 1916:

Waiting to attack is like what waiting for the hangman to come and do his job must be. Everyone is eager to get going, for the uncertainty of being launched into eternity or of coming back in pieces is not comforting in these tense moments.[13]

Fear was not discussed with comrades, and loyalty to the unit and the regiment was a powerful force in overcoming it. A working-class guardsman in the fourth Battalion Grenadier Guards commented on an artillery bombardment in December 1915: 'You see the boys come along crying like children and shaking like old men. Still the shells burst in the air and

skatter [*sic*] death and destruction'. He concluded that 'it [is] better to be a
Dead Hero than [a] living coward'.[14] For most soldiers fear was forgotten
as they went over the top into utter confusion and overwhelming noise.
There are few clear accounts of combat, as normal emotions were numbed.
The chances of being killed in a particular day's battle were under 30 per
cent, usually much less, but random death could slay anyone.[15]

Just as artillery bombardment focused the mind on the prospect of
death, so also did the ever-present decaying corpses. Lieutenant R. G.
Dixon described their impact in 1917. He grew accustomed to the sights
of dead bodies but not to the 'all-pervading stench' of decaying remains,
mingled with high explosive fumes, which hung over miles of Belgian
countryside:

All around us lay the dead, both friend and foe, half in, half out of the water-
logged shell-holes...Their rotting faces stared blindly at us from coverlets of
mud; their decaying buttocks heaved themselves obscenely from the filth with
which the shell-bursts had smothered them. Skulls grinned at us; all around
stank unbelievably. These corpses were never buried, for it was impossible to
retrieve them. They had lain, many of them, for weeks and months; they would
lie and rot and disintegrate foully into the mud....Horror was everywhere, but
one became inured to it in time and somewhat callous.

In retrospect Dixon thought the war affected his sensibilities, 'made
me indifferent about death. Not callous, but so used to it that it stirred
no emotions'.[16] And yet he was sufficiently moved to write vividly
about it.

Trooper W. Clarke of the First Cavalry Brigade, a working-class man,
also described becoming hardened by the regularity of death and the
sheer mass of corpses. His emotional responses became blunted. He
remembered in particular the many dead soldiers who could not be
decently buried after the battle of Loos in September 1915: 'Seeing so
many corpses around became just another sight...Your feelings only
came to the fore when it was a special mate who had been killed'.[17] Frederick Manning wrote that the dead were quiet and still, like wooden
dummies: 'One sees such things and one suffers vicariously with the inali-
enable sympathy of man for man...The mind is averted as well as the
eyes'. Yet they must each move on, 'gambling on the implicit assurance'
of their own immortality.[18]

However soldiers rationalized it, the sight of a recently dead corpse,
especially from their own unit, was likely to trigger intimations of

mortality in many men. Such dreadful sights could desensitize and
harden responses, and individuals reacted differently according to age,
upbringing, sensibility, and years served. Siegfried Sassoon described his
attempt in April 1917 to help a 23-year-old new recruit become accustomed to the unpleasant sight of men killed during the Arras offensive,
mostly shot in the head. Sassoon took the recruit for a walk round the
battlefield, where they saw many of 'yesterday's dead' lying in front of
the trench. Young Casson tried to behave as if his first sight of the horrors
of war was quite ordinary, but Sassoon wrote, 'I was thinking to myself
that sensitive people like Casson ought not to be taken to battle-fields'.
Sassoon had grown accustomed to such sights, but he suddenly appreciated their likely impact on new recruits, and felt that he had shown
Casson 'something obscene' during an evening walk. The new recruit
was killed soon afterwards.[19]

It was necessary for soldiers to try to harden themselves to such sights
to survive, if they could. Apparent indifference was a vital form of self-
defence, to sustain morale and keep fear at bay. They rationalized their
responses to putrefying corpses and men blown to bits, in many ways.
Sassoon acted as if every day might be his last.[20] Others told themselves
that even death was preferable to life in the trenches. Lieutenant H. C. L.
Heywood wrote in his journal at Gallipoli in May 1915: 'Death with its
sense of peace and rest would not seem half as bad as the spectacle of the
hideous battle of life against death'.[21] They all had to try to distance themselves from these constant reminders of their own mortality, by living in
the present, preoccupied with their daily tribulations. They must not
allow themselves to think, as they saw their next corpse, that it could be
their turn next. But the impact of the common stress of such sights was
cumulative, and was constantly reinforced: ultimately it could contribute
to shell shock for some unfortunates.

Above all, most men's defences could not survive the deaths of their
closest friends. The trauma of such a loss was vastly greater if their friend
was blown to bits, died on the barbed wire of no-man's-land, or just went
missing. In such circumstances it was much harder to accept the reality of
death. Men would often risk their own lives to bring back the bodies of
their friends from no-man's-land. They also went to great trouble to bury
comrades with as much reverence and respect as circumstances allowed.
As we shall see later, the loss of close friends contributed to psychological
stress and breakdown.

## Religion and Spirituality in the Trenches

Some soldiers sought comfort in faith on the loss of comrades, but religion only aided a minority. Christianity was challenged from the 1860s by the combined impact of biblical criticism, evolutionary theory, and working-class disillusionment with the churches. The urban working classes had long ago deserted most churches (except for the Catholic Church), especially in the north, and many poor had never really belonged. By 1920 60 per cent of English people were nominally Anglican, 15 per cent Free Church, and 5 per cent Roman Catholic—the Anglicans stronger in the south and the others in the north.[22] Possibly 50 per cent of the population had no meaningful religious affiliation, especially the unskilled urban working classes in the north. Of perhaps greater concern to the churches between 1900 and 1920 was the decline in Christian faith among their core congregation, the middle classes, as many moved towards agnosticism.[23]

Alan Wilkinson observed with insight that 'The war revealed the extent of the alienation of the majority of the English male population from the life and practice of the Churches—it revealed it, it deepened it, but it certainly did not create it'. Bishop H. H. Henson noted after the war that 'organized Christianity does not come well out of the world crisis'.[24] There was no religious revival during the war, and many clergy later regretted the misplaced early bellicosity of some of their colleagues, anxious to join in the patriotic fervour.

Bishop E. S. Talbot chaired a committee of inquiry into 'The Army and Religion', which published a report in 1919, drawing on nearly three hundred responses from many churches. The report concluded that the working classes had been falling away since the Industrial Revolution, but that 'many soldiers were in some measure Christian without knowing it'. Most soldiers who had been killed 'had little use for the church' but they were not godless and Christ claimed them in death. As Talbot observed, 'The soldier has got religion, I am not sure he has got Christianity'. Faith in life after death was also widespread but there was little understanding of its nature, while hell and judgement were largely overlooked. During the war many soldiers prayed to God but felt reluctant to do this in an institutional setting. A major stumbling block was their difficulty in reconciling a loving God with the indiscriminate suffering of the Great War. Fatalism and folk religion made more sense to them than Christianity.[25]

Talbot's inquiry concluded that Church of England Evangelical chaplains were often upper-middle-class men who were puritanical fundamentalists: they were unable to cope with working-class culture and soldiers' complex experiences of daily life in the trenches. Alan Wilkinson noted the challenges for Anglican chaplains at the front in offering plausible explanations and consolation for mass deaths. Their ministry to the dying could be inconsistent and unconvincing, even capitulating to popular demands for public prayers for the dead. Consequently doctrines of immortality were adapted to allow that soldiers who sacrificed their lives in the patriotic cause must go to heaven, regardless of belief or penitence. The concept of the redemptive sacrifice of Christ was extended to include the war dead, as part of the popular language of consolation.[26]

The Talbot inquiry also found that the Church of England lacked the necessary sacramental rituals to enable soldiers to cope adequately with the deaths of comrades and the horrors of the war. The Church of England had no authorized ritual for sacramental confession and absolution before a battle, and no adequate ritual for commendation of the dying and extreme unction. By contrast, Roman Catholic chaplains could offer all these comforting rituals to soldiers on the front line. As Wilkinson observed:

In situations that are totally new and bewildering, rituals can supply boundaries and signposts, so reducing the sense of chaotic novelty; through the familiar rituals a sense of solidarity is established with both 'normal' life beyond the emergency, and with previous generations. Rituals can 'contain' feelings too overwhelming or perplexing to be otherwise expressed. The calm exercise by a priest of his role can give a parent-like as well as a professional reassurance of order, love, and meaning in an otherwise chaotic and unbearable existence.[27]

The experience and observations of Julian Bickersteth, a chaplain at the Front, reinforce Bishop Talbot's conclusions about the failings of the Church of England. Bickersteth was a devout Anglo-Catholic clergyman who cared deeply about the soldiers' spiritual welfare, looked after the wounded, and buried many dead during the battle of the Somme. He was convinced that most ordinary soldiers were indifferent to religion, which rarely touched either their hearts or minds: 'I don't believe 90 per cent of the men out here think twice a day about what or who they will meet on the other side, if death comes their way'. They tried to banish such thoughts with the hope they would be lucky. Commanding officers overlooked their spiritual responsibility and discouraged chaplains from discussing death with soldiers, 'as likely to undermine the morale or at least the cheerfulness of the men'.[28]

As Bishop Talbot observed, soldiers had found some sort of folk religion, but it was not necessarily Christianity, though Christian habits of thought and behaviour survived informally. More pervasive were examples of superstitions, folk rituals, and supernatural beliefs which helped soldiers to make some sense of the terrifying experiences of trench warfare. Moreover the familiar language of the Bible and popular hymns was used to describe the psychic phenomena and folkloric superstitions of the war. Many soldiers combined a nebulous faith in God with a belief in the paranormal, including miracles on the battlefields—such as the angelic figures which appeared to British soldiers at Mons in September 1914. As Jay Winter has explained,

Apocalyptic legends marked the first two years of the war. As the casualty lists lengthened and the war dragged on, the realm of the supernatural was dominated more by ghostly apparitions than by divine or demonic ones...The dead were literally everywhere on the Western Front, and their invasion of the dreams and thoughts of the living was an inevitable outcome of trench warfare.[29]

The bizarre and frightening world of the Western Front almost inevitably encouraged visions of dead comrades and tales of spiritualist phenomena. An unknown soldier, identifiable only as 'Horace' from Leicester, wrote a condolence letter in October 1918 to his dead friend's mother, Mrs Brown, telling her how he and his comrades felt the nearness of the spirits of the dead: 'On our marches, and at the evening rest, we felt that those who had gone were still with us, though we heard their names no more at roll-call'.[30] Soldiers, poets, and artists depicted the Front as hell on earth, nurtured by the horrific landscape and the constant presence of the bodies of the dead among the living.

Spiritualism helped some servicemen to make sense out of chaos and loss, while the support of soldiers gave spiritualism greater authenticity for those at home. The spiritualist movement was a popular alternative source of consolation because it encouraged belief in the possibility of communication with the spirits of the dead through mediums. The movement had spread from the United States to Britain in the 1850s and 1860s, facilitated by seances conducted by mediums and by table-tapping at private 'home circles'. It was often informal, sometimes fraudulent, and concentrated in the north of England. A more serious academic approach was taken from 1882 by the Society for Psychical Research, led by Cambridge scientists and philosophers such as Henry Sidgwick and F. W. H. Myers. Their aim was to authenticate the scientific validity of the phenomena produced by mediums, though some members were agnostics who still yearned for faith. Before 1914 its popular following was limited, despite increasing numbers of affiliated spiritualist societies.

Unorthodox spiritual responses were stimulated by the Great War, challenging soldiers and grieving families to develop alternative responses to violent mass deaths when traditional religions seemed inadequate. The spiritualist movement gained mass appeal during the war: the number of its affiliated societies doubled between 1913 and 1919, reaching a peak in the 1930s with about a quarter of a million members.[31] Its wartime popularity was greatly enhanced by the public conversion and advocacy of two celebrities, Sir Oliver Lodge and Sir Arthur Conan Doyle. On losing his son, Conan Doyle became a full-time evangelist, convinced that spiritualism could be reconciled with belief in Christ. Spiritualism had a more secular appeal to Oliver Lodge, a physicist and leader of the Society for Psychical Research. His book *Raymond*, published in 1916, became a bestseller with immense attraction to other grieving parents, who found special consolation in the belief that the dead themselves wanted to contact the living. The book offered an elaborate exploration of Raymond's supposed life in the spirit world of 'Summerland', which mirrored worldly life to a remarkable degree; but it also attempted a scientific analysis of psychical phenomena. Scientists, Anglicans, and Roman Catholics variously refuted its claims. Both the secular and the religious forms of spiritualism flourished during the war and in the 1920s, as thousands confronted mass deaths and sought to contact the fallen.[32] Spiritualism provided an outlet for intense sorrow and offered an assurance that the dead of the Great War lived on.

Jay Winter concluded that during the war 'millions needed all the help they could get. Should we really be surprised that the magical and mythical realm flared up at a time of mass death and destruction?' The enduring appeal of spiritualism in the Great War was due to the universality of loss and bereavement; its force declined when many mourners at last came to terms with their prolonged grief. The appeal of spiritualism declined in the 1930s and it had far less support during and after the Second World War.[33]

## Emotional Casualties of Attritional Campaigns, 1916–1918

It is scarcely surprising that there were so many psychological casualties of the Great War, since many men lacked the capacity to endure prolonged artillery bombardment and the loss of so many comrades. A diagnosis of shell shock or 'neurasthenia' was one extreme along an extended path of emotional anguish, as stress levels increased with years of front-line service. Many officers noted at one time or another that their nerves 'went to pieces', especially during the prolonged attritional campaigns of the Somme and Ypres. Some cracked suddenly, sometimes after seeing a close friend killed brutally, having previously exercised intense self-control: finally fear became overpowering and the mind seemed to snap. Military authorities in the earlier years of the war interpreted 'shell shock' as feigned illness and labelled the victims malingerers. But attitudes began to change as the numbers of sufferers increased and it was realized that officers were disproportionately affected. By 1916 40 per cent of casualties in combat zones were attributed to neurasthenia. A substantial proportion of these were experienced officers of high social class who could not be accused of cowardice.[34] Wilfred Owen's poem, 'Mental Cases', goes to the heart of this traumatic experience, especially as he himself was a victim:

> These are men whose minds the Dead have ravished.
> Memory fingers in their hair of murders,
> Multitudinous murders they once witnessed.
> Wading sloughs of flesh these helpless wander,
> Treading blood from lungs that had loved laughter.
> Always they must see these things and hear them,
> Batter of guns and shatter of flying muscles,
> Carnage incomparable and human squander,
> Rucked too thick for these men's extrication.[35]

Captain W. H. Bloor of the Field Artillery was killed by a shell-burst in January 1918. His diary for September 1917 revealed his clear understanding of the widespread terror of such a death, but he was even more afraid of shell shock: 'To lose one's nerve must be the very *worst* hell there can be for a soldier in this enlightened 20th century. We have a case in the battery now, and I only hope I am blown to shreds first'.

During the Somme campaign he understood that artillery was the main killer of the war:

It is well known that 95 out of each hundred men are hit by shell fire...The horror and the misery and countless tragedies of this war—even the little of it that I have seen—are much too awful to let the mind dwell upon, and I am surprised that more men do not go mad with the horror of it.[36]

Even the toughest soldier could become 'a nervous wreck' during the appalling attritional campaigns of 1916 to 1918. Charles Carrington was a vicar's son, aged 17 when he took a junior officer's commission. His memoir reveals that he initially saw war as an adventure, and leadership 'a duty and a delight... I was very happy. This was Life'. Even his experience of the fighting on the Somme in 1916 with its 'world-shaking bombardments' did not unduly discourage him, despite its enormous casualties. By Christmas 1916, however, Carrington was not the man he had been earlier: he was 'a nervous wreck' as 'the shell-fire began to tell on me', reinforced by the trauma of battle. But he was one of the survivors, with the emotional and physical resources to overcome his terror of shellfire. He was partly sustained through the increasing hardships by *esprit de corps*: all the terrors could be endured if the men bore them together and pride made a man 'endure what his comrades endured'.[37]

Carrington returned from a long leave in September 1917, hating the war, but longing to rejoin his regiment at the awful campaign of the third battle of Ypres. He was filled with foreboding as he rejoined his men, fearing that he was doomed to die or be crushed by the military machine. He admitted that 'I never could stand shell-fire', which made him neurotic and forced him to make imaginary bargains with fate. But as they went into battle on 3 October 1917 at Broodseinde he noted, 'there is no more thought or feeling, no more fear or doubt' and his brain cleared despite the endless blast of sound. This day was the most wretched of his life. The artillery noise made him more anxious than ever. Four officers and eighty-one other ranks from his battalion were killed and he received a Military Cross for bravery, which he claimed was undeserved. But worst of all, his beloved servant, Stanley, was killed by a bullet which left a ghastly hole in his face:

I am dumbfounded with rage and horror. They have got Stanley, best of friends and loyallest of servants...Stanley is dead, Stanley who gave me confidence in myself...It was Stanley that never left my mind...He had been a part of my life for eighteen months...I began to realise how much was lost to me.[38]

Such comradeship and affection across the classes between master and servant was not uncommon in the Great War.[39] Following that searing experience Carrington's war ended with long leave in reserve positions.

Captain H. J. C. Leland was a staff officer for musketry in the South Staffordshire Regiment. His letters home to his wife give a vivid picture of the cumulative impact of successive deaths of comrades. He noted on 11 December 1916, 'Muck, mud, misery and melancholy reign supreme, and a pitiless bombardment adds to the general discomfort'. Many friends were killed in January 1917, causing him to consider his own possible death. His anxiety about the state of his nerves was justified and by 2 April 1917 he was hospitalized with 'a collapse'. The death of a beloved friend at the second battle of Bullecourt on 6 May left him 'horribly depressed and brooding on the dark side of the war'. They were surrounded by death so completely 'that one has grown in to such a state, that nothing seems to affect us as it should. We are always mourning someone lately'. By 14 May, few of his original battalion were left.[40]

Throughout the second half of 1917 the tragedy of the third battle of Ypres left Leland constantly 'terrified that my nerve will go'. The final stage of the campaign for Passchendaele village in October 1917 was 'real HELL' for Leland: 'Death seems to be barking at me every moment. I don't suppose anyone has gone further through the mill than I have these last four days'. The guns roared continuously even through the night, leaving him 'muddled' if he was too close. His mental state was aggravated because his servant and his groom had both been in the trenches too long and their 'nerves have gone absolutely'. On 9 October 1917 at the disastrous battle of Poelcappelle the heavy rain caused men to struggle in knee–deep mud in terrible conditions. A shell killed three more of his friends—'the loss is serious'—and he was feeling the remnants of dysentery contracted in West Africa. Again he was terrified that his nerve would go: 'the strain is intense at times'.[41]

Late in October 1917 Leland sent his wife some 'horribly sad' letters: 'All my friends have gone. I want to come home. It is cowardly to talk like this, but I do feel so rotten'. He wondered if they would ever share old age together, and if he would ever see his babies in their little green coats. He never wanted to endure another ten days like the last. It was no use pretending that he was not losing his nerve, as the Germans were 'bombing the place to pieces'. On 22 October he told her: 'My heart is very sore tonight. What remains of the Staffs [Staffordshire Regiment] have gone up tonight...Death and glory I suppose they call it. All my friends gone, not a soul to go to even for a chat'.[42]

By 26 October 1917 Leland admitted to his wife that he definitely had shell shock: 'I have lost all I knew and have become absolutely callous'. All he wanted now was to return home, as he felt rotten, sleepless, and affected by tear gas. He could no longer tolerate any noise and had developed a violent temper. On 31 October he observed, 'this was Super Hell', with 120 men dead and 210 wounded, though he predicted that these grim casualty statistics would never be published. He wondered what God thought of the war. He was now dwelling on the dead intensely in a way he had not done earlier, and he recited the names of many dead men known to his wife.[43] We are reminded of a line of Wilfred Owen's poem, 'Mental Cases': 'These are men whose minds the Dead have ravished'.[44]

By 1 November 1917 Leland's only remaining comfort was in writing letters to his wife, 'a conversation with no answers'. He could not sleep and if he did sleep he experienced awful dreams. He had recovered neither from the gas shell nor the explosive shell that had dropped on their billet. Three weeks later he was resting in the officer's hospital, with pain across his body and frightful headaches. He felt 'disgusted with myself' for succumbing to shell shock, even though a specialist insisted that he was actually very sick indeed; 'it is not my fault. I have fought against it for a long time'. The doctors said he must go to England for a month of complete rest away from the guns, at the Special Hospital for Officers for shock and nerve cases in Kensington. He was 'so sorry this has happened' especially as he had stuck it out as long as he could. On 8 December 1917 Mrs Leland received a letter from the hospital, advising that her husband had a breakdown in France due to stress of overwork: he was mentally confused and utterly exhausted, but they hoped he would improve steadily.[45] Alternatively he might have joined the 65,000 soldiers in mental hospitals by 1929.[46]

## The Losses of War in Retrospect

Psychiatrists suggest that the shocking impact of multiple deaths of comrades in war can lead to an 'imprint of death', locking men into the death encounter, impairing mourning and subsequent civilian life. This was Captain Leland's experience, as we saw, and we have no way of knowing if he recovered after his breakdown. Many soldiers used suppression of emotion as a defence mechanism in war, with varying effects. In extreme cases this repression could cause prolonged numbing after the war, leading to a lack of trust in life and feelings, especially if returned soldiers were expected to be unaffected by the war.[47]

The poet Charles Sorley had died in 1915, early in the war, but he had seen enough to know that 'It is easy to be dead... Their blind eyes see not your tears flow'.[48] It could be harder for the survivors, who had to live with grief, guilt, and terrible memories. Adrian Gregory estimates that about three million veterans survived who had direct experience of the horrors of front-line fighting:

Every frontline soldier experienced loss, the loss of comrades who were often intensely bonded with those who survived. The combination of this loss, often horrific and witnessed at close range, with the more general effects of surviving the 'carnival of death' (memories of living with the dead, memories of the fear of death, close escapes from death, memories of killing) produced a complex experience of bereavement, possibly even more intense than the loss of a close relative.[49]

The responses of the veterans to the deaths of their friends in the war were probably as complicated and ambivalent as their feelings about the war itself. They knew too much to accept the simple ritualized rhetoric of commemoration in the 1920s. Many wanted to forget and sought refuge after the war in marriage and domesticity, getting on with the job of living. Most seem to have spoken and written little of their wartime experiences. For some, haunting memories of lost friends and terrible battles resurfaced in recurrent nightmares or in later life, sometimes prompting them to write memoirs of their experiences. Those memories scarred the lives of the emotional casualties of war who spent years in special hospitals.

Charles Carrington noted in 1929 that the 'secret army' of young ex-soldiers in the 1920s seemed to present to the world 'a front of silence and bitterness'; they were a generation apart, reluctant to speak of their experiences. But even in the dark days of 1917, the soldiers were not disillusioned but just 'fed up': there was no hint of the mutinies which afflicted other armies. They had not chosen the war but, however dreadful, they intended to see it through to the finish. If there was disillusionment, it came after the war, not during it. Life seemed pointless to many former soldiers, especially those who were disabled physically or emotionally:

they had known nothing but war and civilians had little comprehension of their experiences.[50]

It is challenging for readers today to see the Great War through the eyes of the soldiers who fought its battles. Over the years contradictory revisionist views of the war have captured the popular imagination through influential books and popular film and television exposure. My focus on death and dying, grief and loss, might seem to reinforce the perception of the war as futile, because it must revisit the more horrific aspects of a terrible war with huge casualties. But it was no comfort to the innumerable mourners to be told their loved one died for nothing in a meaningless war. And it is therefore important to understand how the war's purpose was perceived at the time.

Disillusionment was fuelled for some people in the later 1920s because the war failed to offer the promised land fit for heroes in the interwar years: instead prolonged depression, high unemployment, and industrial unrest suggested that the war had not changed the world for the better, but the reverse. The so-called Anti-War Books written from 1929 by disillusioned veterans, such as Siegfried Sassoon, fuelled this view. Popular notions of the futility of the Great War were further shaped in the 1960s by the revival of the anti-war sentiments of the 1930s against a new backdrop of profound fear of an all-out nuclear war. The visual images of unimaginable horror in the popular television series of 1964, *The Great War*, confirmed the dominant view that the dead died in vain. Paul Fussell's influential book, *The Great War and Modern Memory*, published in 1975, was widely hailed as a classic, ensuring long-term acceptance of the unmitigated futility view of the war, 'fought for no cause'.[51]

In the last ten years, however, historians have strongly challenged the popular perception of the First World War as futile and meaningless. Gary Sheffield, Brian Bond, and other military historians have produced thoroughly researched revisionist history which offers a multidimensional and more balanced view of the war as tragic rather than futile, as wasteful but essential. Their fundamental point is that the war was necessary and, in the end, successful, against the greatest army in the world at the time. The war had to be fought by Britain to maintain the balance of power in Europe and prevent an autocratic Germany dominating Europe. The war had to be a total war, fought to the end, because the aims of the two sides could not be reconciled.[52]

Lieutenant R. G. Dixon wrote an unpublished retrospective memoir in the early 1970s, recalling his service as a subaltern through the 'appalling nightmare' of the Ypres campaign, and the final British victory in 1918 which brought him great satisfaction. He had tried to avoid emotional involvement to survive, but the individual deaths of friends hurt intensely. He believed that such a war changed young men and matured them beyond their years, setting them apart from those who had not endured war and failed to understand their suffering: 'For such experiences alter a man's attitude to life and death and towards his fellows. They change a man's values permanently'. He experienced survivor guilt and still wondered why he was spared. His own experiences of the Great War 'spoiled me, blunted my sensibilities and coarsened my reactions'. It was common in the 1970s to question the purpose of the Great War and portray it as a colossal waste. But, despite his own suffering, Dixon was convinced that it had been necessary to fight both world wars: servicemen and women had a 'filthy job' that had to be done.[53]

## The Influenza Pandemic of 1918–1919: 'the 'flu was rapidly relegated to obscurity'

Alice Reid observed in 2005 that the global death toll from the influenza pandemic in 1918–19 was estimated to be at least twice that of the Great War: 'Yet while the war has been held responsible for the creation of a "lost generation", the 'flu was rapidly relegated to obscurity'.[54] Patterson and Pyle in 1991 reached a conservative estimate of about thirty million influenza deaths globally, but more recent revisions have raised that mortality figure to over fifty million.[55]

The pandemic crossed the world in about six months and was ranked second to the Black Death in the history of epidemic disease. It attacked in three waves; the first in spring 1918 was relatively mild, but the second wave was far more lethal and virulent. It was first reported in Brest, and covered much of Europe in weeks, carried by troop movements, railways, and ships. By the end of January 1919 it had crossed the globe: 'it was probably the most truly pandemic disease in the history of the world at that time'.[56] The second wave was so frightening because of its speed, its virulence, and its huge death toll. Up to 30 per cent of the population experienced symptoms. It was also more threatening because it was often accompanied by pneumonia, against which medicine still had no defence. It had a disproportionate impact on young adults aged between 20 and 40—an additional blow to the generation already severely depleted by the war. Moreover medical science was helpless in fighting flu in 1918—the virus was not identified until 1933. The third wave of influenza in the early months of 1919 was mild by comparison—the damage was already done.[57]

The estimated deaths in England and Wales from the pandemic were over two hundred thousand or 4.9 per thousand of the population, just under the European average.[58] This compares with estimates varying between 560,000 and 577,000 for the total war dead from England and Wales.[59] The *Manchester Guardian* retrospectively placed much of the blame for the virulence of the 1918—19 outbreaks on the war, noting that the three epidemics were believed to have originated in the army, which was 'a huge and mobile force containing masses of men who had come from unhealthy climates'.[60] Certainly the impact of the Great War explained the virulence of the epidemic and England's weak response. The resources and the efforts of the government and the nation were focused at the time of the pandemic on the final stages of a grim war. Britain's hospitals were already heavily engaged with military casualties and about half the doctors and nurses were committed to war service; the war thus severely restricted resources available to fight the pandemic. It is perhaps understandable that the government and military leaders determined that the nation's duty was to carry on as normal in wartime, despite the influenza epidemic.

But the measures needed to fight a lethal war were not appropriate to counter disease. Sandra Tomkins has suggested that the medical profession in Britain bore its share of the blame for the death toll from the influenza epidemic: it was more advanced in public health than many other countries, yet paradoxically its efforts to respond to a virulent epidemic were less effective than elsewhere. British doctors and public health administrators were too confident of the power of the bacteriological revolution and unwilling to admit that existing medical knowledge could not contain the disease. Instead, they deprecated its virulence and played a passive role, even advising people to ignore the epidemic, warning that fear itself could invite infection. The *Manchester Guardian* in December 1918 passed on the medical advice that 'terror is the big ally of influenza'.[61] Admittedly there were severe limits to the efficacy of public responses, when medicine had no cure and no really effective treatment. However, more might have been done to offer symptomatic relief and improve ancillary services, such as home nursing and emergency hospitals, as was done in North America.

Also more effort might have been devoted to emergency burial services. Undertakers could not cope with the mortality rate in the second wave so that bodies were often left in people's houses for days or weeks, adding to the existing health hazards. The Local Government Board gave no advice, leaving local authorities to find manpower and resources as best they could. Birmingham made more effort than most, in late November 1919, following over one thousand deaths in the previous fortnight. The heavy death toll and the manpower shortage placed so much strain on the undertakers and the gravediggers that the city authorities intervened. In many cases corpses remained in private houses, sometimes in the rooms occupied by the living relatives. The Lord Mayor secured additional labour from military authorities and other sources, and organized transfer of bodies from homes to temporary repositories, pending burial.[62]

The Great War almost completely overshadowed the influenza pandemic, despite the unprecedented loss of life from the flu. Subsequently the memory of the killer epidemic was subsumed in that of the war. J. Whyte, a lieutenant in the King's Liverpool Regiment, was one of the countless soldiers killed by influenza rather than by war. His fellow officer, Donald Watson, tried to console Whyte's wife on her 'bitter loss' in mid-April 1919: 'It is, as you say, beyond understanding that after all the hardship and danger which your husband went through and your own long days of waiting and anxiety, that the prospect...should be broken to pieces by this cruel parting'.[63] Others, like J. L. Garvin, suffered a double blow when they lost beloved family members to the epidemic as well as to the war; they tended to blame the war for both deaths, since influenza attacked people already weakened by grief. Garvin had been deeply affected by the death of his only son in the war. His wife and his daughter Katharine went to London without Garvin on Armistice Day 1918. Katharine remembered her mother crying bitterly throughout the celebrations, saying sadly, 'It is too late for me', as she had lost her son. Three months later, when Garvin's wife died from the flu at the age of 43, Katharine described her as 'a war casualty'. Garvin's grief for his wife and son increased as time passed: 'year after year I saw him break into uncontrollable tears when he mentioned my mother'.[64]

The huge numbers of English people killed by the influenza pandemic tended to be seen as war victims, but they were not commemorated in the interwar years, as were the dead soldiers. The tragedy of the influenza pandemic was not remembered in history as the Black Death was, and as it might have been had it struck in peacetime. People wanted to celebrate victory in war in November 1918, not dwell on the horror, loss, and grief caused by an epidemic of disease. So in one sense the epidemic was seen as prolonging the war and in part caused by the war, rather than as a tragedy in its own right. Many writers paid tribute to the war heroes and commemorated their loss in poetry and prose, but there was no equivalent for the influenza victims.

Such public forgetting of the hundreds of thousands of those who died in the pandemic can be attributed to several factors. The vast numbers of horrible deaths by violence of young men in the war blunted the emotions of many survivors—civilians as well as ex-soldiers. Only so much suffering could be fully mourned and commemorated. It was an extreme example of how a prolonged and terrible war could deflect the normal community response to an epidemic disaster. War censorship discouraged accurate reporting of the extent and severity of the epidemic in the press, understating the virulence and death toll, and even advising the community to ignore the epidemic. Moreover, this forgetting of the influenza victims foreshadowed the valorization of soldiers' deaths over civilian deaths in the interwar years. The mass deaths of heroic young soldiers in a victorious war substantially eclipsed those of individual civilian deaths due to disease, foreshadowing the silences surrounding domesticated deaths in the interwar years.

# 2

# Violet Cecil and Communities in Mourning

## 'Grief and Loss is Too Universal'

Countless English people mourned relatives, friends, and neighbours killed in the Great War and their profound grief was often inexpressible. These numerical losses were redressed by increased births within a few years of the Armistice, but continuing sorrow and desolation cannot easily be quantified. Nearly three-quarters of a million British servicemen were killed in the war, but the burden of the loss was unequal, varying markedly by class, region, and family. Adrian Gregory suggests that about three million Britons out of a population of less than forty-two million lost a close relative, a son or a brother. But the secondary bereaved who mourned a cousin, colleague, friend, or neighbour 'encompassed virtually the entire population'.[1]

In absolute numbers the majority of the total casualties were working class, with twenty of the lower ranks killed for every officer.[2] Within the working classes, members of the north country 'Pals' battalions, who volunteered to fight with men from their town or village, were especially hard hit: entire battalions died together and their home towns suffered disproportionately heavy losses. The *Barnsley Chronicle* mourned the town's casualties on the first day of the battle of the Somme in July 1916: 'there is hardly a home that has not experienced some great loss or suffered some poignant sorrow'. But the *Chronicle* was confident that these huge sacrifices would be borne 'with Spartan courage': that the brave women of Barnsley 'will show the same fortitude under affliction as is being displayed everywhere by the women of England'. In a closely knit community like Barnsley, 'the grief and anguish of one of our number is the grief and anguish of us all'.[3]

The middle and upper classes also suffered disproportionately, as their enlistment rates in 1914 and 1915 were higher, most became officers, and their casualty rates were twice those of their men. Lord Killanin refrained from offering condolences to Violet Cecil on the death of her son in 1914 because 'grief and loss is too universal'. One in four of Oxford and Cambridge men aged less than 25 were killed, and one in five of those who served from the elite public schools.[4] The idea of the sacrifice of the 'lost generation' seemed apposite in relation to the heavy losses of the privileged classes. J. B. Priestley belonged to that ill-fated generation which grew to manhood 'watching its dearest friends being killed'; afterwards he believed that 'crowd of ghosts' were the best of their generation.[5] Lady Cynthia Asquith lost a succession of close relatives and beloved friends to the war, recorded in her diary with mounting anguish as the years passed. In November 1915 she wrote sadly, 'before one is thirty, to know more dead than living people'. By July 1917 she had hoped to pay her war dues in full, 'but there is no limit'.[6]

Even among the social elite, some suffered more than others, because their sons became officers in crack regiments, fought in battles with horrific casualties, or were particularly unlucky. Thus, Lord William Cecil, bishop of Exeter, lost three sons and Ettie Lady Desborough two. There is good reason to explore the meaning and manner of expression of such grief among this particular social group, especially as their family archives are so rich. Lady Violet Cecil is my central subject in this chapter because her story illuminates the sorrow and ways of coping of a range of people in her community of mourning, varying in gender, class, and religion. Her atheism provides a revealing contrast to the Anglicanism of so many of her class. Her extensive correspondence with the bereaved working-class families of the other ranks who died with her son gives an unusual insight into class differences in response to loss. It suggests that collaboration across the ranks among the fighting troops on the Western Front may have encouraged rather more interaction and understanding across the classes at home, when united by mass bereavement.

Jay Winter has written perceptively of the development of 'communities of the bereaved' in many towns and villages across Europe during the Great War. Powerful emotional bonds were forged among communities in mourning: 'There was a progression of mutual help, a pathway along which many groups and individuals sought to provide knowledge, then consolation, then commemoration'. Individuals and Red Cross searchers helped to provide precious information on the fate of missing soldiers amidst the confusion and fear provoked by ambiguous bureaucratic statements. Such 'kinship groups' offered consolation and support through participation in pilgrimages to war cemeteries at national memorials as a ritual expression of their bereavement. The grief of individuals was witnessed at such ceremonies and shared by friends, neighbours, and the community, who drew strength from each other.[7]

Where Jay Winter explored such 'kinship bonds' in bereavement primarily through the invaluable work of the Red Cross, in this chapter I will examine the way they worked in the communal life of the English upper class, with Lady Violet Cecil as my focal point. Her community of grief primarily included relatives, friends, neighbours, and political colleagues in her own social class who shared her suffering. It also extended beyond her own class to include the working-class families of the soldiers who were killed with her son, as well as the French community in the village where he died and was buried. Notable in her correspondence of grief was the quite different emotional tone of her letters depending on the gender of the recipient. She shared the emotional anguish of her loss primarily with her women friends; with her male friends and relatives she chiefly addressed the practical problems of searching for her son and finding precious information on the manner of his death.

## Violet Cecil's Search for Her Missing Son

Violet Cecil was born Violet Maxse (1872–1958), the daughter of a Crimean War hero, and sister of a distinguished Great War general, Frederick Maxse, and also of Leo Maxse, editor of the right-wing *National Review*. An active imperialist, she counted among her close friends Cecil Rhodes, Rudyard Kipling, Alfred Milner, and the French statesman Georges Clemenceau. Her first marriage in 1894 was to Lord Edward Cecil, fourth son of the Conservative Prime Minister, Lord Salisbury, whereby she moved into the highest echelons of British society and politics. However, this marriage was affected by differences of temperament and religion (her atheism conflicted with the Cecil family's Anglicanism), and by Edward's long years of absence on military service in Egypt. Violet Cecil lived in Sussex, with the Kiplings and Milner as neighbours, and worked for imperial causes such as the National Service League. Three years after Edward's premature death from tuberculosis in 1918, Violet married her beloved friend of many years, Alfred Lord Milner, who died in 1925. On her brother Leo's illness in 1929 she became for twenty years an active editor of their family-owned journal, the influential *National Review*. Hugh Cecil described her as 'tough and strong-willed, articulate and argumentative': her sparkling intelligence, courage, and humour attracted writers, politicians, and a wide circle of stimulating friends. As Kenneth Rose observed, Violet possessed an indomitable atheism, a combative temperament, a thirst for intellectual society, and an imperious will.[8]

If Alfred Milner became the love of Violet Cecil's life, the death of her 18-year-old son, George, in the first weeks of the Great War, became the profound grief of her life. George had been educated at Winchester School and was the prize cadet at Sandhurst in 1912. Like many upper-class boys from public schools George volunteered immediately war was declared, following his father into the Grenadier Guards. He went to the Front in August 1914 with the first troops of the British Expeditionary Force, and was killed in action on 1 September 1914, only a month after the war began.

George Cecil was reported missing in September 1914 near the village of Villers Cotterets in France, but it was several months before his family learned he was dead. Following the British defeat at the battle of Mons on 23 August, an exhausting thirteen-day retreat had achieved some success by frustrating the Germans' outflanking movement. The Grenadier Guards' ten days of marching and fighting in retreat took them on 1 September into a circular clearing in a forest called the Rond de la Reine near the village of Villers Cotterets: there they engaged in a bayonet charge against the Germans. Months later, searches revealed that the Guards had been fighting for their lives in the enclosed space of the forest: two surviving soldiers reported seeing George running, sword in hand, to forestall a German attack on their flank. Both soldiers saw him shot and were certain he died instantly. But at the time, George was reported missing, and all the men killed, wounded, or taken prisoner.[9]

Violet Cecil kept a brief 'War Diary 1914' in which she jotted down a few fractured phrases on significant days of George's disappearance. On 23 August, the day of the battle of Mons, she noted, 'awakened 6.30am rifle fire'; again on 1 September, the day of his death, she entered '7am rifle fire'. On both 4 and 5 September she mentioned bad fainting fits which left her unable to stand all day: 'these are the days that frighten me'. Then on 5 September, she received news that George was wounded in the head and missing: 'my darling, darling boy—I see him all the time with some terrible irreparable injury in his beautiful face and suffering—suffering'. In an undated 'thanks for sympathy' letter, Violet wrote that ' "missing", with a barbarous enemy, may mean so much'.[10]

Violet Cecil's personal search for her missing son was highly unusual in this very early stage of the war. She called on the influence, wealth, and authority of both her eminent families—the Cecils and the Maxses—especially her brothers, Leo Maxse and General Frederick Maxse—and her friends Rudyard Kipling and Alfred Milner. Her brother-in-law, Lord Robert Cecil, was an invaluable source of help as he subsequently became director of the British Red Cross Inquiry Office for the Wounded and Missing, founded in Paris in autumn 1914.

Violet's pursuit of her son included a remarkable visit to France for several days from 19 September 1914. In Paris she asked her friend, Georges Clemenceau, to influence the French Minister of War to obtain permission for her visit to Villers Cotterets; there she met the doctor and mayor, Dr Henri Mouflier, and his wife, who was a nurse at the local hospital.[11] Thus commenced a lifelong friendship between Violet and the Moufliers. A subsequent letter from Violet to Colonel Gilmour, who commanded her son's regiment, gave an account of her French visit in September. Not surprisingly, even she found it challenging to gain permission to go behind the front line to talk to the troops about casualties in the forest battle. However, the American Ambassador and Mayor Mouflier both assisted Violet, especially as she was searching not only for her own boy, but also other officers of the regiment. Undaunted, Violet went behind the lines to talk to soldiers about her son: 'I found many relics picked up on the battlefield, some of them men's pocket books, and among them some signed by my boy'. She asked the French government to take care of the relics. She also spoke to villagers at nearby Puisieux, who informed her that there were two large communal graves in the wood and khaki caps nearby suggested that English soldiers were buried there.[12]

Meanwhile the search for George was also undertaken by Robert Cecil, Alfred Milner, and Rudyard Kipling. General Frederick Maxse, Violet's brother, interviewed soldiers and attempted to obtain prisoner-of-war lists. In late September, a private search agent hired by Alfred Milner relayed a rumour that George was a wounded prisoner at Aix-la-Chapelle, but the Dutch consul-general subsequently rejected this story. These searches were conducted at the highest levels, emphasizing that the victim was the grandson of a former British prime minister. But by November the director of the search agency regretted that 'only a miracle can afford us better tidings'.[13]

Robert Cecil was able to draw on the resources of the British Red Cross Inquiry Office for the Wounded and Missing, which became the best source of information on the missing. Eventually private enquiry agencies were also established by intermediaries from neutral countries such as Denmark and the United States. Van Asch van Wyck and Cox and Co. Inquiry Office of Craig's Court, London, were both used by Violet and Rudyard Kipling, and were considered to have a reliable reputation. But the *Manchester Guardian* warned against bogus agents such as 'The Dead Soldiers Society' in Cologne which promised results on receipt of remittances but exploited families' grief for personal gain.[14]

On 26 September 1914 the officer in command of George's battalion advised Violet that there was no longer any doubt that George was dead, but Violet's various advisers, especially her brothers, insisted they must continue to follow up all rumours and not just assume the worst. Rudyard Kipling's wife, Carrie, and Violet's other women friends also urged her not to give up hope, as George might yet be a prisoner, or badly wounded in a hospital. Violet agreed that 'my boy is everything in the world to me and I want to leave no stone unturned'.[15]

Violet Cecil was an exceptionally strong woman, capable of keeping her intensely felt emotions to herself. Her deepest feelings during this ordeal seem to have been revealed to her sister Olive Maxse and her friend Alfred Milner. Violet herself had little real hope of George's survival from an early stage. She wrote to Milner on 20 September 1914:

To think that he should have been dead nearly three weeks and I not know it. We have not yet got absolute proof which I think it important to get if we can. I can't help crying a great deal...My darling was killed in defeat. He had no glorious hour of Victory—only that long weary retreat.

But she promised Milner that she would be brave 'presently'. She knew how much she had to live for and she would not fail her family or him. Nor would she close her eyes to her own rich past, which included her beloved son. She accepted that 'These days must be lived through. The Valley must be crossed. Then I will take up my life again'. Meanwhile, despite great sorrow, she promised to take good care of herself. She would not tell her mother and her daughter Helen until she had the 'absolute certainty of having identified George'. She could not bear to think of their intense grief as George was their 'pride and joy'. Once she had definite evidence that he was dead and she knew where he was buried, she would try to make life bearable for them.[16]

Ten weeks later, when she had that firm evidence of George's death, Violet opened her heart to her sister, Olive Maxse. Violet recognized that their mother would never be happy again and that her own daughter was 'sore, tender and miserable':

I am broken too, my old darling, to have lost our darling, to have lost him so young, before he had any chance—to think that all the years of our lives must be lived without him is crushing. I am overcome by it and cannot pretend I am not.

From a selfish perspective she would miss George's companionship, council, and support—in the absence of her husband in Egypt. Far more of a loss was '*the fearful waste* of his promising life', which she would never cease to mourn.[17]

Late in October 1914 Lord Robert Cecil wrote from Paris to his sister-in-law that the government intended to undertake 'some general disinterment and reburial' of the mass graves in the Villers Cotterets area, as Violet had urged in late September. The location had been revealed by English prisoners who had been forced by German soldiers to bury their own dead the day after the battle. Robert Cecil considered it advisable to wait for this official disinterment rather than attempt the more individual 'piecemeal operation' which he thought Violet had in mind. We can only speculate as to this. The major breakthrough came with a thorough Red Cross search of the Villers Cotterets area for the missing officers who fell on 1 September. Lord Robert Cecil and Lord Killanin gained permission to accompany the Red Cross party because they had close relatives among the missing officers.[18] Both men sent accounts of the search to Violet.

Permits were obtained from local authorities to visit the mass graves in the forest at Rond de la Reine, 2½ miles from Villers Cotterets, on 16 November 1914. The Red Cross workers started with a large pit marked by a cross and a French inscription on a nearby tree stating that twenty British soldiers were buried there. After two days' hard work the six workers disinterred and examined over sixty corpses, all other ranks, none officers. It was 'repulsive work' as 'bodies were huddled and entangled, just as thrown in anyhow, one after the other'. There was no question of 'personal recognition' and it was impossible to save men's hair as mourning relics for relatives, though they removed identity discs and pocketbooks. By the end of the third day, when nearly eighty bodies had been exhumed, the Red Cross working party found the remains of four officers, two with identity discs and two without. Lord Killanin identified one of the latter, from his small gold watch, as his brother, who had commanded the Guards. George Cecil was the second officer without a disc, judging by the buttons of a grenadier lieutenant, the size of his large boots and body, and the initials G.E.C. on the front of his vest. This piece of material and three buttons were carefully removed as precious mementoes for his mother. They retrieved in total the bodies of ninety-four men and four officers, and decided to increase the size of the original mass grave substantially to allow room to lay out the bodies in a dignified manner.[19]

Seventy of the ninety-four soldiers were identified by hair, teeth, or other features, but the remaining corpses had decayed too far in the ten weeks since their burial. Moreover, the bodies had been treated badly so that 'faces were quite unrecognizable, often smashed, and were all thickly coated with clay and blood'. Afterwards, the bodies of the ninety-four soldiers were laid out carefully in the enlarged grave. An Anglican clergyman and a Catholic priest said prayers for the dead by the graveside, before the ninety-four bodies were covered with earth. A wooden cross on the soldiers' grave was erected until a permanent monument could take its place. By contrast the bodies of the four officers were buried in pine coffins at the nearby village cemetery in Villers Cotterets, where the two clergymen again read prayers. The funeral of the officers was attended by the mayor and twenty French officers, and marked by a booming cannon.[20]

The contrast between the treatment of the officers and the other ranks in death was marked—not least because the mass grave was only disturbed as an accidental consequence of the search for the officers. However, families of the private soldiers were still fortunate that this intervention took place because they at last received precious information on the fate of their own missing loved ones, who would otherwise have remained missing for ever. Such a search, exhumation, and reburial would not have been possible later in the war, even for officers, once trench warfare became established and the numbers of dead were infinitely greater. The preferential treatment of the officers also contrasts sharply with the uniformity of burial in the war cemeteries approved by Parliament in 1920.

On return to London Lord Killanin gave the lists of the men, with identity discs and other means of identification, to the War Office. His brother's watch was handed to his widow, and George Cecil's buttons and vest initials to his mother. Killanin explained the significance of their achievement to Violet:

Irreparable as is the loss suffered by the death of these officers and soldiers and awful as the work of exhumation was...it is to me an abiding consolation...to know that their remains were rescued from an utterly unknown grave and a most indecorous burial, and have been laid to rest under the circumstances described, when everything possible was done to show respect and reverence and affection and honour to their glorious and loved memories.[21]

Violet's papers in the Bodleian Library include an envelope containing a copy of the inscription on her locket: 'This locket contains a piece of the vest worn by George Cecil the day he was killed in action, in the forest of Villers Cotterets, France, Sept 1st 1914'. Killanin concluded his account to Violet with the statement that he would not offer condolences since 'grief and loss is too universal'. He was correct in believing that such detailed information about the discovery and reburial of her son would do far more to help Violet than any number of condolence letters.[22] This evidence made all the difference between George Cecil remaining 'missing', possibly for ever, and having a dignified funeral, and a known grave which she could visit to remember him.

Violet Cecil now had the consolation of knowing that her son's body was given a respectful burial, but she insisted she must understand more about the circumstances of his death if she was eventually to come to terms with it. She needed to reconstruct his last days and hours in minute detail. She shared this urgent need with Constance, Lady Manners, the mother of her son's friend, Lord John Manners, who went missing in the same battle. Constance's husband, Lord Manners, known as 'Hoppy', had also travelled to the Front to look for his son—'it wrung Hoppy's heart so he could not bear it'—nor could he manage to talk about his son's death—one of many instances of men lost for words in the face of death. By contrast Constance and Violet found it invaluable to share their grief with each other, in letters and conversation—a significant indication of gendered differences in response to loss. They needed all the information available to help them relive in their imagination the final days of their sons' lives and deaths: 'it is like giving a last look at our beloved dead, it is anguish, but it is sacred'. The two mothers comforted each other in frequent letters—as Constance wrote, 'no one else understands' as they did.[23] Indeed the substantial correspondence between Violet and her close female friends and family members, together with their many intimate conversations, formed deep bonds in a community of the bereaved. Mutual help groups such as Compassionate Friends for bereaved parents have an analogous role today.

Where Carrie Kipling offered emotional support to Violet, her husband Rudyard provided essential practical help, an illustration of the gendered support system at work. Rudyard Kipling did all that he could to record George's last days and hours for his friend and neighbour. He tracked down surviving Grenadiers from the Villers Cotterets battle and person- ally interviewed them in hospitals and elsewhere. Afterwards he carefully composed for Violet a detailed reconstruction of the most likely events of George's final days and hours, attempting to resolve conflicting accounts. By 9 December 1914, Constance Manners thought they now had a consistent account of 'our darling boys' last fight: "A man could die no nobler a death than as one of so glorious a band".[24] This written record marked some sort of coming to terms with the stark reality of their sons' deaths. Rudyard Kipling was developing a search and interview procedure that he was to repeat in even more painful circumstances in 1915, when his own son, John, went missing and was never found. Kipling's poetry, including his poem 'For All We Have and Are', written after the battle of Mons, reinforced the chivalric language of sacrifice which helped to console these desolate families, especially in the early years of the war.

## Grieving Families of the Other Ranks

Both Rudyard Kipling and Robert Cecil came to recognize the inequality and intense resentment created by class privilege in the treatment of war deaths and the need for equality in death and burial to match the equality of sacrifice. They both played significant roles in the creation and devel- opment of the Imperial War Graves Commission as a consequence of their private grief for their own families' missing soldiers. Violet Cecil was also moved by her own traumatic experience in 1914 to a compassion for the parents of the lower-class soldiers who died fighting at Villers Cotterets with her son. She knew the details of the soldiers' burial and was determined to offer their families as much information as she could to help them in their grief.

In Violet Cecil's papers in the Bodleian Library there is a remarkable collection of letters from grateful relatives of working-class soldiers who served and died with her son George. Violet wrote to many dozens of families with particulars of the fatal battle in the forest, based on Kipling's assiduous search. She focused in her letters on the reburial in a respectable grave with a religious ceremony, and later sent the families photographs of the mass grave at Villers Cotterets. The many dozens of letters of thanks to Violet are deeply moving. Most offered condolences on George Cecil's death, such as, 'It must break your heart the death of your son'. Many told sad stories of great hardship and sorrow as they learned or presumed their sons or husbands were missing. Catherine Laffey was a 'heart-broken mother' who had lost two sons and considered suicide: 'I got out of drowning as I am getting afraid I drew more trouble on myself'. Elizabeth Wallace wrote from the Liverpool Royal Infirmary: 'My trouble was twofold as I lost my eldest girl & the Father inside ten months and my baby was only nine months the day. He [her husband] was killed so it quite broke my health up'. John Whitcroft of Derby wrote that his son's death was an even greater loss because he himself was an invalid with heart disease and unable to work.[25]

These families were deeply grateful for Violet's kindness in sending them such precious information. Some had received a brief formal notification from the War Office in late November that their sons had been buried at Villers Cotterets in early September, but many others learned only that their relatives were officially deemed missing. George Hannegan wrote that his son was still regarded by the War Office as missing 'despite every possible enquiry'. It was a great comfort to know how and where he died. Eveline Meadows was overwhelmed by relief: 'I could not get to know whether my husband died from disease or wounds, I have sent to the [War] Office twice'. Mrs A. Lineham had heard dreadful rumours of what might have happened to the missing. They were all deeply relieved to learn about the circumstances of the battle. John Meagher wrote that it was 'always a matter of deep anxiety to me and his mother to know how he died, because the only previous accounts all differed and seemed unreliable'. Violet Oldershaw of Rugby was grateful for the particulars which she knew she would never have received from the War Office. She thanked Violet 'from the bottom of my heart': she had agonized about how much her husband suffered or if he was ever buried. George Hannegan was relieved to learn his son died quickly. He and his daughter suffered weeks of pain and anxiety from the thought of him lying there for days in agony, alone and uncared for. Charlotte Jamieson of Ramsgate confessed that her family had 'wondered and wondered how he died' and thought they would never know until they heard from Lady Violet.[26]

Above all, these bereaved families were thankful to learn from Violet that their beloved sons and husbands had been identified and given a dignified burial. They were no longer missing for ever. They would all treasure the photograph of the grave, which probably sat on many mantel-pieces for years. George Hannegan had framed the photo which was greatly prized, and his surviving sons aimed to visit the grave after the war. They recognized that only Violet's kindness had made this possible. A. Brimson of Wapping wrote that many other wives of the missing would never know or see the place where their husbands lay. She intended to save the money to travel to France after the war to see her husband's grave: 'I would not mind what sacrifice I made . . . if for only a few minutes to be able to stand by that grave'. Mrs A. Lineham wrote that 'It is a consolation to have a grave to cry and pray over and to know he was buried with his comrades'. John Meagher was very proud of Violet's letter and photo, and was relieved to know the grave was tended by the French.[27]

These bereaved working-class families knew that despite their great loss, they were more fortunate than many others. They had experienced the ordeal of their sons and husbands being designated as 'missing' for only a few months, because of the accident that the officers' families had conducted a rigorous search for the bodies. They also received far more detailed and comforting information than was officially available to most soldiers' families because Violet Cecil took the trouble to write to them.

These letters from working-class bereaved parents to Violet are espe-cially valuable because unpublished files in the Imperial War Museum on the grief of working-class families are few and often unrevealing. Many working-class soldiers came from a background of grinding poverty and static class divisions. In 1911 one and a half million of the working classes were still domestic servants, and a quarter of the population were farm labourers. The soldiers' unpublished memoirs tend to feature simple descriptive narratives of everyday events, but some tell a story of anguish in a few terse words. Private W. Cook went to visit 'Pozzie' Gibson's mother after his death, finding her near destitution. All she could say was 'I've lost my only boy' and then she became mute with grief.[28] This was the silence of so many of the very poor facing the death of loved ones in the nineteenth and early twentieth centuries.

Len Wade left a brief typewritten note in the Imperial War Museum describing the terrible response of his mother-in-law, Kate Clayden, to the death of her husband, Albert, late of the West Riding Regiment. He was a saddler who survived from 1914 until he was killed at Cambrai during the final German retreat in 1918. Kate suffered a 'severe breakdown, being left with two young daughters to bring up alone. She died eventually in an Epsom mental hospital in 1974'.[29] Some tragedies require few words.

Robert F. Wearmouth was a Methodist army chaplain from Newcastle upon Tyne who wrote over two thousand letters and cards to families in his two years at the Front, advising that their sons were missing or killed. A 70-year-old mother from Lancashire replied in May 1916 that she was 'too broken-hearted' on her son's death to write earlier. It was such a terrible shock that the boy's father, aged 71, did not recover and died two months later. The padre went to visit one bereaved mother on his next leave in Newcastle in 1916: 'her grief was still great and almost unbearable. For a time she wept just like a child'. The fathers' responses were more restrained, and sometimes only their reactive illness or death is recorded. But what stands out overall in these letters is the bravery and stoicism. One father wrote on the death of his son, 'thousands of fathers are in the same position'. A widow realized that 'I am only one in many hundreds'. Several were at least consoled by the knowledge that their loved one was actually buried, when so many lacked even that comfort.[30]

# Grief and Commemoration in Violet Cecil's Community of the Bereaved

The incoming correspondence to Violet Cecil from Constance Manners, Carrie Kipling, and various Cecil in-laws is illuminating on the impact of their losses and their code of appropriate behaviour in wartime grieving.

Their shared trauma drew Violet close to Constance Manners, whose son had died at Villers Cotterets with George, and also to Carrie Kipling, whose son subsequently went missing for ever. They sent each other handwritten copies of their sons' letters written in the final weeks before they died; they also forwarded copies of correspondence relating to the searches for their missing sons. This written evidence was treasured even more when shared with the few close women friends who also suffered and therefore understood. It also helped in the precious detailed reconstruction of the final days and weeks before their sons' deaths.

During the traumatic months of the search for George Cecil and John Manners in late 1914, Constance Manners told Violet that she was the only person she could communicate with: 'no one else understands'. Like Violet, Constance and her husband, Lord Manners, also went to the Front in search of their son. Constance later described them both as 'distraught with anguish' in this 'terrible suspense', which they could share with very few. In 1915 Constance understood how deeply Violet was sharing the suffering of the Kiplings when their son was also posted missing, yet 'it did not re-open your wound: it is always bare and bleeding'. Violet's sister-in-law, Eleanor Cecil, knew that the first anniversary of George's death would be an especially cruel time for Violet: Eleanor thought it must be 'torture', particularly as Violet would never be precisely certain how George had died.[31]

Constance Manners and Violet Cecil later adopted Ettie Lady Desborough as a heroic role model in their own grief: she was an influential society hostess whose two beloved sons, Julian and Billy Grenfell, were killed in 1915 within a few months of each other. Billy Grenfell's body was initially buried, but lost for ever as the fighting continued; and he joined the thousands of the missing whose names were inscribed on the Menin Gate Memorial. For a short time Lady Desborough preferred not to see anyone, even Constance, but trusted that later her 'poor broken body may be mended a little'. But soon, as Cynthia Asquith reported, Ettie Desborough determined to overcome her tragedy through sheer gallantry and willpower:

She inspires one with tremendous admiration. There seems nothing strained and artificial about her marvellous courage, just a sort of alchemy which has translated tragedy to the exclusion of all gloom . . . Her determination to go on fighting with broken tools and to save whatever was still worth keeping was wholly admirable.[32]

By November 1915 Ettie Desborough appeared 'absolutely normal in company', deliberately unemotional, her zest for life apparently unimpaired, and refusing to wear mourning clothes. And yet there was a marked distinction between her public and private faces of grief. As Cynthia Asquith observed, her public performance might be thought inhuman by some, but alone with a close friend, 'tears pour down her cheeks' and she talks endlessly about her dead boys, revealing her 'bleeding heart' and the emptiness in her soul.[33]

Constance Manners wrote to Violet of her visit to the Desboroughs at Taplow Court near Henley, late in August 1915:

It hurts to see such courage and I feel wicked to be so miserable and weak. Ettie won't allow a word of sorrow or bitterness to pass on her lips...Lord Desborough is just broken and the tears trickle down his sad face as he talks of them both and I found that almost easier as I feel like that.[34]

Violet and Constance found the inspiration for their own courage in Ettie's example. That was the way the upper class should behave in grief, and it was also the way their officer sons had been expected to deal with the loss of their comrades in wartime. Constance several times congratulated Violet on her 'wonderful' bearing on public occasions among the Cecil family, especially when celebrating milestones for the younger generation, in her own dead son's absence. Condolence letters to Violet reinforced the expectation of a stoical courage in the bereaved mother of a young soldier. Herbert [H.A.L.] Fisher, the distinguished historian, wrote to Violet in November 1914, certain that her sorrow would be 'transmuted into power and courage' and that her beloved son would 'visit your heart with promptings to a courage akin to his own'.[35] Violet lived up to this ideal. Her brother, General Frederick Maxse, wrote in July 1915 that he was happy to see her looking more like her old self: 'That is the right spirit. We have got to stick it out, all of us, both privately and as a nation'.[36]

While grief was intense for bereaved parents who knew where their soldier sons or husbands were buried and had some information as to how they died, family anxiety was vastly increased where the initial reports were 'missing', even when the bodies were later located, as in George Cecil's case. But the loved ones could suffer protracted pain when the bodies of the missing were never recovered. Thousands of soldiers had no known burial place because their bodies were shattered by shells or scattered by subsequent engagements. Hopes might be raised by search agencies like the Red Cross, but later dashed. Families could suffer continuing anguish by imagining terrible mutilation and smashed bodies. It was almost impossible for families to come to terms with the reality of their soldier sons' deaths without a body and an identified grave. Many may have grieved intensely but privately for the remainder of their lives, traumatized by losses which they could never completely accept.

The grief of Carrie and Rudyard Kipling on the loss of their only son, John, known as Jack, at the battle of Loos on 27 September 1915 has been described by Tonie and Valmai Holt in *My Boy Jack*. Jack Kipling was posted as wounded and missing, but the Kiplings never found either his body or his grave. Rudyard and Carrie conducted a prolonged, obsessive search which continued for years, following initially on the lines of the search for George Cecil. Given Kipling's fame, the extensive searches and enquiries were heavily publicized, especially as he later became a commissioner of the Imperial War Graves Commission, and suggested many of the evocative inscriptions used in the war cemeteries.[37] During 1915 and 1916 Carrie sent Violet a series of agonized letters describing the search. The Kiplings had contacted soldiers at Loos who had offered 'conflicting stories', which increased the confusion. In October 1915 they had interviewed more than twenty wounded soldiers in hospitals, but were 'more at sea than ever'. Carrie worried that Jack might have been captured and lost his mind: 'I often think I shall do the same'. A month later she wrote, 'No news—a great darkness seems to be settling down on it all. But who should know better than you'. By November 1915 Jack's battalion had concluded he was dead, reinforced by Red Cross reports from a sergeant who saw him dead and believed he must have been buried by a shell.[38]

By September 1916 Carrie Kipling shared her husband's despair, writing to Violet: 'All day and every day I cry for some confirmation, some real proof that John is dead and there are thousands of mothers who feel as I do'. But she knew by now that no one could really help her deal with the cruel uncertainty and confessed that she endured some terrible days. She would often like to 'bolt into a car and tear off and out and down all the carefully built up commitments and just be a broken-hearted mother for a little bit'. But of course she never did. As she added: 'What a dreadful place all earth would be if we were able to do such things'.[39] As Tonie and Valmai Holt observe, 'To most outsiders the Kiplings closed ranks and licked their painful wounds in private'. However, Carrie expressed her heartbreak and bleak despair openly in her letters to Violet, who fully empathized. In 1919 John Kipling was pronounced officially dead, on account of the passage of time, though there was no evidence to substantiate his death. Rudyard Kipling's profound pain and desolation never ended and was expressed in his poetry, as in that on Armistice Day in 1923:

> All the empty-heart and ache
> That isn't cured by grieving
> Where's our help from Earth or Heaven?
> (Grieving—grieving!)
> To comfort us for what we've given
> And only gained by grieving.

Throughout, the Kiplings maintained a stoical facade of acceptance, concealing their continuing grief from the world. Their daughter commented later that they bore John's death 'bravely and silently, perhaps too silently for their own good'. Their lives were marked by grief for ever.[40]

Rudyard Kipling, like many intelligent bereaved parents, was powerfully tempted by spiritualism which held special appeal for those mourning for one of that vast army of soldiers whose bodies were missing in perpetuity. Kipling's poetry and short stories show how sternly he strove to overcome the temptation to believe in the presence of the dead and the possibility of communicating with them.[41] Lady Cynthia Asquith noted in her diary the strong appeal of spiritualism for her mother, Mary Countess of Wemyss, following the death of her two sons in the war. Mary Wemyss read parts of Oliver Lodge's book, *Raymond*, aloud to the family and thought it worthwhile to visit a spiritualist to contact her sons. Several friends deprecated her 'dabbling' in spiritualism, while others themselves resorted to table-rapping—so many beloved young men were killed, and so many hoped for some form of connection with those lost lives.[42]

Nearer to home for Violet Cecil were the deaths of the other four young men in the Cecil family, in addition to her own son. Robert Cecil, Marquess of Salisbury, had ten grandsons, of whom five were killed in action. His daughter, Maud, was married to Roundell Palmer, Lord Selborne: their son, Captain Robert Palmer, aged 28, a promising barrister before the war, died of wounds in Mesopotamia in 1916. Kenneth Rose comments that, like her two brothers, 'Maud bore the loss of a favourite son with outward stoicism', though it was the cruellest blow of her life. She responded to condolences with acceptance: 'It is easy to think of him with God, and in time these wounds heal'.[43] But her close family believed that she was never free from sadness thereafter. Lord Selborne's response was similarly stoical but he admitted to his sister-in-law, Violet, in 1916, that he shared her deep grief: 'Yes, I walk hourly in that valley the shadow of which you know so well'.[44]

Lord William Cecil, Bishop of Exeter, and his wife Florence, suffered the devastating loss of three sons in the Great War, as well as an 18-year-old daughter Anne in 1924. Beloved by his flock, Lord William displayed a Christian resignation in the deepest grief which equalled his wife's courage and calmness. Florence's letter to Violet in July 1915 was remarkable, following Rupert's death: she was glad that Violet understood so well what it was to lose a beloved son. And yet, Violet was 'much more to be pitied' than Florence, as George was her only son, while they had others left to comfort them. Moreover, they were spared the 'long agony of suspense' which was so cruel for Violet: 'Yes, your trouble is worse'. But in August 1915, when her eldest son, Randle, returned to the Front, Florence revealed a little more of her heartache: 'The ache gets worse, not better, doesn't it?' In September 1918, when she had lost three of her four sons, she admitted that the world was 'very grey' without them, though 'our pride in them helps us along'.[45] The Bishop of Exeter sought refuge in his deep Christian faith: 'Life must be taken as a whole, the sorrows and the joys'. But he burnt all condolence letters as they compounded his suffering.[46]

## The Consolations of Memory and Commemoration

For Violet Cecil and her family and friends there were several major forms of consolation for such loss. For devout Christians such as the Cecils, their faith was probably the greatest consolation, though they did not broadcast this to the world, and it could not be shared with Violet, who was an atheist. Lord Hugh Cecil, for instance, did not help Violet in 1914 by assuring her in a letter that they would see George again in heaven. As Violet's husband, Edward, confessed, 'It is awful for her to believe that she will never see him again and that he is only dust'.[47] It was unusually difficult for the devout Cecils to find adequate words of condolence for unbelievers. As a consequence, they perhaps placed more than usual emphasis in letters to Violet on the consolations of patriotism and sacrifice. In November 1914 Hugh Cecil reassured his sister-in-law on George's death that 'the glory of a brave death closes his life finely', and that they would be 'richer for the sacrifice'. Lord Hugh seemed to recognize the inadequacy of such high diction to ease a grieving mother's pain: he conceded that 'no words can be a comfort or help' and even urged Violet to 'try not to think always of the one topic'.[48]

For Violet Cecil the traditional religious and patriotic consolations offered little comfort. Religion offered her nothing at all, while the heroic rhetoric became even less meaningful as the carnage of the Great War increased. As Eleanor Cecil—Lord Robert's wife—understood, 'I am afraid it may all seem more and more unbearable to you as time goes on'.[49] For Violet, the knowledge that her son's body had been identified and given a decent burial in a beautiful spot, where she could eventually visit his grave, was the vital consolation. This allowed her to commemorate his death annually at Villers Cotterets and helped to make memory her major avenue of comfort. In the early years of bereavement, photos and memories of George's grave could inevitably renew anguish as well as offer consolation. When Constance Manners received a photograph of their sons' graves in September 1915 she had mixed feelings: 'dear Violet how futile it is to have a *photograph* of John and George's Grave! Though I am so grateful for it I can hardly bear to look at it'.[50] As the awful battles of attrition of 1916 and 1917 moved back over the burial grounds of earlier fighting, their memories of the peaceful grave at Villers were often disturbed. Constance wrote to Violet in June 1917: 'Somehow I clung passionately to the knowledge that they lay in the silence of the Forest, but even that small consolation is denied us, for the guns and all the cruel movement of modern war must be moving over their beloved heads'.[51]

Despite the ongoing horrors of the war, the memory of their sons generally brought Violet and Constance some comfort, especially as time passed. Their exchange of letters on the anniversary of their sons' deaths expressed their dominant sentiment: 'I knew we were thinking of each other and of our darlings—Oh! How beloved they were ... And we have everything to remember, nothing to forget. We have to remain here and endure'.[52] Both Constance and Violet kept remembrance books of their sons' lives and deaths, into which they lovingly copied and pasted correspondence, press cuttings, and memorabilia.[53] On their sons' birthdays they recalled how 'happy and gay' the boys were: 'how one loves to dwell on their fun and laughter!' In August 1915 Constance thanked Violet for a lovely framed photo of George, which she would take upstairs to her bedroom: 'They become almost too sacred to be where someone may ask about them. This day [last] year they still had their beautiful unabated youth'. As Constance wrote to Violet on the first anniversary of their son's deaths: 'Time, which cannot take away our grief, cannot take away either the memory of our happiness with them or dim the lovely picture of them in our hearts'.[54] Perhaps because Violet had no faith in immortal reunion with George, material commemoration of his life and death in this world was all the more important. She treasured her locket which contained the piece of her son's vest, worn when he was killed.[55]

The most significant memorial for Violet was her son's grave at Villers Cotterets, which remained the focus of her grieving for George for the rest of her long life. Violet visited the grave at least once each year and sent funds for its upkeep to her good friends Henri Mouflier and his wife. They exchanged letters, photos, and family news for nearly fifty years. On 20 August 1915 Mme Mouflier wrote to Violet (in French) for the first anniversary 'of the glorious death of your dear son in our country'. She assured Violet that 'the graves of the English heroes, who died for freedom' would be tended with care in the name of all the English mothers prevented by war from coming in person to pray and weep there. The French would continue to honour and remember the English dead, as indeed they did. Mme Mouflier sent photographs of the grave and promised Violet hospitality in her own home when she came on her annual 'pious pilgrimage'. On Christmas Day 1915 Mme Mouflier laid a bouquet of violets on the grave as she knew Violet would be particularly sad during Christmas festivities: 'when all the family is there, the grief is renewed when one of them has disappeared for ever'. Mme Mouflier only handed over custody of George's grave to the head of the British War Graves in France in 1949 because of advancing years and failing health.[56]

Ever since George's body had been found in 1914, Violet Cecil had been determined to give him an appropriate memorial. She had regretted that George's body had been moved for burial to the village cemetery with the other officers, rather than left where he fell in the forest with his men. However, in 1922 Fabian Ware, head of the Imperial War Graves

Commission, approached Lord and Lady Milner (Violet's new title having recently remarried) with a proposal from the families of the three other officers buried with George in the village cemetery. They asked that the remains of all four officers be removed and reburied with their men in the Guards Grave in the forest at Villers Cotterets, in keeping with the democratic spirit of the battlefield cemeteries since 1920. Violet Milner gave willing consent to this reburial in 'an ideal resting place', which was carried out with reverence in 1923 in Mme Mouflier's presence. Fabian Ware advised Lord Milner that there was no doubt of the identity of the four officers' bodies: George Cecil's coffin was located at the top right as specified by Lord Killanin nearly a decade earlier: his teeth, his whistle, and some Guards' buttons were still complete. Ware hoped the Commission would erect headstones over all the graves in the Guards Cemetery shortly.[57] Violet herself at last succeeded in erecting a monument to George by the sculptor François Sicard on the spot where he died in the woods at Villers Cotterets: this became part of a larger ensemble 'Guards Memorial' to all ninety-eight guardsmen killed there in 1914.

Violet Milner's diary for 1934, the twentieth anniversary of George's death, offers a poignant insight into her continuing grief and the vital roles played by memory and commemoration in consoling and supporting her. By then she had lost two husbands—Lord Edward Cecil in 1918 and Lord Milner in 1925—and her brother Leo Maxse in 1933. She had replaced her brother as editor of the *National Review* and was suffering from overwork, declining strength, and an 'intensely lonely life'. On 14 May 1934 she visited Villers Cotterets where she placed flowers on George's grave and sat for a while on the seat opposite the monument to her son: 'it was all heartbreaking'. On 25 June she wrote to Lord Salisbury, her former brother-in-law, to offer him a sixteenth-century painting—Isenbrandt's *Crucifixion*, as a memorial to George in Hatfield Chapel on the twentieth anniversary of his death. On 12 August 1934 she noted in her diary: 'It is 20 years today since I said goodbye to my darling George'. Late August and early September had remained a harrowing time of the year for her ever since. On 1 September 1934, for the first time in her life she placed an 'In Memoriam' notice for George in *The Times*, with a copy in her diary. The notice included the quotation: 'I shall remember while the light lasts and in the darkness I shall not forget'. In her diary she noted: 'It is 20 years ago since he was killed. The sorrow, the loss, the pain, are as great today as in 1914. Perhaps they are greater, from my intense loneliness'.[58]

As late as April 1945 Violet consoled Professor Geoffrey Bickersteth on his son's death in the Second World War, telling him of her own loss in the earlier war: 'And I have not yet recovered. You will not recover. One grows a carapace. That is all'.[59]

## Catholicism and Bereaved Families: The Feildings

Because the principal character in this chapter so far has been Violet Cecil, an atheist, the continuing value of the Christian religion for bereaved families in offering some meaning in death, and some consolation in grief, has been somewhat understated. Condolence letters and other correspondence to Violet, even from her Cecil in-laws, were sometimes brief and awkward because writers could not share with her the solace of their own Christian faith. To compensate for this, and to balance the emphasis elsewhere on Protestants, I will close this chapter by exploring the experience of a devout Roman Catholic family who had to cope with the deaths of two sons in traumatic wartime circumstances. The Feilding family's papers offer a rare archival record, which was not representative of all Catholics in England, since the majority were working-class Irish by origin, but it is nonetheless rich and illuminating. It demonstrates that the Catholic faith offered particular benefits to bereaved families, though the privacy of their communication with their priests inevitably limits the archival evidence.

Though numbering only about two million in England and Wales by 1920, the Catholic Church gained in strength and authority throughout the twentieth century, especially from the 1940s, with large numbers of East European Catholic migrants and new waves of Irish immigration. As Adrian Hastings demonstrates, the appeal of the Catholic Church lay in its certainties and its claims to authority, as well as its ritualism and its sacramental system which had special attraction in times of war and in facing death.[60]

Anglo-Catholics and Roman Catholics often gained powerful support and consolation from the Catholic culture of death, which offered a vital combination of comforting sacraments and traditional ritual. Catholic Christianity suffered less than Protestantism from the challenges of evolutionary theory and biblical criticism. The Catholic belief in purgatory as an intermediate state between heaven and hell also offered more hope of ultimate salvation than the stark alternatives offered by the Protestants. Time in purgatory could be reduced for the Catholic faithful through prayers of intercession and good works. A clearly defined ritual made sudden or violent death less fearful: the familiar sacraments could be deeply comforting in a time of anguish.

The consolations for Catholics are well illustrated by the correspondence of the devout Feilding family of Newnham Paddox in Gloucestershire on the death of two beloved sons in the war. Rudolph Earl of Denbigh belonged to the old Catholic aristocracy in England, and his family included two nuns—Lady Agnes Feilding, the Earl's daughter, and Teresa Agnes Clifford, his wife's sister. Hugh Feilding, a naval officer on the ship *Defence*, was killed at the battle of Jutland on 31 May 1916 at the age of 29. This was the one major naval confrontation between Britain and Germany in the Great War, when fourteen British ships and eleven German ships were sunk. Unlike the land battles of 1916, almost all the casualties were killed, many entombed in the hulls of their ships. The battle was fought in great confusion, making it difficult for observers to give clear accounts of events which might console sailors' families.[61]

The family's grief was greatly aggravated by the absence of detailed information about the manner of Hugh's death and by the lack of a body to bury and a grave to visit. The ship blew up and sank within seconds, taking all her crew with her, but their deaths were described as instantaneous and painless. Condolence letters carried mixed messages: the terrible shock of learning that their son was blown up was somewhat mitigated by the belief that he died quickly and nobly.[62] This information was essential to the family as their son was just as much 'missing' as were the missing of the land battles on the Western Front. In the absence of a body and a precise location and manner of death, at least they could have battle details to reassure them that the sacrifice of his life was not in vain. Many writers offered the comfort that it was 'a sacred sorrow' but a 'noble death—the supreme sacrifice for duty' in an unknown grave 'in the great clean ocean'.[63]

Just as important to the Feilding family was the spiritual implication of Hugh's sudden death. For a devout Catholic family, perhaps the worst aspect was that he did not receive the final sacraments at the end, especially extreme unction. Detailed notes kept by the family on the vital effects of extreme unction in its preparation of the soul for immediate acceptance in heaven indicate their deep concern about its omission. Some naval officers who had offered condolences and participated in the battle understood this anxiety and emphasized that Hugh was 'a splendid example of what a Catholic should be'. Many promised to say mass for Hugh on his noble death.[64] The spiritual intervention of the two nuns in the family vastly increased the family's confidence that Hugh was safe in heaven, since the extra masses shortened his time in purgatory. Lady Agnes Feilding, the Earl's daughter, wrote from her convent in Brighton that 'Hugh is so good that if the Lord has taken him He must have taken him straight to Heaven'. That a nun should suggest Hugh's virtues merited an instant path to heaven gave heart to Agnes's sisters. Lady Denbigh's sister, Teresa Agnes Clifford, a nun at Mount Carmel Vista in Wells, sought to make sure of her nephew's early elevation to heaven:

The Masses have been attended to... The Holy Father decreed that all killed in action were entitled to the equivalent of the 30 Masses of St Gregory for a Mass offered for them and the benefit of a privileged Altar whether the Mass was said at once or not... Your 8 [masses] therefore equal 240... It is a sweet thought to give him such a homecoming to his heaven.[65]

Only sixteen months later Hugh's younger brother, Lieutenant Peter Feilding, was killed at the third battle of Ypres in Flanders on 9 October 1917. Peter was hit by a high explosive shell just as his company of inexperienced men went over the top of the trench. His death came early in an attack towards Passchendaele Ridge, which was to be another costly military failure.[66] None of the condolence writers even attempted to justify Peter's death, as they had for Hugh at Jutland. Little was said about the terrible battle or the shocking extent of Peter's wounds. Instead the family focused entirely on the spiritual aspects of his death—on the 'devout way he received his last communion... Because of his strong and simple faith this last communion was so beautiful and peaceful'. The Catholic chaplain had visited Peter in the casualty clearing station to administer extreme unction—the precious sacrament unavailable to Hugh. Peter was only just conscious enough to say his confession. As his brother Rollo told his mother, Peter's death was dreadful, but it might have been worse: he was buried in a 'real grave' and his body was not missing—as, by implication, was Hugh's in its watery grave. They would be able to visit Peter's grave eventually, but never Hugh's.[67]

Less than two years after Peter's death, Lady Denbigh unexpectedly followed her two sons. Her early death was attributed by her family to the intensity of her grief, which was hinted at in family correspondence. Agnes Arkwright had written to Lady Denbigh on Peter's death: 'you were sent a Cross that is too heavy to bear', while other correspondents referred to the appalling impact of the mother's two 'great sacrifices'. Peter himself had worried greatly about the effect of Hugh's death on their mother in 1916: 'the glory of such a death is its own tragedy and it nearly breaks [mother's] heart'.[68] Lady Marjorie Feilding and her father Lord Denbigh visited the French battlefields in 1920 to see Peter's grave, and doubtless to remember all three who had died since 1916. Marjorie wrote to her father that it was a necessary part of their education to 'see these ghastly battlefields...It has made a very great impression on me—having seen so ghastly a sight one can never forget it'. It allowed her to appreciate more fully what her two brothers had suffered, 'it helps one to carry on with the beloved mother and boys' example'.[69] In the next chapter I will explore more fully the complex reasons why so many families found it necessary and comforting to honour their dead on the battlefields where they died.

There had been variations in emotional responses to the deaths of loved ones in the century before 1914, across time, gender, class, religion, and temperament. But the exigencies of the First World War added a powerful constraint to grief and mourning; and the Second World War in turn reinforced the impact of the Great War. The cultural prescription for approved behaviour in wartime grief favoured stoicism and the English 'stiff upper lip'. Indeed, in letters home serving sons and husbands urged their families to be brave if they died and to grieve for them in silence. The emotional constraints of wartime were more challenging for women than men. In the nineteenth and early twentieth century women's responses to death were likely to be more emotionally expressive than those of men, with greater need to share their sorrow with sympathetic sisters or friends. Though Violet Cecil and her friends drew a clear distinction between the public and private expression of grief, they still shared their sorrow freely with each other. In this there was to be a marked contrast with women's more general constraint in the Second World War.

# 3

# The Bickersteths' Sacred Pilgrimages to the Great War Cemeteries, 1919–1931

## National Commemoration and the Battlefield Cemeteries

Following the Great War grieving relatives of dead servicemen desperately needed reassurance that their loved ones did not die in vain and that their sacrifice would be remembered. The language of sacrifice gave deep meaning both to soldiers' deaths and to the suffering of the bereaved. Several fine scholars—notably Jay Winter, Ken Inglis, Adrian Gregory, David Lloyd, and Mark Connelly—have explored the new forms of public ceremony needed to mourn and honour the sacrifice of the dead and comfort the bereaved.[1] Jay Winter argues that the new public war memorials and remembrance rituals addressed the widespread need to mitigate grief and make sense of loss: 'Commemoration was a universal preoccupation after the 1914–18 war. The need to bring the dead home, to put the dead to rest, symbolically or physically, was pervasive'.[2] In the absence of corpses and individual graves in England, monuments and ceremonies served as focal points for mourning, whereby bereaved people could share their suffering and find comfort through collective affirmation of the value of their sacrifice: they were not intended to celebrate military triumphs.

Traditional forms of burial custom and mourning ritual were unavailable for most dead soldiers of the Great War. Many were buried in hastily dug mass graves close to the Front and many were neither recovered nor identified. Soldiers' burial in England was prohibited, so their grieving families had no funerals and no graves at home which might become a focus for their sorrow. Victorian-style deathbeds and ritualized mourning were impossible and in any case inappropriate. And so new ways were devised to remember the war dead, notably the remarkable rituals at the Cenotaph and the tomb of the Unknown Warrior, and the annual commemoration on Armistice Day. The inspiration for innovative commemoration came partly from the state, but also from the churches and from popular demand. Local civic war memorials were erected in cities, towns, and villages across England, drawing on traditional Christian imagery and reaffirming the community values for which their soldiers had died.[3]

At a national level, the initial urge to salute the war dead with a temporary shrine for a march past of the armies in July 1919 was translated by popular demand into the erection of Lutyens's Cenotaph in Whitehall as the permanent national war memorial. This 'empty tomb' became the symbolic resting place of all dead soldiers: its abstract classical form spoke to millions of bereaved who 'could contemplate the timeless, the eternal, the inexorable reality of death in war', as Jay Winter observes. It became a focus for a public display of collective mourning to honour those who sacrificed their lives for the nation.[4] The impressive burial of the Unknown Warrior in Westminster Abbey on 11 November 1920 carried special meaning for the relatives of those other Unknowns—the huge army of missing soldiers, unidentifiable, lost in mud, or blown to bits. The Unknown represented all his dead comrades: as the Liberal politician C. F. G. Masterman said, 'we were burying every boy's father, and every woman's lover, and every Mother's child'.[5] This new ritual meant so much to the bereaved that one million people visited the grave of the Unknown within a week. Adrian Gregory highlights the emotive power of the silence of Armistice Day in response to 'a particular moment of mass bereavement and mass grief. It provided structure and meaning to an unparalleled outpouring of collective emotion'. Silence was in itself a symbolic response when language was often inadequate to convey feelings of anguish and loss. The Times observed on 12 November 1919, 'Grief has been private. The great result of the two minutes' homage yesterday will be to teach the nation its general loss'.[6]

We cannot generalize about the ultimate value of national war commemoration in England in consoling grieving families and returned servicemen: probably it made the loss more bearable for many, but not all. There were tensions between the dual functions of enabling the bereaved to mourn their dead and honouring the sacrifice of the war heroes: it was not easy to achieve both. Some veterans were haunted by traumatic memories and tried to forget the war, if they could. War memorials and Armistice Day may have been most valuable for those able to structure their grieving around patriotic concepts of honour, duty, and noble sacrifice, offering reassurance that their loved one had not died in vain. Such public commemoration at home was also more likely to mitigate the grief of families with unambiguous information about the cause of death and known grave sites. It may have had less appeal to returned soldiers still suffering anguish at the violent deaths of good friends; and to the numerous families of the missing with no known graves, who may have needed solace most of all. Many such bereaved families and returned soldiers felt an urgent need to visit the battlefields in France and Belgium to see the spot where their beloved son or husband was buried, or, failing that, where they had been killed.

The remarkable man primarily responsible for the creation of the Imperial War Graves Commission was Sir Fabian Ware, who had been sent out by Lord Kitchener late in 1914 to search for missing soldiers with a small mobile unit equipped by the British Red Cross, following the retreat from Mons. Ware had been profoundly moved by his search in October 1914 for a particular friend's grave in the Béthune town cemetery: the twenty or so wooden crosses bearing the names of British officers and men appeared 'pathetically lonely and expatriated'. He was determined that such graves must not be lost. The Red Cross offered financial support for the unit to find and register British graves and erect new crosses. This was the start of the Imperial War Graves Commission, whose role was expanded by the decisions by France and other Allied governments to grant their land in perpetuity to make the cemetery sites permanent.[7]

From 1916 the Commission recognized that it would never be possible to obtain a record of all graves, especially those of the innumerable missing. In many cases all traces of burial grounds were later obliterated by enemy shellfire, while numerous graves of British soldiers within enemy lines were not marked and were lost for ever. From 1916, however, the Commission began to establish authorized burial grounds behind the British front lines, with soldiers employed by the Commission to look after them. The scale of the challenge for the War Graves Commission immediately after the war was immense, especially the problem posed by countless scattered and isolated graves.[8]

There was heated debate in the House of Commons in 1919–20 over the Imperial War Graves Commission's proposal that war graves of all ranks should be marked by the same plain 3-foot headstone: upper-class critics demanded in vain the right of the bereaved to choose their own individual monuments. In 1920 Parliament approved the uniform rows of neat headstones for the British war cemeteries, on the democratic principle of equality of treatment, given the common sacrifice of officers and men. However, it was conceded that families could add their own inscriptions (of not more than three lines) together with personal details of rank, regiment, and date of death. A *Manchester Guardian* editorial concluded in December 1919 that the war cemeteries were currently 'the most beautiful and moving places in which men ever collected their dead' with their 'nobly expressive simplicity'. The war cemeteries were intended to be completed by 1922, when they stretched across France and Belgium in a line from the Vosges to the English Channel. But they had to remain open throughout the 1920s to inter thousands of newly discovered corpses as the War Graves Commission combed the battle areas. Each cemetery was dominated by a Christian 'Cross of Sacrifice' designed by Reginald Blomfield, and by Edward Lutyens's Stone of Remembrance, combining religious imagery with classical influences.[9]

## Morris Bickersteth: Missing on the Somme, 1 July 1916

This chapter will explore the story of one family—the Bickersteths—who made repeated ritualized visits to the Great War cemeteries which brought profound consolation. We will see why this was so, and how the nature of that solace differed within the family for the bereaved parents and the ex-soldiers, and how it altered over the years in subsequent visits. David Lloyd's history of *Battlefield Tourism* examines visits to the war cemeteries as pilgrimages and as tourism, with an emphasis on organized group pilgrimages led by philanthropic societies and the British Legion for ex-servicemen.[10] This chapter's focus is different: it explores detailed narratives of several pilgrimages undertaken over twelve years by the same grieving family, which included the two parents as well as three veteran soldier sons. Where Lloyd examines group pilgrimages of bereaved parents and ex-servicemen separately and at times in some tension, the Bickersteth pilgrimages reveal in remarkable detail the interaction between the responses of former soldiers and grieving parents within the one family.

Lieutenant Morris Bickersteth, aged 25, was killed on the first day of the battle of the Somme on 1 July 1916. His father, Revd Samuel Bickersteth, vicar of Leeds and later a canon of Canterbury Cathedral, belonged to a distinguished Victorian Evangelical family, and was himself the son of a bishop. This upper-middle-class family was the product of public schools, Oxford, and the Church of England, with two sons in holy orders. They were strongly patriotic as well as deeply religious, as were many people of their class in 1914. Samuel's wife, Ella, kept all her soldier sons' wartime letters, together with her own commentaries and press cuttings, in eighteen imposing volumes of 'War Diaries', one of my primary sources for this account. The numerous detailed letters from Julian and Burgon were intended to be circulated throughout the family before they reached the War Diaries. This substantial collection is vividly illuminating about the experiences of wartime grief, loss, and commemoration.[11]

Samuel and Ella Bickersteth had six adult sons, of whom five served with the army—four on the Western Front and Geoffrey in War Office Intelligence. This chapter is chiefly concerned with Morris, Julian, Burgon, and their parents. Julian was an Anglican clergyman, who had been chaplain of Melbourne Grammar School in Australia from 1911 to 1915, when he volunteered as a chaplain with front-line duties on the Western Front. He was devout, energetic, and a born leader—often in heavy fighting, caring for soldiers' spiritual welfare, looking after the wounded and burying the dead. He also won the Military Cross for bravery. After the war he became a headmaster first in Australia and later in England, and subsequently archdeacon of Maidstone. Julian was close to his younger brother, Burgon, an academic administrator and poet, who later spent twenty-six years in Canada as warden of Hart House at the University of Toronto. Burgon served with the Royal Dragoons as a cavalry officer in France throughout the war, often in heavy fighting, winning the Military Cross twice and writing a history of the Sixth Cavalry Brigade immediately after the war. In later life he joined Julian and his aged mother in the service of Canterbury Cathedral. Their nephew later described Julian as tall and debonair, 'a disciplined Anglo-Catholic priest'; Burgon, the younger, was 'wiry and stocky, a wonderful listener, and a devout Anglican layman'. They were both full of ideas, energy, and enthusiasm, and 'fun to be with'.[12]

Julian, Morris, and Burgon Bickersteth were all involved in the Somme offensive of July 1916. They succeeded in meeting near the battlefield on 29 June, knowing that any one of them could die in the forthcoming battle, which would be Morris's first. After her son's death, Ella noted: 'It is a joy to think that the three brothers had that happy meeting two days before Morris went into action'. Ella described the location of this meeting in later years as one of 'the stations of the Cross' on their pilgrimages to Morris's grave. During their three hours together, they spoke a little of their forebodings: 'Not one of us could pretend that we [faced death] without fear.' Julian reassured their parents: 'We did agree, Morris and I, on a previous occasion that death must be very wonderful and not a thing to be feared in itself at all.'[13] However, it was easier to see death as 'wonderful' in theory and away from the battlefield.

The Somme offensive was intended as a diversionary attack on the Gommecourt salient held by the Germans. Morris was one of 20,000 killed of the 110,000 who attacked on the first day, with 40,000 more wounded. He was an acting company commander with the fifteenth Battalion, the West Yorkshire Regiment, better known as the Leeds Pals, formed largely from North Country 'Pals' battalions in the original Kitchener army. Its soldiers volunteered to fight with friends and neighbours from the same local area: this was good for comradeship and morale, but it meant they also died together and their home towns and villages in the north of England suffered disproportionately heavy losses.[14]

Julian was fighting a different kind of personal battle during the 'glorious failure' on the Somme, where he was a Church of England chaplain dealing with large numbers of dead and wounded, as he explained to his family at home:

I have seen sights and heard sounds the last few days which will live with me to my dying day, and filled me with an agony of sympathy for those suffering indescribable things. I have identified over seventy bodies, some of them scarcely identifiable and have seen men wounded beyond recovery; I have been surrounded for three days with nothing but blood, blood, blood. Yet rising out of this sea of misery and pain, human nature, the spirit of man, has won the day. His is an immortal soul. The courage, self-sacrifice and endurance of countless numbers of these men will be an inspiration to me for all time, though I may never blot out from my eyes the hideous realities of these dreadful days. I seemed to have packed into them the experiences of a whole life-time.

It was a challenge to divert thirty men from the fighting to dig a huge trench in the little village cemetery, as individual graves were out of the question. In Julian's battalion over four hundred men were missing— wounded, dead, or prisoners: 'the task of writing to their people is quite beyond me'.[15] Meanwhile Morris had been reported missing at Serre on 1 July, the opening day of the Somme battle, though the telegram informing the family that he was killed in action did not arrive till 5 July. Ella and Samuel were distraught at not knowing how Morris was killed or whether he had 'suffered long hours' before death. On 3 July Julian went across to Serre to find out whether Morris was still alive, 'with my heart full of apprehension, news of the terrible loss of life further south having reached us'. On the way he stopped two Leeds Pals who told him that no officers survived the attack and that they had heard Morris was dead. This news was confirmed by another chaplain, 'almost broken-hearted over the terrible losses'. Morris had encouraged his men and led them bravely over the top, but heavy machine-gun fire cut them down in no-man's-land: Morris was struck in the head and killed instantly. Of the 750 Leeds Pals who had attacked, 230 were killed and over 300 wounded, with no ground gained.[16]

Early in July 1916 Julian reported sadly to his parents that his brother's body had to be left unburied in no-man's-land because of the British retreat. He consoled them:

You will see then, dear ones, that it is quite impossible to get the body back...But I don't worry about that so much and you mustn't either, dearest ones...I never felt so strong in my faith that the dear lad isn't dead but lives...His grave is all the world, and his memory is ours to cherish for all time, and he isn't far from us.

The devout Bickersteth family knew that Morris was spiritually prepared for his likely fate, with a strong, simple faith in God. He had left a letter for his parents in the event of his death, assuring them that death had no terror for him, because in time the whole family would be reunited in eternal life.[17]

But even the most devout Christian faith could not assuage the parents' grief and anxiety after such a violent death, especially as they did not know what happened to his body. They were thankful that it had been identified and they knew he died quickly, but they continued their enquiries to locate the body. Burying parties were unable to reach the corpses in no-man's-land at Serre in July 1916; so much high explosive was used there for days after the battle that recovery was impossible. Nevertheless Julian tried twice to locate Morris's body: on one occasion, a month afterwards, he managed a risky journey across the scarred battlefield to the spot where Morris's comrades said he fell, and where Julian presumed he might be buried: but he was warned by a soldier to go back because heavy shellfire made the terrain too dangerous. He concluded on 9 August that Morris's body had probably been blown to pieces. But some months later he learned that the body had been moved into a nearby cemetery where the ground had been cleared by a chaplain. Serre was not captured by the Allies until February 1917, but in March and August 1918 it was again lost to the Germans, and then retaken: it was continually swept by opposing armies.[18] They had reason to fear that Morris's body might be lost for ever.

On 23 July 1916 Ella Bickersteth noted in her journal that Morris's body still lay unburied, and her suffering was acute: 'We sit in the garden and think of Morris our soldier saint...I can't bear to think of our darling's body lying in the open, and we should love the things he carried in his pockets'. On 24 August she wrote sadly, 'As I write our Morris' body has never been found, nor will it be'. Any normal process of mourning seemed impossible when uncertainty and anxiety about the location and condition of the body persisted. Ella's journal recorded in April 1917 that after nine months Julian was still finding the bodies of his own officers lying unburied at Gommecourt, nor had he abandoned hope in his search for Morris at Serre.[19]

Meanwhile, memory offered a major consolation which reinforced that of religious faith. Late in August 1916 Ella Bickersteth noted how good it was to talk to a friend about Morris's life and death. By September 1916 she reported that she and Samuel were slightly better 'but not strong'. A parcel of Morris's winter clothes had been returned but it was 'hard work unpacking them'. Their youngest son, Ralph, also a soldier, took some of these clothes as a remembrance, having inherited them in Morris's will. There was a poignant moment in 1916 when Ralph presented his parents with a 'most beautiful crayon portrait of Morris' as a surprise commemoration present. The parents were delighted with the lifelike portrait: 'you might think Morris would step out of the frame and speak...[It] is such a joy to us'.[20]

The Bickersteth archives demonstrate the importance of war memorials in local churches, and of commemoration services and honour rolls for those parents whose sons' bodies were missing, or whose graves were not yet located. Just after the first anniversary of Morris's death, his parents erected a memorial tablet on a pillar in Leeds parish church, where Samuel was the vicar. Ella's grief was unabated in January 1918: 'I yearn for Morris with my whole being sometimes'. In June 1918 the parents attended the moving memorial service at Rugby School for the boys killed in the war: 'Our Morris seemed very close at the early service in the chapel'. Afterwards she 'communed with my darling', sitting near Morris's former school house. This sense of the spirits of dead soldier sons being close to their bereaved parents was often remarked on. From Rugby Ella and Samuel proceeded to Leeds parish church to commemorate the second anniversary of their son's death, placing a flowering rose under his memorial in the side chapel. They also left a wreath beneath the roll of honour in memory of all the brave soldiers who fell on the first day of the Somme.[21]

Morris Bickersteth's family did all they could to remember him, in the absence of a corpse and a dignified burial in England, but the memorial tablet at Leeds parish church and the commemoration services at Leeds and Rugby had their limitations. More was needed to help them grieve for a soldier son who died so violently for his country and whose burial place in a foreign land was still uncertain. Many thousands were comforted by the national rituals at London's Cenotaph and the tomb of the Unknown Warrior, but these did not mitigate the grief of all the bereaved, especially ex-servicemen and families of the missing. The primary source of consolation for the Bickersteths, as for many others, was not a state memorial in their homeland, but the spot in France where Morris's body was presumed to be buried.

## The Bickersteths' Sacred Pilgrimage to the Battlefields in 1919

Members of the Bickersteth family visited Morris's grave at least four times between 1919 and 1931. Their journeys reveal not just how sorrow could be mitigated by time, but also how the pilgrimages were themselves altered by the passing years and a changing landscape. I am drawing here on three detailed accounts of battlefield tours by various Bickersteth family members, held in the Bodleian Library Oxford and Churchill College Cambridge. The most significant is a thirty-five-page account of the first family tour from 28 June to 3 July 1919: it was written by the bereaved parents, who were accompanied by their soldier sons, Burgon and Julian. They were among the first mourning families to visit the battlefields after the war. Their visit was timed to coincide with the third anniversary of Morris's death, making it a 'labour of love' and a 'sacred pilgrimage'.[22]

Immediately the war ended the War Office was swamped by enquiries from relatives wishing to visit war graves: they were advised that for military reasons none could be permitted for many months. In April 1919 a frustrated relative wrote to the *Manchester Guardian*:

Many bereaved mothers, widows, and other relatives of fallen soldiers are waiting, with what patience they can command, to make pilgrimages to France to the last resting place of their loved ones, and will know no peace of mind until this journey has been accomplished. It is not evident after five months of armistice, that the right of bereaved relatives to visit the graves is receiving the attention it ought to have. Moreover, there is the fear that when at last the opportunity occurs, this sacred pilgrimage will have to be made in the presence of hordes of pleasure-seekers and of those who merely wish to gratify their curiosity. It is the duty of the people of this country to insist that there shall be no unnecessary delay in arranging that the relatives of fallen soldiers shall visit the graves, and under proper conditions.[23]

By February 1920 only 300 of the 1,500 British burial grounds in France had been taken over by the War Graves Commission: only three of the new war cemeteries had so far been constructed, following the same pattern—each cemetery surrounded by a stone wall and each grave of identical design with uniform headstones for all. There were still problems with supply of labour and transport of tombstones from England. Complaints of inconsiderate behaviour were made as early visitors to the battlefields made fires to prepare meals and pitched tents on consecrated ground.[24]

In this context, then, the Bickersteth family's early visit to the more remote battlefields from 30 June to 3 July 1919 was remarkable. Julian Bickersteth, the wartime chaplain, had by this time already visited Morris's place of death at Serre three times. His third visit of 28 April 1919, when he was still serving with the British Expeditionary Force in France, was described in a letter to his parents and was doubtless made in preparation for the planned family pilgrimage two months later. Julian and two soldier companions took the old Arras–Cambrai road, 'every inch of which we know by heart', finding it utterly desolate. No civilians lived in the destroyed villages they passed. The final eighty minutes of the journey to Morris's grave at Serre had to be made on foot, over devastated country which was largely uncleared.[25]

Morris's cemetery was in the centre of the original no-man's-land, near where he and about one hundred comrades fell. All the graves were dominated by a large white cross. However, it was clear that the 'Graves Registration people' had not reached this cemetery since the Armistice. Many of the temporary wooden crosses had been destroyed by shrapnel as the ground was fought over following Morris's death. The three soldiers considered themselves fortunate to find Morris's grave: the wooden cross was broken at the base, but Julian fixed it firmly into the ground and said a short prayer. All three soldiers were overpowered by the desolation of the land and the profound emotional impact of the cemetery. They were 'brought back into the very heart of the War', forced to revisit painful memories of the sacrifices of their comrades on the Somme nearly three years earlier:

We realized that the bitter and tragic side of War had already begun to be softened and subdued by time . . . Mercifully, perhaps, but certainly one forgets the horror and tragedy of it all as the years go on. We had come back for one afternoon into the heart of it again and the old memories were crystallized again for us and made us sad.[26]

David Lloyd has rightly argued that religion and spirituality played a vital role in British pilgrimages in the interwar years. In this the Bickersteths were not unlike many other pilgrims, though their family included three Anglican priests and their faith may have been unusually deep. Though formal church attendance had declined, religion remained a significant part of British culture. Religious organizations, such as the Church Army and the St Barnabas Society, organized many group visits to the war graves, some at low cost for the poor. Many people who were not active churchgoers still retained nebulous folk beliefs in God and some kind of afterlife, with a general knowledge of Bible stories and popular hymns. The term 'pilgrimage' was widely used to mean a religious journey to a sacred place: like the Bickersteths, many pilgrims believed they were closest to the spirits of their dead on the battlefields where they were killed. Many battlefields became cemeteries and were described as sacred places where heroic soldiers had sacrificed their lives for their country. The notion of sacrifice was central in efforts to make sense of the suffering: at times the pilgrims even likened the soldiers' sacrifice to that of Christ. In every war cemetery, the Cross of Sacrifice and the Stone of Remembrance were seen as Christian symbols.[27]

Pilgrims who visited the battlefields more than once were likely to create their own rituals, but in doing so they often drew on Christian symbols. The Bickersteths' rituals centred on battlefield sites of meaning to their soldier sons and places associated with Morris's death became their stations of the cross. They were inevitably a little disappointed on later pilgrimages when the rebuilding of villages interfered with their memories and their rituals. Some common rituals were less obviously Christian. The Bickersteths carried flowers from their English garden to place on war graves in France and Belgium: in exchange they collected souvenirs from the battlefield, such as soil, stones, or flowers, to take back home as material links with Morris.[28]

The role of memory in the process of mourning and commemoration was almost as important for the Bickersteths as that of religion. Morris's spirit seemed to accompany them as they followed his final journey. They could recapture his last days in remarkable detail through the three sons' numerous letters collected in Ella's 'War Diary', combined with the running commentary of the surviving soldier sons. The heart of their pilgrimage was Morris's grave with its name on the headstone—an individual link with him which distinguished his grave from the thousands of the missing. They felt particularly close to him there. Their narratives were dominated by memories of Morris: their pilgrimages helped them to assuage their sorrow, which became less acute and anguished in later narratives.

Memory worked in a more complex way for pilgrims who were also veterans, like Burgon and Julian Bickersteth, than it did for bereaved civilian parents. Veterans were grieving for comrades who had closely shared their own traumatic experiences of war: they were haunted by intense memories of horrific deaths often seen at close quarters, and sometimes by guilt at having survived. Revisiting the battlefields meant returning to their own painful past, which many preferred to forget. For some, revisiting the battlefields reopened old wounds: for others, like the

Bickersteth brothers, remembering was a crucial part of grieving, and facing up to distressing memories. The active recollection of past battles and dead comrades was clearly traumatic for both Julian and Burgon, but they conceived their pilgrimages in part as an essential tribute by the survivors to the dead. Their narratives revealed little of this likely inner turmoil; indeed their accounts were prosaic and largely unemotional, unlike those of their parents: but they needed to keep remembering in order to come to terms with their painful and complex wartime past.

For Burgon it was also necessary to revisit in his imagination, over and over again, the detailed military strategy of some of the most damaging battles of attrition, to find meaning in the killing and reassure himself of the justification for the war. He doubtless wrote his *History of the Sixth Cavalry Brigade* so soon after the war finished to help him deal with his own demons. The family pilgrimages were a continuing part of the process, even though Burgon's recurring insomnia on those journeys signified their pain. But Burgon and Julian also gained increasing satisfaction with each pilgrimage as they began to focus on the more positive memories. Inevitably what they remembered on these pilgrimages was a mixture of the comradeship, the day-to-day routine, and the horror of mass slaughter. Nostalgia was mingled with sadness when intimately remembered battlefields changed their contours over the years. They were confronting the reality of their past, in an attempt to exorcize the worst of its horrors and find some measure of reconciliation.

Julian and Burgon were well aware of the huge gulf that existed between returned soldiers who had experienced the trauma of multiple violent deaths in battle, and relatives at home who had not. The brothers set out to reduce that gulf for their own family by describing in detail the battles they had fought. They sought to show their parents exactly where, how, and why they fought particular engagements. They wanted to help Samuel and Ella to understand the military objectives of the war, so they in turn would appreciate that Morris did not die in vain. The parents needed to visit Morris's grave to feel his spirit close to them, for they had not seen his body nor had a funeral to farewell him. Walking over the land where he died was a sacred experience for them: it reinforced their view of their son as a hero who sacrificed his life for his country. The broken landscape of the Serre valley in 1919 bore further testimony to his ordeal and his endurance.

And so, on 30 June 1919, the four pilgrims set out from Folkestone for France, for the third anniversary of Morris's death. Ella and Samuel later wrote separate accounts of their pilgrimage, charged with feeling: Ella's was more emotional and more detailed, while Samuel added his 'impressions' to his wife's story. The two narratives are combined here, indicating the author only where that adds meaning.[29] Ella and Samuel stayed first at the Hôtel de L'Univers in Amiens, as they did on later pilgrimages. The first tour created a ritualized pattern for later visits, with both brothers keen to return to the scenes of their own battles, as well as places associated with Morris. So, as they were driven from Amiens to the ruins of Villers Bretonneux where Burgon fought with the Royal Dragoons in 1918, he explained the military action and his role in it at length, while pointing out key military positions. Ella responded enthusiastically: 'It was thrilling to be on a spot where a son of ours had actually taken part in a battle that saved Amiens and the channel ports, where brave deeds had been done and lives lost'. Burgon helped his parents to understand the meaning of the war from the soldiers' perspective and offered a military justification for the conflict which killed their son. The parents created another ritual when they picked up a battered helmet and two bullets, to remind them later of the harsh reality of war.[30]

On 1 July 1919, three years precisely after Morris was killed, they took their car with a driver on the *route nationale* from Amiens to Albert, which seemed to Samuel 'haunted with the vast armies which had rolled along it'. They looked at the results of 'mad destruction': scattered on the ground were remnants of war, such as helmets and cartridges, but also human bones, never buried. The town of Albert had once been substantial but now 'the desolation of its ruins beggars description'. All that remained of houses and the cathedral were a few tottering walls: old women were digging in the ruins and the clearing-up operation was slowly starting. It required a huge effort of the imagination for Ella and Samuel to reconstruct the scenes of the war from the remaining desolation and their sons' commentary. Julian and Burgon vividly recreated the events of their war for they knew the territory intimately. As Samuel noted, every step of their pilgrimage was as familiar to Julian as Rugby School and Melbourne.[31]

Sacred sites of family memory were visited on this drive to Serre. From Albert they went to the village of Bus-les-Artois where Morris had been billeted in his final weeks and where the three brothers had their 'historic' meeting on 29 June 1916. They sought out the farm which had been Morris's battalion headquarters and where his two brothers had proudly watched him commanding his company for the first and only time. It took a while to identify this farm, and to show their parents' Morris's mess and his bedroom, where he wrote his last letter home. This little farm became a shrine for his family. They also identified the crossroads at Acheux where Burgon and Morris parted for ever. Then they moved on to the ruins of the village of Hebuterne where Julian had been based: they found the site of the casualty clearing station where the wounded had lain during the Somme battle. Julian took his family to the nearby village cemetery— overgrown now, but once beautiful. Julian had helped to bury there about seventy of his men, killed on the first day of the battle of the Somme, the day of Morris's death. All of this the parents already knew from Julian's letters home, but to understand more fully they needed to see the cemetery and to hear him tell the sad stories again on the spot, noting how heavy shelling during burials forced the burial teams to shelter in open graves. Such harrowing scenes were relived time and again during the Bickersteth pilgrimages, helping the sons to work through excruciating memories and the parents to empathize with their suffering.[32]

This first pilgrimage was already a highly charged emotional experience for the Bickersteth family. As they visited the 'sacred' locations of the last days of Morris's life, they were vividly aware that this was spiritual preparation for their visit to Morris's place of death at Queens Cemetery at Puisieux, near Serre. The closest a motor car could approach to the front line was at Hebuterne, leaving a full hour's strenuous walk across 'a sea of shell-holes', testimony to the destruction wrought by modern warfare. This must have been hard for the elderly parents, and for Julian, who was only just recovering from trench fever. Samuel depicted this hazardous walk, following Morris's final hours, as the 'Via Sacra' in 'the area for ever hallowed in my memory'. He saw Morris as having been spiritually and personally tested by the challenges of trench warfare; and he hoped historians would one day see the battle of the Somme as the watershed of the Great War (as some have depicted it). Samuel was striving here to justify the purpose of the war in order to reassure himself that Morris had not died in vain: this vital point is repeated again and again in the family narratives. This was especially important given the catastrophic slaughter on 1 July 1916 and its abject failure to meet its strategic targets. Julian described again for his parents the military action on 1 July 1916 and

Morris's final hours, as told to him by his brother's men. So Samuel followed in his imagination as Morris courageously led the eighth wave of his company to the attack, and was struck down before even reaching the British front line:

The rapid cross-firing of machine guns, the noise, the smoke-bombs, the hell upon earth, I was able in my mind to reconstruct, however faintly, something of what our Leeds boys faced that summer morning, led and strengthened for endurance by the cool courage of that young Acting Captain, who had mastered fear, such natural and inevitable fear, so as to be able to do his duty.[33]

The family would never have found Morris's burial place in July 1919 without Julian's intimate knowledge of the area, thanks to his three earlier visits. The area between Serre and Puisieux was a scene of desolation, with the few surviving broken trees bare of leaves and no house standing. As Julian led the family across the shell-torn ground, they crossed over old trenches, avoiding shell holes and barbed wire; they saw the remains of German machine guns and cases of hand grenades and picked up shells and shell cases as souvenirs. The rain was 'torrential' as they reached the front line and the three cemeteries—'not out of keeping with our feelings'. Morris's cemetery was the central one, in the middle of the original no-man's-land. Ella observed, 'It was a dreary scene of desolation and yet we were so glad our dear son was actually buried on the battlefield among his men'. Queens British Cemetery at Puisieux was overgrown by weeds, dominated by a large white cross, and surrounded by wire attached to four corner posts. The heavy rain and the devastated landscape helped the grieving parents to relate to 'the Calvary-like surroundings' of the battle their son faced. Ella described their search for 'our Morris's place of Victory over Death' and for the cross which symbolically marked his grave. Her account revealed how much she had learned from her sons' explanations:

The trenches were filled in, but we could trace Warly trench and what must have been the assembly trench. The long pollarded willows (our front line) were still there and so we identified our bit of holy ground. The ground sloped upwards, Serre lying over the ridge out of sight. On the higher ground were the Germans and they could command the whole slope with their guns. Our men had absolutely no chance, but to see it all made one feel the glory of their advance against such hopeless odds, and their willing self-sacrifice filled one with a never-dying admiration and pride. As Burgon said 'After all, there is something grand about War, the comradeship, the selflessness, the laying down of life willingly for the ideal of liberty and freedom'. We felt when we stood later on the devastated strip of country from Albert to Ypres that one could more easily give up our son, who with others had died to put a stop to such horrors.[34]

This was indeed a 'sacred pilgrimage', though the family used the term sparingly. The 'big words' of heroic rhetoric survive in the Christian language, and were used here by both parents with love and understanding— and none of the irony employed by such writers as Siegried Sassoon or Wilfred Owen. This was not naivety but belief in those great ideals. The high diction, used in both parents' accounts, also demonstrated the genuine patriotism of the family. Even Burgon and Julian, who had more than enough experience of the horrors of the Great War, still believed it was a necessary war fought for 'the ideal of liberty and freedom'.[35]

The pilgrimage itself and their sense of its sanctity were especially important because they could not be certain that the cross actually marked the exact site of Morris's remains. As Samuel explained, 'We found the little cross, which whether it marks it or not, the place where they laid our Morris, is to us a sacred foot of mother-earth'. It was enough to know he died and was buried close to that spot, where they laid red roses from their Canterbury garden and Samuel offered prayers. The flowers from their garden were a symbolic exchange for their souvenirs of war. These rituals had a special value in 1919 because the family did not yet know whether the Imperial War Graves Commission would leave Queens Cemetery untouched or whether the soldiers' remains would be reinterred and consecrated elsewhere in a larger and less isolated cemetery.[36]

It was hard to tear themselves away from Morris's place of death as they drove north to Arras and Ypres. The remainder of their journey took a different turn, with a greater emphasis on the wartime memory of the two soldier sons and their grief for dead comrades. As they passed ruins, 'every place seemed full of memories to one or other of the two sons'. At Arras, part of their own hotel, the Hôtel de Commerce, was gutted from ground to roof, with shell marks on the wall and wallpaper hanging in strips. They saw the ruined buildings around the square, with only the walls standing of the Cathedral and Bishop's Palace. From Arras they drove to the town of Vermelles and the site of the battle of Loos in 1915, stopping at the newly extended cemetery at the town's entrance. This cemetery already held 2,500 dead in July 1919, and was daily receiving more bodies. Samuel would not let Ella walk to the corner of the cemetery where corpses were being reinterred from surrounding small battlefields, given their own uncertainty about the future of their son's remains.[37]

Their final destination was Ypres, which Ella described as 'Holy Ground' because countless British soldiers defended it from the invader for four years, and far too many died in its defence. Samuel noted that they stood grief-stricken 'by the dreadful and dreary desolation, the contrast between what is and what was too overpowering'. This was one of the most poignant of all spectacles. It seemed a hopeless task to rebuild the once-beautiful city, but it was to be done, leaving the thirteenth-century Cloth Hall and Cathedral in ruins, as a memorial to the dead. However, they were thankful to see Ypres before the tourists invaded.[38]

## The Later Pilgrimages, 1926–1931: Rituals, Memories, and Landscape

The second significant account of the family's battlefield pilgrimages was written seven years later, in mid-1926, for the tenth anniversary of Morris's death. Samuel and Ella had made the pilgrimage again in 1921 but no account appears to have survived, and there may have been others. The 1926 narrative is illuminating both for the contrasts it depicts in the landscape of the battlefields and the changes in the family's responses. The parents did not travel this time, probably because Ella was losing her sight. Burgon, who wrote the account, was again accompanied by Julian, and also by their eldest brother Monier, another priest, with his wife Kitty. For this anniversary pilgrimage, Julian returned to Europe from Australia and Burgon from Canada. Kitty died of cancer just over ten years after this tour, which had personal meaning for her because she was also visiting her brother's grave at Vermelles. For Monier and Kitty the emotional impact was greater because it was their first visit.[39]

Their journey took the now familiar route from Ypres to Arras and Serre, revisiting the sites of memory located in 1919. Burgon and Julian were astonished to discover a complete 'resurrection' of Ypres, which had been entirely rebuilt since their last visit with their parents in 1919. Indeed the whole Ypres salient had been transformed, as people returned and rebuilt their homes: it was now a 'marvellous sight'. In 1919 it had been 'still an ugly waste of shell holes, mud, and ruined villages', but was now covered with luxuriant crops and dotted with villages, though no trees had yet grown. Moreover, the villages and churches had been rebuilt in brick rather than the original mud and plaster. The transformation offered hope and consolation. The family stood on a ridge looking back to Ypres, overcome by the 'most moving' view across former battlefields: 'Every now and again shining white among the amazing crops or a group of red roofed farms we could catch sight of cemeteries with their white cross and headstones...What memories! They were too deep for words'. It seems likely that Burgon and Julian again kept the depth of their feelings to themselves, whereas Ella had in 1919 found expression of emotions easier. This reflected a gendered and a generational difference, as well as that between soldiers and civilians. They discovered newly added graves in the cemeteries all along the former Front, especially on the Somme. The chauffeur mentioned that bodies were still frequently discovered: three weeks earlier 117 bodies of British soldiers were found in a single shell hole.[40]

Burgon found himself unable to sleep, as on the 1919 pilgrimage: 'the memories brought back by the old scenes we had revisited were too vivid'. He spent the long nights rereading his own history of the Sixth Cavalry Brigade which he had brought to refresh his memory on the details of military tactics and particular battles. As they drove, he relived for them the battle of third Ypres (Passchendaele) of July 1917—in his view one of the bloodiest and most unjustifiable offensives of the war. And he explained in some detail the military operations of the last two years of the war, and his part in them, for the benefit of Monier and Kitty. The two former soldiers had a special relationship with the war dead and with their own traumatic memories of combat—and it was again important to the rest of the family to share and empathize as far as possible. At Vermelles, a coal mining district, the cemetery for the dead of the battle of Loos was the only place of beauty: Kitty placed flowers at her brother's grave and took photos which she would later cherish.[41]

Finally, the four pilgrims reached the Queens British Cemetery at Puisieux in the open country east of Serre, where Morris was buried. They were obliged to use their chauffeur's guidebook to the cemeteries to make sure that remains from Queens Cemetery had not by now been reinterred at Vermelles: they were relieved to find that nothing had been touched. They walked from the car to Queens Cemetery 'knowing every step of the way': the original wooden crosses were still in place over the two hundred or so bodies and the old wire fence still surrounded the plot. The War Graves Commission did not reach the Queens Cemetery at Puisieux until 1929, thirteen years after Morris was killed. The 1926 Annual Report of the Commission helps to explain why. During the war the Commission had promised soldiers that if they carried their dead comrades to certain authorized burial grounds close to the trenches— often at risk to their own lives—the dead would rest there undisturbed. The Commission tried to keep this promise, except where the original site was entirely unsuitable or extremely small.[42]

The family walked directly to Morris's grave, on which they laid flowers bought that morning in Arras (whereas Ella had brought flowers from her garden). Little or nothing had yet been done to cultivate the land around these three small and isolated cemeteries, where bushes and weeds still grew profusely. The shell holes were clearly visible, but had partially collapsed and were covered with a white flowering shrub. The extensive view from Queens Cemetery brought back many memories of that day, precisely ten years earlier, when Morris fell. The Queens Cemetery at Puisieux was one of the family's few sites of memory to remain intact in 1926. Many houses had been rebuilt since their 1919 visit to Bus-les-Artois, so the brothers could not identify their 1916 meeting place with Morris. They drove to Pozières, which had been entirely rebuilt and where workmen were still filling shell holes and finding corpses.[43]

This 1926 visit and the account written by Burgon contrasted markedly with that of 1919, composed by the grieving parents. Much of this difference derives from Burgon's prosaic and understated prose. His insomnia indicates, however, that his emotions were still powerfully aroused by memories of battles fought and comrades killed. Where the first family tour of 1919 was essentially a sacred pilgrimage to Morris's grave, this 1926 journey was dominated by the two former soldiers' memories and their need to revisit their wartime experiences and to grieve deeply for lost comrades. The 'big words' of heroic rhetoric and even the Christian language of mourning and consolation were largely absent here—reflecting both a generational change, and the contrast in responses between grieving civilian parents and active participants in the war.

The last of these accounts was written by Burgon to commemorate the family pilgrimage to Morris's grave in 1931, the fifteenth anniversary of his death. It was one of the two components of the celebration of Samuel and Ella's golden wedding anniversary. The first was a gift by the sons to their parents: the publication in an edition of 200 copies of a *Memoir of Morris* compiled by Samuel just after the war and revised during the winter of 1930–1. The second was the visit to Morris's grave, almost certain to be the last the parents could manage: Ella was now 73 and blind, while Samuel was only a year younger and destined to die in 1937. It was a remarkable undertaking for such a frail elderly couple—indeed a labour of love and sacrifice. The participants on the pilgrimage were, as in 1919, Samuel, Ella, Julian, and Burgon, but this time they were accompanied by 'Ninny', Elizabeth Peters, the sons' former nurse, who died five years later. The journey took place from 29 June to 3 July 1931: the visit to the grave on 1 July was again the primary purpose, but it was made in the context of a wider tour by car of the towns and battlefields of Belgium and northern France.[44]

Following the Channel crossing the five pilgrims drove in a borrowed chauffeur-driven car to the recently completed Menin Gate Memorial to the Missing at Ypres, opened in July 1927, just ten years after the start of the terrible third battle of Ypres. They admired the new memorial for the magnificence of its simple beauty. They joined the crowd assembling under the huge vault of the Gateway to hear the 'Last Post' sounded at 9 p.m., as it was every evening. Three Belgian trumpeters stood under the gateway facing Ypres and sounded 'the most moving of all military calls—the last post', with everyone motionless. Symbolically the Last Post stopped time and encouraged the pilgrims to remember the dead and ensure they did not die in vain. Ex-servicemen could be overwhelmed with memories and bereaved families with sorrow for their dead. The Menin Gate was the most important British monument to the dead on the Western Front and became the chief destination for British pilgrims. For the Bickersteths this was a high point of this pilgrimage. Perhaps they reflected that they were fortunate in one respect: though Morris was initially reported missing, at least they knew eventually where and how he was killed, and believed they knew—more or less—where he was buried. Other bereaved families lacked this consolation and for them the Menin Gate Memorial symbolized the missing grave. On 30 June the family set out on their ritualized three-day retracing of the British front line from Ypres to Arras and Serre, which would include many landmark sites well known to Julian and Burgon, and familiar to the parents from their earlier visits. They spent that night at Arras, as they had in 1919, and next day toured nearby sites resonant with particular memories of their personal experiences of the war.[45]

At last the family made its way to Morris's grave in the Queens Cemetery at Puisieux, in the valley of the Serre: 'for us it was the holiest ground in all the long battle front'. They walked across an uncultivated field still scarred by shell holes. Yet the three cemeteries had been transformed by the War Graves Commission in 1929: each was now marked by the Cross of Sacrifice designed by Reginald Blomfield and surrounded by high walls. The neat white headstones were almost obscured by masses of brilliant flowers, including a small bush of red roses against Morris's headstone. They placed their own tribute of red and white lilies at the foot of the great stone cross with a message on a card: 'With golden thoughts of your self-sacrifice from Father and Mother, 1 July 1916'. Samuel briefly placed a copy of his *Memoir of Morris* on the headstone of his grave while they took a photograph. They remained a long time in this place of 'extraordinary peace and beauty', leaving as the sun set.[46] That photograph would take its place in their precious collection of mementoes of Morris.

Their day concluded in a lighter mood with dinner at the Hôtel Continental at Cambrai. They behaved more like tourists than pilgrims in their final two days. They laughed over dinner as Samuel pretended not to comprehend the language of the menu—confusing the waiter 'who must have thought English people harder than ever to understand'. Next day, 2 July 1931, the family explored the Hindenburg line, parallel to the British front line, following the route to St Quentin, where they visited the newly restored cathedral. Burgon and Julian attended benediction at the cathedral before visiting an annual circus and fair: such entertainments would have been unthinkable in their early pilgrimages. Their final day was devoted to visits to places with wartime memories for the two brothers before driving to Boulogne to start their journey home to Canterbury.[47]

None of the brothers ever forgot the loss of their beloved Morris: they continued to place an 'In Memoriam' notice annually in *The Times* for nearly sixty years. The surviving brothers, aged over 80, only decided to stop on 1 July 1976, when their final 'In Memoriam' notice read: 'Bickersteth, S.M. In memory of our brother Lt. (acting Captain) Stanley Morris Bickersteth, 15th Bn. West Yorkshire Regiment, killed on 1st July, 1916, on the Somme. E.M.B., J.B.B., R.M.B.'. The brothers continued to remember Morris and their fallen comrades, even when themselves close to death.

The contrast in the Bickersteth archives between their commemoration of family deaths of soldiers and civilians in the interwar years is marked.

There were many volumes of war diaries and there were also several substantial accounts of their sacred pilgrimages to Morris's grave in France, as we have seen. By contrast little survives to remember their family's civilian deaths in peacetime, apart from bundles of condolence letters. There was nothing of substance to match the remarkable Victorian deathbed memorials, apart from their loving records of visits to Morris's battlefield grave.

# 4

# Death, Disasters, and Rituals among the Northern Working Classes, 1919–1939

The dominant narrative of death in the interwar years was that of the commemoration of the Great War soldiers, which eclipsed that of individual civilians who died in peacetime. The two world wars reinforced each other in altering attitudes and practices relating to death, grief, and mourning, but the Second World War had the greater impact. Marked regional and class diversity in attitudes and rituals relating to death and bereavement persisted in the interwar years and beyond. The picture is complex and multi-layered. To compensate for the bias towards the comfortable classes in the south of England in the archival records, I will focus in this chapter on the working classes of the north. Julie-Marie Strange's work has illuminated a distinctive working-class culture of grief in the decades before 1914.[1] My own research for the interwar years points to strong continuities with that past, reinforced by years of deep economic depression.

During the interwar years profound economic and social changes were taking place, especially in the south of England and the cities, but elsewhere older traditions remained powerful and there were distinctive regional and class variations. It seems likely also that generational changes in attitudes and behaviour were marked between the wars. The generations to which the soldiers and their parents belonged were the most deeply preoccupied with mourning and commemoration, especially in the 1920s, while their children were more likely to look to the future and try to avoid the seeming obsession with mourning the dead.

The pace of change in the interwar years was far slower in the areas most heavily affected by the Depression, where the continuities with the past remained strong. To illustrate this I will draw especially on the work of Elizabeth Roberts for Lancashire and David Clark's study of Staithes in Yorkshire. I will also explore one significant segment of the working class which experienced more deaths in peacetime than any others and which responded in ways that were deeply rooted in the past. The coal miners faced appalling disasters, with about one thousand killed annually, some in major disasters caused by explosions, but more in isolated accidents which were common but rarely noted in the press.

## Death and Mining Disasters in the North

In the interwar years the coal miners and their communities suffered exceptionally severely from unemployment and poverty, in part because coal mining was a declining industry in urgent need of reconstruction, with 20 per cent of miners unemployed by 1929. The deep depression of 1929–33 hit those industries hardest which were already badly damaged in the 1920s, and miners' unemployment continued high in the 1930s, still at 25 per cent in 1936. Structural unemployment was heavily concentrated by region as well as industry: it was especially high in the old staple industries such as coal mining, shipbuilding and textiles, located primarily in the north of England and in south Wales. By 1930 these 'depressed areas' of heavy industry suffered levels of unemployment two or three times higher than those in London, the south-east, and midlands.[2] Ross McKibbin has observed that long-term unemployment 'pauperized many working class communities and came close to destroying the integrity of the working culture of the North of England as a whole'.[3]

In 1934 J. B. Priestley published *English Journey* which gave a remarkably vivid portrayal of such marked regional variation. In the autumn of 1933 he visited 'the fourth England', the distressed land of unemployment in the north, seldom visited by outsiders—including parts of Lancashire and the mining villages of County Durham. He noticed that in deeply depressed Jarrow, many shops were closed, but those that sold funeral wreaths remained open and the community turned out in force for the march to the cemetery:

It seemed as if Death provided the only possible spree left here. Once you had escaped from this narrow life your cold body was treated like an honoured guest and made a royal escape. There were flowers for the dead, if none for the living. All the neighbours turned out to witness this triumphant emigration. Here was the remaining bit of pageantry.[4]

Priestley believed the mean ugliness of the environment must either bring the mining community to despair or blunt their senses and harden their emotions.[5] Indeed expressions of sorrow were socially constrained, especially between men, as miners were expected to show emotional strength.

Miners had to tolerate notoriously bad living and working conditions in a tough and highly dangerous occupation, with more than five thousand miners killed and over eight hundred thousand injured in the five years up to 1931. Miners' wives lived continuously 'in the anxious atmosphere of the war years', forever anticipating tragedy, and every miner understood that he risked 'one of several peculiarly horrible deaths'. They were among the most overworked and underpaid men in England. Younger wives were emphatic that their sons would never go down the pits.[6]

Priestley employed the metaphor of war, often used in relation to the miners: 'In these unhappy districts there is a war on, and the allied enemies are poverty, idleness, ignorance, hopelessness and misery'. Miners in the interwar years were frequently compared to the soldiers in the trenches in the Great War, in which a quarter of miners had enlisted, many in the 'bantam' battalions of smaller men. The *Whitehaven News*, reporting on the 1922 colliery disaster, wrote: 'No pen picture can ever hope to bring home to those who have not experienced it, what real warfare means, and no pen picture can visualise the scenes at the pit head following a big disaster. The latter is infinitely worse than warfare'. Herbert Smith, the Yorkshire miners' leader, often commented that the miners were 'always in the trenches'. The high death toll in the mines in the interwar years led the *Manchester Guardian* to refer to the mines as 'the front-line trenches of our most dangerous industrial fight'.[7] At miners' funerals coffins were often draped with the Union Jack to signify war service and brass bands added to the military air.[8]

Strict cultural conventions governed the behaviour of the mining community and the press in dealing with death and bereavement at such mining disasters, which were among the few types of civilian deaths to receive press coverage. In the interwar mining catastrophes, as in the Great War, suppression of emotion was common and necessary to help men survive their ordeal. Miners followed the stoical military culture of silent coping, for they could not afford to admit their distress, even to themselves. The dead miners remained almost anonymous in press reports up to the 1960s. There was no massive media intrusion as there might be today, nor were there support mechanisms such as psycholog-ical counselling. Mutual-help groups were a phenomenon of the future, and even memorial ceremonies for the dead miners did not feature in the community's rituals. In her book, *When Disaster Strikes*, psychiatrist Beverley Raphael in 1968 described how the terror of death and mutila-tion could evoke agonizing post-traumatic stress reactions causing intense anxiety and nightmares.[9] Such expert information was not available before the 1960s.

The press did not intrude on individual sorrow, nor did they pay much attention to the bereaved, unless to acknowledge 'a grief-stricken town'. The bereaved were rarely noted by name, except occasionally during the ritual of identifying bodies. The press acknowledged that the grief of the miners and their widows was indeed deep, though they knew how to mourn with the appropriate dignity. The role models for the bereaved families were the stoical miners and the heroic soldiers of the Great War—an entirely masculine model. The emotional needs of bereaved families were not recognized as they would be today and such losses could not easily be shared. Families would usually receive some practical help and material support from the community, which constituted an expres-sion of sympathy, accompanied by the platitude that time might help. Otherwise, family sorrow took place behind the drawn blinds and closed doors of little cottages. However, the women in these mining families were likely to offer neighbourly support, and they were sadly accustomed to the deaths of their men at young ages. Widows were likely to be pauper-ized by the loss of breadwinners, as their insurance money would not pay much more than funeral expenses. Even if negligence against mine-owners could be proved—and that was highly unusual—a widow gained little compensation for a husband killed in a pit.[10]

Mining disasters in the two small towns of Whitehaven and Bentley illuminate the human responses to these tragedies and the ways in which mining communities coped with death. Whitehaven in Cumberland was a small town of only 20,000 people, largely dependent on the Haig and

Wellington collieries, which extended under the sea to great depths to reach new seams of coal. They had a bad reputation for high levels of methane and frequent deaths. A massive explosion in the deepest section of the workings at the Haig pit on 5 September 1922 left thirty-nine miners entombed under the sea. The surrounding air was full of after-damp, which was mainly carbon monoxide, a serious hazard to the rescue parties, made worse by roof falls.[11]

The long 'watch of agony' maintained by 'stoical' families seeking to suppress their distress was one of the significant public rituals which marked these terrible mining disasters. A crowd of somewhere between 2,000 and 3,000 waited all day and night 'silent and motionless' for news of their loved ones. The *Whitehaven News* observed: 'Women with children in their arms and little hands clinging to their skirts, wait with steadfast patience for possible news of the bread winner, and those around, who realise that all are doomed, dare not tell'.[12] The size of the crowds at the Haig pit gates and in the colliery yard declined as the days passed. Rescue workers were determined to recover all the bodies if possible, despite the risks to their own lives, because miners' families dreaded the remains being entombed for ever below the sea, depriving them of a funeral and a body to bury. They needed a corpse, however damaged, to legitimize their loss. There was little public display of emotion and the town's work continued as usual, despite deep distress. As more bodies were recovered, the colliery yard was 'crowded with dry-eyed but woebegone women'.[13]

Another dreaded public ritual was the identification of the bodies at the official inquiry, presided over by a local coroner. The day after the Haig pit explosion the inquest took place in the electric powerhouse, with the corpses in the cellars below. Eight deceased men from more fortunate families had been placed in handsome coffins with brass mountings, while the majority were just loosely covered over except for their exposed bandaged faces. Many male relatives were still engaged in rescue work, so widows were ushered into the cellar, where the bodies had been rendered as presentable as possible, 'to pronounce the dreaded "yes" or "no"'. The *Whitehaven News* considered this ordeal possibly the worst experience of all for the families. In one case, a widow could identify her husband only by his clogs and stockings; in another by his belt and trousers. The inquest determined that the men were either 'killed by violence' or suffocated by after-damp. Miners Kirkpatrick and Hope had been found lying in each other's arms.[14]

Usually newspapers such as *The Times,* the *Manchester Guardian,* and the *Whitehaven News* respected the emotional privacy of bereaved families at these disasters to a degree inconceivable today. The families were some-times reported as giving evidence of identification of the bodies with 'no emotional scenes'. Most witnesses maintained 'a dignified calm, although the effort to conquer emotion was apparent'. It must have required a huge mental struggle, or low expectation of life, to sustain such composure during this ordeal.[15]

A third vital public ritual followed on 8 September 1922 with the funerals of the victims. Press reports of the funerals were usually short by today's standards, with no intrusion into the grief and the privacy of the families. The reports emphasized the crowds of thousands, including large numbers from neighbouring collieries who shared the sorrow—again we are reminded of the value of such communities of grief, highlighted by Jay Winter. We are usually told that all the blinds on windows were drawn, flags on any public buildings were at half mast, and sometimes the local brass band played.

The accounts of this 1922 Whitehaven tragedy focused on the funerals of just ten of the eighteen buried on 8 September. These ten were buried in the pretty village of Hensingham, 1 mile from Whitehaven, following a 'united' service in the parish church, conducted by both the Anglican vicar and the local Wesleyan minister, as most miners were Wesleyan Methodists. Thousands of people paid their last tribute as the procession passed, and two of the ten were accorded military honours, having fought in the Great War. The most remarkable aspect of this funeral was that these ten dead men were laid in just one long mass grave, probably without coffins. The other eight, identified earlier in their handsome coffins, were probably buried privately in other locations by their more fortunate families.[16]

Miners killed in pit disasters were frequently buried in common pauper graves because of the poverty of their surviving families, who could not afford insurance policies.[17] The condition of the bodies was often an addi-tional explanation for a common burial, particularly when they had been so disfigured by fire that they could not be identified. The only possible consolation was that comrades would be buried together, but that brought little comfort when mass burials carried grim associations with humili-ating Victorian pauper funerals. A second negative association was with the mass graves on the battlefields of the Western Front, where so many miners had fought. Such unpopular common graves were also the fate of many civilian victims of the Blitz in the Second World War—also killed in large numbers, with problems of identification because of mutilation.

On 20 November 1931 a powerful explosion killed forty-two miners at Bentley colliery, near Doncaster, one of the largest mines in the south Yorkshire coalfields. Three days later the affected area of the pit was sealed off, leaving five men buried there. The press agreed it was the worst disaster in twenty years and described Bentley as 'a village of tragedy': 'miners' wives hurried to the pithead with shawls thrown over their heads, and their little children running by their sides'. Since most men in Bentley were miners, most families were vitally affected, so the number of dependents could be as high as two hundred. Money in these families had been scarce for years, with unemployment high, and the Bentley pit working on short time.[18] The *Manchester Guardian* reported on 23 November:

Bentley has become a village of sad, solemn faces. The neat little semi-detached houses, which make Bentley look like a gigantic housing estate, have drawn curtains or blinds almost everywhere. The one topic of conversation is the disaster—conversations conducted in the hushed voices of men and women who live constantly in the shadow of accident and catastrophe...Nobody knows better than wives who hurry to the pithead when news of an accident is received how difficult it is to learn what has happened half a mile or so below ground.[19]

But the full realization of the tragedy came only slowly to the shocked crowds keeping vigil at the pithead. The statistics for the miners dead, injured, and missing kept changing as groups of rescuers emerged carrying stretchers and slender hopes of survival began to disappear. The horror was increased by the awful condition of the corpses, making it impossible for families to identify bodies, charred beyond recognition. The depth of the survivors' suffering was highlighted on 23 November when Arthur Lawton, aged 30, committed suicide on learning that his brother Harold had died in hospital as a result of his injuries.[20]

Meanwhile another pit disaster ritual was being played out. The identification of the thirty-seven recovered bodies took place on 23 November 1931 in the Bentley colliery offices. 'A sad procession of witnesses' walked to the witness chair: some women even 'broke down completely' and needed attention from the nurses in the waiting room. Demonstration of emotion to this degree at an inquest was highly unusual but understandable, especially as their sad stories revealed abundant evidence of hardship, with several families of six or more children. The youngest victim was

Albert Barcock, who was supporting his widowed mother and three dependent siblings, despite his age of 17.[21]

The third major public ritual of the Bentley disaster was the mass burial of thirty-one victims at Arksey Cemetery on 25 November 1931. Like the Whitehaven burial in 1922, this was an extraordinary ceremony, which prefigured the interment of Blitz victims in mass graves ten years later. In both the Blitz and the mines the victims were often disfigured and unidentifiable, with large numbers to be interred rapidly. The miners' families must have been anguished at the prospect of a pauper funeral, but burial in a mass grave was at least preferable to the fate of the five miners entombed for ever in the pit. The *Manchester Guardian* headline announced 'Pit Disaster Funeral: One grave for thirty-one victims. Distressing scenes.' Of the forty-two victims, thirty-one were in the mass grave, five remained buried in the pit, while six were interred privately elsewhere. Police estimated that the dense crowds, ten-deep, which lined the route, amounted to more than thirty thousand people, with a funeral procession 3 miles long.[22]

There seem to have been few, if any, memorials to the victims of mining disasters in the interwar years, whereas most towns and villages erected memorials to the dead servicemen of the Great War. The contrast is again clear between the treatment in death of war heroes and civilians in peacetime. The issue of memorialization deserves further analysis in relation to the colliery disaster of 22 September 1934 at Gresford in Denbighshire, close to the English border, 10 miles from Chester. A series of explosions took place in a very deep pit, killing some miners instantly, while others were gassed, crushed, or burnt to death. The following day all rescue workers had to be withdrawn as the risks of continuing explosions were too great and there was no hope that any trapped miners were still alive.[23]

The pit had to be sealed off, leaving 260 miners entombed for ever. The government inquiry in 1937 noted that it was the worst disaster for a generation, but its cause was obscure and nobody was identified as criminally negligent: moreover, it was considered impossible to reopen the sealed section of the pit to investigate further. Bereaved families sent anguished letters requesting the sealed mine be reopened and they were bitter about the refusal. When mining resumed at Gresford, miners were uncomfortably aware that 260 former workmates were buried in the next section of the colliery.[24]

The human cost of the Gresford disaster was immense. About two hundred women lost husbands and about eight hundred children lost fathers. They mainly survived on the charity of the Gresford Disaster Relief Fund, which sometimes humiliated those obliged to prove their case for relief. The press frequently commented on the remarkable stoicism of the bereaved families, who had lost an entire generation of miners. But neither the press nor the authorities recognized the urgent need of hundreds of bereaved to ensure that their loved ones were not forgotten. The bereaved had to wait until 1982, when the emotional climate had changed, for a memorial to be erected to the dead miners—nearly half a century too late. Even then children of the victims had to campaign for the individual names of the entombed men to be etched onto a monument plaque. As late as 2006, grandchildren were still lobbying the local council for a road heritage sign marking the position of the monument off the Chester–Wrexham bypass.[25]

In 2006 schoolchildren, including many grandchildren of the victims, were told the story of the Gresford disaster in their schools and encouraged to send emails to a disaster website. Several wrote expressing regret that the disused mine site had not been turned into beautiful gardens to remember the victims: 'such a shame that more wasn't made of the site as a memorial to the lost souls'. They were also distressed that a housing estate had been built on or near the site of the disaster: 'those poor souls lying beneath the very ground I live on'.[26]

The 2006 Gresford disaster website is also revealing about the impact of the disaster on a number of individual families in 1934. This is valuable because the press did not intrude into family grief for disaster victims in the 1930s. Practical efforts had been made at the time to assist with money and relief in kind, even including donations of Aberdeen kippers, cases of Campbells soup, and mourning clothes. But the families were left by authorities to deal with their loss privately within their families as best they could. Some of the children wrote to the Gresford website in 2006, as did Alex from Wrexham, 'My grandad lies in the pit still as he has never been recovered'. Samantha Lloyd wrote to say that her grandfather, John White, was killed in the disaster: 'he left behind my gran who brought up 5 children on her own, including a 11 month old little boy, which was my dad'. Thomas Gregg of Wrexham wrote that his father was killed by the explosion:

I sort of remember seeing my mother sitting on the stairs crying and then my next door neighbour came round saying her husband was underground as well. My mother had to get my Grandmother to look after me and my younger sister Patricia. My mother had gone for hour after hour. Then there was my mother standing in the door saying sorry Tom your father has died in a bad mining disaster. My heart sunk. My eyes poured with tears. My mother was 6 months pregnant and when she had them it was twins. I hope a disaster does not happen like this again because I don't want anybody to be as devastated as I was.[27]

Family memories were lost: some bereaved families were obliged by poverty to move away, others were split up for ever, and many children lost a parent. Several website writers asked for help in tracing the families of men lost in the disaster. Andrea Wilson explained that her grandfather, William Crump, was killed, leaving his wife and four young children. When his wife died six years later, all family possessions from the house were disposed of, so the children were deprived of photographs and memories of their parents which they would have cherished.[28]

# Folk Religion and Working-Class Death Rituals in Yorkshire

During the interwar years newspapers revealed nothing of the grief behind the drawn blinds of individual miners' houses. We know from various sources that expressions of emotion were culturally constrained—even more so for miners than for the working classes generally, and more for the miners than for their wives. We can only speculate on the effect of so many violent pit deaths on the private family rituals that once accompanied a death in the working-class family. The rituals described in the press which took place during and after a colliery disaster were all public rituals—the long vigil at the pit-head, the identification of the bodies, and the funeral. The only major public ritual which was part of the normal business of death was the funeral, with its impressive community support and its ceremonial processions. But we learn nothing of the more private family rituals, such as the laying-out of the corpse and the wake held around it. The circumstances of colliery disasters often made these impossible: many victims' remains were buried in the pit, while those which were mutilated and unidentifiable went directly from the pit to the mortuary.

James Obelkevich and others have argued that 'modern industrial society makes secularisation inevitable', as Christian faith and church-going declined. But Peter Clarke has warned against overstating the extent of this change: 'The religious affiliations of an earlier generation left a long-lasting residue'. Institutional religion held its own more powerfully than some critics suggest, particularly the Church of England, though Nonconformity fared less well, its numbers reduced by 50 per cent between 1901 and 1966.[29] By 1920, half the population in the larger northern towns had no official religious affiliation, but about 20 per cent still attended chapel. Moreover, the decline of the churches did not necessarily mean the end of religion defined more broadly: although fewer working class people were weekly churchgoers, many believed it was not necessary to attend church regularly to be a Christian. By 1950 more people were indifferent to institutional religion, yet a majority continued to believe in God and about half had faith in some kind of afterlife.[30]

The Christian religion played a diffuse but pervasive role in response to death and bereavement in the interwar years. Several historians have especially underlined the continuing influence of 'folk religion'. Obelkevich's research on South Lindsey in the early nineteenth century revealed a rich mixture of unofficial beliefs, orthodox church faith, superstition, and magic. Ruth Richardson and Julie-Marie Strange demonstrate that such unorthodox beliefs among the working classes were a vital part of death rituals in the Victorian period.[31] Medical sociologist David Clark has argued forcefully for the survival of such folk religion well into the twentieth century, and emphasized its continuing impact on death rituals and behaviour in bereavement: 'death represents one of the few aspects of human experience still relatively immune from secularising forces'.[32]

Clark reached this conclusion through his investigation in the 1970s in Staithes on the north-east Yorkshire coast, where he interviewed its older inhabitants about their experiences over the previous half-century. The concept of folk religion was at the heart of Clark's argument. He defined it as a blend of folk and formal religion, together with superstition and occasional visits to church. He observed that sociologists had tended to focus their analysis on official church attendance statistics, which were misleading for villages like Staithes. Institutional religion in Staithes was not moribund, but continued to survive, despite low attendance, alongside spiritual practices, superstitions, and rituals outside the church. The spiritual life of the villagers extended beyond institutional Christianity, providing an ethical code which helped make sense of death, and popular beliefs which added diversity to the rites of passage accompanying death. Folk religion contributed greatly to the prolonged survival of a rich framework of beliefs and customs for dealing with death and loss: it lasted most effectively in isolated communities like Staithes, supported by closely knit kinship networks. However, folk culture was highly localized, with substantial regional variations, which may have been challenged in the later twentieth century by the increasing unification of a modern society.[33]

Clark's superb portrait of the rituals of death in the village of Staithes allows us to imagine the elaborate rituals of death as they might have been in earlier times in other Yorkshire working-class communities. Staithes was an isolated fishing village, 10 miles from Whitby, which also had some mining; Clark undertook his research in 1975–6, allowing him to reconstruct Staithes' past, in part through the oral testimonies of elderly villagers. He vividly describes the sort of customs and rituals denied to the miners when charred corpses of loved ones were not available to the families as a focal point for their grief.

Clark observes that folk religion blended with the institutionalized religion of chapel and church in Staithes, providing a rich variety of folk responses to life's rites of passage, especially death. He reminds us that death, like birth, required ritualized activities and superstitions to regulate responses in traditional societies: these survived in isolated Staithes far longer than in most places. He pieced together the death customs in Staithes in the early twentieth century, showing that the rituals within the home were at least as vital as those outside. Death itself would usually take place in the home. The community layers-out performed the vitally important custom of laying out the body, with love and pride, knowing that the correct ritual was essential to make the corpse presentable for public viewing. They used the traditional laying-out board, stored in the workshop of the village joiner, who doubled as the undertaker. The women washed the body, tied the jaw, wrapped the corpse in a white sheet and carefully laid it on a board in the centre of a double bed. A white sheet covered the corpse, with a white handkerchief over the face. Such rites were traditionally intended to protect the family from the contagion of death. Members of the family took turns to watch over the body, as neighbours, friends, and relatives paid formal visits to view it and touch it, as expressions of sympathy and respect. During the middle phase of the rite of passage, between the death and the burial, clocks were stopped to signify the suspension of time and normal patterns of behaviour, the curtains were drawn, and mirrors and pictures covered.[34]

Meanwhile funeral preparations were under way. The undertaker–cum–joiner built the coffin, the women baked the funeral foods, and the female 'bidder' knocked at each cottage door in the village to announce the time of the funeral. On the day of the funeral, the family gathered around the open coffin in the house as the minister offered a prayer of thanks for the dead person's life. The lid was then attached to the coffin which was placed on two chairs in the street, as mourners sang the first verse of a funeral hymn, leaving the door of the house open to permit the departure of the dead person's soul. These were all traditional folk rituals which held great meaning for villagers who were anxious to follow them correctly. The coffin bearers (female relatives if the deceased was a woman), lifted the coffin and walked to the chapel as the villagers continued singing the hymn. The bearers were followed by the 'waitresses' who were to serve the tea, wearing black hats and sashes with white lace shawls, and then by the minister, the bereaved family, and the villagers, with the women all in black.[35]

Following the chapel service, Clark tells how the coffin was carried 1½ miles to the graveyard at nearby Hinderwell (as Staithes lacked a cemetery). The impressive procession sang as they climbed up a hill and along the cliffs to the graveyard, where they sang 'Gather at the river', or its equivalent, after the committal. Later they returned to the village for the funeral tea, dividing up into small groups to fit into the little cottages, where the 'waitresses' served smoked ham and fruit cakes. This was the first of the rites of incorporation, as the group formally recognized the death and prepared the bereaved to return to normal life, marked by opening the curtains and removing covers from mirrors. In the ensuing months the bereaved family had to follow mourning customs which fell especially heavily on the women, who had to wear black mourning dress with a black bonnet and remain indoors for several weeks. Slowly and steadily these rules were relaxed so that the mourners returned to their usual roles in the community.[36]

Clark shows how these traditional rituals were lost or modified in Staithes in the years between the early twentieth century and the 1970s. Death itself was as likely by the 1970s to take place in hospital or a nursing home as at the family home, while a professional funeral director took over the family's former roles in the week of the funeral. The corpse would often be taken directly from the hospital to the funeral director's chapel of rest, where the funeral director laid it out. The most significant change, however, was that 40 per cent of bodies were cremated in Staithes by the 1970s—a smaller proportion than the national average of over 50 per cent, but still a massive shift for conservative Staithes, especially as the nearest crematorium at Middlesbrough was over 20 miles away. Staithes villagers had a marked aversion to cremation, reflecting the hostility of the working classes more generally up to the 1940s. For hundreds of years their dead had been buried at nearby Hinderwell, where they could perpetuate their memory by caring for the graves regularly. Grave visiting had a ritualistic significance for them, a powerful link with the world of the dead, whereas they could envisage no lasting memorial at the crematorium. Moreover, the burial took place locally and it was still possible to retain some of the older rituals, including impressive chapel funerals, and funeral teas in the chapel school room, with ham sandwiches still served by 'waitresses'.[37] Traditional death and mourning rituals among the working classes would have declined in similar manner elsewhere in the north, but more rapidly in cities, towns, and less isolated places.

## The Lancashire Way of Death

Elizabeth Roberts offers another valuable perspective on death in the working-class north, especially on the role and attitudes of women. She interviewed 160 older people from the three very different towns of Barrow, Lancaster, and Preston, between 1971 and 1981. Her book, *A Woman's Place 1890–1940,* is complemented by her thoughtful essay on 'The Lancashire Way of Death'. The Lancashire women interviewed were conservative in their views and had a strong sense of community and of continuity. Most had connections to a church: some attended church services and sent their children to Sunday schools, so most children were brought up with some Christian teaching. Many families still lived with kin or their near relatives lived close by, even in the same street. Links between women, especially neighbours and relatives, were powerful, offering friendship, sociability, and reciprocal services.[38]

Roberts noted, 'Judging from the time, money and attention lavished on the dying, the dead and the bereaved, death was a very important part of working class life in North Lancashire in the period 1890–1940'. Cultural traditions and social needs were more important than religious faith and yet spiritual beliefs remained influential. They explain people's readiness to accept death, in the hope that their loved ones would go to heaven. Families accepted the loss of babies and very young children stoically but sadly: they nursed them and grieved for them but felt there was little they could do. Death helped to socialize children who learned early that death was natural and inevitable, as they encountered it frequently, often at home. Over 20 per cent of interviewees experienced as children the death of a sibling or a parent, and most children saw a dead body before the age of 14. The custom of viewing and touching corpses was common in 1900 but had almost disappeared by 1940: it was an accepted practice, supposed to assist in grieving, so that more children and neighbours viewed bodies than attended funerals.[39]

The performance of long-established rituals was seen as vitally important in providing comfort, and the corpse played a significant role, as Roberts shows. From 1900 to 1940 death, like birth, remained in the experienced care of female family members and their helpful neighbours, while male undertakers merely transported the body from the house to the church. The important business of laying out the body followed a similar ritual to that in Staithes. A female relative might undertake the task, but it was more often a respected neighbourhood layer-out, often an untrained and unpaid midwife, who would also arrange the funeral tea. She washed the body, plugged the orifices, dressed the body in a clean nightgown, placed pennies on the eyes and a binder round the chin. The body was often left for an hour with the windows open to allow the soul to escape (and perhaps also the odours). This loving procedure helped to demystify death and to offer sympathy and respect. The body in the open coffin was kept at home in the front parlour surrounded by flowers, with curtains drawn, as kin and neighbours paid their last respects.[40] Christine Kenny has argued that mourners in Bolton gained comfort from the corpse once they became accustomed to it. She also notes the disapproval of overt and dramatic displays of grief around the body at home, or at the church: there was a 'matter of fact' attitude to death among the older women.[41]

Respectable and even impressive funerals were considered vitally important in Lancashire (as in the Yorkshire and Cumberland mining villages). A 'good send-off' was crucial. Roberts noted that only one family in her sample of 160 interviewees did not pay death insurance for each family member and so faced the prospective indignity of a pauper's funeral. Most families made their contributions to a death club or an insurance company, because funerals were not only more significant than weddings, they were also more expensive. A 'big turn-out' for the funeral procession, with appropriate black clothes and pageantry, was vital. Funerals were acknowledged to serve the needs of the living, to allow them to confront the reality of the death and start the grieving process. It was a significant rite of passage which recognized the separation of the dead from the living. In Lancashire, as in Staithes in Yorkshire, burial remained more popular than cremation until the 1970s, and for the same reasons. Funerals gave a sense of continuity with earlier generations: families often had a grave site with space for more and they wanted to be buried together, with their graves as a focus for commemoration. We are reminded again of the working-class hostility to cremation and their common dislike of the bleak crematorium.[42]

The funeral tea with ham sandwiches was prepared for mourners after the funeral by the layer-out or neighbours, sometimes using borrowed crockery. As Roberts notes, 'the funeral tea was a time for family solidarity with stories and reminiscences about the dead person'. The family then went into mourning for a considerable time, though the twelve months usual before 1914 declined somewhat in the interwar years. They wore black mourning clothes and severely reduced their social activity:

People were given time to grieve, indeed they were expected to grieve. There appears to have been little expectation that they should smile brightly and pretend nothing had happened. The dead were constantly remembered, they were talked about, their photographs were displayed and their graves visited.

Mr Boyle, interviewed by Roberts, remembered that the dead were talked about as if they still lived. Family members went to the cemetery most Sunday afternoons to tend the graves: 'And they went on living, so to speak, in conversation and memory for some considerable time'.[43]

Sheila Adams found similar patterns in her study of the role of layers-out in Foleshill, near Coventry, in the interwar years. This was a close-knit working-class community excluded from formal care by poverty. The neighbourhood layer-out was essential to the pattern of informal care organized by women to deal with births, sickness, and deaths. She would often already be caring for a dying person when death came and the bereaved family would be part of her local network. Adams also argues that the important role of the layer-out was gradually replaced by the formal professional care of doctors, nurses, and funeral directors. With the introduction of the National Health Service in 1948, health care became more a matter for the hospital, and home nursing was supervised by the district nurse. The site of death was transferred from the home to the 'public sphere of the hospital, hospice and mortuary associated with male scientific rationality'.[44]

From the 1940s death was increasingly taken over from the community of women by male professionals, notably funeral directors and doctors. Working-class attitudes to death changed very slowly over several decades and many old customs were gradually abandoned or attenuated. But as Roberts notes, such changes were not necessarily imposed on an unwilling working class. There is some evidence in Adams's interviews of growing distaste at the 'smell of death' in front parlours of overcrowded houses if funerals were delayed: an undertaker's 'chapel of rest' had advantages, as also did care of the dying by medical professionals.[45] Nevertheless, the speed of this process of change should not be overstated, and its rate varied greatly by region and class. Geoffrey Gorer's 1965 survey of attitudes and practices relating to death in England shows that a surprising number of rituals described by Clark and Roberts survived among the northern working classes into the 1960s, albeit often in a reduced form.[46]

In 1999 Nicholas Taylor, a Norfolk funeral director, was interviewed by the Millenium Memory Bank about his family's work as local funeral directors since 1890. He regretted that funeral directors had been seriously affected by the unfortunate trend towards the disintegration of the community since the 1950s. Taylor believed it was vitally important that the whole family, including the children, were involved when one of them died, but since the 1950s that had often ceased to be the case. Previously there had been more widespread acceptance of the deterioration of the body, the meaning of death, and its inevitability:

Before the 50s the vast majority of people who died would stay at home. They'd stay in the house in the front room. The curtains would be drawn, which is advertising isn't it, that there's been a death. And the neighbours would come round, the children would be there, and they would see it as being very much a very real part of life. It was there, they could see the body, and deal with it and they were supported by the community. Now that disappeared in the 50s and 60s and 70s. Instead people came to the Chapel of Rest, most people died in hospital, rather than at home . . . It meant that children especially, were spared the grief of having to witness this, now I actually feel that was a great shame.[47]

# 5

# Sir Sydney Cockerell: Cremation and the Modern Way of Death in England

## Cremation: The Modern Way of Death

Cremation symbolizes the modern way of death in England, accounting for 80 per cent of funerals in 2000, compared with only about 20 per cent in the United States. A century earlier the pioneers of cremation lauded its sanitary advantages in reducing the pollution of the earth by putrefying corpses. Later it appealed to environmentalists as a clean and efficient solution to the problems of land shortage and overcrowded cemeteries. Cremation has followed cultural change rather than helping to create it. It was widely seen as modern in discouraging ceremony: tight schedules, industrial hardware, and functional buildings seemed to suit a society increasingly inclined to keep death at a distance. Its simplicity appealed to a modern age which reacted against elaborate Victorian funeral display. The practice of cremation has advanced as religious belief has declined, though in recent years it has been increasingly patronized by the Christian churches.

The growth of cremation also coincided with the slow decline of the traditional mourning rituals which were thought by Victorians to offer therapeutic and social benefits to ease the pain of grief. Victorian convention guided many bereaved people in determining appropriate social behaviour during the week of the funeral and in the months or years of grieving. Public rituals included funeral etiquette, the wearing of black mourning dress, and the customary time required for each stage of grieving. Among the working classes more emphasis was placed on the correct manner of laying out and viewing the body.

Powerful cultural, religious, and demographic changes impacted on mourning rituals and methods of disposal of the dead from the late nineteenth century, not least the slow development of cremation as a primary secular mode of disposal. The decline in mourning rituals can be traced back to the efforts of the National Funeral and Mourning Reform Association from 1875: it encouraged cheaper and less ornate funerals, shorter periods devoted to grieving, and simpler mourning dress for women. This process of simplification was accelerated by the Great War, not only because undertakers, gravediggers, and funeral operatives were conscripted. Geoffrey Gorer vividly remembered his mother as a tragic figure in full black widows' weeds, visibly withdrawn from the world, when his father drowned with the *Lusitania* in 1915. He recalled that widows in full mourning were common in 1915 and 1916, but the 'full panoply of public mourning' became exceptional thereafter. It was argued that national morale would suffer from mass mourning and a 'pageantry of funeral gloom'. As Julian Litten observed: 'At such a time of great national suffering and sorrow, individual displays of funeral pomp and panoply did not sit comfortably on the conscience'. It also seemed inappropriate to display extravagant public grief and stage grandiose funerals in England when the soldiers killed for their country had to be buried overseas, often in mass graves with little or no ceremony. Advocates of cremation took full advantage of the war to promote their cause: dismal, expensive, 'funeral gloom' should be replaced by simple, sanitary cremation.[1]

I will explore the English cremation movement largely through the lens of Sir Sydney Cockerell's life and career, which offer valuable insights into attitudes and rituals relating to death, grief, and cremation among the intelligentsia and the upper middle classes in the first half of the twentieth century. They are important because they did so much to build the early cremation movement, which did not begin to be adopted by the working classes until the 1940s. Sir Sydney Cockerell was an extraordinary man whose many associations with death, bereavement, and cremation were closely tied to his professional position as director of the Fitzwilliam Museum, Cambridge. He was an influential advocate for cremation in its early years, anxious to develop new secular rituals with appeal to intelligent and imaginative people.

My account of the early history of cremation will be brief, as Peter Jupp has recently published a substantial history. Only ten officially recognized cremations were performed in Europe before 1877. Sir Henry Thompson, surgeon and president of the British Cremation Society, opened the debate in Britain in a powerful article in the *Contemporary Review* in 1874, presenting the sanitary and utilitarian arguments: cremation would eliminate graveyard pollution of air and water, and reduce the costly ceremonial of burial and the wastage of land. The landmark Cremation Act was passed in 1902, legalizing the practice of cremation in England, Scotland, and Wales, thereby indicating that public opinion by then at least tolerated it. But the pace of change was still extremely slow after the 1902 Act with only 105 cremations in London in the first five years and just over one thousand in 1914. Not until the 1960s were half of those who died cremated.[2]

The progress of cremation in England in its first half-century was so slow largely because religious sentiment against it remained powerful. The political decision in favour of cremation in 1902 was exclusively based on sanitary arguments, which influenced politicians, doctors, and the intelligentsia, but failed to persuade the working classes. Two thousand years of Christian burial tradition and an emotional distaste for the concept of cremation still strongly influenced the attitudes of most people, even those who no longer attended church services. A diffuse, residual religious sentiment combined with the conservatism of the working classes to create passive resistance to cremation.[3]

Bishop Albert David of Liverpool noted in 1936: 'The chief reason for the continuance of the burial system is the innate conservatism of people in all matters connected with death, but among the more educated and wealthy sections of society little short of a revolution in funeral customs has taken place during the past fifty years'.[4] That tiny minority of people who supported cremation in its early years was drawn largely from the scientific and literary intelligentsia in the professional and upper middle classes. It was a secular and progressive movement led by agnostics, atheists, and doctors. Peter Jupp has described cremation as 'an ideal battleground for the challenge by the radical of the traditional, the past by the future, the religious by the rational and the manual by the mechanical'.[5] The council of the Cremation Society included at various times Herbert Spencer, Sir Leslie Stephen, John Everett Millais, and Anthony Trollope, as well as other literary and professional people, including doctors, scientists, artists, lawyers, and even clergymen.

If the decline in Christian faith was one significant factor in the rise of cremation, the impact of the Great War was another, especially as the war further weakened a Protestant faith already under strain. Moreover, the horrors of trench warfare violated faith in the sanctity of the body and the grave. Many soldiers were sickened by memories of makeshift burials on the Western Front, and piles of unburied rotting bodies in no-man's-land. Cremation increased its appeal precisely because it was so different from earth burial. It was quick, sanitary, and unsentimental, and carried no bitter memories of the war, though the war prepared a wider section of the population to endorse it. For mourners who preferred not to think too deeply about the meaning and the material consequences of death, cremation seemed less offensive than burial, as Joanna Bourke has argued: 'The allure of a clean death was pervasive. The vision of death during war—painful, humiliating, ugly—intensified the urge for its immaculate counterpart'.[6]

Bourke observes that before 1914 the supporters of cremation emphasized the 'disgusting decay' of burial, reinforced by its capacity to pollute and cause disease. But by 1918 the rhetoric changed as ex-servicemen wanted no reminders of the indignities of slow decomposition. The Cremation Society's posters altered their focus to highlight public health and 'purification by fire' instead of the pollution of burial, with the cremated remains scattered in beautiful gardens.[7] And so crematoria buildings were designed and grounds landscaped to promote a sense of peace, beauty, and dignity. There was no architectural precedent for the style of a crematorium, as Hilary Grainger notes. The architects of the late Victorian crematoria at Woking and Liverpool chose mock Gothic, which echoed the style of much church architecture and perhaps offered reassurance. Ernest George, the architect of Golders Green, instead followed Manchester's bold use of Northern Italian Romanesque, which resembled a cloistered monastery with a peaceful timeless quality, combining humanity with spirituality, and dignity with grandeur.[8]

Given such a slow start it is remarkable that England experienced a massive growth in the cremation rate in the twentieth century which outstripped that of most other countries. In the early 1930s only about 1 per cent of the population was cremated, but by 1967, this had risen dramatically to 50 per cent, following substantial public acceptance and nearly four decades of growth. The statistics in *Pharos*, the journal of the Cremation Society, are illuminating for comparative evaluation in 1992, when the UK cremation rate had reached 69 per cent. This compared at the higher end of the scale with Denmark at 68 per cent,

Australia at 48 per cent, and the Netherlands at 46 per cent (all predominantly Protestant countries). At the lower end, the USA stood at 9 per cent, France 8 per cent, and Italy 1.5 per cent—with the lowest levels in Catholic countries.[9]

The most rapid growth in support for cremation took place after the Second World War but important foundations were laid in the interwar years. The 1930s witnessed a fourfold increase in cremation from 0.9 to 3.7 per cent in England and Wales, while the number of crematoria grew from twenty-one in 1930 to fifty-four by 1939. There were two reasons for this interwar growth. One was the energetic promotional and organizational work of the Cremation Society, which held annual conferences to target local authorities, undertakers, medical officers of health, and churchmen. Its quarterly journal *Pharos* was published from 1935 to promote the cause and disseminate positive information: this was aimed especially at the education and conversion of the working classes, since its limited existing support was still predominantly middle and upper class.[10]

The second reason was the vital role of local authorities in promoting cremation, which Peter Jupp rightly highlights. They saw cremation as far cheaper than burial, as available land for large cemeteries grew scarce, and as existing cemeteries exhausted their space. Valuable land in city centres was required for the needs of the living—for houses and recreation—and neglected overgrown cemeteries continued to be perceived as health hazards in congested population centres. In searching for solutions to the perennial problems of cemetery neglect and land shortage, cremation seemed to offer a complete answer to issues of space, health, and environment. Thus the advantage of economy was added to that of health. In the interwar years many local authorities therefore responded to land shortage by building new crematoria when existing cemeteries filled up. The Cremation Society's motto, 'Save the land for the living', emphasized the cost effectiveness of cremation for local authorities, especially in the cities, where the cremation rate was 6.2 per cent, compared with the national average of 1.5 per cent in 1935.[11]

Where the Protestant churches had earlier been in general opposed to cremation, during the Second World War they softened their view, especially as public support was slowly increasing. Individual bishops and clergy had long supported cremation. Bishop Albert David of Liverpool had stated in *Pharos* in 1935: 'It is already agreed among the best educated Christians that the quickest, cleanest, and most seemly disposal of the dead is provided by cremation'.[12] In 1944 the Church of England determined that the doctrine of the resurrection of the body did not preclude the practice of cremation, though its rationale was more pragmatic than logical. Canon Guy Rogers of Birmingham stated that this change would bring relief to many people anxious about the disposal of the bodies of their loved ones, especially those blown to pieces by shells or bombs.[13] Further support was offered by the cremation of Archbishop William Temple in 1944 and Archbishop Cosmo Lang the following year.

The disposal of ashes presented a challenge for the supporters of cremation in the earlier years, especially as the Church of England conceived the scattering of ashes as a pagan practice until the 1950s. The early cremationists preferred to bury ashes in consecrated ground, drawing on the work of the monumental mason for traditional tombstones as memorials. From about 1910 more people adopted the new practice of preserving ashes in memorial niches in colonnades in walls of chapels or columbaria at the crematorium. From the mid-1920s the Cremation Society began to encourage the scattering of ashes, despite the Church of England's prohibition. The Cremation Society's secretary observed in 1936 that the growing popularity of scattering ashes was transforming memorialization. Ashes could now be scattered at a crematorium in a garden of remembrance which inspired individual memorials such as bird-baths, seats, or fish ponds, adding to the garden's natural beauty; or trees, shrubs, and flowers could be planted in the gardens, marked with simple labels of dedication. By 1936 ashes were scattered after 65 per cent of cremations.[14]

## Sir Sydney Cockerell: The Promotion of Cremation as a Modern Secular Movement

Adrian Hastings has argued that the most important new intellectual orthodoxy in England in the 1920s was 'a confident agnosticism' inspired by Darwin and biblical scholarship. The leaders were 'cultivated upper class post-Darwinians', including G. B. Shaw, H. G. Wells, Gilbert Murray, Bertrand Russell, G. M. Trevelyan, D. H. Lawrence, and Virginia Woolf. Hastings includes Sydney Cockerell in this group of modern cultivated men who took agnosticism for granted and did not understand the religious frame of mind. The gulf in faith and ideas between Cockerell and his Catholic friend, Dame Laurentia of Stanbrook Abbey, was illustrated by his admission that 'the dyke that separates us is one that cannot well be crossed by either of us'.[15]

For Cockerell and his enlightened colleagues cremation was the appropriate means of disposal in the age of modernity: they conceived it as a vigorous secular movement which rejected outmoded Victorian assumptions about faith, ritual, and aesthetics. They dismissed what they saw as Victorian bad taste, with its ugly cemeteries cluttered with over-elaborate monumental masonry and its excess of sentiment. Crematoria should be peaceful places of meditation which consoled the bereaved, encouraging quiet acceptance of loss rather than immoderate displays of grief.

Sir Sydney Cockerell's life is richly revealing about the history of death and cremation among the elite up to the 1950s. Cockerell bequeathed seventy volumes of correspondence and eighty volumes of diaries to the British Library, and these constitute the major sources for my chapter. Cockerell (1867–1962) was an influential and unusual man who was director of the Fitzwilliam Museum, Cambridge, for nearly thirty years from 1908. He acted as literary and estate executor for many eminent friends, offering advice on cremations and death rituals. He was also a notable obituarist for *The Times* and collector of books and medieval manuscripts. His enthusiasms included a passionate advocacy of cremation in its pioneer years, and a willingness to act as executor for his friends, who were often generous benefactors of the Fitzwilliam. His many asso-ciations with death and cremation were for thirty years closely tied to his professional position, so he was in constant contact with death and bereave-ment on his own terms.

His character was complex and even apparently contradictory. His friend and biographer, Wilfrid Scawen Blunt, the poet, described him vividly: 'Cockerell was short and stockily built, pugnacious and some-what alarming on first acquaintance but soon revealing, to those who won his approval, innate kindness and a warm heart. His enthusiasms were infectious, and his zest for life remained undiminished to the end'. He was an agnostic with no belief in a future life and an aversion to overtly expressive public mourning: in his view, noble lives should be celebrated at death with minimal ceremony, and the utmost in dignity and simplicity.[16]

Cockerell's life needs to be understood in the context of his 'extraor-dinary empire' over his innumerable friends.[17] He cultivated the art of friendship over a lifetime; Siegfried Sassoon congratulated Cockerell in 1956 on his 'ministrations to some of the most "worthwhile" people of your time'.[18] Hugh Whitemore described him more critically as 'prickly, pedantic, a collector of gossip and famous people, a man who pursued friendship with tireless energy'.[19] Cockerell's astringent tongue made enemies but his loyalty, kindness, and willingness to help those in need won him many more friends. He was an aesthete who chose his art and literature, as well as his friends, with deliberation, and it is tempting, but perhaps unfair, to be sceptical of his motives. His career depended on his connections with people of wealth and good taste for their generous gifts to the Fitzwilliam.

Cockerell's father was a London coal merchant whose early death, when Sydney was 10, obliged him to enter the family coal business for several years from 1889. An early admiration for the work of his two greatest heroes, John Ruskin and William Morris, encouraged him to contact both in 1887, leading to significant changes in his life. Designer, poet, and socialist, Morris in 1892 gave Cockerell more congenial work as secretary to the Kelmscott Press. Cockerell's friendship with Ruskin developed during a French holiday in 1888. Ruskin and Morris became the two most profound influences on Cockerell's life, with their shared interests in socialism, art, literature, travel, and architecture. Cockerell was an efficient private secretary to Morris and cared for him throughout his last illness in 1896. For four years from 1900 he entered a partnership with his closest friend Emery Walker, in his engraving business.[20]

This artistic and business experience, combined with his considerable talents and contacts, secured Cockerell his position as director of the Fitzwilliam Museum at Cambridge in 1908. W. S. Blunt described his achievement there: 'he transformed a dreary and ill-hung provincial gallery into one which set a new standard of excellence which was to influence museums all over the world'. As Cockerell noted, 'I found it a pigsty; I turned it into a palace'.[21] Enthusiastic and resourceful, he reorganized and rearranged the displays, and massively increased the collections, besides adding two new galleries. This 'scrounger of genius' pursued benefactors unmercifully, making lifelong friends with many. On retirement from the Fitzwilliam in 1937, having been knighted in 1934, he moved to Kew in Surrey, where he was active until his seventies: even when he became bedridden he was tended by devoted friends as the 'sage of Kew', until his death in 1962, aged 95, from heart failure.[22]

In 1907, when he was 40, Cockerell married Kate Kingsford, a talented artist and manuscript illuminator. They had two daughters and a son, Sir Christopher Cockerell, inventor of the hovercraft. Soon after their marriage, Kate Cockerell developed disseminated sclerosis and finally became bedridden. Cockerell's friend, W. S. Blunt, observed that Cockerell loved his wife and grieved, 'but did not allow this personal tragedy to interfere with his work'.[23]

Cockerell favoured cremation over burial from an early age, reacting against elaborate Victorian funeral ceremony which he perceived as undignified and distasteful. He also preferred to dispense with the religious connotations of the traditional methods of disposal of the dead, though he welcomed church music. The first cremation he attended was that of his sister Olive in 1910—the family tradition began early. His aversion to burial in cemeteries was frequently expressed in his diaries. He attended Fairfax Murray's funeral at Isleworth in bitter weather in January 1919: 'A dreary cemetery and a garbled service', he noted.[24] The burial of Thomas Hardy's brother, Henry, in December 1928 was equally uncongenial, with no music, not even a hymn, at the funeral at Stinsford church, while the 'graveside portion' was miserably cold and forlorn.[25] Other burials were described in similarly disparaging terms.

Cockerell's preferred way to dispose of bodies was by cremation at Golders Green Crematorium in London, with simplicity and dignity. After a walk around the extensive and beautiful grounds in 1938 he explained in his diary why cremation held such appeal for him:

I found it all very peaceful and appropriate. The absence of pretentious memorials and the general good taste are a blessing. Death is dealt with as a natural and inevitable thing, almost cheerfully and not as a horror. I came away feeling that on a fine summer day it is one of the most inspiring and creditable features of London.[26]

The keywords for Cockerell were 'peaceful', 'natural', and 'inspiring'— each repeated many times in his diary entries on the numerous cremations he attended at Golders Green. When his friend Emily Guest was cremated there in November 1919, he noted that it was 'a dignified ceremony without a touch of vulgarity'.[27] The remarks of Cockerell's friend Caroline Doughty in 1926 on the cremation of her poet husband, Charles Doughty, add to these positive perceptions of Golders Green. The crematorium service was beautiful, in her view, especially as it was 'the shortest and

simplest' possible. She was inspired by 'the glimpse of those lovely puri-
fying flames [which] made me so happy, his spirit still here in the dear
girls'. This was surely an unusual response to the crematorium flames in
1926, when the usual aim was rather to conceal them, but it probably
reflected the views of enthusiasts. Caroline Doughty explained that her
husband had earlier wanted his ashes scattered at sea, but changed his
mind to allow their ashes to be buried together in the Garden of Rest at
Golders Green: this was a sacred place for them, as well as a lovely, well-
kept garden, not in the least like a traditional cemetery.[28] She echoed
Cockerell's belief that cremation could be inspiring—both secular and
sacred.

A more detailed account of the cremations of Cockerell's two closest
male friends at Golders Green reveals more of the nature of such individual ceremonies and the ritual which attended them. They span the
years of the early growth of cremation, from 1915 to 1933. The first was
that of Philip Webb, one of Cockerell's dearest friends—an architect and
another member of William Morris's intimate circle, aged 82 at his death
on 17 April 1915. On learning that Webb was dying, Cockerell noted in
his diary, 'Sad to say, this is really welcome news as his mind has quite
given way lately'. Therefore it was a time to praise Webb, not to mourn
him, because he had lived a productive life and finished his work. Cockerell found his old friend still alive at Worth in Sussex, but unconscious,
attended by Margaret Dickinson, his housekeeper, and a helpful male
nurse. A few hours later, Webb's breathing became weaker and he died
peacefully. This was the first time Cockerell had actually been present at
a death, and in the case of such an old man he found this 'a natural event
attended with no horror'. By contrast Mrs Dickinson, who had taken care
of Webb for fourteen years, was severely distressed. Cockerell preferred to
avoid such excessive display of emotion and went out to send telegrams,
leaving her female family members to soothe her.[29] This was only one of
many gendered responses to death and the emotions it evoked, that are
recorded in the Cockerell Papers.

Three days later Webb's coffin went off by motor hearse to Golders
Green, while Cockerell, Walker, and Mrs Dickinson followed by train to
London, to find many mutual friends from Morris's circle gathered in the
crematorium chapel. J. W. Mackail, classical scholar and poet, read the
passage from Ecclesiastes, 'Now let us praise famous men', suggested by
Cockerell and setting the tone of celebration rather than lament. Cockerell

was happy to draw on rich passages from the Bible where they illuminated his secular purpose. Part of Mozart's Requiem was played on the organ, accompanied by 'a great strewing of primroses' brought by Cockerell from Webb's home, adding an element of natural beauty. All was 'seemly and dignified', establishing for Cockerell a model for future cremations. Three days later, Cockerell and Walker, as executors, spent a day sorting Webb's letters and papers. Cockerell's big bundle of his own letters from Webb initiated another personal ritual, as he found that reading them through in the next few days renewed many old memories.[30] Cockerell also sought comfort in talking through memories of Webb with other friends from the Morris circle, often over a meal. In the absence of religious faith, memory and conversation were vital sources of consolation. Affectionate and often repetitive conversation about the recently dead was a common form of consolation in the nineteenth century, especially among women, but it became less so after 1945. Its value has again been recognized since the 1970s.

Other modern rituals were established by Cockerell and his friends at this 1915 cremation, which required considerable thought as they were aware they were creating precedents. Apart from the cremation service itself, there was the tricky question of what to do with Webb's ashes. The initial decision was taken that the simple and natural choice was to scatter his ashes, but the location for the scattering was more problematical. Another close friend, Charles Hornby, printer and collector, followed up Cockerell's suggestion to write to the warden of New College, Oxford, seeking permission to scatter the ashes on college ground. Hornby did so, but with little hope, as he explained to Cockerell,

I am a little afraid that their orthodoxy will shy at the idea of any remains resting in unconsecrated ground. Why not scatter them in some Oxford garden—New College—or John's or Trinity—without permission? It could probably be done quietly and unseen, that is to say if the bulk is small—I don't quite know what cubic measure a cremated body rises to.[31]

It took Cockerell, Hornby, and Emery Walker three months to decide on the appropriate location, the warden of New College having presumably turned down their unorthodox request. Finally, on 10 July 1915 the three men went together to Uffington to scatter Webb's ashes at the top of White Horse Hill in Berkshire—'a glorious spot', dear to them all, close to Kelmscott village, home of William Morris. At his own request, memorials for Webb were to be simple and appropriate: these included the sharing of memories of their friend's life and achievements over meals. On 9 July 1915, after supper at a local inn, Cockerell, Walker, and Hornby attended a meeting in honour of Webb at the Art Workers' Guild, where his designs were on display and his life and work discussed.[32]

The second instructive cremation of a beloved friend was that of Sir Emery Walker himself in 1932, eighteen years after Webb's death. Cockerell observed in his diary that they had loved and trusted each other since the days when they worked together on the Kelmscott Press with William Morris. Cockerell recorded Walker's final illness, death, and cremation in affectionate detail. From mid-1931 Walker, aged 82, was an invalid, but he kept rallying, despite severe heart attacks. Cockerell spent considerable time in London at Walker's home at Hammersmith Terrace, running errands for him and trying to raise his spirits. On 10 December 1932 Cockerell heard Walker was critically ill, but found that he had rallied again, so they were able to have an excellent talk: 'he spoke easily of death'. Such courage and composure in the face of death, allied with a positive attitude of sangfroid, were vital qualities for Cockerell in facing death well. But that also required mental clarity: he feared senility most of all, and was delighted that his friend's mind was still lucid.[33]

By 1932 Cockerell was regarded as an accomplished obituarist who wrote for *The Times* on the deaths of his many friends and literary acquaintances. Older people often took the newspapers for the obituary news. Quality newspapers like *The Times* highlighted the obituary feature article, often written by experts like Cockerell. The best dailies made a practice of keeping up-to-date prepared obituaries on a broad spectrum of worthy people. Cockerell regarded the writing of a good and balanced obituary as a significant tribute to his friends; in the absence of immortality, an accurate account of a life well lived was essential to preserve its memory. Cockerell had an alarming tendency to rush off from deathbeds to *The Times* obituary office and back again. And so, knowing Walker could not last much longer, on 16 December Cockerell mapped out an obituary. He offered it to *The Times* only to find they already had one on file, which he deemed inadequate and undertook to improve. He devoted the next two days to creating a fitting obituary, which was lovingly written, and deposited it with the editor of obituaries at *The Times*.[34]

During the next few months Cockerell visited Walker regularly, reporting more excellent talks about the old days, some temporary improvements and further heart attacks. Walker, Cockerell's 'dearest man friend', finally died on 22 July 1933. Cockerell was pleased that their last meeting on 13 July was 'a singularly happy one. Indeed we were quite merry together and I am fortunate to have this final sight of him to remember'. He saw Walker's daughter Dolly for an hour after the death, and spent the next day with her at Hammersmith, writing letters and talking with her. Cockerell noted: 'I felt great exaltation at the thought of Walker's well spent life'. This prompted him to return to *The Times* office to check the proofs of Walker's obituary notice, written six months earlier, when he had seemed close to death.[35]

Cockerell maintained his equanimity in the face of genuine deep sorrow by diversions and good cheer. On 24 July 1933, he returned to Dolly Walker at Hammersmith Terrace for lunch after his visit to the lawyers to examine the will. In his capacity as executor he wrote letters until the coffin arrived, when 'I superintended and finally saw it screwed up'. Afterwards, he went 'to dine and sleep and talk of old friends' with Sara Anderson, another old friend. However, this was not just a distraction from gloom—it was also an immersion in the poignant pleasures of memory, to strengthen his nerve for the cremation next day, when he accompanied Dolly Walker and other mourners to Golders Green Crematorium. The chapel was packed with friends, for 'a quite perfect ceremony'. As at Webb's funeral in 1915, J. W. Mackail, classical scholar, read appropriate passages from Ecclesiastes, again setting the tone of celebration rather than lament, aided by suitable organ music.[36] The custom had been started in 1915 and copied at so many cremations in the eighteen years since that a ritual was now well established. Undoubtedly all was 'seemly and dignified', as in that earlier service. The main difference between the two was the gap in the ranks of mourners attending, so many friends having died in the meantime. Just two weeks after Walker's funeral Cockerell took Dolly Walker for a month's cruise on the *Atlantis*—a favourite escape from the blues.[37]

Cockerell acted as executor to several celebrities whose obsequies were sometimes unorthodox. Though he disliked Victorian-style burials in cemeteries, he clearly approved of the eccentric interment of his old friend, the poet Wilfrid Scawen Blunt, in September 1922. Blunt had directed that he be buried in the simplest manner without a ceremony or a coffin, but wrapped in his old Eastern travelling carpet: he was to be buried in a specific spot in the wood in the grounds of his home in Sussex. The day before the burial Cockerell supervised the digging of a huge grave with steps leading into it, having personally lined it with boughs of oak, chestnut, yew, elder, and ivy, to add the beauty of nature to the occasion. Cockerell superintended the sewing of Blunt's body into the Eastern carpet, which was then carried to the grave by six men from the estate, followed by eleven family members and friends. Cockerell considered it 'a most beautiful and dignified burial, like that of an ancient Pharaoh'. This funeral satisfied Cockerell's wish for a simple, dignified, and non-religious ceremony for Blunt, at one with nature—if cremation was not permitted. He observed in his diary, 'Nothing seemed lacking. All was exactly as he had wished and the little company dispersed afterwards with full hearts'.[38]

On the death of the famous poet and novelist, Thomas Hardy, aged 87, in January 1928, Cockerell was joint executor with Hardy's widow Florence. Cockerell regarded Hardy, an agnostic, as a friend, having known him since 1911. Florence summoned Cockerell to their home in Dorchester on 10 January 1928, but Hardy died of pleurisy next day. Almost immediately Cockerell phoned *The Times* to report the death and to discuss an obituary. Then he returned to try to comfort 'the brave unselfish widow', talking to her into the early hours, before trying to sleep in his clothes in the dining room. Next day Cockerell was pleased that Hardy's expression was 'noble, majestic and serene—that of the Happy Warrior. It is wonderful that he should have ended his long life peacefully and with his mind clear to the last'.[39]

Cockerell regarded his role as executor to Hardy as a heavy responsibility, but he also enjoyed his own reflected glory and authority. His chief concern was to obtain the consent of the Hardy family to a state funeral in Westminster Abbey. The initiative for this seems to have come from Cockerell, but was met with outrage by Dorset opinion and by Hardy's brother Henry, who wanted Thomas buried in the local churchyard at Stinsford, alongside his family, in his native Dorset where his novels were set. Florence Hardy was distressed about the Abbey proposal, but Cockerell triumphed, following intense lobbying in London. An extraordinary compromise was arrived at, whereby Hardy's heart was to be removed before cremation at Woking and buried in Stinsford churchyard, while his ashes would be simultaneously interred at Poets' Corner in Westminster Abbey at a national funeral. Cockerell had pulled powerful strings to achieve his goal and rose to the challenge of organizing the Abbey ceremony:

Another very busy morning seeing the undertaker, seeing journalists, five of whom came to see the body, and telephoning to London about arrangements. Mrs Hardy full of doubt as to the decision to bury in the Abbey, instead of at Stinsford.[40]

Cockerell was obliged to miss the cremation because his invalid wife Kate, 'in terrible pain', summoned him home to Cambridge, but she recovered sufficiently to allow him to attend Hardy's impressive funeral in the Abbey on 16 January 1928.[41] Cockerell's friendship with Hardy's widow suffered irretrievable damage.

## Cockerell Faces His Own Mortality

Cockerell's dealings with death in his immediate family tell a more complex story. This was partly due to timing, in that—apart from his sister Olive who died in 1910—his other four siblings lived to an advanced age, dying in their seventies and early eighties between 1943 and 1948. Cockerell's wife Kate followed them in 1949. Cockerell had retired from the Fitzwilliam Museum in 1937 to live in Kew: in the decade or so after retirement, when even his frenetic life slowed down, he came face to face with the deaths of five close family members, and at last confronted the prospect of his own mortality. His retirement ended his professional obligation to encourage legacies for the Fitzwilliam and to act as executor for the estates of wealthy people with artistic tastes. It is no coincidence that from 1941 onwards his formerly prolific diary entries for deaths, cremations, and obituaries diminished, and he attended few funerals, whereas for most people the opposite occurs with advancing years.

Cockerell became increasingly concerned about his own mortality, as he watched four siblings go one by one within five years. A new emotional element now came into play, which he had usually suppressed in his semi-professional interactions with the deaths of numerous eminent people. The closest he had come to showing his feelings openly had been at the deaths of his dearest friends Philip Webb and Emery Walker. His diary also revealed his powerful but hidden emotions each year on the anniversary of the death of his beloved hero William Morris on 3 October 1896.

As Morris's private secretary Cockerell had cared for him on his deathbed: forty-four years later, on the 1940 anniversary, he was still describing this in emotional terms:

It is the 44th anniversary of William Morris's death. I was in his study across the passage from his bedroom on the ground floor of Kelmscott House, but I did not actually see him die. He was the first person that I ever saw dead...When I had been previously left alone [in the death chamber] myself I burst into an uncontrollable paroxysm of tears and was led back into the study, where for some time I went on sobbing. When it abated I set to work on all there was to be done.[42]

This impassioned late-Victorian response to death by the young Cockerell seems far removed from his habitual emotional restraint and composure in the twentieth century: this did not usually signify indifference, so much as avoidance of a public demonstration of his feelings. Thus he frequently left women in bereaved families to cope with the intimate and painful details of death, while he rushed off to see solicitors or have lunch with friends who would divert him. To an extent this might be construed as a gendered division of labour at death. He most admired friends like Anne Mew—sister of Charlotte Mew the poet—who faced a painful death from cancer heroically, 'with wonderful sangfroid and courage'.[43] He disliked witnessing suffering, and believed in a positive approach to pain and to death.

This apparent insensitivity to suffering appeared not infrequently when Cockerell's siblings were dying, when his search for self-possession, his efforts to conceal his emotions, could seem cold. The death of his brother Leslie in April 1943, aged 70, probably hit Cockerell hard because Leslie was five years younger, as he noted in his diary: 'This is the first break in our family since Olive's death in 1910—which of us will be the next to go! The remaining four of that generation may well depart almost hand in hand'. And so three of them did. This was the first intimation of mortality for Cockerell, though he had probably seen little of Leslie who had been a mining engineer overseas.[44] When he heard in July 1944 that Una, aged 77, was close to death from cancer in Oxford Infirmary, he noted in his diary: 'She has had great pain and is under morphia which renders her oblivious of her surroundings so it is useless for me to try to see her again'. He did not attend her cremation in Oxford, instead spending the afternoon at a Noel Coward matinee to escape his gloom.[45]

His brother Douglas Cockerell, a distinguished bookbinder, died at 75 in 1945, and Theodore, an eminent naturalist, followed three years later, aged 81. Cockerell was obliged to confront the ominous fact that he was the only survivor of the six siblings, but 'for how long?' However, in November 1947 his increasing awareness of the approach of his own death had forced him belatedly to settle his affairs. Walking in Kew Gardens he reflected that even his immediate family would not know how to proceed if he also died suddenly. So he took action, calling on his way home on some kind neighbours to ask if they would set the process moving in case of his sudden death, pending the arrival of his executors. They were to insert a brief notice in *The Times*, noting 'Cremation private. No flowers and no mourning, by his direction'. He requested: 'Arrange for cremation—No religious service—Music by Handel, Bach or Purcell, not a doleful nature'.[46]

The death of Cockerell's wife, Kate, on 18 September 1949 was the most difficult in every way for him. In 1949, Neville Lord Lytton deplored the tragedy of her prolonged paralysis with sclerosis: 'This amputation of the expression of her talent and the way she bore it showed a divine patience'.[47] The many volumes of Cockerell's diaries scarcely mentioned his wife and children, though he clearly loved them. On 21 August 1949 Cockerell described 'Kate's sudden illness': she lost her speech and the doctor diagnosed thrombosis, a slight stroke, from which she might not recover. In despair he moved Kate to the Nightingale Nursing Home in Twickenham—'a sad event as I fear she may never see her home again'. He visited her nearly every afternoon for the next twenty days, taking only one day off when he was exhausted. The news that she died peacefully on 18 September came as a relief after days of suspense, and he was thankful her intolerable half-life was not prolonged. He considered her life happy on the whole despite thirty years of disablement.[48]

Cockerell, now aged 82, made arrangements with the undertakers for Kate's cremation, and announced in *The Times*, 'Cremation private. No flowers please'. Only Cockerell and his two adult children Margaret and Christopher attended the cremation on 21 September 1949. Kate's coffin arrived soon after them and they followed it into the chapel at Mortlake:

We three were alone, but for an attendant or two, when the coffin moved slowly through the opened doors, which closed after it immediately. It was all very dignified and just what I should desire for my own coffin, when the time comes.

I had brought the five books that Kate wrote as well as illuminated. We looked at these in turn for half an hour, and then came home, Margaret returning at 4.30 for the ashes…I went early to bed feeling thankful that this difficult day had passed off so satisfactorily.

Next day Cockerell arranged for tributes to be published in *The Times* and a week later went to stay with his old friend Cicely Hornby for a week in the country.[49] Such an escape was his usual response to deep grief, perhaps to remember the better times.

Two years after his wife's death Cockerell was himself confined to his bedroom in Kew, and he stayed there for eleven years until he died from heart failure in 1962. He was not afraid of death or extinction but he feared a painful death from cancer, which had killed several close relatives. He wanted a peaceful sudden end. In March 1962 he had a difficult night: he sent postcards of spring flowers in Kew Gardens to his family and close friends, with the inscription, 'I think I am dying'. W. S. Blunt visited soon after to find him in excellent form.[50] Cockerell had no belief in a future life: 'As to hereafter I know nothing, nor whether I have lived before, and this ignorance does not worry me at all'.[51] On his 86th birthday in 1953 Cockerell noted in his diary that he was well looked after: 'many dear friends and other visitors have made my imprisonment a happy one'. He kept Kate's ashes in a casket on the top of a bookcase in his bedroom, awaiting his own death when they could be mingled—perhaps the most telling testimony to his affection for her.[52]

Cockerell's story illuminates the attitudes of increasing numbers of his class to death and dying, and their enthusiasm for cremation as the appropriate modern and secular way of death; it also demonstrates their efforts to promote simple, dignified, and inspiring rituals and ceremony. Cockerell ceased to be an active advocate of cremation after his retirement, but he was no doubt pleased by the rapid advance in its popularity up to his death in 1962. Peter Jupp has shown that cremation was in line with the new Labour government's aim to create a welfare state from the cradle to the grave. Nearly one in ten London funerals in 1938 had still been pauper funerals, so the government introduced a national insurance benefit for funeral expenses in 1946 to make funerals cheaper for the poor. The building of crematoria in Britain reached its climax in the twenty years from 1950 to 1970, increasing from fifty-eight to 206.[53] Cockerell did not live to see the statistical landmark in the history of cremation in 1967 when its numbers exceeded burials and it became the principal mode of disposal. A contributory factor was the cautious lifting in 1964 of the late nineteenth-century Vatican ban on cremation for Catholics, so that those who chose cremation were no longer denied the sacraments. As the hospitalization of the dying increased, the medical profession also became more supportive of cremation, as did funeral directors who recognized its inevitability.[54]

Cockerell would doubtless have been pleased at the growing popularity of cremation which affected 70 per cent of British funerals by 1991. However, he would have deplored the bleak utilitarian architectural style of the crematoria and the failure to develop inspiring secular rituals for the growing mass market. He would have shared Alan Bennett's view of one of the new municipal crematoria erected in the 1960s:

It looks like the reception area of a tasteful factory or the departure lounge of a small provincial airport... This is the architecture of reluctance, the furnishings of the functionally ill at ease, décor for a place you do not want to be... Unsolemn, hygienic and somehow retail, the service is so scant as to be scarcely a ceremony at all, and is not so much simple as inadequate.[55]

James Stevens Curl, a passionate advocate of burial, in 1972 dismissed crematoria as 'really horrible places... where death is played down and made apparently insignificant'. In his view, if cremation was to become universal it should be conducted with the conviction and panache of the Victorians, with meaningful symbolic rites of words and music for family and friends to farewell their loved ones.[56] Cockerell and his friends achieved this in the first half of the century among the social and intellectual elite. But it proved a more challenging task thereafter to create a ritual and ceremony which were secular and appropriate, while also inspiring the mass market.

# PART II

## The Second World War

# 6

# The People's War:
# Death in the Blitz

English ways of death changed profoundly in the years after 1914. There was a gradual shift from a dominant Christian culture of acceptance of death and more open expression of grief in the Victorian period to one of avoidance and reticence. The two world wars had a cumulative impact on this process of change, which was still very uneven in the interwar years, varying by region, class, religion, and gender. The Second World War marked a more profound break with the past: silence and stoicism in the interests of morale and a successful war effort were immeasurably reinforced by the experience of the Blitz.

## The Myth of the Blitz

The bombing of British cities killed ordinary men and women in an unprecedented manner, especially as it was concentrated on specific locations and in the nine months from September 1940. In the entire war about sixty thousand British civilians were killed by enemy action, including about forty-three thousand in 1940 and 1941. The total civilian losses amounted to about 20 per cent of military fatalities, half of which occurred after mid-1943.[1]

Angus Calder's 1991 book, *The Myth of the Blitz*, argued that the 'myth' of the 'people's war' with its emphasis on civilian sacrifice, stoicism, and good humour, was well established by the end of 1942 and came to dominate the popular memory of the war in Britain in the next half-century. Calder saw the 'myth of the Blitz' as including Dunkirk, the Battle of Britain, and the Blitz—all vital components of a victory of good over evil:

'heroic mythology fused with everyday life to produce heroism'. This was the epic story of how Britain was saved from defeat and invasion in 1940–1, with British 'phlegm' reaching its finest hour in the Blitz. The 'myth of the Blitz' helped people make sense of the chaos, horror, and distress of wartime bombing: 'Its construction involved putting together facts known or believed to be true, overlaying these with inspirational values and convincing rhetoric—and leaving out everything known or believed to be factual which didn't fit'.[2]

The myth was based on a core of truth which highlighted special qualities of the British national identity, including heroism, stoicism, defiance, solidarity, humour, and self-sacrifice. Propaganda slogans such as 'We can take it' and 'We'll give 'em hell' helped to create a behavioural norm which was reinforced by Churchill's speeches, J. B. Priestley's broadcasts, and the BBC. Reported behaviour in the London Blitz established a model of how people should behave and consequently influenced how they did behave, in the provincial towns as well as the capital. As Calder put it, 'Chaos never became ungovernable. The effect of...continuous blitz was to spread the habit of adaptation from those who were brave and active to those who were not'.[3]

Such a view of the Blitz was largely accepted as a consensual memory until the 1960s, when questions began to be asked: were most people really so heroic and self-sacrificing in 1940? Revisionist historians were keen to note exceptions—such as Dunkirk, which may have been heroic but was also a disaster. Examples were cited of poor morale in the Blitz—of hysteria, cowardice, and panic. On the whole, however, historians have agreed that there was no extensive cover-up regarding the habits of 1940–1. Philip Ziegler concluded in 1995 in *London at War* that 'Few Londoners behaved badly, many more conspicuously well; and the population of London as a whole endured the blitz with dignity, courage, resolution and astonishing good humour'.[4]

However, significant omission allowed the myth to persist: it was largely concerned with sustaining positive morale, with cheerfulness and courage in the face of devastation and misery. Death and destruction could not, in fact, be concealed from the public in Britain in 1940–1, so people had to be encouraged to overlook the dark side of their existence in the war and to change their perspective. Censorship of the press naturally played a significant role here, especially in suppressing the most distressing aspects of stories. The devastation of houses and city centres and awful deaths by burning had to be reconciled with the needs of survival and everyday life. Many people cooperated because it was vastly preferable to conform to the heroic stance approved by the authorities than be overwhelmed by despair.

Indeed the fundamental aim of the myth was to conceal or reduce the actual devastation and death inflicted by the Blitz, perhaps by transforming it in the imagination. The dark side of the Blitz could be very black for certain people in certain cities at certain times. The myth did not dwell on the trauma of the burnt bodies left behind after a raid and the intense distress of wartime bereavement. Journalist Mollie Panter-Downes was critical of the BBC's efforts to minimize the 'horrifying' destruction in London in October 1940: 'To someone newly facing grief, the chirpy statement that "casualties were slight" has a way of sounding callous'.[5] An angry listener also protested to the BBC about use of the phrase 'slight material damage': 'but of course you cannot see thousands of hearts broken, they are not *material* damage'.[6] The creation of the myth of the Blitz was essential to an effective war effort, given that the major aim of bombing civilian populations was to smash morale. The myth was largely effective in maintaining civilian morale. Perhaps even the victims could more easily accept their loss within a context of national defence and sacrifice. Before the war the authorities had anticipated far higher mortality rates from air raids and feared they would have to deal with mass civil disobedience. It took them some time to realize there were many fewer dead and far more homeless than expected. It was in practice easier to promote the myth because most people in England were not directly affected. Civilian casualties were concentrated largely in urban areas more accessible to air attack, and within the months from September 1940 to May 1941. Moreover, since industrial areas of cities were common targets, the working classes and the poor suffered more than the middle classes and the wealthy. [7]

# A Hidden Core of Trauma and Grief: 'Try not to dwell on what we have lost'

The myth of the Blitz played a significant role in the history of death and grief in twentieth-century England. Until the 1930s the stiff upper lip about death and loss had been more common among males, the lower working classes, and the upper classes; but it became more pervasive from the 1940s, irrespective of class and gender. Death, loss, and grief were inevitable parts of the experience of the Blitz that did not fit the paradigm and had to be minimized or concealed to reconcile horror and destruction with the needs of survival. Nor was it in the interests of the war effort and morale to reveal numbers and details of countless bodies blown to bits and collected piecemeal in sacks, or loved ones terribly burnt. Therefore the dark side of the Blitz story, which necessarily included such appalling information, was suppressed or sanitized. To sustain morale, wartime censorship prohibited detailed reports on gruesome deaths and mass burials. At the heart of the myth of the Blitz, then, were countless individual lives which were directly destroyed by it, and numerous families wounded by sorrow that could not be expressed: grief at the loss of loved ones had to be internalized, sometimes for years. People in the target areas could live in conditions akin to battlefields but they must 'take it' in silence. Individual bereaved people were left to grieve privately, displaying outward stoicism and courage.

The churches and the clergy reinforced the myth of the Blitz in their response to death and grief. On 22 November 1940 Dr Mervin Haigh, the Bishop of Coventry, addressed the mourners of the 172 bomb victims buried in a common grave after the devastating Coventry raids:

Remember that the eyes of millions of people are upon you…We must try not to dwell too much on what we have lost, but to turn our thoughts and our hands to the tasks we can do to help for the sake of our city and of our nation…The Germans can kill our loved ones, but it rests with us whether they shall break our spirit. This evil air raid has brought us together in a great bond.[8]

The sorrowing relatives of the 172 victims must 'try not to dwell' on their horrific loss, but instead maintain their courage and good humour—an effective psychological strategy in wartime. This was a far cry from the emotional responses to community disasters in England in more recent years, as at Aberfan and Hillsborough, where bereaved relatives were actively encouraged to talk through their loss with therapists.

So the awful carnage at the heart of the Blitz was implicitly acknowledged with the proviso that it must not be lingered over. The myth of the Blitz was widely accepted and morale on the whole remarkably good, reinforced by press censorship. Information on some of the worst disasters—including the Bethnal Green underground station disaster in

March 1943, which killed 173, and the Bank tube tragedy of January 1941 with its toll of 111—was largely suppressed by authorities in the interests of public morale. But to gain some kind of understanding of the profound impact of the Blitz on the families, friends, and communities of the sixty thousand dead victims, a few individual tragedies need to be explored here—and mentally multiplied by several thousand.

The worst period of the Blitz lasted nine months from 7 September 1940, with its primary aim to demoralize the population of London and force Britain to surrender. The German bombers returned to London every night that first month, killing about 5,730 people and seriously injuring up to ten thousand. The numbers of fatalities seemed horrific at the time because it was the start of the aerial bombing, though civilian deaths from Allied bombing of German cities in later years often far exceeded these in Britain. On Saturday 7 September 1940, later known as 'Black Saturday', the raiders killed 430 people, followed by 400 on the second night and 370 on the third. The raids were chiefly aimed at the East End, leaving the docks blazing. Since industrial areas were common targets, the working classes and the poor suffered disproportionately. Winston Churchill visited the slum area of Silvertown which was the worst hit. His rhetoric set the tone: 'Pessimists had predicted panic and bitterness in the East End, but I saw nothing of the kind...Smiles, cheers and grim determination showed already that "London can take it".'[9]

A two-page account in the Imperial War Museum of the loss which befell the Furniaux family on that first night of the London Blitz gives a vivid impression of its wider impact on the relatives of the 1,200 victims over the first three nights. Thirteen members of the Furniaux family took refuge in a public air-raid shelter in the Columbia Road, home of the Flower Market, along with numerous other poor residents of Shoreditch. About forty people were killed and many more wounded when a bomb exploded in a ventilation shaft. Rose Furniaux wrote most of the brief account. She described an 'almighty explosion' from within the shelter, causing chaos and extensive casualties. She saw that her sister Flo, nearest the air shaft, and her two children, were seriously injured, if not worse. Her parents also appeared badly hurt. Most people had shrapnel wounds of varying degrees. A pregnant woman was killed outright by the explosion, and her dead baby was expelled from her body. Utter chaos followed. Rose tried to fetch Flo's husband but instead collapsed herself from injuries and shock. Amidst the chaos the fifteen family members were taken to various different hospitals, each frantic about the fate of the others. Flo Furniaux and her two children had in fact died. Flo's parents suffered severe shrapnel wounds but survived. Flo's mother discharged herself from hospital to attend the funerals of her daughter Flo and her two grandchildren, Dolly and Ronnie. Like so many victims of the Blitz they were buried with their fellow victims in a communal grave at Manor Park Cemetery, denied the dignity of an individual funeral, grave, and memorial.[10]

Two nights later on Monday 9 September 1940 370 people were killed. Six hundred East Enders had been bombed out of their homes and taken to a rest centre in a primary school in Canning Town. A bomb killed seventy-three of those sheltering in the school: the roof caved in, burying people under concrete slabs and layers of bricks, as Juliet Gardiner shows:

No one even knew for sure who had been sheltering there, or how the various body parts that were pulled from the wreckage—and carefully carried to the local swimming pool that had been turned into a temporary morgue—could be pieced together for identification, to give families the bodies to decently rest in peace. ARP workers and local volunteers went on digging for twelve days before conceding that of course they'd never bring out anyone alive, or even whole, now. Entire families had been wiped out. The seventy-odd known dead were buried in a mass grave. But the locals reckoned nearer 200 had died, and believed that more than a hundred still lay incarcerated in the site the authorities concreted over.[11]

Nearly a month later 154 people died when a bomb blasted a public shelter in a basement in Stoke Newington, trapping and crushing people and rupturing water mains and sewage pipes; the victims drowned or were blown to bits and twenty-six were never identified. It took ten days to dig out survivors.[12] In the early stages of the Blitz, Air Raid Precautions workers and firefighters were unable to cope with the huge scale of disasters, and civil administration collapsed in some areas of the East End. Many who found the bombing intolerable fled, though some later returned. Over the first two months most people who remained in London learned how to cope.[13]

Mea Allan was a journalist reporting on the war for the *Daily Herald*, describing the devastation and the high morale of most Londoners, who seemed to her more angry than depressed. Her first experience of a raid was 'near hell upon earth...You felt you really were walking with death'. Allan learned to distrust deep shelters because of the dangers from gas leaks, burst water mains, fire, and entombment. This view was strongly reinforced by her experience of covering the Bank tube disaster early in January 1941, when 111 people died, crushed by the blast or thrown in front of an approaching train. Mea was the first reporter to gain access to the 'hell-hole of the disaster—a crater containing the whole bally circus...Beneath were dead shelterers whose bodies were, one by one, being brought out...The blast was as bad as the actual bombing...people were picked up like pieces of paper and hurled along passages and on to the line—every bone in their bodies smashed.' As Mea explored the underground passages she found the station still used by shelterers, despite the carnage: 'I can't describe the sordid awfulness of these dreary passages...Chaos, noise and death—and amid it all the regulars are settling down to sleep. Not thinking they are brave. Just Londoners, carrying on in the good old wartime style'. In June 1941 Mea had her first panoramic view of the extensive damage to the City: 'It was like the knocked up remains of a film set...Hardly in all that square mile a building that was whole. And most of them razed to the ground. An occasional half-building still standing—but windowless, burnt out, gaunt, empty as a skull'.[14]

The provincial cities had less total damage than London, as bombing was not continuous over many months; but small cities suffered a concentrated attack over significant central areas which could be devastating, as in Coventry, where 100 acres of the city centre were ravaged on 14–15 November 1940. Nazi propaganda coined the term 'Coventrate' to mean the physical and psychological destruction of a whole city. The German bombers set the medieval city centre on fire and gutted its superb cathedral in a terrifying attack lasting ten hours, killing 554, seriously wounding 865 people, and making one-third of the houses uninhabitable. The small, compact size of Coventry (213,000 people in 1938) made this experience worse for many than the London Blitz, as most people knew someone who was dead or missing. Three observers participating in Mass Observation's social survey noted that the numerous refugees fleeing Coventry believed 'Coventry is finished'. There were more 'open signs of hysteria, terror, neurosis' observed in one evening than in the previous two months in all other areas. Coventry became a ghost town as many citizens fled to the countryside around.[15] Yet despite serious damage to production, machines survived, employees returned, and economic life gradually continued. The people of Coventry were no less brave than those in London, but their experience was probably more terrifying and it took time to adjust.

In the spring of 1941 the east coast became a target: Hull suffered an estimated 1,200 deaths, mostly between March and September 1941. In early May an intensive German attack badly damaged the docks and killed 280 civilians. R. Peat volunteered for the Cyclist Messenger Corps, which had to accompany ambulances to bomb sites and move casualties to public shelters. He found his first experiences 'terrifying'. Peat's account was punctuated by references to the dead people he saw while he worked—a policeman lying on the road, people stuck in a burning house for whom nothing could be done, firemen lying dead on the road: 'Arriving back at the First Aid Post we were given toast and cocoa and sat in a semi circle dead quiet. Some of the men were crying. We received instructions not to talk to civilians about the fires to try and stop panic'.[16] Two hundred of Hull's unidentified victims of that early May raid were buried in shrouds rather than coffins, and in a mass grave.[17]

The raids on Hull continued. Peat and his brother were in the First Aid Post on 11 July 1941 when a heavy raid started and a bomb fell into the room, just as they were about to move out with the ambulances. They were completely buried as the floor opened and the school collapsed on them:

My arms and legs were trapped and I was unable to move at all, I was totally buried. I had seen people burnt and gassed to death in Incidents I had attended and I knew this could happen to me. I wished a bomb would drop nearby and blow away the debris burying me; I was absolutely useless and knew only God could help me. There was no sound from my brother and the others who had been in the room with me but I could hear someone screaming in the sitting-room area. I could feel the ground vibrate when bombs fell and later the drills of the rescue parties so I knew that they were looking for us.

Peat was fortunate to be dug out alive but nobody else was rescued alive from the control room, including his brother. A total of seven people were killed in the blast. The brief six-page diary ends there, without remark on how Peat coped with his brother's death.[18]

## Shattered Bodies and Mass Burials in Common Graves

The horror of the Blitz must have been intensified for many by the manner in which corpses were treated after a raid and by the mass common burials often deemed essential by the authorities. Those corpses which could be retrieved after a bombing raid in London were usually laid out on the ground in rows, covered by sheets or sacking, often bloodstained. They were removed to the morgue in mortuary vans which had once been butchers' vans or even council dustcarts. But sometimes the remains of the dead could not be retrieved, though they might be discovered when buildings were eventually demolished months or years later. And many could not be identified because they were too badly shattered by blasts. Wardens were expected to collect baskets or bowls of 'unidentified flesh' which would be taken to the mortuary. Frances Faviell was an artist who had studied anatomy and was helpful in the grim attempts at reassembling body parts, often without conclusive results:

We had somehow to form a body for burial so that the relatives (without seeing it) could imagine that their loved one was more or less intact for that purpose. But it was a very difficult task—there were so many pieces missing and, as one of the mortuary attendants said, 'Proper jigsaw puzzle, ain't it, Miss?' The stench was the worst thing about it...It became a grim and ghastly satisfaction when a body was fairly constructed—but if one was too lavish in making one body almost whole, then another would have sad gaps...I think that this task dispelled for me the idea that human life is valuable.[19]

Bereaved London civilians usually knew little of the macabre details of the retrieval of bomb victims. But many must have been shocked and dismayed by the burials in mass graves of unidentifiable or unclaimed Blitz victims and those who were killed together in large numbers. One female journalist always guarded her handbag closely as it contained her identity card: if she were killed it would spare her from 'one of those ghastly cardboard boxes in which civilians, unclaimed, are dumped'.[20] The importance attached to individual burials was clear in a note by Philippa Strachey, referring to a friend killed in a shelter:

I have also had a most distressing conversation with poor Mr Fenlon who told a harrowing tale of the death of Ethel Coombe in an air raid. Her body was not recovered for six days during which he spent every moment he could spare on the spot in order to prevent her being buried as an unidentified person and to have the consolation of placing her in a grave near her mother and Ellen.[21]

Individual tragedies of violent and untimely deaths in the London Blitz were compounded by the indignity, lack of respect, and loss of identity symbolized by impersonal mass burials. Common graves reminded people too vividly of the dreaded burials of paupers, and of horrific mass graves on the Western Front in the First World War. Moreover, communal burials in the Blitz inevitably made grieving families fearful of the likely condition of their relatives' corpses, especially if they were unidentified after explosions.

The communal burial which caught the popular imagination was that of over forty London schoolchildren from Lewisham in January 1943. Though the most sustained and continuous period of the London Blitz ended in May 1941, intermittent bombing raids continued until 1943. Photographs of the bodies of the children were considered too distressing for publication. The children were buried in a mass grave in the presence of several thousand of their families and neighbours. The long communal trench was lined with laurel and fir, holding its extended row of small white coffins. The slow funeral procession was led by the Bishop of South-wark and other dignitaries, followed by the crowds of neighbours. Finally came the 'pathetically long line of wan-faced fathers and mothers, sisters and brothers. Many a father had his arm round a stumbling woman in black who held in her hand not an elaborate wreath but a bunch of spring flowers, narcissi, violets, or snowdrops'.[22]

The impact of the devastation of Coventry, with 568 fatalities in November 1940, was also compounded for many bereaved families by the way the bodies of loved ones were treated afterwards. Numerous corpses had been stacked in the mortuary with identification labels marked in indelible pencil. But the roof of the mortuary was destroyed in the raid and the labels rendered illegible by rain. Relatives had great difficulty in identifying shattered bodies, so clothes were removed and placed in sand-bags; and victims were identified by clothes and belongings instead of physical remains.[23] Before the Coventry disaster, many identified victims still received private burials; but that was changed by the sheer scale of the Coventry deaths and the overwhelming problems of mutilation and iden-tification. The Coventry Emergency Committee argued that two huge mass funerals and communal graves would be less painful and less expen-sive than numerous individual burials spread over weeks. They tried to persuade grieving families it was preferable to remember their loved ones as they were in life.[24]

Coventry families were obliged to accept a highly unpopular decision by the authorities. As the *Manchester Guardian* put it, 'relatives and friends of the civilian dead laid their hopes in a common grave and turned away'. On 22 November 1940, Dr Mervin Haigh, the Bishop of Coventry, led the mourners to the trenches in which 172 of the bodies were laid. (Trench formation was considered more likely to give the appearance of separate graves.) The *Guardian* saw it as 'the strangest burial since the Christian service came to the world'. Several services had to be read: a Roman Catholic ceremony was combined with Free Church prayers and an Anglican bishop's commendation. Mourners had found something black to wear, even if only a veil or a black raincoat over stained dungarees. Only officials had been allowed in the cemetery when the 172 coffins were carried in on lorries covered with tarpaulins, with labourers as pall-bearers.[25] An official directive of November 1940 had ordered that bodies should be lowered into the mass grave before the relatives were permitted into the cemetery.[26] Close by in the cemetery a mechanical excavator was meanwhile preparing for the next mass funeral. The clergy all came from wartime duties, pulling clerical robes over gumboots and steel helmets. The long line of mourners came into the cemetery later, many of them also directly from rescue work, including Home Guards, servicemen, and ambulance and Red Cross workers. They walked slowly past the cypress and yew trees and the bomb craters which had even disfigured the cemetery. A few days later a similar mass funeral was held for another 250 unidentifiable victims, whose bodies were still being recovered during the first ceremony.[27]

Many mass burials in communal graves in other cities were recorded in the *Manchester Guardian*. These included a 'long grave' for the 'martyrs' of the raids on Norwich; and two large communal graves for raid victims in Bath in early May 1942.[28] Liverpool was heavily bombed late in 1940, and again in March, April, and May 1941. But the bombing of the first week in May 1941 was devastating, leaving 1,900 people dead, 1,450 badly wounded, and 70,000 homeless. It was the worst disaster in Liverpool's long history, destroying the centre of the city with its many famous buildings. An unspecified but substantial number of unidentified bodies of the victims were buried on 13 May in a large communal grave at Anfield Cemetery. The Bishop of Liverpool, Dr A. David, declared that the mass grave would always be honoured as 'a specially sacred place', which hopefully would be marked one day by a monument enshrining the memory of the brave people of Liverpool. But it was impossible in May 1941 for officials or clergy to transform a vast common grave into a sacred place, when popular memory still associated mass burials with ignominious pauper burials.[29]

Julie Rugg's research in civic records in Hull, York, and Bradford illuminates the official management of civilian deaths caused by enemy bombing in Yorkshire. Rugg emphasizes the continued attachment to traditional burial practices in the north in the mid-twentieth century. She found tensions between the government's aim to reduce costs and resources needed for emergency interment and the desire of local authorities to give decent burials. The government opposed cremation, even though it might have been cheaper and more hygienic: only 3.7 per cent of the population had been cremated in 1939 because of continuing community opposition on cultural and religious grounds. Moreover, the few crematoria available were inadequate to process the large numbers of bodies anticipated in wartime. The early preparations for managing civilian war deaths were regarded as highly sensitive and publicity was to be avoided. Subsequently the Ministry of Health decreed that local authorities in Hull, York, and Bradford were responsible for collecting, identifying, and burying those victims not claimed by relatives: their bodies should be wrapped in sheets and interred in mass graves. As we have seen, this was the form of Public Assistance Committee burial sometimes adopted for poor miners killed in major colliery disasters in the interwar years. It revived powerful memories of humiliating pauper burials in the past; it was also a reminder that even as late as 1938 nearly 10 per cent of London burials were in Public Assistance Committee common graves for the destitute.[30]

The local clergy and cemetery authorities anticipated substantial public hostility to mass graves, which signified utter lack of respect for the dead, especially as the use of shrouds instead of coffins could prove 'gruesome' for relatives. Yet local governments were ultimately forced to concede that heavy raids with hundreds of casualties left them no option but to proceed with the shallow trench grave for 200 unidentified victims in Hull on 8–9 May 1941. The authorities attempted to compensate by the use of military rhetoric, in a futile effort to replace the pauper stigma with the suggestion of death on active service. Mass funerals were tightly controlled, with no publicity. Each victim was usually allowed only one close relative as a mourner, who attended by special permit, and costs of common funerals were reduced by discouraging display, even the personal touches of family flowers.[31]

# Individual Experiences of Death and Sorrow

In July 1945, with the end of the war in sight, the *Manchester Guardian* regretted the massive human price paid for victory: 'It is a high price, and, of course, the tables of killed, missing, and wounded are dumb when it comes to that further toll of victory, the suffering of those who bear these losses silently within their families'.[32] As we have seen, the myth of the Blitz with its paradigm of a courageous and stoical response to loss and grief was extraordinarily powerful. Some horrors of the Blitz were indeed for many people too dreadful to be dwelt on: many doubtless found the path of least resistance was to fall in with the official view of silent grief and try to forget.

Since mourners were discouraged from expressing their sorrow freely, the historian suffers from relatively limited primary sources. However we do have two surveys which offer some insights into attitudes to death and dying during the Second World War. Mass Observation was the pioneer social research organization founded by Tom Harrison in 1937 which sought continuing commentaries on themes in everyday life. During the war its nationwide panel of voluntary observers was officially deployed to report on issues directly relevant to the war effort, including civilian responses to the Blitz. London reports for 1940 revealed that people spoke remarkably little about death, despite its daily threats. As Harrison observed: 'the normal human capacity to sweep death under the carpet was if anything accentuated by blitzing'.[33]

This conclusion was confirmed by psychologist Harold Orlans's 1957 study of the 530 personal statements in Mass Observation's London files for May 1942. These observers were asked in 1942 to comment on the impact of the war on their personal views about death and dying. Orlans concluded that their thoughts about death during the war were complex, contradictory, and vacillated according to time and circumstance. However it was clear that many observers, especially those closely involved in the war effort, became more 'fatalistic, indifferent and callous'. Many confessed to becoming strangely detached: a soldier contemplated death and dying as little as possible, as did a subway-station attendant. Indeed many respondents exercised mental control to switch their thoughts in other directions, to remain detached, and to block out memories. Those who allowed themselves to consider death and dying more often and more directly were generally women and the elderly. About half the women and one-third of the men had some sort of belief in an afterlife, however nebulous, but more saw death as annihilation. They were more afraid of dying than death, especially of dying slowly and painfully, trapped under a building in an air raid.[34]

Another study was conducted by sociologist David Field in 2000, drawing on Mass Observation's questions in 1994 about the personal

experiences of death and bereavement of fifty-four English correspondents aged over 65. Field concluded that their experiences of death during
the Second World War had clearly played a significant role in shaping
their subsequent lives: the ubiquity of death in war had taught them to
detach themselves and accept death as a consequence of war, 'regrettable
but not unexpected'. The war made everyone aware 'of the imminent
possibility of death'. Their fatalistic response to death could seem callous
from a peacetime perspective. They had to become accustomed to seeing
dead bodies in gruesome condition during air raids or in battle. Even the
death of friends could sometimes seem like another dreadful incident in
an epic struggle.[35]

There are also a number of private diaries and memoirs in the Imperial
War Museum which throw some light on a variety of individual ways of
coping with the deaths, disasters, and grief of the Blitz. Three narratives
of individual experiences of the Blitz illustrate the range of responses.
Audrey Hawkins, a well-educated middle-class writer from Plymouth,
joined the Women's Royal Naval Service in 1939 and served as an officer
throughout the war. The diary she kept during the war suggests she was
a sensitive, intelligent young woman, who still lived a fairly sheltered
existence at home with her parents in 1939. She commented in some
detail on the severe bombing of Plymouth in March and April 1941,
when much of the small city centre was destroyed, and 932 people were
killed. Audrey's family did not escape the devastation: her fiancé Terry
Deacon's family was made homeless and a relative was killed. Audrey
admired the courageous response of the people of Plymouth but felt a
heavy price was paid for this 'sangfroid': many people felt they had to
become emotionally 'cold' to deal effectively with death and personal
tragedies in wartime:

At first we expected to see the town very much knocked about after a raid, especially if we had actually heard any bombs; but after a time everybody got used to
it and now takes it with a calm which is almost horrible. The whole business is
so cold: you hear a whistling and an explosion, and anti-aircraft gunfire, and
then you come out and go on where you left off. And somewhere you see a pile
of rubbish where there was a house or a shop, and you're told that people were
killed there. And you hear, and carry on—deciding whether you will plant
turnips or parsnips for next Spring, or something equally petty. I suppose it is a
good thing: the nervous strain would be very great if it were not so, but it seems
horrible that we can have settled down in this cold-blooded way to accept raids
and their consequences as part of ordinary life.[36]

She could see why people felt they must live for the moment to stay calm but recognized that this response could dull emotional sensitivities and blunt compassion. She had been very afraid of the early raids which left her shaking uncontrollably, but had learned through experience that 'I'm not petrified with fright during a raid'. But she knew that she was no hero: 'the only way I cannot be frightened is not to think about it, except in a casual way'. She had adapted, like so many others, becoming stoical and fatalistic. She had learned a kind of courage which allowed her to 'sit tight and look brave'; but it came at some cost.[37]

Mrs E. Hudson, a housewife, served in Air Raid Precautions in London during the Blitz. She wrote a revealing letter in 1941 which emphasized the way civilians had to become desensitized to violent wartime deaths, at least those of strangers:

We have adjusted our minds to the fact that tragedies do happen. We accept them and look at them in the same light as we do the rest of life. Thank God for the adaptability of the human mind for to continue to be overwhelmed by...each horror would most certainly lead to insanity. [38]

Hudson tried to forget the horrific results of bomb blasts and to regard them as impersonally as she might a murder story. But this did not make it any easier for civilians to come to terms with the deaths of their own relatives and friends, especially when the myth of the Blitz imposed silence on its darker aspects. The maintenance of strong public morale called for the stiff upper lip in response to the death of a loved one and the need for silent grief in private.

Betty Holbrook's story of her experience as a radar operator in the Auxiliary Territorial Service (ATS) in 1944, drawn from her memoir in the Imperial War Museum, offers another perspective on wartime responses to destruction and loss of life. She was stationed at an anti-aircraft gunsite in Victoria Park, Hackney, while the V1 rockets known as flying bombs were terrorizing London, starting on 13 June 1944, a week after the successful landings in Normandy. In the first two weeks the casualties equalled those at the start of the Blitz: each flying bomb on average killed two people, with 2,340 flying bombs in London killing 5,475 people. Londoners responded as they had to the Blitz: defiance was followed by depression, and then a measure of adaptation. Although the new weapon created great fear, it was easier to cope than in 1940 because Hitler now seemed doomed to fail.[39]

Betty Holbrook described the impact of the numerous flying bombs over Hackney during the second week of the attacks. Several exploded nearby, shaking their ATS hut at the camp. They were in and out of bed at night, dashing under the bed as the flying bombs approached their camp: 'there is something so demoralizing about lying under a bed waiting to be killed'. One night a flying bomb landed on working-class houses adjacent to the camp; Betty was thrown from her bed amid screams and chaos. She tried not to think about the numbers of factory workers who occupied each house destroyed by the bombs, as they would all have been asleep in bed when they fell.[40]

The last hut in the line at the gunsite had been taken over as an enquiry office, where a long queue of white-faced, distraught people waited for information. An official running in and out informed Betty that twenty-nine people were already reported dead, with dozens seriously injured and hundreds slightly hurt. Later in the afternoon the rescue squad brought an old lady on a stretcher out of one of the demolished houses, with 'a great weariness in her face', covered with yellow-black dust. Betty wrote, 'The helpless, bewildered expression in her blue eyes hurt me. It was as though someone squeezed my heart dry of blood and then tied it into a hard, hurtful knot. I thought, "oh God, if you are, have mercy!!".' The woman asked where her husband was and Betty tried to reassure her that he would be waiting at the hospital. Betty then went to check on the old lady's husband at the enquiry office, only to find that his body was one of the first to be removed from the rubble. Betty was in tears when she heard later that the old lady had died too.[41]

As Betty and her friend Joy walked along the edge of the camp towards the First Aid huts she noticed a strange-looking sight:

We saw a row of boots, shoes and slippers, all pointing upwards. Each pair was tied together and with a label attached. Shoes in that position must have feet in them. Bodies were attached. Covered over with sheets and counterpanes. How very silent and still are the dead. Odd to think that boots and shoes are the only clues to the owners. This time, yesterday, the feet inside those shoes and boots were moving around the streets. Now only the boots and shoes were of any use. At the end of the long row of bodies were several very large, white enamel bowls, also covered over. 'I wonder what they are for?' someone said. Someone else made a movement to move a cover. 'Leave them alone!' The words came from behind us. We all turned. It was one of the male sergeants. 'Why?' we asked, automatically. In ferocious tones he spat out the words between clenched teeth, 'If you must know—those bowls are filled with pieces of people. There are seven

hands, three feet, two halves of heads and a two week old baby in three pieces . . .'
'Shut up, damn you!!' Joy spoke for all of us.[42]

The Vicar, his face covered in dust and streaks of congealed blood, came to join them. He looked along the row of bodies with a stricken and perplexed stare, as he told them there were thirty-two dead and sixty seriously injured. To Betty's disbelief he added, 'God moves in mysterious ways', as he continued looking at the enamel bowls of pieces and the row of bodies. She was angry as they returned in silence to their battered Nissen hut to clear up the mess left by the V1, and noted, 'we were cold and desolate'.[43]

That night flying bombs came over at five-minute intervals, as fire engines and ambulances tore round the streets outside their camp, with bells ringing frantically. Yet their Captain told them they could sleep that night. 'My spirit was very low', she wrote:

More dead, more injured, more rows of bodies tied together at the feet, more big white enamel bowls were being lined up somewhere around. We could sleep tonight. A Flying Bomb crashed very near. The solid concrete building was shaken to its foundations. I lay and thought for a long time, until I became too tired to care about anything. What did it matter what happened. Maybe I would be killed within the next few days; feet tied together, or pieces in a white enamel bowl. Or, if I wasn't killed should I become so used to rows of bodies and large white enamel bowls that I wouldn't care anymore? Maybe no one was to blame. Not God, not the enemy, not us. You can sleep tonight. . . . I must sleep tonight; to get strength for any tomorrows that might be left.[44]

A few days later Betty was on leave with her boyfriend George at a riverside hotel 30 miles from London, where it was quiet and peaceful, and the events of the previous week seemed incredible. Later they had a drink at a country pub where a jolly crowd of people played darts, and laughed, chattered, and sang. As twilight fell, she looked out at the lovely evening view, and suddenly she vividly recalled the awful scenes of the previous Sunday: 'the bodies of people, the wounded sitting in gutters with blood pouring out of them; the white bowls; the row of bodies covered in counterpanes. And the little old lady looking at me from her sad blue eyes. Something broke inside me'. Tears rolled down her face; George found her crying and led her to a private seat in a rose garden. She sobbed in his arms as she had never done in her life before. Her anguish was excruciating, 'I guess it was my reaction to the last week. It was awful'.[45]

Betty Holbrook's intense emotional response to her traumatic experiences of the second week of the flying bombs can be put in the context of its time. The British propaganda of the Blitz strove to maintain a cool, positive morale amongst the population, whilst the German aim was precisely the opposite. The government needed good humour and sang-froid, even from victims of the Blitz and the flying bombs. Emotional 'breakdown' amounted to undermining the war effort, even cowardice. In 1940 seven special centres for treating cases of neurosis due to air raids had been set up but few patients were admitted and numbers actually declined during the Blitz. In February 1941 the *Manchester Guardian* reported that the British people were not being turned into 'nervous wrecks' by bombing. The Chief Medical Officer of the government stated that only about 5 per cent of victims incapacitated by air raids suffered from psychological disturbance. He was amazed at how well people stood up to the Blitz and recovered from its raids.[46]

But victims of raids were given no encouragement to report psychological trauma—precisely the opposite. Civilians, like RAF aircrew, were expected to be courageous: reporting war neurosis meant acknowledging failure to cope, even cowardice and behaviour harmful to the war effort. So, like Betty Holbrook, they bottled up their feelings and expressed them, if at all, to a sympathetic friend or relative. They carried on as best they could. Some people were able to cope, but others experienced difficulties in later years, as we shall see in subsequent chapters. The attitude to cases of neurosis during the Second World War was very different to that during community disasters today, when victims, relief workers, and grieving relatives are often encouraged to talk through their trauma with sympathetic counsellors, if they need help.

The silences surrounding the death and destruction of the Blitz affected commemoration as well as grieving. It may have been a people's war but there was no people's memorial to pay tribute to their sacrifice and console bereaved families. A letter to the *Manchester Guardian* on 19 September 1944 had expressed concern that the civilian victims of the German raids might not be commemorated as adequately as military casualties. Wilfred M. Short praised the 'magnificent spirit' of the people of Britain in withstanding the terror of German air attacks—'that spirit of courage, fortitude, and heroism'. He called for an appropriate State memorial in memory of the 56,000 civilians who had already lost their lives to the raids. The most fitting place for commemoration would be St Paul's Cathedral,

which had been the chief target for destruction, but still stood in its grandeur amidst the surrounding devastation. He would like to see a sculptured memorial, symbolic of the virtues he had attributed to the victims,
as 'a tribute in homage to those who have lost their lives, enshrining for
all time the memory of that sacrifice'. It might, he thought, be some small
consolation to their grieving families and friends.[47]

In the 1990s Rose Furniaux's son added some retrospective comments
to his mother's earlier account of their family tragedy on the first night of
the Blitz. He was angry that there had been no counselling for the family
nor any compensation for death or injuries when Flo and her two children
had been killed in the September 1940 blast. Indeed Rose Furniaux, like
many other victims, had received a hospital bill for the cost of her treatment: Rose refused to pay, and died in 1990 with shrapnel fragments still
in her body. Her son deeply regretted the subsequent failure to commemorate the victims of the Blitz; his comments reflected the changed cultural
climate of the decades since the late 1960s:

There has been no recognition for the suffering of London's civilians, no plaque,
no epitaph. The 50th anniversary of the start of the Blitz over London passed in
1990. There were no remembrance services, no politicians paid tribute. One
member of this family did lay a simple bunch of flowers in Columbia Road in
memory of that night.[48]

# 7

# Missing Airmen and Families in Anguish: 'There could be no mourning'

Bomber Command in the Second World War suffered an appalling attrition rate. About fifty-five thousand British and Commonwealth airmen died in combat or accidents—a loss of over 36 per cent of all flying crew.[1] The American army air force made a similar contribution to the war effort with equivalent casualties, but my focus here is on the British. Mark Wells argued in 1995 that the casualty rate for Bomber Command was higher than any other section of the British armed forces, comparable to the subalterns of the Great War.[2] On one dreadful night, 30 March 1944, 670 Bomber Command air crew died in seven hours during a raid on Nuremberg—more than all the RAF casualties in the Battle of Britain, when 544 British airmen were killed over nearly four months.[3] Yet it was the heroic fighter pilots of the Battle of Britain who captured the national imagination, while the men of Bomber Command were denied their share of recognition for more than half a century. After the war Bomber Command was largely forgotten, its memory tarnished, with notable exceptions, such as Paul Brickhill's successful film, *The Dam Busters*. On the fiftieth anniversary of VE Day Bomber Command received little acknowledgement of their contribution because they were still shadowed by the controversy over area bombing, highlighted by Dresden.

Richard Overy has presented both sides of the balance sheet in the heated controversy over area bombing, which is beyond the scope of this chapter. On the negative side, area bombing was condemned by many critics who saw it as a strategic blunder, or even a war crime, which did little to reduce German war production and did not help to decide the outcome of the war. Bomber Command was accused of killing somewhere between 180,000 and 250,000 German citizens and smashing the beautiful old city of Dresden because of a flawed strategy.[4] As Mark Connelly has demonstrated, the negative view of Bomber Command's air offensive over Germany prevailed for half a century after the war ended. In the 1950s the strategic air war was officially marginalized: the glorified 'myth' of the war centred on the Battle of Britain, the Blitz, and Dunkirk, when Britain fought bravely alone. People wanted to forget the huge death toll and the horrors of the war. The popular television series *The World at War* in the 1970s represented the strategic air offensive primarily as a costly failure which pointlessly killed German civilians.[5]

Bomber Command pilots who survived were bitter at their perceived vilification, as they looked back fifty or so years later. John Gee, a former pilot, wanted courageous air crew to be remembered for a major contribution to a tough war, not 'as a lot of murderers', as he saw them portrayed.[6] Jack Watson, a veteran of seventy-seven operations, had returned from the Nuremberg raid to discover that twenty-eight friends were dead: 'I feel bitter. It's sickening to think that all those men died to keep this country free and their memory is being tarnished. I am proud of what we did'.[7] Many former air crew were so distressed at the continued attacks on their reputation that they fell silent over the years and tried to forget. Reg Davey, a navigator who had lost many friends in the raids, saw them as brave patriots trying to stop the Germans taking over Europe: 'a lot of people who were in Bomber Command in the war don't talk about it. They have pushed it out of their minds'.[8] Crews dispersed and lost touch. They buried their past until, for some, squadron reunions drew them back together decades later, when they began to see their years of silence as a betrayal.

Only in the last fifteen years have historians such as Richard Overy and Mark Wells explored the positive side of the balance sheet. They argue that Bomber Command's significant contribution to the war effort went far beyond the area bombing of Germany, in supporting the advancing armies, assisting both the land campaign and the war at sea. Bomber Command provided a vital tactical and psychological weapon in the early years of the war, with significant impact on British, American, and world opinion. It also increased domestic morale in the early and desperate years of the war when Britain and the Dominions were fighting largely alone. It was the only way to take the war to the enemy and avoid a war of attrition on land while the army was not ready for an offensive. The air raids

played an important part in the defeat of German air power and the decline
of German domestic morale; they damaged the German economic war
effort and prepared the way for the invasion of Europe by smashing open
the invasion ports. There was also a widely held view at the time that
Britain was fighting a ruthless enemy and that in modern warfare civilians
would be killed; that it was vital to national survival to crush a brutal
enemy before it invaded Britain.[9] As Connelly noted, Bomber Command
air crew were condemned for doing what most of the nation wanted during
the war, but later preferred to forget. In 1943 six out of ten Londoners
approached by the Mass Observation social surveys approved the bombing
raids over Germany.[10]

The death toll in the strategic air war was appalling, as over one-third
of the air crew never returned home. As John Nichol and Tony Rennell
observe, 'They died for their country in terrible ways—shot, burned,
drowned, literally blown to pieces in the sky. It is hard to take in the
reality behind the numbers'.[11] The casualty rates were higher than any
other section of the British armed forces. If a bomber crashed, usually all
crew members were killed. By 1942 Bomber Command air crew on heavy
bombers had a 44 per cent survival rate on the first tour, but less than 20
per cent on the second.[12] Death was random, except for higher losses in a
crew's first few operations. Many losses occurred in non-operational accidents and many were due to aircraft or equipment malfunctions in combat,
as well as poor weather, or sheer bad luck.

Death and the fear of death were unavoidable realities. All crew recognized the odds against survival and were probably afraid much of the time,
acknowledging that the real test of courage was the capacity to repel fear.
Many crew probably feared cowardice as much as they feared death. They
rarely spoke about death or their chances of being killed, though the scale
of the casualties could not be concealed. Some responded to this knowledge with fatalism, and others did their best to avoid thinking about it by
keeping busy. But the stress was probably cumulative and men could reach
their breaking point. Seeing friends shot down repeatedly could cause
some to become resigned to their own inevitable death.[13]

The culture of Bomber Command obliged airmen to suppress their
feelings, influenced in part by its original upper middle-class composition
(though this was gradually changed to the necessary recruitment of all
classes). Pilot Officer M. A. Scott was killed on 24 May 1941 on his first
raid. He left two letters for his parents in the event of his death: 'As a

family we are terribly afraid of showing our feelings, but war has uncovered unsuspected layers of affection beneath the crust of gentle-manly reserve'. He was one of many affected by an English 'stiff upper lip culture'.[14] As Henry Medrington, another former public schoolboy, noted, 'I'm not usually one to unpack my heart'.[15] Bomber Command reinforced this English male reticence, with its potentially harsh treat-ment of emotional casualties. The tiny proportion of men who broke down under intolerable stress and fear could be treated as weak and cowardly, though the official charge of lack of moral fibre was rare. Their habitual stoicism did not denote lack of feelings, especially at the loss of comrades, though their emotions were less visible than those of their American counterparts.[16]

Bomber Command air crews feared death and saw far too many planes crash, killing friends and comrades in terrible ways. But they revealed little of this to their families, for obvious reasons, and seldom talked about it with other air crew. In 1995 Mark Wells explored some of the grim realities of death in the air. The fear of being horribly burned or maimed was the more vivid because air crew had seen it many times. Numerous aircraft were shot down in flames: 'some aircraft simply exploded instan-taneously in balls of fire when hit'. Even when crew had time to bail out, parachutes were not always worn in flight due to their bulk, and hatches could be too small:

Those who managed to survive the harrowing, and sometimes heroic, circum-stances of leaving a damaged aircraft frequently faced the rigours of high altitude bail-out, which included oxygen deprivation and frost-bite. Many had already been terribly wounded before coming out of their aircraft. Moreover, parachute landings—often in wooded or mountainous terrain—were extremely perilous. In many instances pure luck determined survival. Finally, those unfortunate enough to land among angry civilians were often killed despite negotiating all the earlier hazards.[17]

Ninety-five aircraft were lost at Nuremberg in March 1944, with an attri-tion rate of 12 per cent of the crew. Navigator Reg Davey wrote years later, 'Aeroplanes were exploding everywhere. They would catch fire then fly along for a few seconds and then explode. I think everybody prayed very hard'. Flight Sergeant R. Rhodes recalled 'the emotional shock and physical shock each time I saw another machine and seven men hit the ground or torn to pieces in the air. It felt as if I was sitting on a platform overlooking the end of the world'. But they just carried on doing their

jobs and never discussed these horrific memories. As Eric Banks later
noted, 'There could be no mourning and no pause for discussion or
inquest, whatever our private thoughts and regrets'. They could not stop
to count the cost.[18]

The recollections of Women's Auxiliary Air Force stenographer Olive
Noble illuminate the awful consequences of such crashes. She had
chosen the RAF because she was fascinated by flying: had she been a
man she would have trained as a pilot. Instead she had to settle for being
a stenographer—a mobile clerk to take on special duties as needed. One
of her most traumatic postings was the RAF burns unit at Rauceby
General Hospital, Lincolnshire, where she typed hundreds of medical
case sheets. The hospital cared for air crew who had been shot down,
dragged from burning planes, and rushed to hospital with terrible third-
degree burns. There they were sent to the Burns Unit to suffer often
excruciating pain in solitary confinement, deprived of family support
and entirely dependent on the nursing staff. Sometimes it took a year or
two before these 'sweet, brave young men' could be released.[19]

Olive Noble found her work in 1944, in P4 Casualty of the Air Ministry
in London in the 'Missing' and 'Death' sections, even more stressful than
the Burns Unit. In the 'Missing' section she had to type an ever-mounting
pile of files of evidence relating to airmen categorized as 'missing' and
'missing believed killed'. These files included vivid and explicit accounts
of all that was known of what happened to the crew and the aircraft. The
details were often horrific, with graphic accounts of trapped airmen struggling in burning aircraft, provided by air crew who escaped. The already
colossal workload for the few typists grew even heavier as the numbers of
bombing raids over Germany increased and with them the numbers of
aircraft shot down. Olive did not see herself as 'squeamish' but she was so
shaken by this work that she had awful nightmares. The endless official
letters to 'next-of-kin' were equally depressing work, though these brief
formulaic statements excluded the horrific details. While she was working,
Olive imagined the impact of these letters on relatives, and after her nightmares she often woke in a sweat with throbbing headaches. The strain was
augmented by the impact of the V2 rockets on London as these meant she
spent her sleeping hours in air-raid shelters. Olive began to black out
while typing as a result of stress and sleep deprivation. A transfer to the
'Death' section of P4 Casualty involved almost equally harrowing work,
compiling precis of reports on 'dead airmen', intended for the archives.[20]

# Relatives of Missing Air Crew Reveal Their Feelings to the Anglican Chaplain

Squadron Leader the Revd G. H. Martin was an Anglican chaplain with No. 7 Squadron, RAF Bomber Command in 1944, based at Oakington in Cambridgeshire. In the earlier years of the war he had been a conscientious senior chaplain in the Middle East Command. Martin's Oakington files on 'Missing Personnel' make depressing reading. Martin gave dates of birth, religion, and next of kin for each man missing, noting that he wrote to all the families promptly on the day the crews were posted missing or the day after. For example, the crew of a Lancaster bomber was reported missing on 12 October 1944: of the seven men initially posted missing, a later annotation stated that four became prisoners of war, the engineer and navigator were killed, and there was no information on the rear gunner. Few lists record any details of what happened, but the high fatalities are in no doubt.[21]

Martin's extensive files in the Imperial War Museum contain a wealth of correspondence from the relatives of airmen who were categorized as missing or missing believed killed in 1944–5. I have sampled over three hundred of the many hundreds of such letters, which offer an illuminating source for the responses of distressed families.[22] Martin's side of the correspondence has not survived, but the relatives' replies reveal that he offered compassionate advice that a husband, son, or brother was missing in action, or presumed dead, with as much information as possible about the circumstances. The responses from relatives make a powerful impact on the reader, even now, by their courage, anguish, and stoicism. Despite their distress, most families expressed gratitude to Martin for his practical sympathy and his considerable efforts on their behalf. They thanked him for 'words of comfort and cheer', and for offering some hope that their loved ones might yet be alive as prisoners of war. W. T. Hurst of Newbury wrote on 28 May 1944, 'We sympathise with you on what must be a heart-breaking job, that of writing to so many who have to face these things. God bless you in your labour of love'. Mrs Joan Taylor was grateful that Martin took the trouble to visit her in person with the news that her husband was missing: 'Yours is a difficult job'.[23]

In reading through hundreds of relatives' responses to Martin's letters, I was surprised that these families placed so little emphasis on their own grief and suffering. They repeatedly insisted that their beloved sons or husbands would have wished them to be strong and stoical, implying their understanding that expressive grief was self-indulgent and unhelpful to the war effort. Irene Wellington of Colchester sought consolation in her brother's courage: 'we owe so much to all the men like him, and it is our duty to be brave in gratitude to them'. Betty Caldwell of County Durham was 'trying to be the brave wife' that she knew her courageous missing husband Bob would wish her to be. Mrs J. Bulson of Glamorgan found the news that her pilot officer husband was missing on air operations 'such a great shock: but for his sake I am keeping my chin up'.[24] In many cases it was clear that their lost airmen had specifically asked them to 'keep a stiff upper lip' if they were missing or killed.

Those few relatives willing to confess to their grief and despair were all women, and their anguish was compounded in several cases by their fear they might lose their Christian faith. This is not to say that some men did not share these bleak sentiments, rather that they did not reveal them. Four women, in particular, expressed their despair in stark terms. Mrs B. Baldwin of Erith in Kent had received confirmation that her husband was killed, and she sought from Martin an explanation for his death, to enable her to carry on her life:

You know how absolutely heart broken I am, nothing seems worth living for. When my dearest went, everything seemed to go from my life. I had faith in God that he would bring him back safely to me each night, prayed every night and morning, but he never answered my prayers. I feel that I shall never pray again, do you think you can help in that respect?[25]

Irene Scotland's case was similar, and her faith was also challenged by the death of her husband: 'I don't feel that I shall be able to endure life without him'. She did not feel she would ever be able to pray again or teach her children, both aged under 2, to believe in a loving God. The baby's christening had to be postponed until she could participate with some sincerity. She would be grateful for Martin's advice in restoring her faith in God, to prove herself worthy of her husband's courage and love. Mrs K. Richardson of London SE3 had been married for seventeen years, with boys aged 15 and 8, when her husband was posted missing: 'really I am right down in the depths of despair', she wrote, for they were devoted to each other.

Margaret Burnside was a nurse at RAF Station Mildenhall in Suffolk: her husband went missing just two months after their wedding. She was returning home to her family for a while to cope with shock and despair as she waited for news: 'I feel I cannot go on. Hank was my whole life'.[26] The daunting prospect of life without him was too much for her.

In general, the women amongst Martin's correspondents seemed to be more comfortable in articulating their emotions than their menfolk, perhaps finding some comfort in sharing their grief. And yet the majority of the female correspondents made substantial efforts to emulate the masculine code of meeting likely death with stoicism and fortitude. They often repeated their mantra that they must try to be brave as their loved one would have wanted. Joan Watson from Surrey admitted that

Life is very hard sometimes. I have already had three great losses in the past twelve months and now that Harald has gone, after we had been married less than two months it seems unbearable. However, I keep reading your letter and trying to carry on, as my husband would have wished.[27]

To some extent, then, there was a gendered shift apparent in that many mourning women were trying hard to bring their more open and emotional female patterns of grieving into line with those of men—a process that was more marked than in the Great War.

Whether the chaplain's letter advised that an airman was missing or dead, the initial response was usually shock and disbelief. Some, like N. Whitehouse of Norwich, found it hard to accept that an airman son was missing after surviving so many RAF operations and seeming invincible. Joyce Knight of Oxford learned from Martin that her husband had been killed: 'I still cannot believe all this. I dare not think of the future at all and am very thankful my two small children keep me so very busy'. But the baby 'breaks my heart' when he tries to say 'Dad–dad'.[28]

Distress was exacerbated by lack of information, long delays in receiving news, and conflicting statements. A correspondent from Hertfordshire expressed utter frustration with the silences of the RAF and the Air Ministry concerning the fate of missing airmen. He/she was grateful for the chaplain's letter which 'provides the one human touch among all the grim formalities'. The response of many families to Martin's initial letter reporting their airman relative missing was to request further information from possible eyewitnesses in other aircraft. Kathleen Green of Earls Court wrote a letter which can stand for many others: 'Could you find out if any of the other planes that came back saw what happened to my dear boy? The suspense is so great I would far rather know the worst. I pray God to give me courage to carry on for my other children's sake'.[29]

Mrs R. Simmonds of Southend wrote to Martin on 14 December 1944 regarding her son Flight/Sergeant Simmonds, missing in action for two months. She had received quite different reports from the Red Cross and from the plane's engineer: the latter stated that all six bodies were found in the crashed plane, but the Red Cross report disagreed. Consequently, she wrote, 'I cannot believe now that my son has past on [sic]'. The stress and grief were so great that she had been forced to sell her business to move to Southend due to her husband's failing health: 'My husband opened that Telegram on that morning, he has never got over the shock he has developed TB in both lungs and lays in bed still waiting for my son to return'.[30]

The physical health of several relatives of the missing airmen was adversely affected by shock, anxiety, grief, or uncertainty—Mrs R. Simmonds's husband was not alone. J. W. Starmonby of Liverpool advised Revd Martin that the news that his son Joseph was missing was 'a very hard blow'. Joseph's mother had a bad heart attack caused by the shock and stress of Joseph's RAF operations, reinforced by the bombing of Liverpool. Consequently she had been an inmate in a mental hospital for two months and must not be told that Joseph was missing in action or it might kill her. The father was lost for words when his wife asked to see Joseph's letters home. They were both proud of their only child and would have liked 'to walk out with him' in his RAF uniform had he come home.[31]

More than half these letters convey a sense of a community of families in mourning, suffering a collective loss. There was widespread understanding that the death rate in Bomber Command was extremely high and that many families would suffer bereavement. The corollary was that individual grief must be borne silently with courage. Henry Devlin of Northumberland learned that his brother was missing in action: 'His absence is going to be a great strain on mother, but of course we realize that everyone else has to suffer grief and hardship in these times'. Mrs J. Hughes of Sudbury, Suffolk, echoed Churchill's words in responding to the news her son was missing: 'Now the burden so very many are carrying we must ourselves bear with courage and confidence'. Mrs Goulding of East Ham, London, took the news that her son was missing as 'a great blow', yet she also saw it as a community loss: 'I know I am sharing the

British troops killed in the push near Monchy le Preux being buried in a cemetery in the line. The burying party was being shelled the whole time, 29 August 1918.

Three army chaplains (Church of England, Roman Catholic, and Presbyterian) attend the reverent burial of four of the fallen heroes, n.d.

Lijssenthoek Cemetery, Poperinghe, Belgium, with its original wooden crosses, being tended by Imperial War Graves Commission gardeners.

Le Tréport Cemetery, as completed by the Imperial War Graves Commission.

The panorama of Ypres from the Cloth Hall, 1919. The Bickersteth family was grief-stricken in July 1919 by 'the dreadful and dreary desolation, the contrast between what is and what was too overpowering'.

Whit Monday mourners in Ypres, 1919.

Photo taken on the day of the Gresford colliery disaster on 22 September 1934. Hundreds of miners waited for those killed by the explosions. The pit was later sealed off and 260 miners were forever entombed.

Funeral of Edwin Orchard at Clapton Park in 1927, with horse-driven carriages.

A coster's funeral in Battersea, London, in 1949. The coffin rests in the parlour of the house where the dead man lived. His relatives have gathered to pay their last respects and wait for the coffin to be carried down to the hearse. Floral tributes from his family surround the coffin.

left; Portrait of Sir Sydney Cockerell, Director of the Fitzwilliam Museum, Cambridge, and promoter of the cause of cremation.
right; Golders Green Crematorium, London.

The smoking ruins of Coventry after a German air raid on 14 November 1940, with 554 dead.

Rescue workers, police, soldiers and civilians attempt to reach the buried children at Sandhurst Road School, Catford, SE London, 20 January 1943. Forty-four were killed.

The burial of thirty-eight London schoolchildren and six teachers placed beside a long trench grave, awaiting burial in January 1943. Sandhurst Road School, Catford, SE London, was bombed during school hours, 20 January 1943.

The mushroom cloud over Nagasaki after the explosion of the second atomic bomb in August 1945.

C.S. Lewis, by Arthur Strong, 1947.

Mourning for Princess Diana, 31 August 1997. Massed floral tributes outside Kensington Palace.

same anxiety of hundreds of other mothers and it needs great courage to bear this loss of one so loved by his family'.[32] It is worth noting that such sentiments about a community loss were common in condolence letters to families of all servicemen, not just airmen.

Most of these families, however, identified particularly closely with the RAF Bomber Command community, and more particularly with the families of their son's or husband's crew members. Of the correspondence sampled, well over half asked the Revd Martin for the addresses of the other crew members' families. Primarily they wanted to exchange information on the fate of relatives and loved ones with families who might have obtained news from other sources. They also sought to establish or extend vital emotional links with their beloved son's or husband's friends and their families, through sharing comfort and sympathy with them. This 'community of the bereaved' was akin to those described by Jay Winter, which had forged powerful emotional bonds in the Great War. It also has some affinity with the mutual support groups of widows and bereaved parents established in recent decades. Many said they wanted to offer whatever help they could to these other families in similar pain, because they understood their suffering in a way others might not. They wanted to draw strength from each other.

Mrs N. Downs of Camberley sent a poignant letter to Martin, alluding to the close bonds formed between members of Bomber Command crews, and the need for mutual consolation amongst the families of missing airmen. Her own brother was missing from a raid and his likely death was 'even more tragic' since he was soon to have been married. She wished to write to the relatives of the crew, 'a fine lot of lads', two married with young children. The stepson of Mrs Rose Glossop of Sheffield went missing in December 1943: 'it was a very big blow to us all and a source of great anxiety'. But she hoped to share any news with relatives of his crew, 'and in any other way to help them or they may help us. These are sad days for us all and a testing time for courage'. Mrs A. Wadham of Cowes wrote to Martin that she had entertained all her son's crew and knew they were very close. She wished to write to the parents of all the boys and had already invited Mrs Ellis of Tottenham, whose son was also missing, to spend a week with them.[33]

Many families mentioned to Chaplain Martin the two chief consolations which strengthened them in facing their ordeal. Most families expressed a deep pride in their brave lost airmen who did their duty nobly and were prepared to die for their country. Mrs J. Baker of Staffordshire found the news that her husband John was missing in action 'a terrible blow', yet her letter focused on her pride in her husband:

I have at least got that consolation if the worst has happened, it was the best he wanted to do to make this a free and happy country for all of us. Also as my little boy grows older I know he will feel proud that his Daddy had helped in this war.[34]

J. Spencer of Halifax honoured her son who 'laid down his life for the principles of good fellowship and freedom'. A number of grieving relatives wrote of their pride in the context of their missing airman's early passion for planes and the RAF. Mrs J. Watson of Dumfries paid a tribute to her son Jack: 'we who are at home owe them a great debt for their courage and sacrifice... We are very proud of him as he was of his uniform and his comrades and the Lancaster. As a little boy it was his delight to be playing at planes and I know that he was happy flying'.[35]

The second major source of comfort to about half of these families was the Christian religion, even if for some it may have been a diffuse, residual sort of faith, more akin to folk religion. Dorothy Masters from Hampshire learned from Martin that her husband had gone missing following a raid over Germany. Her long letter focused on religious faith as a means of consolation and support:

I have been praying for strength and courage, and I am sure that this, and other people's prayers for me, have helped me a great deal to feel brave about all this. I have a great faith though, that my husband and the rest of the crew will return some day... I felt terribly upset on the day that I received the dreadful news, naturally it shocked me, but prayer is very comforting.[36]

Mrs Beatrice Brandwood of Preston revealed a similar degree of faith in divine help in her husband's safe return. This was the second time her husband had been posted missing; 'The first time it was a miracle that he and his crew were found at all—and I believe in miracles and God'. Many next of kin mentioned Christian faith only briefly but clearly regarded it as important. About half wrote that they would pray for their loved one's safety, and many asked the chaplain to add his prayers. Violet Grant-Smart of Southend wrote that her dear missing husband was 'a fine and true Christian' and her constant prayers for him could not be in vain. Ruth Davis of Stroud had 'faith that God will return him to me'.[37]

By contrast, as we saw earlier, few admitted to the chaplain that the dreadful news had left them overwhelmed by such despair that they feared the loss of their faith.

## Tracing and Burying the Missing

Some saw the category 'missing in action' as positive because it still allowed them to hope. A number of stoical next of kin expressed a firm belief that their husband or son was alive and vowed never to give up hope. Such hope often led them to pursue enquiries with the Red Cross, contact families of other crew members, and seek further information from Revd Martin. Mrs Rose Glossop's stepson went missing in December 1943, and she wrote to Martin the following month, 'Until we get definite news that he has been killed we have a definite ground for hope'. Mrs C. Bolt of Chorley expressed pride in her husband, affirming that she would 'never give up hope' of seeing him again.[38]

For some the final formal announcement of presumed death came as a terrible shock which ended hope. The terse, formulaic official verdicts of 'missing in action' or 'presumed dead' seemed to many families worse than a definite announcement of death. Ethel N. Hosgood was distraught when her son was finally officially 'presumed' killed, since that decision was based entirely on the passage of time since his plane crashed, not on actual information received. In the intervening months nothing had been heard of the crew: none could be prisoners of war after such a long silence and the Red Cross could discover nothing. She still felt she must try to do something more to find out what happened: 'I feel heart-broken—to my mind this of all things is the most cruel...never to know the end of someone dearer than life itself'. Mr L. Nathanson of Tottenham had to suffer the terrible shock of the missing in action verdict twice, as one son had been reported missing from Bomber Command in March 1944 and the other just three months later.[39]

Others, like Mr and Mrs Maddocks of Orpington, responded more positively when the long uncertainty was ended and their son's fate finally confirmed: 'It was a crushing blow to us when we received the telegram. At the same time, it has eased our grief to learn that Jack has departed this world, leaving behind so good an impression. He has always been one of the best'. Mr Maddocks asked where Jack was buried, so they might visit in the future and Revd Martin responded with a plan of the cemetery and the grave number.[40]

Where death was confirmed and burial had been possible, bereaved relatives like the Maddocks were eager and grateful for details. Next of kin recognized they were privileged if burial took place, since plane crashes left few bodies which could be recovered, and so many remained 'missing presumed dead'. Only four families in my large sample were actually able to attend funerals, due to an accidental crash in England on 5 May 1944 which permitted air crews' bodies to be sent to family homes for burial. Stephen J. Knight of Welwyn Garden City thanked Revd Martin for conducting a beautiful service at his son's graveside in Cambridge, and for sending photographs of the funeral, which were a great comfort to the family. The funeral service and the photographs were treasured as a memorial all the more because 'We *are* proud of our boy—the last one of our four children left to us—and we loved him dearly'. We may suppose that one or more other children also died in the war.[41]

Following this accidental crash three other grateful families thanked the chaplain for helping to arrange for the bodies to be sent to family homes. J. Spencer of Halifax wrote on 13 May to advise that the body of his son Kenneth was buried at All Souls church, Halifax: 'we feel more content to know that we can visit his grave at any time we desire'. G. Matthews of Birmingham informed Martin that his son's funeral was now over: it was an 'exceedingly bright service...God provided the sunshine and we the flowers'. His son had been a choir boy and Sunday school teacher at the church where he was buried. The father found the service a 'great comfort' and was sure that 'God will give us the strength and fortitude to carry on in the future'. Gertrude Young of Southampton had been greatly shocked to lose her son in the same crash: 'I can hardly realize it yet. I shall miss him terribly'. Her son's coffin had been taken to the church in Southampton, where he had once been confirmed—but this time for his funeral service.[42]

These four bereaved families asked Martin to advise them of the findings of the Court of Inquiry into the accident. That inquiry might conceivably have offered less comfort to them than the funerals. In 2003 Reg Davey recalled a painful experience he had around Christmas 1944 when he was an experienced Bomber Command navigator and a veteran of the Nuremberg raid. When his tour finished he became an instructor at RAF Feltwell in Norfolk. Two Lancaster bombers with pupil crews on board collided while doing circuits at the airfield. Following the explosion little was left of the crews, but fourteen coffins were filled, mostly with sand to make up the weight. Davey had to represent the squadron at the funeral of one of the dead airmen in Birmingham—the first funeral he had ever attended. He found the ordeal traumatic, especially as he didn't know the dead airman:

It must have been shattering for them. How should I react? What excuses could I make to them? I had seen so much death, so many empty bed spaces, friends killed, but meeting the parents of someone who had got the chop affected me more than anything.

The situation deteriorated. The grieving parents had a candlelit vigil by the coffin on the night before the funeral and the mother wanted the lid removed to see her 21-year-old son. Davey was appalled and invented excuses which alerted a family member to the likely reality of a coffin filled mainly with sandbags. The mother's attention was fortunately diverted. It was a Christmas funeral in the snow and Davey was shocked to see the parents so utterly distressed. It made him consider how his own parents would cope with his own funeral: 'and the pain and anguish caused by the deaths of so many fine young lads'.[43]

For most bereaved families of Bomber Command crew there was no funeral, traumatic or otherwise. In the absence of a body to bury, and a funeral, the personal effects of the dead men assumed far greater significance. The few tangible reminders became precious relics, among which photographs of the dead men were especially prized. H. S. Clifford of Ilkeston asked the chaplain for a copy of the photo showing his son and gallant crew in front of their bomber, taken a few days before he went missing. Mrs B. Baldwin of Erith, Kent, thanked the chaplain for his letter with the last photograph of her husband: 'it is a letter and snap that I shall treasure for the rest of my life'.[44]

The Missing Research and Enquiry Service of the Air Ministry (MRES) had been set up in 1941 to find the remains of missing air crews in response to the questions posed by such grieving families. Many had refused to give up hope until they received definite official information that their airman had been killed. MRES was swamped with enquiries from 1944, when it had to rely on the International Red Cross or neutral sources for information, but from VE Day, fieldwork on the ground to track down crash sites at last became possible. In January 1946 Flight

Lieutenant C. Mitchell was one of many airmen transferred to MRES, in his case to Hamburg. Mitchell's short unpublished memoir explained that this was a tough assignment, since officers were required to identify bodies which had been badly burnt or fragmented, from personal effects. The scale of the task was as daunting as its nature, as Bomber Command lost over fifty thousand flying crew killed in action or missing believed dead. MRES officers had to be willing to endure long hours of mental and physical fatigue. Mitchell's commitment was in part inspired by his own misfortune in witnessing the deaths of many of his first crew at the start of his operational tour. His sense of moral responsibility and respect for the dead airmen was powerful and doubtless reinforced by seeing other crashes:

It was my belief then, as it is now, that we, both as a nation and an Armed Service, had a moral and ethical responsibility to trace all those who had been lost. Inevitably there would be some whose earth [sic] would never be known with any degree of certainty, but the erection of a monument containing 50,000 names would not, in itself, ease the grief and distress of the next of kin. It was equally unthinkable that so many of the bereaved should forever remain ignorant of how their loved ones died or where they were buried.[45]

The task was gruesome in the extreme but it was vital to soothe some of the continuing sorrow of the relatives of missing airmen who remained desperate for any information. Mitchell likened the task of gathering evidence to meticulous police detective work, corroborating and discounting accounts based on rumour, hearsay, or press reports. Investigators commenced with casualty reports from Air Ministry P4, typed by stenographers like Olive Noble. They then visited the local area of the crash to talk to the police and burgomaster and check the cemetery and crash scene. If the evidence warranted, they proceeded to exhumations to verify identification, but were hindered by massive inaccuracies in German records on Allied burials. Mitchell stated, 'I was not prepared to allow airmen to remain unburied without coffins in unconsecrated ground any longer than was absolutely necessary'. At least in some cases Mitchell was able to give these missing airmen a more dignified burial and offer their families long-awaited final information and comfort. The Air Ministry had decided that RAF airmen would be buried in a series of concentrated war cemeteries in Germany, where their graves would be cared for and shown the utmost respect.[46]

Mitchell's memoir underlines the overwhelming task facing the Air Ministry and MRES. Many missing airmen could not be traced because they had been lost at sea or in mid-air explosions, or collisions between planes. The only verifiable evidence usually came from eyewitness reports of comrades in the other planes on the same raid, where these existed. Throughout his memoir, Mitchell emphasized that he saw this difficult work as a 'privilege and an honour': he was content if his efforts brought 'a little comfort' to relatives. He kept in mind the feelings of the relatives of missing personnel at all stages of the investigation: 'any error could have far-reaching consequences—not least of which might cause avoidable grief and distress to the next of kin, quite apart from embarrassment to the Air Ministry'.[47]

The grief of next of kin of missing and dead airmen would no doubt continue after the war ended in 1945. Many of the missing remained so, including those who crashed at sea. Despite the valiant efforts of the MRES after the war, many remains could not be found or identified. And in some cases it was years before aircraft were discovered and remains given a decent burial. Many families of the missing airmen suffered for years. Some of them may have been trapped in a state of perpetual mourning, with no certainty of death and awful mental images of the fate of their loved ones. Numerous parents and wives continued to search for missing airmen, sometimes long after hope might have been expected to evaporate.

For all these grieving relatives, their pride in the courage and the heroic contribution of their beloved airman was a significant consolation and helped to make sense of their loss. It was vital to know that these fifty-five thousand deaths had not been in vain. Indeed the phrase 'his sacrifice was not in vain' was used repeatedly in these family letters to Chaplain Martin and in many condolence letters to relatives of men killed in the other armed services. It is almost impossible for us now to conceive the psychological and emotional impact on these long-suffering next of kin of the treatment of these airmen in the half-century that followed. The airmen were condemned for area bombing and their vital contribution to the war effort was marginalized. They were not recognized as heroes like the Battle of Britain pilots, but were instead accused of killing German civilians. John Nichol and Tony Rennell in *Tail-End Charlies* described the continuing hurt for the survivors of Bomber Command at the post-war damage to their reputation.[48] That hurt extended to the grieving relatives of the victims. However, at last in 2006 a fitting permanent memorial to over fifty-five thousand air crew of Bomber Command was unveiled at Lincoln Cathedral, which had once been welcomed by weary crews as a homecoming beacon. But it was half a century too late for many bereaved families. Perhaps the dead airmen were forgotten also because their high casualty rate was too powerful a reminder of death in a society that preferred to forget it.

# 8

# Experiences of Wartime Grief

One has no business to spread one's own sorrows, especially when tens of thousands of others are suffering in silence far worse pain than we are.

Geoffrey Bickersteth

Emotional restraint was part of the customary prescription for the bereaved during and after the Second World War. This new model of suppressed, privatized grieving had long constrained upper-middle-class men; in the two decades after 1945 it had a broader influence. Open and expressive individual sorrow was culturally discouraged, as mass bereavement overshadowed the individual heartache of ordinary civilians. It was considered selfish to 'spread one's own sorrows', when thousands of others were 'suffering in silence'. These cultural norms were very powerful, especially when they were represented as vital to the war effort, and they probably had a deeper coercive effect on women. It was unacceptable for women to dwell on feelings of sorrow, which should be concealed beneath a smiling face.

This restraint was exemplified by a working-class widow of a Royal Artillery gunner, Trevor Pale, who died in 1943 as a prisoner of war in the Far East. When the news came two years later it was a terrible shock to Nancy Pale, especially as her family had already lost all their possessions during the air raids and Trevor's mother had just died of cancer. Yet Nancy tried hard to be positive and 'look on the bright side' in a letter of October 1945:

I shall just have to face up to things and make the best of life, fortunately I have a good many very good friends so cannot be lonely. Some days I feel very depressed, others I don't feel so bad, don't think I go about with a mournful face, I can smile and laugh with anyone, I don't wear my heart on my sleeve, for it doesn't do.

Trevor's sister-in-law, Muriel Pale, noted approvingly that Nancy 'had behaved so splendidly', responding just as her husband would wish.[1]

There was a veil of silence over the suffering of the English bereaved in the Second World War: they were meant to bear sorrow internally, with fortitude, as their dead sons and husbands would have wished. The dearth of archival evidence suggests that many lived up to this tough assignment. However, I draw chiefly on two remarkably detailed and reflective records of grief and loss during the war. They are, of course, not necessarily representative of the broader population of the bereaved, since grief is such an individual matter and no one experience is likely to be quite the same as another. But both writers were obedient to the cultural prescription of the 1940s that they grieve quietly in private. One concealed her sorrow inside the covers of a very private diary, published by her daughter thirty-five years later. The other kept his anguish from his wife and children, but wrote about it at length and in private to his aged mother and to his brother.

These two accounts of wartime grief tell us much about the ways in which two sensitive and intelligent people mentally and emotionally traversed a terrible loss. Peggy Ryle was responding to an initial 'missing' report on her pilot husband, which was later amended to 'killed in action'; Geoffrey Bickersteth was dealing with wartime death by accident. Geoffrey was an upper-middle-class male who lost a son, while Peggy was a middle-class woman who lost a husband. He was a devout Christian intellectual whose crisis of faith was central to his response; she was a regular church-goer, whose faith had less impact on her grief. Their two diverse experiences of wartime death include elements of the ordeals of many others.

Evidence in earlier chapters has suggested a general tendency for women and men to grieve in different ways: men were more inclined to contain their feelings, and women to express them. These gendered differences may go beyond cultural conditioning, and were even more pronounced in the nineteenth century. The cumulative impact of the two world wars in England was to discourage open and public expression of grief: but given female expressiveness, this convention had a greater coercive impact on women. There are clear signs of these differences at work in the narratives of Peggy Ryle and Geoffrey Bickersteth. Both suffered profoundly on the loss of a loved one during the Second World War: it would be impossible to claim that one was hurt more than the other. Yet their expressions of their pain were quite different. Peggy Ryle bared her heart in an outpouring of emotion in a private diary while speaking to no one about her intense suffering.

In contrast, Geoffrey Bickersteth was more cerebral in his analysis of his own feelings, which undoubtedly caused him acute pain, and he shared them with his aged mother and his brother in a series of intimate letters. He acknowledged that women and men reacted to life and death very differently: that his wife, Jean, was behaving with great self-restraint and courage, whereas he felt the 'want of a man to talk to'. He believed in this case that, as the father, he experienced the loss more intensely than the mother, 'whose *heart* rather than whose *mind* is broken by his premature death'.[2] Geoffrey Bickersteth was correct in his belief that gendered differences existed, but he seems to have misread their nature and practical implications. His wife almost certainly needed to share her suffering with someone sympathetic, preferably her husband, even more than Geoffrey did. She must have had a hard time in her grief and it was sad for both of them that they could not talk to each other about their shared loss. But the wartime emotional constraints generally imposed a heavier burden on the women, who had learned their lessons too well to be easily able to reverse the conventions of grieving in the years which followed.

We need to bear in mind that individual bereaved people had no guidelines during the Second World War to help them understand their grief or cope with it, except the wartime prescriptions which aimed to deal with public morale rather than personal sorrow. They faced their loss before psychiatrists had constructed theories of grief which impacted on the broader culture. And whereas today, bereavement counsellors encourage the bereaved to talk through their sorrow, in the 1940s the bereaved were expected to grieve largely alone and in silence. This cultural prescription applied even more powerfully to servicemen grieving for their dead comrades, though it was arguably less difficult for men than women.

## Peggy Ryle's Ordeal: The Diary of a Missing Airman's Wife

The extensive correspondence between Chaplain Martin and the next of kin of the missing and dead from Bomber Command is harrowing but illuminating, as we saw in the previous chapter. It is also tantalizing because it contains so few letters from each family. There is limited information about their subsequent experience of bereavement to tell us how they coped with their loss, grief, and anxiety; and for many the material is further restricted by their determined effort to be stoical and courageous.

But the extraordinary story of just one of Martin's correspondents—Peggy Ryle—illuminates the personal experience of loss in a remarkable way.

Peggy M. Ryle of Surbiton in Surrey, aged 38, wrote just one short letter to Chaplain Martin on 6 May 1944, thanking him for the 'lovely letter' of sympathy when her husband, Squadron Leader George Ryle, went missing over Friedrichshaven. She observed that 'life is pretty terrible at the moment'.³ The other letter in Chaplain Martin's correspondence which relates to Peggy Ryle's ordeal was from Judy Lockhart of Colchester, whose husband Wing Commander Guy Lockhart was pilot of the same missing plane. Judy Lockhart's letter revealed exceptional stoicism in the face of an unusually tough ordeal:

I am trying awfully hard to take this—as I know Guy would expect me to. But, this—his third time missing—I am hardly able to cope with. I am not trying to appear martyred—but having lost my small son a year ago—I feel God has been rather brutal and it is like a cat playing with a mouse—if its time Guy left this earth, why didn't God take him the first time? It's almost more than the human frame can stand.⁴

Judy still had her little daughter who loved her father 'more than anything in this world—and I am feeling very bitter and not at all brave. I am almost afraid to hope again'.

In most cases Chaplain Martin's correspondence ceased after a few letters, so we learn no more of the outcome. But in this instance Peggy Ryle kept an unusual diary, addressed to her husband, 'telling you all I have done since that ghastly morning, Friday 28th April'. This extraordinary diary of 166 pages has been preserved in the Imperial War Museum under the title 'Missing in Action, May–Sept 1944' and was only published by Peggy's daughter thirty-five years later, when Peggy would have been 73.⁵ It illustrates the ordeal many women suffered in the months following the 'missing in action' notification: the shifts between hope and despair and the huge effort to remain courageous while continuing silence from the authorities signalled diminishing room for hope. George Ryle was Peggy's second husband: she had two daughters by her first marriage which had broken up when she fell deeply in love with Ryle, also divorced, and they married in 1942.

George Ryle's final flight took place on the night of 28 April 1944, ten days before Peggy Ryle began her diary on her husband's birthday: 'your birthday, darling, and I don't know where you are or even if you are alive'.

On that 'ghastly morning' she waited a long time: when she heard his plane had failed to return, she told her younger daughter Sally, and went down on her knees in prayer. That morning she made a resolution to drink no more alcohol until George returned; sobriety was necessary to conceal her heartache and maintain strict control. Group Captain Combes came from the base at Oakington to see her later that morning 'and was very shy and awkward', finding appropriate words difficult to articulate— doubtless suffering from the effects of the British 'stiff upper lip'. She phoned her father, asking him to spend the night with her, to talk the situation over to help her 'sort myself out'. On Peggy's first Saturday evening alone, Group Captain Combes and two other RAF colleagues of her husband came to see her, bringing chocolates:

[They] did all they could to show their appreciation of the way I was keeping my chin up. I didn't let you down, Georgie. I think you would have been proud of me. The Group Captain told Judy Lockhart I was taking it very well. But none of them can possibly know what an awful agony it is. I have heard people talk of heart-ache and never known what it meant or thought anything about it. But I have a pain round my heart night and day and I feel raw inside. I have lost a stone and a half in ten days.

During that first awful week Peggy left her accommodation near the airbase to move to Surbiton, to stay with her father and his third wife Jean. At the end of the first week Judy Lockhart phoned to say that George Ryle's plane was not amongst those that had landed safely in Switzerland. From this point, Peggy had to fight continually against her knowledge of the impact of air crashes on the crew: 'I try to keep my mind off all the awful things that may have happened to you, because if I think too much, I shall go off my head'. She slept very little, despite the prescribed sleeping pills: 'I never lose the pain or worry, waking or sleeping'.[6]

Peggy knew she must keep busy and be distracted by other people to enable her to continue to 'take it well' and 'keep my chin up'. Some time was consumed by the considerable paperwork required to deal with her husband's pay and the alterations to her own allowances now he was officially missing. But that was not enough for her. She bravely went to the firm where her husband had worked in peacetime, asking to take over her husband's job as 'I must have work to ease my mind'. Three days later her husband's firm advertised his former position. She was reduced to playing bridge, reading, or going to the cinema alone, in addition to social activities—which helped her 'not to think so much'.[7] She was forbidden from taking a man's job to distract herself but still expected to take her grief like a man.

After the first week she could not avoid wondering if her husband was alive or dead: 'Darling, if you have been killed, I don't want to go on living, but I don't believe you have been or I should feel you nearer me, I'm sure'. She was writing this diary because she hoped he would return: 'I have been praying so hard, my beloved, that this confidence in your being alive may not be false'. When he had been gone for two weeks, it felt to her like two years: 'I think I shall try and die if you are not coming back to me, beloved'.[8]

Peggy found a little comfort in material mementoes of her husband as tangible reminders of the physical presence she missed so much. She had an enlargement made of a photo of her husband and his closest friend, Ray Ridley, who was also missing: and later took a copy of this photo to Ray's wife, to bring her consolation. The photo often cheered her, as if he were saying, 'Chin up, Pippy darling, of course I'm coming back to you!' She had a new strap put on his watch, which she wore all the time. She also continually wore the little brooch he had given her, to bring him luck. Peggy even reclaimed George's tunic from storage 'so that I can smell you. The smell upset me terribly when I was packing [his clothes], but now I just long for it and don't care how sad it makes me. It's *you, you, you* I want'. Her head was splitting and her eyes swollen with crying, so she needed to stop writing her diary in order to compose herself.[9]

In the third week of her husband's absence, from 14 to 20 May 1944, as the initial shock wore off, she became more deeply depressed and far more anxious about her husband's possible suffering. A phone call from Judy Lockhart provided the trigger, 'and depressed me beyond words'. Judy passed on information from an Australian pilot who had seen nine Pathfinder planes in trouble over Strasbourg the night George went missing—two had blown up and seven were in flames. 'Oh dearest, I pray you are not badly burnt and suffering agonies'. From this point Peggy could not push these awful possibilities out of her mind. A constant refrain in the diary in the weeks that followed was, 'O, Georgie darling, I hope and pray you are not burnt and in pain. You can't think how awful this not knowing anything is'. She could no longer wish him alive without acknowledging the likelihood of intolerable pain and disfigurement.[10]

Another turning point came on 20 May when Peggy's stepmother, Jean, moved her over to a single bed—one step on the road to potential widowhood. Some days the awful suspense was intolerable, and she agonized over George's likely wounds that needed care: 'No one can guess quite what this hell I am in is like. Knowing nothing, perfectly helpless and trying, trying, trying not to let my imagination run away with me'. She was no longer able to conceal the strain and anxiety from her family and friends, despite her great efforts at control. 'Everyone seems to be treating me as if I have taken leave of my senses', she wrote, because they knew how much she loved George and that 'the pain in my heart is agony', despite her usual outward composure. She knew she was 'terribly strung up' but was trying very hard to conceal it. Women tended to be described as 'strung up' in the 1940s and 1950s when stern self-control escaped them. Peggy cried herself to sleep on many nights: 'it is the only time I get to myself and I cry for you and pray for you every night, my beloved'.[11]

Six weeks of separation marked an important step towards accepting that George might be dead. On 4 June 1944 Peggy noted in her diary, 'Very sad tonight, darling, just can't help missing you so desperately and keep thinking I may never see you again on earth, it's ghastly...I can't go on without you'. Next day she ordered a black dress to be made for everyday wear, signifying that she was in mourning: 'You know darling, I think I was numbed at first by shock, because now the pain gets worse and worse every day'. But it was not just numbness that was wearing off, it was hope as well. She occasionally feared that this torment was retribution 'for taking you from your first wife'. She began to wish that she might die, but then had to remind herself that George might still be alive somewhere. She had also started bargaining with God in her prayers at night, promising to be a better person if George returned safely.[12]

By Derby Day on 17 June Peggy wondered if they would be together on the next Derby Day, 'or if I am going to be on my own all my life'. Her fragile hopes that George might still be alive veered up and down from day to day. She felt desperately sad without him. She had only dreamed about him three times: it was 'heaven' to be with him, even in a dream. On 1 July she hoped the church service would comfort her, but was rather 'shattered' by the hymns 'which were all about our valiant dead'. They led her mind back to awful thoughts of the effects of a crash on her husband's body: yet, 'blind, no arms, no legs, anyhow, I want you for ever and ever and will love and look after you all my life'.[13]

At the ten-week mark despair began to conquer hope. On 7 July she wrote: 'I am losing hope, George—what shall I do?' She felt so terribly lonely and unhappy, and had ruined another page of the precious diary by crying all over it. She could not relate to ordinary life and people: 'I can't be civil to anyone because I begrudge them being here when you are not'. She felt miserable seeing happy couples together. Even major disruptions to daily life seemed scarcely to impact on her, merely to provide distractions, as when their London flat at Great Portland Street was bombed and several days were needed to sort out the mess. Peggy dreaded lunches with Judy Lockhart, who had become so pessimistic and talked so much of the fearful possibilities.[14]

By July Peggy was reduced to prayers for miracles. Yet she tried to keep faith with George's request that she allow him a full year in the 'missing' category before abandoning hope. In late July Group Captain Combes wrote that he was not hopeful after three months. She felt overwhelmed by misfortune:

If I was sure you were dead I would try and come to you...I lie in bed and try and will your spirit to come to me; sometimes I think I can feel you near, then I think it is only because my thoughts are so concentrated on you all the time. I have your picture always by my bed and it makes me cry every time I look at it.[15]

By 4 August, she began to be resigned to the prospect that he would never return, and 'made a fool of myself' by crying in front of her two daughters for the first time. On her wedding anniversary she at last admitted that 'if you were alive you would have somehow or other got in touch with me by now'. She began to focus instead on happy memories of George with her family in the past. As various capitals of Europe were being liberated in August, she knew it was too late for any good news of her beloved husband. Victory meant little to her without George: 'Nothing means anything in life any longer, my beloved, without you. I can't think that I can continue my life without you. I might have to live another forty years. It could be such heaven together'.[16]

September 1945 marked the fifth anniversary of the war and increasing acceptance of George's death. On 3 September Peggy went to church and was relieved not to break down in tears. But afterwards she met an airman who asked after George, and it 'upset me terribly' to tell him:

Have felt bloody miserable all day...I am so desperately lonely and miserable without you...I don't want to go on living...I do hope you are not hungry, and

now the weather is breaking, cold. Oh god I must not let my thoughts run on.
I imagine you ill and dying without me and it nearly kills me.

This diary entry reflected the depths of her despair. On 7 September 1945
a letter from the Air Ministry stated that there was little hope that her
husband was alive, confirming her fears of the last month: 'it seems so
much more definite written down'.[17]

While the Air Ministry's statement deeply distressed Peggy, it also
reduced the terrible uncertainty which had paralysed her. She now knew
that she had to face George's death directly. She marked this significant
transition by ending her self-imposed months of temperance. On the day
she received the Air Ministry's letter she had her first alcoholic drinks at
the local Duck pub where she used to drink with George. She had about
five whiskies alone at the Duck, and later wrote, 'I felt so desperate'. Soon
afterwards Kate, George's mother, wrote to say she wished to announce
in the Manchester press that her son was missing, but Peggy asked her to
wait another month. It took Peggy only another week to come closer to
practical acceptance of George's likely death. By 15 September she was
reluctantly considering starting a business on her own: 'I want a big
worry other than *you*, it may help to take my mind off things for a bit.
You can't be a prisoner now darling, you must either have been killed or
be in hiding'. Yet she knew the latter was too much to hope for. Peggy
wondered what she would do at Christmas and New Year and all the
other nights without him. On 25 September she reached the end of her
special diary at page 166. Two days later she heard that Guy Lockhart's
body had been found: 'there were five unidentifiable bodies there which
means you my darling. God help me'.[18] There her diary ended. Her
beloved husband was awarded the Distinguished Flying Cross for his
bravery in action. The definite knowledge that he was no longer missing
was perhaps some compensation for the terrible information that his
remains were unidentifiable.

This remarkable diary illustrates the trauma of many of the next of kin
of the missing who corresponded with Chaplain Martin. Peggy Ryle had
given no hint of her own intense torment in her letter to Martin. She
wrote and spoke of her grief and despair to no one—not to her parents,
her daughters or her friends. Least of all did she 'break down' with her
husband's comrades, respecting the conventional military code of silence
and courage in the face of pain. Only in her private diary addressed to her

lost husband did she reveal her intense emotions—her private 'hell'. Peggy Ryle was unusual as an Englishwoman in the 1940s in contemplating starting her own business, having inherited 'a little money' from an uncle, and having been divorced. She felt she was capable of starting life again independently if she had to, though she dreaded the prospect. She had touched the depths of despair in those five months of diary keeping and would undoubtedly have many difficult months and years to follow. Other wives of air crew with fewer material means and inner resources would face an even more challenging situation when their husbands went missing—especially as they were permitted no outlet for their grief. The effort to keep a 'stiff upper lip' could be overpowering and counterproductive, but the loss of stern self-control led to the charge of being emotionally 'strung up', perhaps the female equivalent of lack of moral fibre.

## Geoffrey Bickersteth: Meditation on Grief, Faith, and War

During the Second World War Geoffrey Bickersteth lost his son Julian, killed in Greece in 1945. This inevitably revived memories of the death of his brother Morris at the Somme in 1916, commemorated by his family's interwar pilgrimages to the battlefields. Geoffrey had been in War Office Intelligence during the Great War while four of his five brothers served on the Western Front. Aged 60 in 1945, Geoffrey was a professor of English literature at Aberdeen University, where (as he said himself) he had spent his life in the study of literature, theology, and philosophy.[19] He had two daughters and three sons: he lost Julian in January 1945, killed by a shell on the final day of the fighting of the Greek civil war. The chance nature of Julian's death compounded the emotional devastation for his father on the loss of a son 'of superb physical beauty and a brilliant intellectual'. The wound was reopened on the death of his eldest son, Tony, during a walking holiday in Italy in 1948, when he was struck by lightning. Geoffrey's Christian faith was severely tested by the 'utter purposelessness' of both his sons' deaths. The course of Geoffrey's grief was movingly recorded in a series of intense letters to his blind aged mother, Ella, whom we met earlier on the interwar pilgrimages to Morris's grave. Ella was a continuing inspiration and support to her afflicted son: she compensated for advanced age and blindness by serenity of spirit and a host of friends.

Geoffrey Bickersteth largely internalized his terrible grief on Julian's death, discussing it little even with his wife Jean and his three children still at home. As he explained in letters to his mother:

We [the family] are struggling—like how many more—to meet this terrible bereavement bravely, as Julian himself would have wished... One has no business to spread one's own sorrows, especially when (as I am fully conscious) tens of thousands of others are suffering in silence far worse pain than we are. But I have in fact done so to no-one except to you and Julian [his brother in Canada], and for the sake of my own relief—just to get it off my chest, as I must not because I ought not to do it in my own family here.[20]

In Geoffrey's case this vow of silence was mitigated by his ability to dissect his thoughts and feelings in lengthy letters to his mother and his academic brother Julian in Canada. He did not mean to be selfish or treat his wife harshly: he was influenced by the wartime constraints as much as Jean, but they affected him in different ways.

Geoffrey's silence was probably difficult for his wife Jean and his elder daughter Elfride, who were both 'wonderful...unselfishness and efficiency incarnate', the greatest help and comfort to him, despite their periods of 'deep, black gloom'. The shock to the whole family was 'shattering'. Elsewhere in his letters he noted his assumption that grieving was easier for his two daughters because they were young and had not lost a son. He assumed significant gender differences in bereavement (which probably reflected the views of many men of his class). Where he needed to know every last detail of his son's death, he thought Jean would prefer not to know: 'She is his mother, and women are made like that'. Geoffrey believed that the father of a gifted son felt his loss more than the mother, 'whose *heart* rather than whose *mind* is broken by his premature death'. He did not really know how women survived bereavement, since he believed they reacted to life and death in a very different way from men.[21] Jean is a shadowy figure in these letters, generously fulfilling the cultural prescription of a brave grieving mother, suppressing her emotions as far as possible, even in private. Geoffrey told his brother Monier on 1 March that Jean was behaving with great self-restraint and courage but he felt the 'want of a man to talk to'.[22]

Geoffrey Bickersteth had formed a bleak view of the impact of the two world wars on his own generation. Late in 1944 he told his mother Ella

that the trials of people living in the first half of the twentieth century
were much more challenging than those which had faced their Victorian
ancestors. His generation, he thought, faced a more severe test of character
because they had been exposed to sudden death on the battlefields of two
terrible wars:

I sometimes think that on the Day of Judgement, we of the period 1914 to 1944
will have a right to say to the Creator, 'You can't judge us as you judge others . . . we
are almost a special race, submitted by you to great trials . . . We deserve Heaven
merely because we lived in such a hell'.[23]

Geoffrey's own supreme test came soon afterwards, when he learned the
bare minimum of facts about Julian's death in Greece on 4 January 1945.
A week later he had received only a terse confirmation of his son's death,
with not even a date provided. And he received Julian's poignant last
letter. It took weeks for the family to learn more—a delay which caused
Geoffrey intense anger and distress. As it later emerged, Julian was not
actually killed in action, but accidentally hit by an 'unlucky mortar',
lobbed into Athens by ELAS, the Greek communist guerrillas, while
Julian was technically off duty. As the Germans left Greece late in 1944,
civil war had broken out between ELAS and the Greek government in
exile in Cairo, and was quelled at immense cost in British lives. Julian
was unlucky enough to be blown to pieces on the last day of this phase of
the war.[24]

Geoffrey's first two long letters of grief to his mother were written in
January 1945 before he knew any of these details and assumed only that his
son was killed in combat. On 10 January he wrote that Ella's letter was
especially comforting from one who has 'passed through the same terrible
testing experience and whose faith has survived the test'. But he was
already aware that this great loss would challenge his own faith, and he
could even now define the terms of this test. On the one hand he knew
he should be unselfish enough not to resent his son's removal to a heavenly
existence characterized by vitality, life, and joy. It was a consolation to
think of his son now in the company of so many who loved him, including
his Uncle Morris, killed on the Somme in 1916. And yet selfishly he
resented God for blighting his own future. Like most bereaved parents,
Geoffrey also begrudged the bleak fact that it was all 'the wrong way
round', as the father should die before the son: 'would God I had died, for
him, my son, my son, instead of him'.[25]

In these early outpourings of grief, Geoffrey was suffering from shock and disbelief—especially as he had just received Julian's last letter. He told Ella, 'I still cannot really believe that I shall never have another letter from him, never see the writer himself or hear his voice again'. Geoffrey's anger and resentment against God were predictable: anger is a common component of grief and for a deeply religious man God was a natural target. It made Geoffrey shudder to think that God might also take Tony, who was facing the 'unspeakable *horrors*' of war in the Burmese jungle at the young age of 23. This justifiable fear of losing Tony as well as Julian haunted him throughout his bereavement. Condolence letters to his family constantly reminded him of the immensity of his loss and would 'tear open the wound again'.[26] They were no more help to Geoffrey than they had been to William Cecil in the Great War.

Geoffrey Bickersteth's letters to Ella in his second month of bereavement were different in tone and content. The note of self-pity was replaced by a more powerful anger and bitterness, which were now directed not so much at God as at the army and its officers:

The suffering continues worse than ever, and is made so much harder by all this waiting, which I am thankful you (we all) were spared in the case of Morris. It prevents me getting the *material* aspect of Julian's death over and done with. I cannot, till I know how he died and much more too.

During the first four weeks Geoffrey had heard nothing from his son's regiment about the details of his son's death. A letter of condolence at last came from Julian's commanding officer on 7 February 1945, informing him of Julian's accidental death by mortar bombs. But Geoffrey in his grief and anger was not to be appeased: the letter 'served to keep the wound open and greatly intensify the pain', as he contemplated the full extent of his loss in the future and 'the outrage that death is to youth'. The most hurtful news was that Julian was not killed in action but due to the sheer bad luck that another soldier had wanted a cup of tea in the officers' mess just as the bombs fell. The circumstances left him feeling 'a little bitter and rebellious': 'The War Office cares nothing for the feelings of the bereaved and never has. It is perfectly soul-less and perfectly heartless, and inefficient to boot'.[27] It was also the inevitable scapegoat of many other angry bereaved parents.

Memory did not help Geoffrey in the least in the first two months of grief. Quite the contrary:

Memories beset me: the beautiful face of the boy, shattered by that horrible missile of death, yet looking out beseechingly to one from his picture. I miss his letters: the silence, unbroken and never again to be broken, is more than I can sometimes bear. My very consolations convert themselves into instruments of torture.

There were constant reminders all around. Occasionally when he mistakenly imagined the anguish was reduced, another memory revived it more poignantly than ever. The only effective remedy would be to banish Julian entirely from his mind and forget the memories, but that was impossible when every detail of family life vividly recalled them.[28]

The celebration of Easter Day 1945, in the fourth month of his bereavement, forced Geoffrey at last to confront the major challenge to his faith. Geoffrey, Jean, and the children attended a three-hour Easter service at Aberdeen Cathedral, hoping for some message of comfort. Instead it was 'a complete wash-out...silly to expect any comfort...comfort comes in the next world not this'. Geoffrey protested angrily in his letters to his mother that Christ's passion lasted only a few hours, whereas his own seemed likely to last until he died, far in the future. The expectation of reunion with Julian 'in the life beyond the grave' was supposed to ease his sorrow, but it did little to compensate for the loss of the real Julian in the flesh: 'Julian in paradise might just as well be non-existent'. His suffering was intensified by the return of the case containing Julian's clothes: 'we packed it together. I unpacked it alone. For where was he? It's exhausting, is grief. Really tiring'.[29]

VE Day on 13 May 1945 was not a celebration of victory for Geoffrey and his family, with Julian dead and Tony still fighting in Burma. But Geoffrey was at last able to reflect more positively that his faith had somehow survived the awful challenge. His faith had never been extinguished, even when he felt 'most desperately sad and depressed', and it would ultimately reconcile him to his son's death. He would continue to love and miss his son and long to see him again. He still had the sensation of living in a dream—'the reality is where he is'. There was a huge gulf now for Geoffrey between his life before and after the war. At the age of 60 his more limited resilience could not cope with the combined strains of bereavement and a world war: 'one carries on...but the thrill has gone, gone irrevocably'.[30]

At least Geoffrey's elder soldier son, Tony, survived the tough war in Burma, where he was fighting with the Fourteenth Army under General

Sir William Slim. The family felt very anxious for Tony on his brother's death: that he was grieving alone, so far away in Burma, more homesick than ever.[31] In August 1945 Tony was injured by a jeep, which expedited his return home by late December 1945, in time for the anniversary of his dead brother's birthday. Geoffrey noted: 'how acutely and incessantly [Tony] misses Julian is clear enough, tho' like all of us, he says little about it'. This comment reinforces the point about the suppression of their sorrow as a family. Geoffrey's grief intensified over Christmas and New Year, as the anniversary of Julian's death approached. The loss of a son in 'the flower of his youth and promise' was terrible. Still, he must try to concentrate on his four living children and the recent gift of Tony's presence.[32]

On Julian's death, Burgon Bickersteth in Canada had told Geoffrey he considered him 'well equipped by the great comforts of Christianity, philosophy, and literature to meet such an overwhelming blow'.[33] But the first bereavement was more dreadful for Geoffrey than his brother anticipated, and the cumulative blow of a second loss, nearly four years later, probably even worse.[34] On a walking holiday in Savoy with his sisters in 1948 Tony was struck by lightning which hurled all three to the ground but killed only Tony. It was a terrible ordeal for his sisters who were remarkably uninjured. The grieving father found his son's death inexplicable as Tony was doing nothing risky and the accident seemed to serve no purpose. It was a sore trial of the family's faith—indeed a second such trial. It was hard to reconcile the manner of Tony's death with a loving God: 'Though we are doing our best, my wife and myself, to bear our sorrow as both our boys, now gone from us, would have wished, we are finding it, and shall increasingly find it, unspeakably hard to face life without them'.[35] Again we see the repetition of the familiar Second World War mantra—bearing grief with silent courage as the dead sons would have wanted.

## Soldiers' Grief for Their Comrades

Countless returned servicemen would continue to grieve for their dead comrades largely in silence for the rest of their lives. Soldiers were often closer to each other in wartime than to their families, yet their suffering is sometimes neglected when we consider wartime grief. Their military code of behaviour prohibited shows of emotion which undermined service morale and could be misinterpreted as weakness. Therefore few accounts of their feelings for dead comrades survive. After the war, such sorrow might be permitted expression only at annual service reunions as they grew older, especially from the 1970s when cultural change encouraged more open expression of emotion.

Gary Sheffield, a military historian, argued in 2001 that the methods of fighting battles in the Second World War built on the prototypes of the First: the chief weapons were more powerful and reliable, but essentially similar. The battles of the Second World War were more mobile but no less attritional, with much static fighting, as in Normandy and at Stalingrad, and with artillery a dominant weapon in most theatres of the land war. Sheffield noted that 'All this resulted in "butcher's bills" that exceeded those of the earlier war'. Britain's lower mortality rate for the Second World War partly reflected its reluctance to commit to a large-scale ground campaign in Europe until 1943. Yet 'casualties in individual units and campaigns exceeded those of the Great War...In 1945, as in 1918, high intensity warfare took a fearful toll of soldiers' lives'.[36]

Soldiers' experiences in the exceptionally arduous campaigns in Italy and Burma show how the nature of front-line combat impacted on soldiers' attitudes and ways of coping with death and loss. As John Ellis noted, the shell shock once deemed a unique feature of the Great War was actually 'an ineluctable consequence of all modern combat'.[37] J. S. Lucas enlisted as a private in 1942 at the age of 19, serving first in North Africa, where he was captured and later liberated. In September 1943 he was transferred to the Queens Royal Regiment for service in the grim attritional fighting of the gruelling Italian campaign. The Allies reached the German fortified positions in northern Italy, the 'Gothic' Line, in late August 1944. By the time Lucas reached Faenza in December 1944, after his regiment suffered thousands of casualties, he was at the end of his tether. Earlier in the year he had already been declared 'bomb happy', but had rejoined his battalion in September 1944. Before the action at Faenza, he was reunited with an old friend from the Tunisian campaign called Doug, who was killed by one of the many exploding mines just as Lucas turned around to find him a cigarette. Lucas's stunned response was movingly described in his memoir:

My hand was still opening the tin of cigarettes and even as I ran to where he lay, my mind refused to accept the fact of his death. One moment tall, a bit skinny, wickedly satirical and now—nothing—only a body with a mass of cuts and abrasions and a patch of dirt on his forehead. There were questions; who was he, what was his name, how long had I known him—God knows—it had seemed a life time and yet it was barely two and a half years. As Infantry Friendships go that was almost an eternity for the Angel of Death sat on all our shoulders and friends in the rifle companies vanished quicker than midsummer morning dew.

Where had he gone? His passing had been so quick. Quick. The quick and the dead only now he was no longer quick; he was dead. God knows, he wasn't the first I had seen die so suddenly. They had fallen at my right hand, they had been demolished on my left. Before me and behind me death had struck continuously.... I felt sure that some part of his soul must still be hovering about. But he had gone—forever. As quick as we all hoped we'd go when our number eventually and inevitably came up. No tears, no weeping nor wailing, just to go between asking for a fag and getting one.[38]

At the battle of Faenza it was clear that Lucas was suffering from extreme combat stress. The terrible losses from artillery and mines at Faenza took a further toll on him: he reached the end of his endurance as the remnants of his company took cover from the shelling on a black December night. Unable to sleep because of extreme stress, cold, and hunger, he brooded on the deaths of his comrades:

Before my eyes there passed, in review, a procession of the mates I had lost— faces of chums who had gone in Africa, below Rome and in the battles above Rome. But most clearly I saw those who had died that day. Doug reeling backwards as the concrete mines exploded and Corporal Rich's gentle eyes as he turned away with a goodbye 'ciaou'. The whole assembly of these dead comrades stood in a sombre semi-circle around me as if they were waiting; waiting and watching until the time should come when I joined their ghostly company.... Not only Doug and Rich, but now all my old mates who had survived thus far were dead or captive. The whole fabric of my life was being torn to pieces.

Next day the medical officer recognized that Lucas was 'all in' and diagnosed 'battle exhaustion'. Lucas was sent to the Base Psychiatric Hospital at Assisi, where he continued to be assaulted by intense grief over the loss of his friends, complicated by guilt at having to abandon them. The medical officer in the hospital had to work hard to persuade him that his grief was justified but his guilt was not, especially as he had contributed far more than his share to the war effort. Lucas was transferred out of the infantry and spent the remaining months of the war in convalescence, fighting his demons of grief and guilt, which may have terrorized him for years.[39]

George MacDonald Fraser provided a compelling account of the impact of attritional warfare on soldiers' experiences of death and loss during the 'forgotten war' in Burma in his 1993 memoir, *Quartered Safe Out Here*. There was great ignorance of the Burma war in England. Fraser described in detail his first fight to the death with the Japanese enemy at close quarters in the battle in the Temple Wood, 'an insignificant moment in the war; its importance is personal'. The platoon was in the wood near Meiktila for four hours: according to the regimental history they won the battle, with 136 Japanese dead to their 7 dead and 43 wounded. But for him 'it was a hectic murderous confusion' and his memory was patchy, though sixty seconds of it were unforgettable. Four men were hit around him in less than a minute, including Corporal Tich Little. Later, amid much confusion, he saw Gale killed as he was about to toss a grenade inside an enemy bunker: 'Gale was lying dead with two men bending over him, the whole wood was echoing with shots and explosions and yelling voices'.[40]

Retrospectively Fraser analysed his emotions and responses to this first experience of death in hand-to-hand combat. Going into the wood he was 'scared stiff but not witless'. But once the shooting started, 'the higher thought takes a back seat'. He was both shocked and enraged at seeing Gale killed: 'I wanted a Jap then': his joy on shooting a Japanese soldier was the strongest emotion he experienced that day. He felt real hatred for the Japanese enemy, which persisted into the 1990s. It was hard to say where fear and excitement met: 'a continuous nervous excitement was shot through with occasional flashes of rage, terror, elation, relief and amazement'. He thought most men were like that, though only a few really enjoyed it. Behaviour in battle varied considerably.

Fraser considered the aftermath almost as interesting as the battle, especially viewed from the perspective of 1993:

Fiction and the cinema have led us to expect certain reactions from men in war, and the conventions of both demand displays of emotion, or a restraint which is itself highly emotional. I don't know what Nine Section felt, but whatever it was didn't show. They expressed no grief, or anger, or obvious relief, or indeed any emotion at all.

Their conversation after the battle was limited to a brief reference to Gale's death and the prospects of the wounded. Nothing was said about Tich Little's death, and an outsider might have thought, mistakenly, that the section was unmoved by the two deaths: 'There was no outward show of sorrow, no reminiscences or eulogies, no Hollywood heart-searchings or phony philosophy'. And yet a remarkable ritual took place, which was new to Fraser. Tich Little's military effects and equipment were placed on a groundsheet for anyone to take and substitute their own possessions. Fraser was rather shocked, thinking it coldly practical, even ghoulish. He only slowly realized that everyone was silently taking a much-treasured memento of Tich:

It was not callousness or indifference or lack of feeling for two comrades who had been alive that morning and were now names for the war memorial; it was just that there was nothing to be said. It was part of war; men died, more would die, that was past, and what mattered now was the business in hand; those who lived would get on with it. Whatever sorrow was felt, there was no point in talking or brooding about it, much less in making, for form's sake, a parade of it. Better and healthier to forget it, and look to tomorrow. The celebrated British stiff upper lip, the resolve to conceal emotion which is not only embarrassing and useless, but harmful, is just plain common sense.[41]

Fraser then offered an interesting comparison between his own experience and the media's encouragement of public displays of emotion since the 1980s. He contrasted the soldiers' understanding of the value of the stiff upper lip in the 1940s with the changing cultural norm nearly half a century later. In the opinion of this reserved old soldier the modern media 'seem to feel they have a duty to dwell on emotion, the more harrowing the better, and to encourage its indulgence'. Cameras focused on stricken families at funerals, following disasters, and interviewers pressed relentlessly to uncover pain and grief. Fraser believed that the public 'shapes its behaviour to the media's demands', encouraging the bereaved to weep for the cameras.[42] He was particularly savage about what he saw as the fashionable vogue for counselling in the 1990s for those who suffered loss, and about the recent assumption that most soldiers would need psychiatric help for post-traumatic stress disorder. He wondered how Londoners survived the Blitz or servicemen of the 1940s returned successfully to civilian life 'without benefit of brain-washing'. He admitted that a small minority needed help with the awful mental scars of war, but in his view these numbers would only increase if people were conditioned to believe it was valuable to indulge their emotions.[43] Fraser's perspective gives us an invaluable point of comparison with the significant cultural changes in expressions of grief in England in the late twentieth century, to be discussed in the Epilogue.

# PART
# III

# A Changing Culture
# of Death and Loss
# Since 1945

# 9

# Hidden Death: Medicine and Care of the Dying 1945–1970

In the modern view [death] is pathological, not normal: it is horrible, not welcome, it is not allowed on the National Health.

Dr Richard Lamerton, *Care of the Dying* (Penguin, 1973)

Much has been written about the variation of attitudes and ideas about death and grief between different cultures. Far less research has been devoted to change over time: people within the same culture can perceive death and respond to grief differently across time and different generations. Change over time is demonstrated starkly by the marked contrast between death attitudes and practices in Victorian England and those in the twenty-five years after the Second World War. There was a gradual shift from a dominant Christian culture of acceptance of death and more open expression of grief to one of constraint and silence between 1918 and 1945. The challenge for the historian is greater because acceptance and avoidance can exist side by side in the same society, as well as in the same individual. We have already seen this complexity in the patterns of change in the interwar years, with substantial variations across regions, class, and religion.

The Second World War saw the process of change move more rapidly: we have observed the growing silences in response to loss among bereaved families of Blitz victims, RAF Bomber Command crews, and other casualties of the war. The community coped with the huge losses of both wars by a complex mixture of remembering and forgetting, which are also contradictory aspects of the grief process itself. But the emphasis was more on remembering after the Great War and on forgetting after the Second

World War. The English already had a traditional reserve about expression of emotions, more marked among men and particular groups such as the upper class and the lower levels of the working class. This emotional constraint was enhanced by the impact of both world wars, but more so the second.

During the interwar years the Armistice Day ritual had tried to make sense of the suffering of the Great War in terms of the traditional elevated ideals of patriotism and sacrifice, often expressed in Christian language. But that had ended in disillusionment once it was clear that the Great War had failed to prevent another war. It was more difficult in 1945 to find symbolic meaning for the slaughter after the mass deaths of civilians, the Holocaust, and the dropping of the atomic bombs. As Jay Winter observed, 'After Hiroshima and Auschwitz, the earlier commemorative effort simply could not be duplicated... After 1945, older forms of the language of the sacred faded, and so had the optimism, the faith in human nature on which it rested'.[1]

Moreover, the mood in England in 1945 was to support the Labour Party's positive agenda in building a new welfare state rather than dwelling on the catastrophe of war with its massive casualties. And so, instead of erecting new monuments in 1945, names of the Second World War dead were generally added to those of 1918. The debates in autumn 1945 among members of the war memorial committees of Lancashire echoed those elsewhere. Instead of stone monuments they wanted memorials which served 'a practical human need' in helping the survivors, those for whom the dead sacrificed their lives: 'The sculptured monument has small place in these commemorative suggestions, and the post-war piety of twenty-five years ago, which strewed the country with pointing obelisks and embattled groupings seems a thing outgrown'.[2] The committees opposed monuments in favour of utilitarian buildings for the future, including old people's homes, hospital wings, community centres, or gardens of remembrance. The debate on national memorials in the House of Lords in February 1945 followed similar lines, emphasizing the need for dignity and simplicity, honouring the dead by assisting the survivors in building a better future. However, all were agreed that the Imperial War Graves Commission must continue its invaluable work in creating new cemeteries for the dead of the Second World War, on the model of those of the last war, to be tended and honoured for all time.[3]

The American decision to use atomic bombs on the two Japanese cities of Hiroshima and Nagasaki in August 1945 ended the war quickly, as intended: it also immediately raised the awful spectre of 'the total extinction of human civilisation', as the Emperor of Japan warned. The prospect of nuclear warfare from August 1945 adds a quite awesome dimension to my more limited story of death and grief in war and peace in England. The story of the 1945 atomic bombs has been addressed at length elsewhere, but I do need to consider briefly the potential impact of that nuclear threat on English attitudes to domesticated deaths in the years that followed.[4]

On 6 August 1945 the American bomber *Enola Gay* dropped an atomic bomb on Hiroshima. Estimates of the death toll vary greatly between a hundred thousand and two hundred thousand: many more people subsequently died awful lingering deaths from radiation sickness. A few days later, philosopher Bertrand Russell wrote his first paper on 'The Bomb and Civilization':

It is impossible to imagine a more dramatic and horrifying combination of scientific triumph with political and moral failure...In an instant, by means of one small bomb, every vestige of life throughout four square miles of a populous city has been exterminated. As I write, I learn that a second bomb has been dropped on Nagasaki. The prospect for the human race is sombre beyond all precedent...In the next war, if atomic bombs are used on both sides, it is to be expected that all large cities will be completely wiped out...Either war or civilization must end.[5]

Looking back now, after the Cold War, the rise of China and India, and the new anxieties about climate change, it is a challenge to relate to the widespread fear of potential global destruction from 1945 to the early 1960s. But as Samuel Brittan recalled in 2001: 'The fear of mutual annihilation in horrifying circumstances was a dominating concern between the Hiroshima bomb in 1945 and the detonation of the first H-bomb in 1954'.[6] That anxiety was fuelled for many by horrific newsreels at the cinema and by newspaper reports. The 'Russell–Einstein Manifesto' warned in July 1955 that one H-bomb could obliterate vast cities like London and New York, while many H-bombs could bring global death, sudden for the minority and 'a slow torture of disease and disintegration for the majority'.[7] Bertrand Russell became a leading figure in the Campaign for Nuclear Disarmament which started in Britain in 1958 as a powerful protest movement. Its marches and its propaganda had considerable impact during the early 1960s. It subsequently declined because most people preferred not to dwell on the prospect of nuclear annihilation, and increasingly the costs of war appeared to exceed the rewards.

Those two decades of existential fear of universal nuclear death coincided with a period of profound reticence about death and loss at an individual, family, and community level in England, as we shall see: it seems unlikely that such a deep-rooted anxiety about the potential annihilation of human civilization would not have contributed. Adrian Gregory observed: 'There was a new silence in 1945, the silence after Auschwitz and the silence after Hiroshima. The silence in which nothing meaningful could be said'.[8] Writing in *New Society* in 1965 Richard Hoggart had a similar view of the impact of the war and of the atomic bombs:

Perhaps we talk less about death *not* because we are running away from it but because in the light of recent experience, we have all too fully accepted it—as massively impersonal, imminent and immanent, and perhaps as meaningless: that we are not so much evasive as dourly or drably stoic.[9]

Writing a book on suicide in 1971 and looking back on the quarter-century since Hiroshima, Alvarez noted: 'Death is everywhere and on such a vast scale that it becomes indifferent, impersonal, inevitable and finally, without any meaning'.[10] The sense of helplessness and existential dread may have haunted many. The threat of mass extinction had the capacity to make individual domesticated deaths seem relatively insignificant. In the broader context of potential nuclear annihilation, personal sorrow for a loved one might seem an indulgence, to be borne quietly alone, powerfully reinforcing those earlier silences in response to wartime deaths.

## Neglect of the Dying

The mass production of penicillin from 1943 raised extraordinary expectations of modern medicine because it was so effective against a broad spectrum of bacterial infections. The therapeutic revolution of the 1950s brought a broad range of impressive new drugs which became more widely accessible through the newly created National Health Service. The doctor's power to cure seemed to have no limits. As medical science and modern technology advanced, terminal illnesses increasingly moved from home to hospitals where intervention was possible to prolong life. But the miracles of modern medicine could unfortunately carry disadvantages for the dying. Death was gradually removed from the control of the family at home to that of doctors in sterile institutions concerned with technical efficiency. The death of a patient could represent failure once doctors began to believe their power to cure was invincible. Some doctors were tempted to carry out unwanted interventions to keep people alive, placing their urge to cure above the desire of many terminal patients for dignified deaths.[11] The palliative care movement and the voluntary euthanasia campaign responded quite differently to these new ethical challenges of modern medicine, as we shall see.

The German philosopher Norbert Elias argued in his book, *The Loneliness of the Dying*, in 1982, that there was a strong tendency in advanced western societies to conceal and repress the 'unwelcome idea' of death. He believed such avoidance operated at an individual level, through socially instilled defence mechanisms, and also at a broader level in society. The dying were hygienically screened away from the activity of normal social life since the living were embarrassed by their presence and did not know how to communicate with them. The withdrawal of the living from the dying continued after death, as the care of the dead and their graves were transferred to paid specialists. For Elias these trends were part of a broader shift in emotional history, whereby many people were unwilling or unable to express strong feelings in public, and sometimes also in private.[12]

Philippe Ariès also contended that in the mid-twentieth century 'an absolutely new type of dying' emerged in the industrialized western world. A total reversal of customs occurred in one generation: 'society has banished death'. He partly ascribed this to the 'hidden death in the hospital' which began slowly in the interwar years and became widespread from 1950, with the complicity of families: 'The hospital has offered families a place where they can hide the unseemly invalid, whom neither the world nor they can endure'.[13]

Elias and Ariès were writing in sweeping dramatic terms about dying and death in advanced western societies, and from the perspective of continental Europe and America rather than England. But there is substantial evidence of a similar if more muted view of death in England in the twenty years after the war. Sociologist Peter Marris considered in 1958 that the English 'are shy of death and prefer to forget it', and that they attached a certain stigma to bereavement.[14] Both Geoffrey Gorer and Philip Toynbee were convinced in the mid-1960s that there was a fundamental refusal in English society 'to face the fact of death at all'.[15] Psychiatrist John Hinton believed that in the 1950s and 1960s many people 'in our culture' were not prepared to meet their own death, and they avoided dying people. Even doctors preferred to talk about cure and were likely to see death as a medical failure.[16] The phrase 'death-denial' was used in the 1950s and 1960s to cover a range of related meanings, including suppression of emotions, minimization of rituals, and avoidance of discussion about death and loss. The term was commonly applied in contrast to 'acceptance' of death, but I use it here sparingly, as it is value-laden and has different meanings for psychologists, sociologists, journalists, and others.[17]

We might suppose that the creation of the National Health Service in 1948 would have improved the care of the terminally ill in the years after the war. After all, the welfare state of the 1940s was a major plank of post-war social reconstruction and was popularly assumed to apply from 'the cradle to the grave'. Unfortunately, in practice the Labour government did not give the elderly or the dying high priority. Physician Ian Grant noted in 1957 that the welfare state achieved much for young people but it needed to do far more for the aged dying in providing adequate and appropriate hospitals and nursing homes. This was especially the case for the working-class poor, living in overcrowded slums, forcing many elderly to die in squalid and overcrowded conditions.[18] In its first twenty years the National Health Service fell considerably short of its aim to provide a modern health service for all, in part due to the financial constraints of prolonged post-war austerity. Little money was available for new modern hospitals and remodelling old ones until the 1962 Hospital Plan.[19]

Little has been written by historians or sociologists about the actual care of the dying in England in the twenty-five years after the war ended, with the exception of two excellent essays by medical sociologist David Clark.[20] The rare sources available were written by psychiatrists and medical practitioners who were working with dying people and becoming increasingly concerned about their neglect. An understanding of the causes of neglect of the dying after 1945 hardly prepares us for the shock of the grim reality. First we need the statistics of the major shift of care of the dying from home to hospital. This is clearly identified by an invaluable report into terminal care, *Peace at the Last*, prepared by H. L. Glyn Hughes in 1957–8 for the Calouste Gulbenkian Foundation. Out of 506,357 deaths from all causes in England and Wales, 246,743 (or nearly half) still took place in the homes of the deceased. The other half died in institutions: two-fifths in hospitals, and the rest in nursing homes, mental hospitals, and other institutions.[21]

The proportion of hospital deaths had been growing steadily since the 1930s, marking a dramatic change since the nineteenth century when death at home was the norm. Richard Lamerton estimated that by 1973 over 60 per cent of British people died in hospital, compared with Hughes's figure of about 40 per cent in 1957. Moreover, whereas 50 per cent of deaths took place at home in 1957, by 1965 this was reduced to 38 per cent, and ten years later to 30 per cent.[22] As David Clark put it, death was moving from the home and community into hospitals and institutions, where it could be 'sanitized, sequestered and removed from the public gaze'.[23]

Glyn Hughes's 1958 investigation provided the first wide-ranging report into the problems and neglect of care of the dying, in consultation with six hundred family doctors and all medical officers of health. Medical practitioners found local facilities deficient in care of the dying in more than half the country. Hughes's report exposed 'a serious gap' in the National Health Service which underlined the need to consider all problems of terminal care thoroughly.[24]

In revealing the deficiencies of terminal care in these years, Glyn Hughes's report can be supplemented by the books of John Hinton in 1967 and Richard Lamerton in 1973, since both men had years of practical experience with terminal care. Hinton was a professor of psychiatry at the Middlesex Hospital Medical School from 1966 to 1983, with extensive experience of working with dying patients. His 1967 book *Dying* remains as much a classic as Parkes's book *Bereavement*. Lamerton was medical officer at St Joseph's Hospice in Hackney and later worked at St Christopher's Hospice and in general practice. All three believed that where possible people should be helped to die at home, where many families continued to give devoted care to the dying. But they recognized the strain of home care, with facilities often inadequate and carers themselves frequently elderly and frail. Families did their best but women were increasingly needing to take on outside work, and both families and houses were declining in size.[25]

Hughes, Hinton, and Lamerton agreed on the need to increase and improve terminal care in institutions because of serious problems in domiciliary care. Some such deficiencies in home care were revealed by a national survey of cancer patients nursed at home, carried out by the Marie Curie Foundation in 1951. Drawing on 7,050 cases, they found that 70 per cent of patients were over 60: many suffered acutely from neglect

and loneliness, and some also from squalid conditions and gross over-
crowding. More than half were bedridden and 68 per cent had moderate
to severe physical suffering. Many had extreme pain which required more
regular treatment and many more trained nurses, as well as better ancillary services. The Marie Curie Foundation responded by opening its own
homes for terminally ill cancer patients in the early 1960s.[26]

Given the increasing numbers who died in hospitals and other institutions, these were the chief focus of attention. Only the minority of the
dying were located in acute wards in National Health Service hospitals
and those were often regarded as medical failures. Lamerton commented
on the needless misery suffered by too many patients with cancer in acute
hospital wards, with inadequate pain control and bedsores:

The emotional isolation is even worse. So often the patient is told lies about his
diagnosis and the family are advised that he should never know the truth.
Communication with him thus ceases, compounded in hospital by his being
hidden in a side room, omitted from the consultant's ward round, and sedated.[27]

Hinton shared Lamerton's opposition to acute care for terminal patients.
Occasionally modern technical apparatus could indeed save people from
death, but doctors were reluctant to care for the elderly dying whom they
tended to see as 'blocking' beds for curable cases. The dying required
more gentle and continual care, while their sudden transfer to a lone side-
ward carried grim implications.[28]

The actress Sheila Hancock wrote in the *British Medical Journal* in 1973
of her mother's death from cancer in an acute hospital ward: 'I had very
little experience of any sort of illness and no first-hand experience of
death whatsoever'. Her first response was to panic, out of fear that she
might increase her mother's suffering because of her inexperience and
inability to cope. She found again and again 'an attitude in the medical
profession of appearing not to want to know about the incurably ill'. She
believed this was because medical education was geared to cure, and dying
represented failure. But she also encountered hospital nurses who were
insensitive to terminally ill patients, partly because of a similar sense of
failure and also because of lack of education about the appropriate psychological approach to dying people.[29]

However, in many cases National Health Service hospitals for the
chronic elderly and terminally ill could be even worse places to die than
acute care hospitals, especially if they had formerly been workhouses for

the poor. Most terminal patients were indeed located in chronic or geriatric wards in the former workhouses or public assistance institutions, taken over as hospitals by the National Health Service in 1948. J. H. Sheldon, in his 1961 report to the Birmingham hospital board on geriatric services, condemned them as grim 'human warehouses' and 'storage space for patients'. He described large wards with four rows of packed beds, neglected patients, and appalling sanitary arrangements. Hinton commented that many such institutions were 'quite unsuited to function as modern hospitals', with their large, cold, damp buildings and cheerless interiors: 'they could be about as homely as traditional barracks, life ordered by rules and prohibiting notices'. The staff were too few, with insufficient training or nursing skills, 'performing a task with no sense of purpose'. The evil reputation of these old workhouses made some dying people all the more determined to die at home, despite inadequate home care.[30]

More light is thrown on the plight of the dying people in these grim old hospitals by a massive survey published in 1962 by sociologist Peter Townsend, of 173 residential homes and institutions for the elderly. His passages on care of the dying are few, but illuminating and sombre. He explained that the government had aimed in 1948 to close the workhouses quickly, but little was done by 1962. The forty thousand beds for the elderly in the old workhouses in England and Wales represented half of local authority accommodation. The high ideals of the new National Health Service in 1948 met resistance due to increasing numbers of frail older people, financial constraints, and the prejudices of local councils in favour of delay. Most local authorities argued for the retention of the old workhouses for at least twenty years, or the foreseeable future. Chief welfare officers insisted that the workhouses were economical for large numbers, especially for the so-called 'anti-socials': 'the hard core of low grade people, the mentally defective and dirty people, are happier here'—a horrific description of thousands of people aged over 70. Townsend explained such frequent comments as due to administrative inertia, ignorance, and crude social prejudice.[31]

Townsend's concern about the plight of the elderly in the former workhouses began in an earlier visit he made in the 1950s to a 'grim and sombre Victorian work house containing several hundred residents housed in huge overcrowded dormitories, and bleak day-rooms'. Changes since the 1948 legislation seemed scarcely perceptible. Forty old men sat in one day room in high-backed chairs, not speaking and staring down at the floor. 'Life seemed to have been drained from them, all but the dregs...they had become inured to pain and robbed of all initiative'. When a staff member told the matron that somebody had died in a distant room and asked if this would upset the residents, she responded, 'they hardly notice'. A few years later, during Townsend's subsequent investigation, one nurse regretted that she missed the satisfaction of seeing patients improve and return home: 'you know it can only end in death'. A considerable number of residents were sent to hospital when their condition deteriorated and they died there. But many others died in these forbidding institutions: between about 17 and 25 per cent of residents might be expected to die each year, especially if infectious epidemics struck them.[32]

In over half these former workhouses the policy was to withhold information about deaths from other residents. 'Most of the staff did not care to face up to unpleasant truths about death: "we try to keep it from them—the old hospital routine, you know. No wreaths. No one goes to funerals. No last respects"'. One such matron just told residents the dead person had 'gone away': they screened the body and moved it swiftly elsewhere when residents were in the day room. A minority of such former workhouses were more lenient and might allow residents to attend funerals if they asked. But most 'hushed up' deaths, thereby making frail elderly people feel even more insecure about their own future fate. Some were fearful of death, but many were probably reconciled to it by advancing years and loneliness, as Townsend observed:

The death of others disturbed them less than the concealment of it...Dishonesty in this most serious of matters created distrust over minor affairs. And to avoid the rituals observed in an ordinary community had other consequences. Prompt removal of a body was not only, old people felt, the final indignity which a resident suffered but it gave no chance to those who were left of paying their last respects to someone who had lived among them, however remotely.[33]

However, by 1960 local authorities in England and Wales had opened about 1,100 small homes in converted premises for the aged and infirm with about forty-five beds each, mostly owned by voluntary and religious associations. These compared well with the old workhouses in amenities, staff, and comfort, though they still suffered the disadvantages of institutionalization and there were no qualified nurses in half the homes. The Ministry of Health stated that such homes should try to care for residents when they were dying, but many homes transferred them to hospitals, claiming they had no provision for such care. Where dying residents were kept in the homes, practices varied, but there was often little respect for privacy, or for the dignity of the dying, and secrecy generally prevailed. Stories might be fabricated to conceal deaths, so as not to upset the residents. One matron said, 'I put them in the front lounge if they are dying. I don't let them die in front of the others'. Another commented: 'if someone dies we put them in the bathroom. We use it as a mortuary. The other residents don't know about it...I get the undertaker to come in at night...None of them go to a funeral'. Most matrons assumed that deaths never affected the residents: 'No one talks about it...They take it in their stride. Old people don't seem to care'. Most such homes failed to create a sense of community which could deal with death and grief, other than by silence.[34]

A minority of homes, however, allowed dying residents to stay in their own rooms. One humane matron said she would not move dying residents to a sickroom or an attic, which were seen in some homes as 'the death room'. She allowed residents to see the bodies of companions and say goodbye, if they chose: 'And [the coffin] goes through the *front* door in the most respectful manner'. Residents helped pay for wreaths and some went to the funerals. That way they felt more secure about their own impending deaths. But that matron seems to have been unusual.[35]

Most deaths which occurred in 1956 outside the National Health Service occurred in private-for-profit nursing homes, which Hughes considered 'totally unsuitable and unable to provide adequate standards of terminal care'. Conditions were often bad, sometimes involving actual neglect, with patients 'in their last days existing in tragic conditions'. Such nursing homes tended to be overcrowded because funding and staffing were too low. Hughes recommended that many such homes be closed, or restricted to long-stay chronic patients needing little care. The homes should be properly registered and made legally accountable.[36]

Hughes further recommended that terminal care should be integrated fully into all hospitals, and into general medical care: all hospitals should care properly for the dying, who should not be isolated in small separate institutions. Priority should be given to building appropriate new hospitals and demolishing the old workhouses. And where possible improved ancillary services and better planning should allow more people to die at home, which many preferred, if they had adequate control of distressing symptoms.[37]

# Pioneering Palliative Care: Cicely Saunders and the Hospice Movement

However, Hughes's recommendation to focus reform within hospitals, rather than isolating the dying within specialized institutions, was not the immediate way forward in England. The pioneer work of several dedicated doctors in the 1960s highlighted the unnecessary pain and distress endured by dying patients in leading hospitals. In the early 1960s A. N. Exton-Smith and John Hinton carried out systematic studies into the effectiveness of relief of pain and distress in the dying. These were the first such investigations since that by the physician Sir William Osler in 1906—in itself a further indication of the 'denial' of dying in the half-century or so since. Hinton emphasized the urgent need for their research, since the general reluctance to talk about dying had led to a dearth of information. He concluded that about one-fifth of dying patients in hospitals suffered severe unrelieved pain, while mental distress and fear of dying could be intense: 45 per cent of his dying patients were severely depressed and 37 per cent anxious about dying.[38]

Such concerns were reinforced by growing anxiety about the so-called 'medicalization' of the dying in large acute-care institutions primarily interested in cure, even if these were located in efficient modern buildings. Dying patients were liable to be hidden away in side rooms or else exposed to the sight of all in large crowded wards—neither option satisfactory. Dr Richard Lamerton criticized 'the cold noisiness, the illusion of efficiency, the uninvolved staff fascinated by my liver function but not by me'.[39] During the 1960s the public also became more anxious about the isolation and depersonalization of dying people within general hospitals, which aimed to save lives rather than manage deaths. Winifred Wooster of Enfield in London expressed her own fears to Geoffrey Gorer in 1965. She gave a moving critique of 'how horrible it is to die alone' in a hospital—almost her own fate recently, after an operation to remove a cancerous growth. She made a powerful plea that such experiences should be made more humane:

Hospitals should have quiet rooms in which patients can spend, if they wish, their last few days in comfort and not insist on that awful hospital routine, when dying, of being disturbed by trollies, bed pans, 6 o'clock morning awakenings, patients being sick after operations, to be allowed a window open if one wishes. Also to allow visitors to see them any time, without them having to worry whether they are disturbing other patients, and to know their grief is not being displayed in public.[40]

Two remarkable charismatic women physicians played a key role in improving terminal care and even contributing to a vital change in the emotional culture relating to death and dying. Elisabeth Kubler-Ross, the eminent Swiss-American physician and psychiatrist, succeeded brilliantly in popularizing psychological ideas about death through the mass media and through her 1969 book, *On Death and Dying*. Her impact went far beyond the 'death awareness' movement she helped to build in America. Her relatively simple five-stage theory of the emotional stages of dying was influential and remains popular in the work of therapists. For many medical and psychiatric experts her model has appeared overly simplistic and rigid, ignoring the variety of individual responses to dying and loss. But the broader impact of her message in changing attitudes to death was more important than weaknesses in her theory.[41]

The power, clarity, and emotional appeal of Kubler-Ross's work helped to change both medical and popular responses to death and bereavement. As a charismatic speaker with a mission her evangelical world tours spread her gospel in the 1970s and 1980s. Her moving stories about the experiences of dying people had a remarkable impact on audiences across the world, accustomed to silences surrounding death. Her books and lectures appealed to the media and the public, with their combination of charismatic evangelism and heartbreaking stories. She explained in simple terms why western societies handled death and grief badly, and how that could be improved: dying people should be allowed to die a good death with dignity, and it was beneficial to express their feelings openly. The enthusiastic response to her message showed that the 'death awareness' movement was long overdue.[42]

Cicely Saunders was the second of these charismatic women, 'bringing the subject out from under the carpet and revolutionising the care of the dying and the bereaved'.[43] Like Kubler-Ross, Saunders had a significant international impact, though she was working from within England, rather than America, and her aims and methods were different. Saunders has told her own story in numerous articles, while David Clark, in two fine essays, has explored her key role in the evolution of palliative care. That these two pioneer women should be tackling the same problem at the same time but from two different countries, highlights the influence of the changing cultural climate.[44]

Cicely Saunders trained at St Thomas's Hospital in London, first as a nurse in the 1940s, and later as a doctor during the pharmacological revolution of the 1950s. Then followed seven years of clinical care and research at St Joseph's Hospice, London, investigating the best methods for relief of terminal pain. She was all too well aware that many dying patients were suffering unduly.[45] As David Clark observes, despite the research into terminal pain in the twenty-five years after the war, there were no major innovations in service delivery: 'no powerful medical lobby had sought to raise the profile of terminal care within the NHS', nor to call for the implementation of the Hughes report.[46] Serious care of the dying was very limited in scope and relied mainly on religious and philanthropic organizations.

In the late 1950s and 1960s Saunders published a series of substantial articles on the results of her intensive research into care of the dying. She believed in listening carefully to her patients and learning from them about the nature of their pain and their needs. Her work at St Joseph's Hospice had shown that dying patients could be free of pain, yet still alert, and that tolerance to morphine and drug dependence did not develop. She noted that she could keep suffering within bearable limits in 90 per cent of all cases. She advocated a holistic view of a dying patient's care which treated all aspects of the physical, spiritual, and emotional suffering, which she depicted as 'total pain'. More than this, she developed a remarkably ambitious project to address the proven gap in the National Health Service provision for the terminally ill. But she rejected Hughes's proposed solution to integrate terminal care within hospitals for the acute sick. Instead she promoted the concept of specialized homes devoted to terminal care, operating independently of hospitals. She also believed the practical first step was to place the emphasis on terminal care of cancer patients, an area of recognized urgent need which had already been the focus of early research, including her own.[47]

As Saunders explained in her articles, from 1959 she had a clear vision of the future St Christopher's Hospice in Sydenham, Kent. She systematically lobbied potential supporters and advisers with detailed papers setting out her case. As David Clark shows, she called on her own immense energy, enthusiasm, sense of mission, and charismatic appeal. She was motivated by a strong sense of personal calling and religious commitment which led her to conceive St Christopher's, initially, as a religious community. But she was sufficiently pragmatic to recognize that this approach might alienate some senior medical supporters and inhibit vital fundraising. She wanted a model which could ultimately be widely adopted within Britain and overseas, so the emphasis must be on promoting the highest medical and professional standards of terminal care: therefore St Christopher's would be influenced by religious ideals, but not dependent on them.[48]

And so Saunders wrote thousands of letters to influential individuals, drawing on her own extensive networks among the upper middle classes, and sent out many grant applications to charitable bodies. She disseminated her vision for the hospice through numerous publications, drawing on the moving stories of particular patients at St Joseph's Hospice. She established valuable links with other leaders in the field, including Colin Murray Parkes and John Bowlby. Visits to the United States enabled her to study terminal care there and extend her networks. Saunders was remarkably successful in generating enthusiasm and broad-based support for her cause long before 1967.[49]

St Christopher's Hospice opened in 1967 in Sydenham, Kent, as the first modern hospice, with a building for fifty-four patients, a sixteen-bed residential wing for older people, and plans for a bereavement service. Essential home-care outreach commenced two years later, funded by the National Health Service: by 2001 ten times more patients were cared for at home than in the hospice itself. Saunders had always wanted her ideas to be disseminated internationally, using St Christopher's as a model for inspiration and adaptation elsewhere, but recognizing that different models might be appropriate. She was gratified that St Christopher's stimulated varied models of palliative care in Montreal, New York, and Connecticut, and that all three types were widely adopted elsewhere. It became accepted that the principles of hospice care could be practised in home care and subsequently even in acute hospital wards (as Hughes had proposed) as well as in independent in-patient hospices. In time the concept of hospice care came to be seen as a philosophy rather than a location. Cicely Saunders offered a holistic approach which addressed symptoms rather than cure, and cared for the patient rather than the disease. The hospice and palliative care movement she founded was largely focused on the English-speaking world and northern Europe. In 1990, Ian Maddocks, Professor of Palliative Care at Flinders University in Australia, commented that the 'remarkably popular response amounted to a social movement':

The fervor of the response [also] suggests that something with deeper spiritual meaning is occurring; a calm strength is appreciated in hospice care, which confronts death with a confidence which somehow has been missing in Western culture... The first hospice programmes touched the conscience of medicine and called up tremendous support from the health professions and from families and community groups who recognized a message which reaches both heart and head; inspiring and compelling, sensible and necessary.[50]

# Euthanasia and the 'Medicalization' of Dying

There was an alternative approach to the existing neglect of the dying, supported by a group of radical doctors and anxious citizens, mostly from the comfortable classes. The movement attempting to legalize voluntary euthanasia was formally established as a society in 1935. It was led by a small but vocal group of concerned physicians, supported by a number of prominent authors and reformers, including Vera Brittain, H. G. Wells, G. B. Shaw, and G. M. Trevelyan. They were motivated by humanitarian concerns about the inadequacies of care of the dying in the interwar years, reinforced by statistical evidence that deaths from cancer had doubled over thirty years: this naturally meant a substantial increase in the numbers of painful deaths. In fact this rise in numbers was largely due to the demographic reality that many more people were living longer and becoming susceptible to cancer.[51]

In 1936 Lord Ponsonby introduced a bill into the House of Lords, on behalf of the society, to legalize voluntary euthanasia for patients with fatal and incurable illnesses involving severe pain. The bill was rejected by thirty-five votes to fourteen. Some of its strongest supporters were physicians. Indeed, the chief ammunition for the campaign in the early years was provided by the revelations of prominent doctors that they had practised 'mercy killing' by ending the suffering of elderly people in pain from incurable cancer. In 1947 Dr E. A. Barton of Kensington, aged 85, admitted sparing several dying people the suffering they feared: he was aware that other physicians had similarly intervened, though they dare not acknowledge it publicly. Under the law at the time they were guilty of murder.[52]

A similar bill in 1950 met with greater hostility because the shocking revelations of the Nazi euthanasia programme of racial purification from 1936 had tarnished the society's reputation—even though their definition of 'euthanasia' differed. The case of Nazi Germany was seen by many as a powerful statement of the 'slippery slope' argument that voluntary euthanasia could become involuntary; this was often used by the churches, especially the Catholic Church, as a grim deterrent. The Catholic Church argued forcefully that the Bible upheld the sanctity of life and that euthanasia was murder. It was inevitable that the 1950 bill in the House of Lords would meet massive opposition. Quite apart from the impact of the Nazi atrocities, most people in 1950 were more interested in positive efforts to build an infant welfare state than in a negative campaign for euthanasia: the moral climate was hardly conducive. The movement's leadership was generally elderly and many were retiring, while the campaign also lacked support from the working classes.[53]

The fortunes of the voluntary euthanasia campaign improved markedly in the 1960s for several reasons, as N. D. A. Kemp has shown. Most significant was the change in the cultural and moral climate during this remarkable decade, challenged by the so-called 'permissive society'—the era of sexual liberation for women and the legalization of homosexuality. There were also major changes in relation to issues of life and death. In 1961 suicide was legalized, the death penalty was abolished in 1969, and in 1967 the abortion law reform bill was passed. The legalization of suicide might seem to encourage the concept of an individual's right to die, but that was counteracted by a prison sentence of up to fourteen years for those who assisted suicide. And yet this legislation overall increased individual freedom and seemed to offer a propitious time for the euthanasia movement.[54]

However, Dr John Hinton argued in 1967 that the case against voluntary euthanasia remained powerful. Religious beliefs prevented some people from assisting in euthanasia, while many doctors were convinced that physicians should not deliberately kill patients. He pointed to the problems in devising adequate safeguards and the 'awesome' challenge of selecting patients suitable for euthanasia. 'A dogmatic prohibition of killing' acted as a barrier against the erosion of the value of human life, as happened in Nazi Germany. Individual doctors might be careless in administering euthanasia or misguided by pity. Moreover, a patient who was distressed by suffering or pressured by relatives could make a faulty judgement. And, if euthanasia was legalized there would be less incentive to spend money on improving the care of the dying. As the *Lancet* argued in 1961, the correct response to the euthanasia campaign was to make death more comfortable through better palliative care. The assumption that medical men would deliberately kill suffering people with a lethal drug was profoundly disturbing and doctors should not take the first step.[55]

Between the 1960s and 1990s there were some shifts in the attitudes of physicians, and a gradual change in the climate of opinion in England. In 1965 a national opinion poll showed that 36.4 per cent of a sample of 1,000 doctors would administer voluntary euthanasia in some form, if legalized. By 1994 a poll of 273 physicians indicated that this figure had risen to 46 per cent. The medical profession also became more comfortable with the concept of not prolonging life unnecessarily: the distinction between killing and allowing patients to die was vital. But despite some increase in public support for voluntary euthanasia in the years after 1970, its legalization was prevented chiefly by the fear that it would facilitate the slippery slope to involuntary euthanasia. As the House of Lords' select committee report noted in 1993, the potential for abuse remained: vulnerable patients and frail elderly people might feel pressure to volunteer for euthanasia. Patients with Alzheimer's or in a vegetative state would be unable to give consent. It was still too difficult to set clearly defined limits and frame adequate safeguards against involuntary euthanasia.[56]

The euthanasia campaign was also energized by the increasing anxiety in the community from the early 1960s about the potential for harm in the care of the dying caused by the technological revolution in medicine. As Roy Porter explained it:

These developments had an enormous impact upon the handling of death, traditionally associated with the home. With new monitoring machinery, quasi-surgical interventions and the growth of respirators and all the other technology associated with the intensive care unit—the hospital became the place, not where the patient came to *die* but where the apparently terminal patient might almost miraculously be *rescued* from death…Medicine strove to develop high-tech machinery and the protocols to accompany it, the aim being prolongation of life at all costs.[57]

Miracles of technology undoubtedly saved many lives and confidence in medical progress soared with developments in many areas, including anaesthesia and immunology. By the 1970s, however, there was growing concern about the capacity of modern medicine and biotechnology to prolong the process of dying and create complex ethical problems. Increasingly the critics of the modern medical revolution used the term 'medicalization' in a pejorative manner to claim that medical technology was out of control. In 1976 Ivan Illich launched a savage attack on the 'medicalization of death', as he termed it, albeit from a North American perspective: 'Society, acting through the medical system, decides when and after what indignities and mutilations [the dying] shall die'. Illich argued that hospital beds were filled with bodies 'neither dead nor alive' and that patients had lost control over their own deaths.[58] Decisions about medical treatment of the terminally ill became more complex, as they had ethical, legal, and philosophical implications. The distinction between death and life was less well defined, since heartbeat and respiration could be maintained artificially. Doctors were more likely to focus on effective intervention in the hope of cure rather than management of symptoms in the context of likely death.

To some extent the anxieties expressed were overstated, especially by Illich, and they had less application to England than the United States, where the process had advanced further. The debate about the medicalization of dying tells us relatively little about care of the majority of terminally ill people in England from 1945 onwards. As we have seen, most did not die in intensive care units or acute care wards where the use or abuse of medical technology might be a significant issue. They were more likely to die at home, or in hospitals for the chronic sick or charitable homes for the dying, where the problem was more often neglect than the prolongation of life by modern technology.

There has been substantial progress in care of the dying since 1945, especially in palliative care, but there have been some limits to these achievements. Seale and Cartwright observed in 1994 that one-quarter of all hospital beds in the United Kingdom were occupied by patients in their final year of life and that 60 per cent of deaths occurred in hospital.[59] Moreover, futile technical interventions at the end of life were hugely expensive and continued to prevent dignity in dying. And while the success of palliative care in aiding terminal cancer patients is undeniable, massive additional funding is required to extend its benefits substantially beyond cancer patients. David Clark cautions that in integrating palliative care within the broader health-care system there is some danger of compromising its early ideals, in allowing medical technology and hospital routines to restrict its spiritual and psychological aims.[60] Despite such caveats, the progress in care of the dying, when viewed over the half-century or more since 1945, is remarkable.

# 10

# Widowhood, Grief, and
# Old Age 1945–1963

It is a particular challenge for a historian to explore the nature of a culture of death and bereavement which is characterized by silence and avoidance, as in the two decades in England after 1945. The lack of sources on the seven or eight years immediately following the war is especially notable, as community attention turned to the creation of a new social order—that land 'fit for heroes' promised in 1918 but not then delivered. Commemoration of the dead of the Second World War was notably muted, and the dark side of the war, censored while the war lasted, continued to be a forbidden subject.

The experiences of widowed people are the focus of this chapter, because they were a large, clearly defined group who suffered bereavement in a particularly intense form, and their numbers were increased by war deaths. The plight of grieving widows was largely ignored in England until Peter Marris's 1958 study of seventy-two widows in the East End of London, which will be a significant part of the evidence for this chapter. There were over six hundred thousand widows aged under 60 in England and Wales in 1951; these numbers increased to two and a half million if widows over 60 are included. My emphasis is mainly on the 1950s and primarily on widows whose experiences of grief, while variable, fell within what might be considered a normal rather than pathological range.

War widows received little attention or community support in the decade after the end of the war. We met Audrey Hawkins in Chapter 6, and noted her perception that emotional sensitivities had to be muted to cope with deaths in the Blitz in Plymouth in 1941. She was an intelligent young woman who had to face her own personal tragedy in May 1944.

She had married Terry Deacon, an army officer, in 1943, and they had a happy fifteen months together before he was injured by a flying shell fragment which led to his subsequent death following a stroke. Audrey was devastated, though her comrades in the Women's Royal Naval Service (WRNS) were kind, as she recorded in her diary: 'But it doesn't help. I just don't know how to start again. I had looked to Terry for support and comfort for so long; absolutely everything was bound up with him. I feel dazed, and every now and then it hits me again, and I realize something new about it. I wish I had not to go on living'.[1]

To cope with her intense grief at Terry's premature death, or to avoid dealing with it, Audrey sought refuge in frenetic work. On D-Day, which was the day after Terry's death, she commented as she returned to duty, 'It settles my problem for the moment—of how to deal with life—by giving me an excuse for not facing it'. She refused to take leave and turned down kindly meant offers of a transfer. But Audrey could not avoid the constant reminders of her husband's death, commencing with his funeral on 7 June 1944, which she found harrowing but helpful. Even on the day of the funeral she returned to duty immediately afterwards. Three days after Terry's death she began to worry about her poor short-term memory and her meagre physical energy—common symptoms of grief which made it difficult to tackle a demanding job as if she was perfectly well. She was again forced out of denial about Terry's death when his comrades handed over his belongings and her last letters to him were returned unopened.[2]

The Normandy landings allowed Audrey to throw herself into vitally necessary war work, dealing with a mass of important signals traffic. Her husband's death seemed unreal in the early weeks, especially as she was mentally blocking her grief through hard work and exhaustion: 'It all seems more remote now. I still have not really got down to putting things together again, and have been practically apathetic during the last day or two. Every now and then I realize some particular aspect—but the fact still has not registered, apart from the initial shock'. Reminders of her life with Terry made Audrey feel miserable. People thought it brave of her to return to duty, whereas for her the work was vital to distract herself from grief. Shock, apathy, and exhaustion were dominant.[3]

In September 1945, fifteen months after Terry's death and following a nine-month gap in her diary, Audrey reread her account of Terry's accident and death:

I can't bear to read it—and yet I had to read part of it; all of it. One thing is still true—that I'm not facing life. I have never yet managed to straighten out my ideas—to work out a basis for living. I don't actively want to die now, and I'm a little past the state of caring whether I live or die—with a slight animal bias in favour of living. But I'm still dodging the spiritual problem.

She acknowledged that for fifteen months she had lived without purpose, 'in a blind unthinking state of numbness mentally'. Soon after this she left the WRNS to turn to a successful career in social work, commencing with a post with the Plymouth Council's Department of Social Services. Audrey's diary ended with an introspective and poignant entry in early 1948, four years after Terry's death, noting that her marriage and Terry's death had in the longer term changed her life and her outlook. When Terry died nothing mattered and life was purposeless: 'I genuinely wanted to die'. She had tried hard to find a philosophy which would enable her to 'assimilate the catastrophe' into her life, and give it some meaning. But she gradually gave up the struggle and relapsed into a prolonged state of apathy because she was so tired mentally and grief had thrown her off balance. Apart from a few 'hysterical occasions' she had remained in that state of apathy since. Religious consolation seems to have played an increasing role in her final recovery, after several years of severe depression and apathy. Her diary hints at continued churchgoing and long talks with the vicar in an effort to find solace in what had earlier been a fragile faith. In April 1948 Audrey asked the vicar of her local church to place Terry's name in the Book of Remembrance—'I think he would have liked me to do it'. Perhaps that gave her some sense of coming to terms with a grief that may have lasted so long because she tried to avoid it, and those around had colluded in the silence.[4]

Audrey Hawkins's story could doubtless be repeated many times among other war widows who sought refuge from sorrow in apathy and avoidance while the community looked away. One further example will suffice, drawn from the 1960 BBC radio programme *The World of the Widow*, edited by sociologist Peter Marris. He recorded the experience of an anonymous war widow, aged 27 when widowed: 'it was a very great shock to me naturally and I felt completely at sea and it took me a long time to recover my feeling for life at all'. She was utterly at a loss for three years or so. An art and design course proved too challenging because her emotional problems 'crowded in on me'. She eventually went abroad in the hope of starting a new life: 'That's the trouble I think, one has to live one's life on two levels—after the actual break you're very, of course, emotional, but then you recover sufficiently to put on a good face'. She noted that most people had no idea what sort of effort it cost widows to 'appear normal on the surface'. She had felt obliged to 'put on a good show' because she had no choice and the community did not want to hear about her grief.[5]

## Working-Class Widows in London's East End in the 1950s

Peter Marris's *Widows and Their families*, an empirical study of the bereavement of seventy-two working-class widows from the East End of London published in 1958, was a landmark in early research into experiences of grief and loss in England.[6] Psychiatrist Colin Murray Parkes noted in *New Society* in 1964 that psychiatrists in England had not yet explored the effects of bereavement on adults, other than clinical patients.[7] John Bowlby, the pioneer of attachment theory, introduced Marris's book with the statement that society urgently needed a study of the social, emotional, and economic implications of widowhood, whereas the focus to date had been psychiatric.[8] Bowlby omitted to mention the great value of Marris's work for future historians in understanding a culture and a decade in which death and loss were characterized by silence, avoidance, and an absence of primary source material.

Sociologist Peter Marris and anthropologist Geoffrey Gorer, writing between 1955 and 1965, agreed that the existing literature on grief and mourning was scanty and heavily biased towards the psychiatric study of abnormal responses to loss. Sigmund Freud and Eric Lindemann dominated the early work on grief. Freud's influential 1917 essay on 'Mourning and Melancholia' expressed a psychoanalytical approach to the pathological condition of melancholia. His few paragraphs on the 'normal emotion of grief' seemed to derive from his developing theories regarding psychoanalysis, rather than from empirical evidence. Freud's brief statements on normal grief had considerable influence on a number of psychiatrists who followed him. Freud argued that normal mourning was not a pathological condition, but it had similar painful characteristics. Successful grieving required determined 'mourning work' to ensure that 'all libido shall be withdrawn from its attachment to [the loved object]'; it required time because of the intense opposing desire to cling to the lost 'object' through 'a hallucinatory wishful psychosis'. This involved time, pain, and 'cathectic energy', but respect for reality usually triumphed, leaving the ego again uninhibited.[9]

Freud's 1917 essay was the foundation for the influential concept of 'griefwork' with its prolonged struggle to reconcile contradictory impulses. In 1944 the American Eric Lindemann was the first psychiatrist to observe the symptoms of grief empirically, in studying 101 bereaved hospital patients. He differentiated between those suffering from normal and pathological grief on the basis of the intensity and duration of their symptoms. Lindemann concluded that the duration depended on the success of the mourner's 'grief work' in gaining release from 'bondage' to the deceased and readjusting to a new environment.[10]

Marris and Gorer were alike concerned on several counts about the limitations of the existing literature on bereavement by the 1950s and 1960s, including the lack of studies relating to England. Most research on grief until the 1950s had chiefly aimed to address psychiatric problems, with some inference that grief was a mental disorder, to be perceived in medical or psychotherapeutic terms. Marris and Gorer made vital, innovative contributions by exploring loss and grief in the context of family and community in England, with an emphasis which was social, cultural, and economic rather than primarily psychological. Marris emphasized that his study was concerned with the practical evidence of the social life of English mourners and their interactions with their families, whereas Lindemann's American subjects were lone hospital patients with no other occupation but 'grief work'.[11] Marris and Gorer both emphasized that the intensity, pain, and duration of grief might be affected by considerations that were social as well as psychological. Lindsay Prior later emphasized that social processes were involved, not just private and individualized innate emotions. Sociological factors influenced the duration and intensity of grief since the concept of normality in public grieving behaviour was socially constructed. Prior concluded that grief is socially variable in its public manifestations and that 'the experience of grief is, in some part, reflected in its public expression'.[12]

Marris's book, *Widows and Their Families*, focused on the bereavement experiences of seventy-two women from Poplar, Stepney, and Bethnal Green in London's East End, who were widowed between 1953 and 1955. Their husbands were all aged under 50 (so as not to confuse their experiences of widowhood with those of ageing), and had worked at the common semi-skilled trades of the East End—in the building and furniture trades, the docks, and the markets. The experiences of these seventy-two working-class widows provide a valuable comparison for the historian with the predominantly upper- and middle-class bias of the archival evidence. These widows were interviewed in the early 1950s, the period of greatest reticence regarding death and loss in the decades after the war ended. Their average age was 42, with an average of sixteen years of marriage each and a total of sixty-one children between them. Since their husbands' average age at death had been 42, it is perhaps surprising that there was no mention of death related to war service, another possible consequence of the silence surrounding this subject.[13]

Marris's study illuminated the sad plight of the six hundred thousand widows, aged under 60, in England and Wales, mostly with dependent children, and so with low incomes. However, these East London widows had the considerable advantage of coming from a caring neighbourly community of extended families, living in terrace cottages or council houses, which offered mutual help in times of trouble. Out of the original sample of 104, seventy-two women were interviewed by Marris to explore the economic and social problems of widowhood, and their emotional reactions to bereavement. Marris encouraged them to talk freely in their homes, with their children around them. Some brought out family photographs during the interviews and prepared dinner or answered callers at the door. Most seemed relieved to 'unburden their feelings' and share their emotional problems as they described their reactions to loss. This study was most unusual at the time, as it was a social investigation in the context of a community (rather than a clinical study of psychiatric or hospitalized patients), and it was the first to focus on widowhood in England.[14]

Marris argued that powerful emotional reactions to bereavement underlay all the other effects of widowhood. Implicitly drawing on Freud, Marris maintained that it might take two years or more to become reconciled to bereavement: 'the working out of grief seems to proceed uneasily, by contradictory impulses'. Bereavement involved a fundamental conflict between the refusal to accept that the loved person was dead, and the opposing wish to come to terms with that loss with its painful associations and build a new life. The effort to live in the past and idealize the lost happiness, with all its memories, naturally conflicted with the constant reminders of reality, bringing poignant grief whenever the power of self-illusion failed. For Marris, as for Freud, only the second course of new life could resolve grief in the long term.[15] Some sociologists in recent years have suggested, in contrast, that there is not necessarily a conflict between the two impulses, and that the outcome may be improved if they can both be accommodated.[16]

However, despite this prescriptive emphasis on building a new life, the thoughts and behaviour of many widows were still directed towards their dead husbands: many interviewees said they continued to act as if their husbands were still alive. Thirty-six reported a distinct sense of their husband's presence, for example: 'I see my husband digging in the garden... he's still there'. Marris quoted one woman at some length:

At first I just couldn't understand it. It didn't seem real... I just couldn't cope for a long while, there was nothing to do for it. My sister and the minister told me to pull myself together, but I said 'What for?' They said I had to for the children, but I still felt there was nothing to do for it. It was a month before we got used to his not coming in... I've gone to open the door thinking it must be him.[17]

Many said they thought of their dead husbands all the time, and were obsessed by painful memories of their last illnesses and deaths. A few even experienced or cultivated a sense of their husband's presence—talking to his photograph and imagining he advised them (as did Peggy Ryle when her pilot husband died). These so-called hallucinations could continue for many months or even years, but usually the recurrent memories became too painful. As one widow said: 'It was like a nightmare afterwards, there were so many memories, we couldn't get away from them'. Thirteen women talked of wanting to escape from the house which contained such distressing memories.[18] Some sociologists today suggest that 'continuing bonds' with the dead loved one may be helpful, but in the 1950s they were seen as abnormal hallucinations which would hinder recovery.[19]

Marris did not represent these characteristic grief reactions as sequential stages, admitting that his classification of symptoms of grief was arbitrary, 'as any attempt to impose a pattern on the complexity of human feelings must be'. Rather, they were reactions experienced by many over varying time periods: they could happen simultaneously or, for some, not at all. In general, as the struggle between the contradictory impulses grew intolerable, with acute distress of mind, many widows relapsed into a state of complete apathy, feeling their life was utterly futile. Marris considered apathy the most common of all emotional reactions to the loss of a husband, mentioned by forty-four out of seventy-two interviewees. For some, deep depression set in, leading them to believe they had 'nothing to live for', so death would be preferable. Yet they somehow had to find the willpower to earn money to look after their children.[20]

During this prolonged period of apathy and depression many widows sought to withdraw from public life and its social activities. They often became isolated, in part because they were such poor company. Some felt guilty that they were in some way to blame for their husband's death, anxious that they had not cared for him well enough. They also tended to reject those who offered sympathy, either because it revived distress, or from a broader hostility, which seemed to be a facet of grief itself. One woman noted, 'when I'm depressed, I hate everybody'. Twenty-four admitted to 'violent feelings of resentment and blame', while equal numbers confessed to avoiding people, and to general hostility. Some blamed their doctors, and thirteen turned their bitterness against God or the Church, which they perceived to be responsible for their cruel fate—as Geoffrey Bickersteth, and several families of missing RAF pilots had done. It is notable that only nine of the seventy-two were practising Christians, and most found little solace in the Church or its doctrines concerning the afterlife. But this is hardly surprising, as working-class East Londoners had been known for their irreligion for more than half a century (another illustration of the remarkable regional variations across the English working classes). Only fourteen out of seventy-two widows considered themselves reconciled to their loss after two or three years— several said 'you never get over it'.[21]

Marris's research suggested that the practical help of families and friends helped to ameliorate the suffering of bereavement: 'Family life in the East End of London provides a system of mutual services that spreads the burden on each household'. Relatives and neighbours offered advice, helped with the funeral, paperwork, and shopping, looked after children, and gave loans or gifts of money. These services made it possible for many widows to earn a living to support their children. Family and friends also provided much-needed companionship during the final illness and through the early months of bereavement. Twenty-two of the women interviewed went to stay with relatives, or had them stay at their own home for several weeks after the death. Most were supported by at least one close relative or friend; mothers, daughters, and sisters, in particular, helped with companionship, housekeeping, and looking after children.[22] This again points to the continuation of traditional patterns of community responses to death and loss among the working classes in particular regions.

Despite close family relationships and gratitude for support, most widows sought independence as soon as possible, though they were not anxious to marry again. Only twelve of the seventy-two widows remarried, and nearly half of those were childless, aged under 40, and only able to earn low incomes. The majority strongly believed they could never love another man as much as their dead husbands, and remarriage would have seemed disloyal to the dead.[23] Again, this is consistent with the recent suggestions about the value of 'continuing bonds'.

However, the independence sought was elusive when women were paid less than men and had an inferior social status. It was difficult to organize jobs around children's school hours and the mothers lacked the skills for many positions. Their earnings were very low and, if they reached a certain specified level, their National Insurance pension was reduced, causing deprivation for many. Widows felt victimized by the earnings rule and humiliated if they were obliged to appeal to the National Assistance Board. Such poverty reinforced the depressive tendencies of grief, apathy, and isolation. Widows were reluctant to participate in social activities and to put on a show when they felt thoroughly miserable. They were expected to 'return to normal' far too rapidly when friends ran out of sympathy. They also had to deal with the problems of bereaved children who were also coping with the loss of fathers.[24]

Marris observed that his sample of seventy-two widows was not intended to be broadly representative, as it was confined to East London and to semi-skilled working-class families. Six years later, Celia J. Hobson expanded the sample by interviewing forty widows from a small market town in the Midlands which she called 'Blacktown'. The widows were all under 60 and had been bereaved for periods between six months and four years. Their physical and emotional symptoms were very similar to those reported by Marris for East London. All experienced health disorders, seventeen having lasting ill health. Twenty-six found it difficult to realize their husbands had died, while thirty-two reported that they often sensed their husbands' presence. They initially cherished their memories of the deceased, but as the months passed these memories became so painful they wanted to 'run away and forget'. Twenty-nine widows described a state of apathy, nineteen reported social withdrawal, and twenty-two were intensely resentful of their fate.[25]

Hobson's sample was also mainly working class, though somewhat higher up the scale than Marris's, with five husbands who were clerical workers, twenty skilled working class, and fifteen unskilled. The chief difference between the two projects was that Blacktown was a 'more hostile area' for widows than East London, where community spirit and a mutual-help network were far more substantial. There were no particularly strong ties in Blacktown between widows and their close female relatives, nor did bereavement enhance them. Practical help and some financial assistance for the children were only offered in the first month. Though most widows were intensely lonely, as social activity was almost non-existent, all but two remained in their own homes and sought to build an independent life. None had yet remarried, and six actively opposed it because they could never love another in the same way.[26]

The new social status of the Blacktown widows was vastly inferior to their married status, and was reinforced by financial problems and poverty, with employment opportunities far more limited than in the East End. There were few vacancies for untrained women, and no extended kinship system to help care for young children. They were reduced to the meagre widows' allowance, which was cut back after thirteen weeks. Like the widows in the East End, those who did obtain employment found their benefit cut because of the mean-spirited earnings rule, while unemployed widows were humiliated by having to seek help from the National Assistance Board.[27]

Margaret Torrie, a Quaker and pacifist, became aware of the suffering of such widows during the 1950s in the course of her work at the Citizens Advice Bureau. Consequently, in 1959 she established the CRUSE bereavement care organization for widows, initially to provide practical services and meeting places, with associated doctors and social workers. Margaret was supported in this endeavour by her husband, Dr Torrie, a psychiatrist, whose own therapeutic work had made him aware of the need. In 1960 the Torries were interviewed for a BBC radio programme edited by Peter Marris called *The World of the Widow*. This programme highlighted arguments in Marris's book about the nature of grief, especially the little-known fact that its painful symptoms were widely experienced and usually normal. The Torries explained that the CRUSE club was urgently needed because many widows felt completely isolated, as most people avoided the subjects of death and grief.[28]

Several widows who had joined CRUSE were interviewed for Marris's BBC programme. One said she had come to CRUSE a month after bereavement: 'It's done me wonders—I don't know what I would have done without it', since it allowed widows to share similar troubles with each other. Another woman said CRUSE had been a great comfort as she had previously never known a widowed person and had no idea what grief was like: 'friends sympathize but I feel they don't really understand'. It was a great consolation to have the companionship and sympathetic bond of CRUSE: 'You just can't explain the feelings [of grief] to others who have not experienced it'.[29]

Dr and Mrs Torrie had been delighted with CRUSE's early achievements in the first eighteen months, with numerous requests to extend the organization and open up centres across England. They emphasized that it was vital to bring widows together for mutual help and support from other widows and caseworkers, who provided the springboard for widows to return to their ordinary community with a sense of renewal. However, the development of the CRUSE organization had to be professional and efficient: 'We want a serious counselling service', they insisted, and not 'a party of wailing women'. The Torries had to establish the confidence of the medical profession, statutory groups, and voluntary societies.[30] There was considerable emphasis in the early years on Christian consolation, combined with practical advice about dealing with social and economic problems. CRUSE ultimately achieved remarkable success, becoming Britain's leading bereavement agency, with increasing focus on psychological and emotional counselling. As Tony Walter notes, by the 1990s CRUSE had become an entirely secular organization in which knowledge of psychology and popular grief theories had replaced religious faith.[31]

## Bereavement in Old Age

Since most people who died in England after 1945 were over 60, and therefore outside the investigations of Marris and Hobson, I will explore bereavement among older people in this final part of the chapter. I will also place the emphasis here on the experience of men, to assist in correcting the gender imbalance. In the 1950s sociologist Peter Townsend carried out a survey of old people in Bethnal Green, in the East End of London. He concluded that the poorest people, emotionally, socially, and financially, were those most isolated from family life, especially widowed men over 80 who were living alone. Several who had lost a spouse in the previous ten years said they would never get over it: 'loneliness is the worst thing you can suffer in life'. Years after their loss, some still thought they heard their wives calling—yet another example of continuing bonds. The loss of husbands in old age was not quite such a disaster for women, who had often been less dependent on their husbands and found consolation more readily with their families and female friends. Even so, many widows missed their husbands deeply: one widow who had been bereaved for eight years said 'I get so lonely I could fill up the teapot with tears'.[32]

Colin Murray Parkes and Beverley Raphael, contemporary psychiatrists with an expertise in bereavement, have also explored the particular challenges of losing a spouse in old age. Death in old age is often assumed to be 'timely' and easier to accept than the sudden death of young people; there is time to anticipate and prepare, and the intensity of grief and distress might be less severe. But old people were more vulnerable to the effects of bereavement on their physical health, and their life expectancy was often reduced. Raphael emphasized the profound shock of the loss of a comfortable relationship of many decades, often the only really close relationship left. Helpless distress, loneliness, and anger were often combined with fear of the future and intense longing for the past. As the future for the elderly was short, there was a greater tendency to hold on to their lost relationship in private for their remaining years.[33]

We gain a deeper insight into attitudes to death in old age and ways of coping with loss from the experience of Captain Ernan Forbes-Dennis on the death in 1963 of his wife, Phyllis Bottome, a popular novelist with an international reputation. Ernan Forbes-Dennis, aged 80, was a psychologist who had fought in the Great War, in which his brother was killed. Whereas earlier narratives in this chapter have been drawn chiefly from the experiences of younger and poorer working-class widows, his experience was that of an older man from the professional middle class. He and his wife had both suffered from tuberculosis, meeting as patients in St Moritz before the Great War, and travelling widely for their health afterwards.[34] On Phyllis Bottome's painful death, apparently from cancer, after two years in which she fought 'hard and bravely', there was an overwhelming response to her husband in condolence letters from friends, family, and fans of her novels across the world. Clearly Phyllis's long ordeal was 'fraught with discomfort and disability', though the word 'cancer' was not mentioned—another illustration of the common death avoidance of the period. Many correspondents recognized that the last few years of caring for his wife had imposed an 'almost unbearable strain' on Ernan, who had been a tower of strength and loving support.[35]

Three correspondents in particular understood from personal experience the utter grief and desolation Ernan must be feeling, and how hard it would be to adapt in old age to a life alone after so many years of devoted companionship. Oliver Calder wrote a moving letter from Oxford in October 1963, warning Ernan of the huge challenge of adjusting to life alone at the age of 80:

Living alone, one gets used to the quiet and the absence but one does not get over it at my age and at yours. My wife, I know, wishes me to be happy, to enjoy life and not to grieve for her over much because it distresses her. The dead never desert us but pray for us unceasingly as we do for them. I live with her presence always in the house. I think of her as having caught an earlier train.

Ernan replied three months later, showing his appreciation of Calder's letter which had tried to deal with bereavement honestly rather than superficially, as was so often the case in condolence letters. Ernan agreed with Calder's comments on the special problems facing elderly bereaved people, though he could not share his friend's complete conviction about meeting his loved one again in the future, despite some hope it might be true. He thought it might still be too early for him to be conscious of anything but the irreparable loss: 'It is as if a hurricane had demolished everything, and though one feels the duty to rebuild, it seems impossible to know where and how to begin'.[36]

Ruth Aspinall, a fellow writer and friend of Phyllis, wrote three compassionate and thoughtful letters to Ernan in the first year of his bereavement. She placed her emphasis on the need in the early months of grief, to try to enjoy the everyday things in life, such as the beauty of nature and Jane Austen's novels. Even though Ernan was bruised and wounded, life would gradually reassert itself if he permitted it, though she admitted she had never been hit quite so hard as Ernan. She had found comfort on bereavement in the belief in the 'resurrection of the dead, and the life in the world to come'; but recognized that if Ernan did not share her Christian faith, it would seem like self-deception to adopt it in the hour of need. However, even without such faith, the spirit of a beloved person who had died often seemed to return to give comfort, further evidence of the long history of trust in the 'continuing bonds' between the living and the dead. Several other condolence letter writers (including Oliver Calder) also noted that Phyllis's spirit would always remain close to Ernan. Aspinall told Ernan to feel free to share his deepest thoughts with her, if it would help: 'sometimes one cannot lift the weight off one's heart for fear of distressing other people too much'.[37] This testified to a continuing belief that sharing the suffering of grief in conversation or letters could be valuable.

Ernan's responses to Ruth Aspinall were enlightening and frank. He agreed that nature could offer some comfort after an intolerable loss, but he found that 'all beauty stabs as well as comforts', since he was painfully reminded that Phyllis had intensely shared his love of beauty. And he made the vital point that on bereavement much depended on the length of the partnership, which had been sixty years for them, so 'the depth of the habit of sharing' was intense. Moreover, the age at which bereavement occurred was crucial: 'At my age it would be quite impossible to "get over" such a loss, whereas I think younger people could in time do so. Much depends on the strength of habit and the person's vitality. The old person can only mark his time until his turn comes to leave'.[38] Ernan's comment reminds us of Peter Townsend's finding that several lonely old widowers in the East End of London were also sure they would never 'get over' their loss.

Further, Ernan considered that much also depended on whether the bereaved person was convinced there would be a reunion in the afterlife, as was Ruth Aspinall. Ernan had formerly believed in 'the life in the world to come' and had tried to reassure Phyllis in her last illness that it was a true and reasonable faith:

But after her death it was shattered. Death seemed too monstrous and insulting. That it should have complete power to blot out a personality, built up through so much hope, and courage and pain and love and striving, seemed too final a blow. I could no longer believe in the survival of her soul—her whole self was her soul...Phyllis has gone. I cannot feel any nearness, only an illimitable gulf... I do feel we ought to know more about death and how to meet it. It is an unspeakably terrible thing—I mean the death of a beloved friend—and perhaps it should not be hushed up.

Like C. S. Lewis three years earlier, Ernan had his own traumatic experience of searching for the spiritual meaning of a prolonged and excruciating

death; but after a long personal struggle Ernan had reached the opposite
conclusion from Lewis about the existence of God. Ernan's solicitor had
insisted that the obituary notice for Phyllis must state that she died peacefully, to reassure friends; but Ernan told Aspinall that 'it was not peaceful'
but 'beyond words shattering' for those who loved her. Ernan concluded
that he might never be able to accept his wife's death and the dreadful form
it took, but he must at least try to avoid self-pity.[39]

Other thoughtful friends insisted that Ernan should create a new life for
himself to ease his pain, an approach more readily available to the comfortable classes. Anne Slemons urged him to follow her own example: after
her husband Morris died she had taken a slow boat to Malta and made
some new friendships there after the wrench of selling her old home.
Other friends agreed that it was an excellent idea to get right away from
England after the 'gruelling months' of Phyllis's slow and terrible death.[40]
Ernan sold his Hampstead house in November 1963, just three months
after Phyllis's death—and then spent some lonely weeks in a London hotel
at Lancaster Gate. Up to that point he had refused all invitations as he was
uncertain he could be a 'tolerable guest'. He found the prolonged business
of selling his Hampstead home and relocating his elderly housekeeper to
Ireland 'exhausting and rather heart-breaking'. It was tough to part with
the house he had shared with Phyllis, but it made no sense to live there
alone with his sad 'memories of the past to undermine the present'. He
took his friend's advice to travel to Malta by sea, to spend the winter there
recovering his health, which had been adversely affected by his wife's
prolonged death. But the December voyage to Malta was bad: the cabin
was cold, the food awful, and the boat rolled.[41]

From Malta, Ernan confessed to Oliver Calder that he was still living
in a 'kind of vacuum', but if he could remedy his physical ailments
he could face the spiritual and emotional troubles with greater courage.
A kind doctor in Malta was helping him with his physical problems, but
in bereavement his ailing body and mind were continually interacting.
Evidently he was miserable in Malta until his nephew, the writer Nigel
Dennis and his wife Beatrice joined him there for two weeks in February.
He loved them both and regarded Nigel as a son. Later Ernan planned to
travel through Italy to Lago d'Orta, to the house left to him by his
uncle, to spend a month there with Nigel and Beatrice.[42] Unfortunately
the correspondence ends there, but the indicators suggest that in time
Ernan would succeed in creating a tolerable life for himself, aided by his

wide circle of friends, his determination, his positive personality, his comparative wealth, and his constructive analysis of the challenges of bereavement. In only six months of what he called 'marking time' he had already accomplished much in the most acute period of grief following a sixty-year partnership.

This chapter has explored some of the variables involved in the experiences of widowhood in England in the 1950s, especially those of gender, age, and class. The overall picture was still complex and multi-layered, though to a lesser extent than in the interwar years. The emphasis of the experts on studies of widows reflects the continuing importance of gender. Sociological researchers such as Marris and Hobson brought a new focus to bear on the social and emotional factors involved in bereavement, complementing the earlier psychiatric emphasis. The next chapter will examine the results and significance of a far broader investigation of death and loss across all of England, conducted by Geoffrey Gorer.

# II

# Gorer's Map of Death:
# Declining Rituals and
# Prolonged Grief, 1963

You do your mourning quietly, alone. The same as you might do praying.

Geoffrey Gorer, *Death, Grief and Mourning* (Cresset Press, 1965)

The harrowing experience of his brother's death motivated Geoffrey Gorer, a social anthropologist, to write his book, *Death, Grief and Mourning in Contemporary Britain*, published in 1965. Raymond Mortimer wrote perceptively in a review in the *Sunday Times* that Gorer's social investigation would interest future historians 'as an account of feelings and behaviour in the 1960s'.[1] Indeed it does, especially in view of the dearth of other such evidence. On publication of Gorer's book, psychiatrist Colin Murray Parkes concluded, 'I thought the book a good one and its case successfully proven'.[2] By contrast, sociologists have recently tended to neglect or downplay the study, perhaps measuring it unfavourably against recent theoretical work on grief. Sociologist Tony Walter also found it flawed, but acknowledged its importance: 'no one had ever dreamed of conducting a representative social survey of bereavement through an entire society'. And regrettably such a survey has not been done for England since. Gorer's work remains invaluable for its empirical evidence and its commentary on behaviour, attitudes, and emotions in 1963.[3] It is an exceptional historical source and its relative neglect thus far is remarkable, despite the personal bias of some of Gorer's arguments and his occasional controversial opinions.

Geoffrey Gorer was an anthropologist and writer, born to upper-middle-class parents in London in 1905. In the 1930s he travelled widely in Africa, the Far East, and the United States. He became a close friend of American anthropologists Margaret Mead and Ruth Benedict, who instructed him in social anthropology, though he did little intensive fieldwork. He published a series of popular investigations of national character—of England, Japan, America, and Russia. Independently wealthy, he settled in 1950 in a farmhouse in Sussex, as a freelance social scientist, with a focus on the study of English culture. He is probably best known today for his controversial 1955 essay on 'The Pornography of Death', and for *Exploring English Character*, published in 1955. He remained a bachelor, and enjoyed annual holidays with his closest friend Margaret Mead. His social inquiries were well known and highly regarded in the 1950s and 1960s, though his work is inadequately acknowledged today.[4]

## Gorer's Personal Experiences of Death and Grief

Gorer's pioneer social investigations provide excellent empirical source material for the historian, especially when supplemented by his personal archive at the University of Sussex. *Death, Grief and Mourning in Contemporary Britain* was not widely known at the time of its publication in 1965, suffering perhaps from the community's wish to avoid the subjects of death and loss. Gorer was prompted to undertake the study by his personal experience of bereavement and his own concerns about contemporary social and cultural responses to death. In 1948 the widow of a close friend had told Gorer, two months after bereavement, that she had been 'socially almost completely abandoned to loneliness' by friends and neighbours. On the deaths of his mother, two elderly uncles, and an aunt, in the 1950s, there was no social ritual except for cremation 'with the minimum of elaboration' and condolence letters. His direct experience made him more conscious of the failure of mourning rituals and the lack of support for the bereaved from contemporary British society. This led him to write his short essay for *Encounter* in 1955 on 'The Pornography of Death', which became more widely known in Britain and the USA than his later book. Gorer argued in the essay that death in England had become unmentionable in polite society, just as sex had been a century earlier: the decline in the Christian belief in the future life had made natural death 'too horrible to contemplate'.[5]

Gorer was prompted to develop these early thoughts by the death of his brother Peter, an eminent scientist, from lung cancer in 1961. Peter's prognosis was twelve months of debility and pain, though in fact he died within a month. This was an appalling shock for Gorer and his family, especially as Peter was happily married with two children and a highly successful career. Gorer felt emotionally unprepared: his response to his brother's death was so powerful that he cried himself to sleep in 'rather noisy sobs' on many nights for months. Gorer's distress was vastly increased because Peter's doctors had decided to hide the truth about his impending death from the patient himself, as was common in 1961. Gorer privately shared Margaret Mead's view that Peter should not be forced to live out his final days in a conspiracy of silence which he would come to distrust. Mead thought this bad decision meant 'a nightmare of suffering and responsibility' for Gorer and for Peter's American wife, Elizabeth.[6]

Although Elizabeth responded courageously while Peter was dying, she dealt with her bereavement by trying to act as if nothing had happened, not even attending the cremation:

She could not bear the thought that she might lose control and other people observe her grief; and she wished to spare the children the distressing experience. As a consequence, their father's death was quite unmarked for them by any ritual of any kind, and was even nearly treated as a secret, for it was very many months before Elizabeth could bear to mention him or have him mentioned in her presence.

This fear of loss of emotional control in bereavement—usually expressed by women—was common in the two decades after the Second World War. None of Gorer's family had 'any sort of religious belief'—indeed Gorer described himself as an atheist, for whom the Church of England service in the crematorium had little meaning. Instead of attending the cremation, Elizabeth had taken the children for a picnic and they 'had a good day', followed by a visit to friends in Somerset, before life had to be resumed.[7]

Gorer's experience of bereavement in the months which followed made him realize that 'our treatment of grief and mourning made bereavement very difficult to live through'. Gorer himself grieved freely, cried copiously in private, lost weight, had disturbed sleep and frequent dreams of Peter. He wore a black tie for three months and met chiefly with close friends. When he refused invitations to cocktail parties his explanation that he was in mourning was received with 'shocked embarrassment'. He felt there was no longer any guidance from traditional ritual as to the treatment of mourners, and people were afraid the bereaved would 'break down' in public. For Elizabeth the situation was worse, as she believed their friends avoided her 'as though she were a leper'. She was only socially acceptable if she pretended nothing had happened, as Gorer explained:

This fear of the expression of grief on the part of the English professional classes unfortunately matched Elizabeth's New England fear of giving way to grief, of losing self-control. She did not wear black clothes nor ritualize her mourning in any way; she let herself be, almost literally, eaten up with grief, when she most needed help and comfort from society she was left alone.[8]

Elizabeth became very dependent on Gorer's support as he made generous settlements for her children over the years after she moved back to the United States. She confessed later that she found it difficult to put intense feelings into words, and she appeared not to welcome expressions of sympathy.[9] Three months after Peter's death one friend wrote to Gorer that he was relieved Elizabeth had now apparently worked through some of 'her melancholic reaction', and he was sad that well-meaning friends were not capable of more help and comfort. Eight years afterwards another friend suggested that Elizabeth required longer-term psychiatric help partly because of unresolved grief at her widowhood.[10]

## Gorer's Social Survey of Grief and Mourning in 1963

Since relatively little is known today of Gorer's work on death, grief, and mourning, my aim here is to highlight his major contributions within their historical context and to analyse the chief features of his evidence and his argument. The strengths and significance of his data were not always evident to Gorer himself because of his own assumptions and biases. Gorer began his study with the hypothesis that since most recorded societies had developed formal mourning rituals and rules of behaviour in bereavement, these might be seen as characteristic and valuable human responses to death. Therefore societies without such rituals and cere-monies could potentially be dysfunctional: they might fail to provide support for the bereaved, thus contributing to prolonged grief, like that of

Elizabeth. Indeed, in Gorer's opinion, the virtual disappearance of shared customs and rituals regulating the behaviour of the bereaved was one of the most significant and least recognized social changes of the previous half-century. The aim of his book was to examine the extent of this decline for all classes and regions in Britain, and to enquire into its consequences.

In May 1963 professional interviewers asked a carefully selected initial sample of 1,628 people of both sexes, aged over 16, from all social classes and regions, if they had attended a funeral or cremation within the last five years. This sample was reduced by excluding those who responded in the negative, and further limited by selecting only those closely related to the deceased, leaving a total of 359 respondents. In addition, Gorer himself personally interviewed eighty of the 359 at greater length to provide more detailed contextual information, and included interview extracts in the book.[11] Although Gorer's title specified Britain as his target area, the main focus of the book was on England. Wales was included only as part of the region identified as 'Wales and the south-west', and it was not mentioned at all in the subsequent interviews. Only about 11 per cent of the original 1,628 respondents were Scottish. Gorer tended to link the Scots with the northern English, often suggesting that the Scots were even more conservative and traditional than the northerners.

The results Gorer obtained from the survey provide a wealth of information for the historian on customs, rituals, and attitudes to death, grief, and mourning in the two decades after the war. I will follow these through, as Gorer does, from the death, through the funeral and burial rituals, to the customs and behaviour in the months of mourning which followed. The survey results are useful even where they simply provide empirical information about such matters as the place, cause, and circumstances of death. It is helpful to know that by 1963 half the deaths in the main sample of 359 had taken place in hospital (situated between H. L. Glyn Hughes's figure of 40 per cent in 1957, and Lamerton's of 60 per cent for 1973).[12] Also, of the eighty interviewed by Gorer, nineteen of the deaths reported were from cancer, and all nineteen, like Peter Gorer, had been kept in ignorance of impending death by doctors. Those who had died in hospital were more often younger people, while older parents were more likely to have died at home, suggesting a generational change relating to the place of death. It is remarkable that most people died alone, except for the occasional presence of nurses or doctors: only 25 per cent of the sample of 359 individuals were present at the death, and most of those were women, again highlighting women's customary role as carers for the dying. Presence at the death was most common amongst the unskilled working class and least among the upper classes.[13]

The chief focus of the survey was on the rituals and customary behaviour associated with grief and mourning. Gorer found throughout that rituals tended to be preserved more tenaciously in the lower ranks of society, having been gradually abandoned by the middle and upper classes since 1914. It was highly significant that two-thirds of the main sample of 359 still viewed the body of the deceased to pay their respects before the funeral, usually at a family gathering. However, this was most common among the unskilled working classes in the north, where the proportion rose to over 75 per cent, compared with less than 50 per cent among the upper middle and professional classes of the south-east. In the north of England most households continued to follow the custom of drawing the curtains to reveal to the community that a death had taken place, whereas less than two-thirds did so in the south-east. Gorer's upper-middle-class bias was evident in his failure to acknowledge and discuss the significance of the widespread survival of these crucial traditional rituals among the unskilled working classes in the north. Instead he chose to offer just three extracts from his interviews which described viewing the body as distasteful or unhelpful, presumably coinciding with his own views.[14] Certainly this statistical evidence of strong regional and class variation weakened his argument about the general collapse of rituals.

The disposal of the body was nearly always accompanied by a religious service, usually that of the Church of England. Since this ritual was almost universal, it is remarkable that Gorer paid so little attention to its meanings and value as a vital rite of passage and a potential cathartic point in the affirmation of the reality of the death. Julie-Marie Strange has shown how the burial service among the working classes between 1870 and 1914 could be interpreted variously to suit the needs of mourners, whether they followed folk religion, formal Christianity, or superstition. Mourners could bring their own meanings to the burial service, which might carry comfort for some.[15] There is no reason to believe this had changed substantially for many people since 1914. Withholding burial rites was widely regarded as a source of great shame, as we saw earlier, when miners were unidentified after explosions and civilians' bodies were shattered in the Blitz.

Gorer's own atheism may have precluded his exploration of the possibility that some religious rites still held meaning, and might even be revitalized in the future. He may have simply assumed that religious faith was likely to decline further with secularization and so deserved little attention, explaining the weakness of his discussion of this subject. He merely noted that few clergy followed up with bereaved families after conducting funerals, but did not explore the causes of the presumed decline in the churches' leadership in relation to death and bereavement.

Of his sample of 359 people, 61 per cent were Anglican, 11 per cent Catholic, 6 per cent gave no affiliation, and most of the remainder were drawn from smaller Protestant denominations. The distribution of denominations by region and class was again marked. The Church of England adherents were concentrated in the south-east and midlands and most numerous among the middle and upper classes, while the Catholics came mainly from the north and tended to be urban and working class. But many respondents were nominal Christians: only 14 per cent of the men and 21 per cent of the women worshipped at church weekly, and they were chiefly drawn from the lower working class and the upper middle class. Only eleven respondents out of 359 held orthodox Christian beliefs about the afterlife, and not one believed in eternal damnation. One-quarter had no faith in a future life, and another quarter was uncertain. Amongst the believers, the most popular concept was of rejoining loved ones in heaven, held by 17 per cent of the women and only 3 per cent of the men.[16]

Gorer's account of the rise of cremation at the expense of burial was brief and unhelpful because his sample of interviewees was small and his commentary was again coloured by his upper-middle-class and atheist preconceptions. His brother Peter's cremation had been consistent with his own preference for cremation and modernity, accompanied by minimal religious ritual. Gorer shared Sydney Cockerell's distaste for burial and the 'cult' of graveyard visits, noting that cremation 'obviates such a cult'. Yet his limited evidence pointed to the surviving preference for burial among many unskilled working-class and rural people. All but four of those who chose burial had erected headstones over the grave and most visited them regularly to tend them and remember their loved ones. A gravestone was so expensive that three poor mourners had to save for over a year, and some made weekly visits a significant part of their life.[17] Gorer had limited inclination to explore the meanings of such continuing working-class rituals in the north and the Celtic fringe.

Gorer's survey of 359 people found that the most widespread mourning ritual remaining in Britain in 1963 was the gathering in the home of the bereaved family after the funeral. This was near universal in the north of England (and in Scotland) and still widely held in the larger towns of the south. Otherwise, he regretted the decline in mourning rituals, such as the wearing of elaborate black mourning clothes by women for prescribed periods of time. Gorer saw this as a major change in English customs since the Great War, in his view almost a reversal of the traditional practices of Christian Europe. But again he tended to draw from his own knowledge of those with the money to purchase expensive widows' weeds. Yet working-class women had long shown respect for their dead by making do with black clothes that were borrowed, dyed, second-hand, or even pawned afterwards.[18]

Only half of the women and four-fifths of the men interviewed signified that they were in mourning by their dress, though this called for only a black tie and armband for men. A few women made small alterations to their dress, but half made no concessions at all, even for the funeral. Those who maintained mourning dress for longer periods were usually poor widowed women from the north, while those who abandoned it were largely from the professional and upper middle classes of the south, the midlands, and the larger towns.[19] Peter Marris's much smaller study of working-class widows in the East End of London in the early 1950s adds a helpful dimension. Marris commented that mourning customs seemed 'perfunctory' among the families in his sample, and the arrangements were often left substantially in the undertakers' hands. He noticed a generational change in attitudes to mourning rituals. Parents often still believed in prolonged and deep mourning: fifty-six of the sixty-one widows in his sample wore mourning for at least three months, and twelve for a year. Forty-seven had visited the grave, including twenty-four who did so at least once a month. But Marris thought younger people were more dismissive of mourning rituals.[20] He also noted the likelihood of generational change in the move from home to hospital as the place of death.

Surprisingly, Gorer had relatively little to say about the growth of the funeral business and its implications. Yet one of the more significant changes from the 1930s was the transfer of the dead body from the care of the women in the family at home to the funeral director's private chapel of rest. Closely associated with this move was the gradual decline of the important working-class rituals of laying out the body and paying respects to the deceased in the home. Glennys Howarth observes that the demands of the Second World War obliged survivors to further reduce mourning rituals, as they had done in the Great War, and continued to do after 1945. Innovations such as funeral parlours, motorized funerals, and embalming, commenced before the Second World War and advanced afterwards. Undertakers sought respectability as professional funeral directors, providing a skilled and necessary service for the bereaved, usually at a reasonable price.[21]

Customs regulating social behaviour in the months after the funeral had declined significantly in England between 1914 and 1963. This contrasted starkly with widespread adherence to social rituals governing mourning behaviour in the nineteenth century, when the bereaved were expected to wear mourning dress and to refrain from social activities for prescribed periods. Gorer believed such rituals and social guidance were valuable in most traditional societies. But his 1963 survey showed that only a small minority of respondents gave up their normal social life in bereavement, while the vast majority acted in public as if nothing had happened. Indeed there was a 'general conspiracy to pretend that death has not occurred and that nobody is grieving', especially among the middle and upper classes in the south, midlands, and larger towns. Friends were generally more supportive towards older mourners in smaller towns, especially if they were widowed and in the lower levels of the working class.[22]

The eighty people interviewed by Gorer were questioned about their behaviour in contacts with neighbours, friends, and workmates in the months following their bereavement. There was no accepted social ritual to ease communication between mourners and community, so neighbours and workmates feared embarrassment, difficult silences, or provoking an emotional outburst. Only twenty-eight of the eighty interviewees said they were grateful for help and sympathy from neighbours and workmates: Gorer saw them as dealing well with their grief and well adjusted socially. But twenty people found receiving public sympathy painful or embarrassing, as had Gorer's sister-in-law, Elizabeth. These included a significant group of chronic grievers and mourners in despair, who will be examined later. Some preferred to keep silent about their loss because they found 'meeting people was terrible', while others were afraid of being overwhelmed by their own emotions or those of others.[23]

In conclusion Gorer argued that avoidance of grief and mourning in the weeks and months after the funeral was the most typical reaction of the majority of people in England in 1963: 'Giving way to grief is stigmatized as morbid, unhealthy, demoralising... The proper action of a friend and well-wisher is felt to be distraction of a mourner from his or her grief'. When conventional rules for behaviour in mourning were discarded, appropriate responses became a matter of individual choice, including the time usually needed to grieve. At most, only about twenty-five out of his eighty interviewees (or 31 per cent) seemed to Gorer to be mourning normally, as he saw it. Gorer believed that the lack of accepted ritual, guidance, and support from church or state could result in maladaptive behaviour, despair, and long-term apathy. And the majority of English people had no such customary guidance. Without a belief in the future life or some equivalent, 'death and physical decomposition have become too horrible to contemplate'. Gorer concluded that there was no secular and public recognition of the human need to mourn in response to grief and often only the minimum of private expressions of emotion: the assumption was apparently made that sensible people could control their sorrow by willpower. He proposed that this harmful situation might be improved by devising and providing inspiring secular mourning rituals for the bereaved and the community, though he did not volunteer suggestions.[24]

   In the final few pages of his book Gorer indulged in some unfortunate hyperbole, linking denial of mourning with maladaptive social behaviour such as destructive vandalism, and generalizing from psychoanalytic theory in which he appeared to lack expertise. Philip Toynbee noted in his review in 1965 that Gorer had 'allowed his personal prejudices a most illegitimate fling' in his 'absurd hotchpotch of conclusions'. It was a pity that these few unhelpful final pages coloured the book for some reviewers and subsequent readers who may not have read the main body of his work.[25]

## Prolonged Grief and Despair

I will focus in the second half of my chapter on a highly significant part of Gorer's study which has tended to be overlooked. Yet Gorer made a valuable contribution in the challenging area of chronic and prolonged grief, sometimes called complicated grief, particularly in his perception that this had been a particular problem for middle-class women since 1945. Gorer argued that many people would respond to the public attitude that mourning was embarrassing and self-indulgent by grieving quietly in private, so as not to offend. But others would doubtless internalize the current prescription of what was culturally acceptable:

There are many, I believe, who accept the implications of the current social attitude uncritically and deny their feelings of mourning to themselves, as well as in public, and fight against giving them any expression...If one can deny one's own grief, how much more easily can one deny the grief of others.

Gorer believed that the decline of traditional rituals combined with the stigma against 'giving way to grief' would inhibit the complex psychological and social adjustments needed. The consequences could be harmful for individuals and for society in general: 'the outcome is liable to be either the permanent despair of depression or melancholia, an impairment of the capacity to love in the future, or various irrational attitudes towards death'. The lack of social support and advice during bereavement could be very costly in 'misery, loneliness, despair and maladaptive behaviour'.[26]

Psychiatrists and psychologists have long recognized a particular type of extreme reaction to bereavement usually described as 'prolonged', sometimes 'complicated' or 'pathological', though there is still no clearly defined label. Colin Murray Parkes saw many patients in the 1960s suffering from such grief, both in therapy and outside in the community. Usually it was identified because it was intense and long-lasting, with no progress made over several years. Parkes observed that severe and abnormally prolonged grief was a relatively common problem in the 1950s and 1960s, which was more likely to afflict people who kept a stiff upper lip and controlled their feelings. It usually manifested itself in highly intense forms of the more common responses to grief, for instance in years of continued pining for the lost loved one, and obsessive preoccupation with memories of the lost life. Parkes argued that such people could be severely distressed, socially isolated, and confined at home alone. They might define themselves almost entirely in terms of the lost relationship, to such an extent that they cut themselves off from the living for years. Normal functioning and working capacity could be affected, with intense depression, and suicidal thoughts. Experts over the years since Gorer's book was published do not seem to have differed greatly in their commentary on prolonged grief.[27]

Geoffrey Gorer believed widows were especially prone to suffer the trauma and despair of prolonged grief, more particularly those from the comfortable classes. Widowhood was the likely fate of many British wives, since women lived longer, but they received no preparation for bereavement. Widowhood was often a time of poverty, even for women from the middle and professional classes who had previously enjoyed larger incomes, and now had to exist on smaller pensions than men. It was also a time of loneliness for many women as they were no longer encouraged to share houses with married children, so there were numerous solitary older women in relative poverty with no accepted role in society. Few remarried. Many had to take unskilled jobs, do their best to appear cheerful and 'keep busy', as the only antidote to grief. The alternative was 'a lethargic, empty, solitary life in a house much too big for them, where they feed themselves inadequately and wait for death'. The emptiness of their lives seemed dreadful to Gorer.[28]

The majority of people identified by Gorer as 'hiding grief' were women. This appears to conflict with the historical evidence that women traditionally were more likely to show their sorrow openly than men, as in the century before 1914. But, as we have seen, the cumulative impact of the two world wars, along with demographic, religious, and medical changes, had altered cultural norms so that women felt that they should grieve in a more contained manner, like men.

Of the eighty people Gorer interviewed at length, he identified about a dozen as 'hiding grief' (about 15 per cent) including several middle-class women without jobs. These women had internalized the wartime prescription that the appropriate way to deal with grief was to 'keep busy' and carry on in public as if nothing had happened. Nine of the twelve were widows and three had lost their mothers. Several stated that 'giving way to grief' was morbid or unhealthy, so that endless distractions were the most effective way to fight it. One case cited by Gorer was a 45-year-old shop-keeper's widow from the north-west who was carrying out her husband's wishes in hiding her grief: he had not wanted her to go into deep mourning and be miserable. This was common. We saw earlier that many wartime widows and bereaved families had noted the frequent injunction by their soldier husbands and sons not to mourn for them. The women interviewed by Gorer had lived through the war and internalized this advice. This shopkeeper's widow said 'you had to put a brave face on', another common wartime response. Looking after the shop kept her busy, which she considered therapeutic, and self-pity was 'ghastly'. Moreover people who came into the shop never mentioned her husband's death. She did not even give way to tears at home because she saw that as unfair to the family.[29]

The widow of a 70-year-old civil servant in the south-west of England used the well-worn wartime phrase, 'the only salvation is to keep busy', in her case by running a bed and breakfast establishment in an effort to create a new life. She considered her husband's life was shortened by his fighting experiences in the Great War, which she believed had 'left their mark on that generation'. As we have seen, wartime experiences had left their mark also on the generation who fought in the Second World War, and on their bereaved families: it is likely that war had also impacted on this widow, helping to condition her current responses to bereavement. The same may well have been true of a 49-year-old Methodist woman, married to a director of a small southern firm, who was still intensely mourning the death of her beloved adoptive mother: 'You've got not to upset yourself or make people unhappy around you... Well you must [hide your feelings] from those around you; you do your mourning quietly, alone. The same as you might do praying'. This woman's grief was prolonged, in part in Gorer's view because she denied it outward expression.[30]

In addition to the twelve interviewees seen as 'hiding grief', Gorer identified nine mourners out of the eighty (11 per cent) as 'in despair', a term he preferred to melancholia or depression. He also feared that one or two people from his 'hiding grief' category might be in danger of becoming 'despairing', given more time. That 11 per cent of his sample was in despair seems substantial. Five were widowed, two had lost sons in young adulthood, and two middle-aged men had lost mothers. One widow had hanged herself between the two interviews. Only two of the eight who were in despair had engaged in formal mourning: these two were practising Christians and were the only two to choose traditional Christian burial rather than cremation. Gorer noted that the despair of these nine interviewees was palpable to him as the interviewer, in their long silences, toneless voices, and grudging speech. Several said 'I'll never get over it' and seemed to mean it. One widow aged 66 was not eating and a widower aged 65 appeared to Gorer to be trying to kill himself with overwork. They were all solitary and had been mourning intensely for at least twelve months when interviewed: the extent of their anguish was in Gorer's view equivalent to that more common in the early weeks of bereavement.[31] He was surprised at the number of people in despair, explaining it largely in terms of the absence of any ritual to guide them or society around them. Certainly the decline of mourning rituals must be seen as a vital explanatory factor, but it was not the only one, and it needs to be seen in a broader context, as I will argue later. Gorer's explanation fails to recognize that the decline of mourning rituals was one symptom of far broader social and cultural changes, with complex causes.

Two of the dozens of readers who wrote to Gorer in the 1960s endorsed his picture of widows in despair. Mary Zobel, herself a widow without supporting family, wrote that 'I found no-one who could even begin to understand and encompass my grief'. She described her own and other widows' experiences of containing their grief and becoming 'frozen and dead' inside as a result. Widows should not have to be 'marvellous', she wrote, but should be allowed to mourn and express desperate grief. Muriel Skeet wrote from West London that she was recently widowed and had also found friends embarrassed by her grief. They told her, from an early stage in her bereavement, not to keep dwelling on her dead husband but to look to the future. She found this attitude most marked among her professional friends, especially the doctors. Both letters confirm Gorer's conclusions about the more rapid and pronounced shift away from mourning customs and rituals amongst the middle and professional classes in the south-east.[32]

# The Ordeal of Prolonged Grief for a Middle-Class Widow in the 1950s

Dorothy Addison's ordeal in widowhood offers a chilling and detailed example of such prolonged grief in the 1950s, and it could equally well have occurred in the following decade. Her extensive diaries in the British Library are heartbreaking to read, reinforced by the likelihood that other widows in the two decades after the war may have suffered in a similar way. The primary subject of Dorothy's six detailed diaries was the story of her traumatic bereavement. She was the second wife of Christopher Addison (1869–1951), a distinguished physician and Labour Party statesman, who was Leader of the House of Lords from 1945 to his death in 1951. Viscount Addison's first wife, Isobel, died of cancer in 1934, mourned by many. Dorothy Low was the daughter of a solicitor: when they married in 1937, Dorothy was aged 40 and her new husband was 68. Her unpublished memoir acknowledged the twin challenges of age and class differences in their marriage: Dorothy was seen as a middle-class woman who was unaccustomed to London society, not least by her husband's colleagues in the House of Lords. Yet Dorothy's memoir described a happy marriage lasting fourteen years, living in the village of Radnage in Buckinghamshire, where she became involved in village affairs, and also regularly attended House of Lords' debates. She enjoyed the social role of political wife and was a supportive and accomplished helpmate to her ageing husband, looking after him well during his final illness from cancer in 1951.[33]

Dorothy was devastated by her husband's death and her intense grief lasted at least five years. From the age of 55, hers was an extreme experience of prolonged chronic grief, exacerbated by the prevailing cultural climate of silence about death and loss following two world wars. She continued for many years to define herself almost entirely in terms of her lost relationship with her husband, inevitably reducing her opportunities to develop new friendships with the living. Her relations with her four grown-up stepchildren deteriorated rapidly during her first year of widowhood. Some of the ill feeling may be attributed to the fairly common antipathy between a second wife and her stepchildren, but more was probably due to the impact of intense grief on Dorothy's behaviour. Her stepchildren became a prime target of her anger and her need to find people to blame, so she failed to respond to their early gestures of goodwill.

Dorothy Addison despised women who sobbed at funerals, as she noted in her diary on the day of her husband's funeral in Radnage church in December 1951. She had displayed this same resolve to maintain total control when she had learned that her husband had cancer: 'I was determined not to break down and to keep complete control of myself'. Her efforts to keep command of her emotions in public are reminiscent of Peggy Ryle's diary entries in 1944. Dorothy's diaries also show that she used alcohol and phenobarbitones to 'stop my emotions' and to deal with the stress of the funeral and subsequent bereavement. The medication helped her to cope, but its combination with alcohol took its toll over time, possibly prolonging her grief and depression.[34]

Widowhood for Dorothy Addison was the more challenging because her reduced financial situation meant that the family house in Radnage had to be sold. She blamed her stepchildren unfairly for this loss, increasing the ill feeling between them. Her first Christmas alone was dreadful, and she knew she must contemplate a future with little capital. Dorothy's job options were limited by her age at 55 and her lack of recent work experience. The prospect of facing life alone with limited opportunities as older age approached was daunting—far more so for women than for men. Dorothy felt numb in those first few weeks of widowhood, but the full depth of her grief and loneliness hit her in the next few months when she suffered from acute insomnia and cried frequently. She missed her husband desperately. Dorothy often expected to hear the sound of his voice, and found herself talking to him, as if he could hear her. She knew people would think she was deranged, but it comforted her, as if he was really there.[35] It was common for bereaved people to believe they could see and hear their dead loved ones, but it was rarely spoken about until recently, precisely because it might be seen as abnormal.

In 1952 there were no advice books for widows to tell them what to expect in bereavement: people did not talk about it and there were no bereavement counsellors or organizations like CRUSE for widows to help. Dorothy's housekeeper, Mrs Stone, her sister Rosemary, the vicar Maynard Burdett, and his wife Marian, all offered comfort, but left her feeling she should 'snap out of her troubles' and move on. Increasingly she could not be bothered to prepare food. The vicar's wife became very worried, and took her to see the local physician, Dr Levekus, who gave her Vitamin B to help her appetite. In May 1952 the house was sold and she left the village after laying a bunch of white narcissi on her husband's grave. By July she believed that she was on the verge of a serious nervous breakdown which she was only holding back by rigid self-control. She began to feel intense anger and bitterness, primarily directed against her stepchildren, but also towards her lawyer and anybody else who upset her.[36]

After her first acutely miserable six months of bereavement Dorothy found the courage to go for five months to South Africa, where she had family links, in an effort to take control of her life and earn some money. But in South Africa in August she was still subject to black fits of total depression and again contemplated suicide. She hoped to gain a job which would occupy all her energies and distract her from grief, while she continued to pretend all was well and to keep up a cheerful front. She found a job in late October, looking after the office of an art gallery for three months, but even the demanding work and the long hours failed to distract her sufficiently from her despair.[37]

On 9 November 1952 Dorothy felt intensely depressed at the approaching first anniversary of her husband's death and had no idea how she could continue to live. She wrote perceptively: 'I am so unfortunate in living at a time when people are bored with excessive grief'. Society insisted she should behave as normal even when her heart was breaking. She had just read a biography of Queen Victoria, who had the 'luxury of grief' on Albert's death: everybody sympathized with the Queen, who had work, status, and her family to help her through her loss. Dorothy considered the contrast with her own situation was stark: she felt she had nobody to rely on, though she had a little money and some status, and she was denied that 'luxury of grief'. She felt desperate and wished she was dead.[38]

Late in December 1952 Dorothy returned to England, where she took two successive jobs as cook and companion to older ladies: this status incongruence could not have been easy. She spent much of 1953 hunting for a suitable cottage, and trying hard to establish a life of her own. Early in 1954, at the age of 57, Dorothy at last moved into a cottage near Wycombe, but time did not heal her misery. She believed she concealed her grief well and nobody guessed how terrible she felt. She was behaving as society expected her to do, pretending to be cheerful, but making no progress. She was also trying to regulate the intake of alcohol and medica-tion to avoid the temptation of an overdose. Dorothy's friends Maynard and Marian, the vicar and his wife, responded to her despair in March 1954 with further encouragement to 'snap out of' her troubles, engage in useful work, and take solace in religion. But she responded that she had tried all these consolations, to little or no avail.[39]

It is clear from the diary that a significant part of Dorothy's problem was probably physical from at least 1954. She learned at last in June 1956 that she had serious gall bladder trouble, causing bouts of agonizing pain, which finally required surgery. It seems likely that this had been undiag-nosed for a considerable time, while her symptoms were all mistaken for the effects of grief and depression. She had complained of lack of interest in food from the first year of widowhood, and by 1956 doctors considered her severely malnourished. Yet as late as January 1956 a hospital specialist still recommended that she find a job or console herself through religion.[40] Following surgery, Dorothy lived on for some years after the last entry in this seemingly interminable diary of despair.

None of the friends, relatives, clergymen, or doctors in Dorothy's diminishing circle seem to have talked directly with her about her prolonged grief. Her sad experience illuminates the problems of bereave-ment in the 1950s when little research had been carried out by psychiatrists and ignorance was pervasive at a popular level. She had little information, advice, or medical support in those first four and a half years. Less than a decade later she might have been helped by C. S. Lewis's book, *A Grief Observed*, or she might have consulted CRUSE counsellors. Today she would have access to advice books, mutual-help groups, and therapists, as well as to antidepressant medication and better informed general practitioners. Most experts across the years have agreed that the most severe cases of prolonged or complicated grief might need help, though they have differed as to what form that support should take. Parkes in 1964 suggested vitamin preparations, psychosomatic drugs, and possible psychiatric help. Nearly forty years later Ruth Malkinson recommended medication for the depression and psychotherapy for the grief.[41]

## The Significance of Gorer's Study

Gorer's empirical work was outstanding in presenting an evocative picture of the changing ways of death, grief, and mourning in the decades between 1945 and 1963. His analysis was remarkable both for its considerable insights as well as for its prejudices. His explanations for the cultural and emotional changes he described were somewhat limited and inconsistent: he seemed at times to suggest that the decline in rituals was in itself the primary cause rather than one of several related factors. In a review of Gorer's book in *New Society* in April 1965 Richard Hoggart depicted the explanations for the changes in attitudes to death and bereavement over the previous half-century as far more complex. For Hoggart the causes lay partly in profound secular changes in attitudes and partly in the impact of the Second World War and the threat of the atomic bomb. People increasingly felt the menace of mass annihilation made death itself seem impersonal and even meaningless: 'we are not so much evasive as dourly or drably stoic'.[42]

Hoggart was, of course, correct about the complexity of the explanations for the changes in attitudes, behaviour, and emotions relating to death and sorrow, as we have seen throughout this book. The decline in prescribed ritualized behaviour in mourning was in the main a response to more fundamental cultural shifts, though it did contribute to the reduction in expressive grieving. More significant causal factors during the half-century from 1914 to 1963 included the traumatic impact of two world wars, demographic change, advances in medical science, and shifts in intellectual and spiritual views of this world and the next. Gorer tells us little of these broader forces. In particular he failed to see that the Second World War had played a major role in encouraging a stoical refusal to dwell on death and dying.

Further caveats about Gorer's assumptions are in order. No doubt influenced by his personal atheism, he seemed to take for granted the inevitable secularization of English society, though he was not alone in this conjecture. He did not enquire into how and why the role of the churches was declining, nor how that role might be rendered more positive and meaningful in relation to death and bereavement. Oddly, Gorer seemed unaware of the publication of C. S. Lewis's influential book, *A Grief Observed*, in 1961, two years before Gorer conducted his survey. Lewis's book vividly described a Christian response to grief: it became a best-seller and helped thousands of the bereaved.[43] It might have alerted Gorer to explore the potential value for some people of faith and spirituality in dealing with loss.

The assumptions Gorer brought to his analysis powerfully reflected his privileged upper-middle-class upbringing in south-east England. His survey results pointed frequently to the contrasts between the behaviour in bereavement of the unskilled working classes and the upper middle classes, between urban and rural areas, and between the north and the south. Yet he tended to generalize in his argument about the widespread decline of ritual, instead of recognizing the two rather different cultures of death and mourning, based on class and region, detailed in his survey. He failed especially to perceive the significance of his own survey data for the unskilled working classes, which revealed a slower decline of death and mourning rituals, with a surprising degree of continuity and survival of traditional modes.

Some psychiatrists and sociologists have suggested recently that people may grieve in different ways: men may be more likely to contain feelings while women may find expressing emotions more helpful. Gorer's evidence substantiates this and he was ahead of his time in taking the category of gender into account. His survey was unusual in 1963 in including almost equal numbers of males and females in the sample. Marris and Parkes had focused on women, apparently assuming their experiences also reflected those of men. Gorer highlighted the preponderance of women among his 'hidden' and chronic grievers, though he attributed that more to their circumstances as widows, than to their gender. He made the further assumption that the healthy way to mourn was by expressing feelings openly instead of containing them and seeking distraction. This was a viewpoint increasingly advocated from the 1970s, especially by middle-class women, as we will see later.

Overall, Geoffrey Gorer gave us an invaluable picture of customs, behaviour, and emotions pertaining to loss and grief in the two decades after the Second World War. His contribution to the history of death and loss in twentieth-century England is substantial. It has been ignored for so long in large part because of the very silences about death and loss against which he protested. We need a successor to Gorer to carry out a similar study to enlighten us about death, grief, and mourning in England in the twenty-first century, with all its variables, such as class, region, gender, religion, and race.

# 12

# Observing Grief: C. S. Lewis and C. M. Parkes

It is difficult to appreciate today how widespread and deep-rooted was the ignorance, silence, and embarrassment about grief in the 1950s and 1960s, and how pervasive the advice to the bereaved to keep busy and cheerful and to move on. As Geoffrey Gorer observed, it was far more difficult for the bereaved to appeal directly for help in a society 'where the majority wish to ignore grief'.[1] In his review of Gorer's book, *Death, Grief and Mourning in Contemporary Britain*, Philip Toynbee, a novelist and journalist, agreed that in the 1960s the English were determined 'to deny the facts of death and loss'. In the years since 1914 they had arrived at 'an attitude which almost makes a pariah of the mourner': they tried to 'avoid the facts of death' and many bereaved passed into a permanent state of despair or apathy.[2]

Bereavement could be an isolating and frightening experience up to the 1960s, with society offering limited emotional and social support, and little advice. Harold Orlans observed in 1957 that the growing literature of modern psychology had thus far failed conspicuously to deal with the fundamental human problems of death and grief, which had traditionally been left to theology, poetry, and philosophy.[3] Psychiatrists were still chiefly concerned with the severe problems of complicated grief among clinical patients. Even the churches were not offering the leadership in relation to death and bereavement that might have been expected, until the publication of C. S. Lewis's book, *A Grief Observed*, in 1961. This chapter will explore the character and influence of the work of Lewis and of psychiatrists such as Colin Murray Parkes, on the understanding of grief in English society.

# C. S. Lewis, *A Grief Observed*, 1961

Public understanding of bereavement in England in the 1960s and 1970s was probably influenced less by psychiatrists than by a remarkable Christian scholar and commentator. C. S. Lewis's short book, *A Grief Observed*, published in 1961, was an elegant and complex analysis of his own experience of sorrow. It became an instant best-seller and has continued to sell well ever since, helping thousands of the bereaved. In 1965 the poet W. H. Auden considered it by far the best first-hand account of bereavement he had ever read.[4] Trevor Huddleston, Anglo-Catholic priest and later archbishop, thought the book would be invaluable to many grieving people: 'it refuses to compromise or to sentimentalise over the issue of death, yet it remains a profoundly religious and theological document'.[5] Passages were drawn from it to illuminate Richard Attenborough's popular film *Shadowlands*, starring Anthony Hopkins as C. S. Lewis and advertised as 'one of the most extraordinary love stories of our time'.

The Second World War had further disrupted habits of Christian practice in England, and its worst features raised basic questions about God's goodness. Adrian Hastings notes that the war also rekindled a sense of spiritual revival and a time of remarkable literary creativity, led by C. S. Lewis, T. S. Eliot, Dorothy L. Sayers, and Charles Williams. Lewis's best-known and most popular theological writing included *The Problem of Pain* and *The Screwtape Letters*, written in 1940, with both books reaching six impressions in two years. *The Screwtape Letters* sold more than a million copies, making Lewis a household name. He was also a hugely popular broadcaster: his *Mere Christianity* was aired by the BBC on five Sundays in 1942. During the 1940s and 1950s his justification of Christian orthodoxy was internationally celebrated and he became almost a cult figure. Hastings observes that, 'In the field of religion no other writer of the mid-century is comparable to Lewis', who exercised an immense influence on the generation of the 1950s. He combined uncompromising faith with rational scholarship and literary creativity. Lewis's most lasting imaginative achievement in Hastings's view, was probably the famous Narnia stories which captivated generations of children.[6] *The Lion, The Witch and the Wardrobe* became a major Hollywood film.

Clive Staples Lewis was born in Belfast in 1898 and he suffered severely when he was 9 from the death of his mother from cancer. Lewis admitted to a friend in 1953 that his mother's loss went deep into his unconscious to produce a trauma: 'there has never really been any sense of security and snugness since'.[7] His biographer, A. N. Wilson, argued that Lewis's quest for his lost mother dominated his relations with women for the rest of his life. His father had repressed his own grief on his wife's death and, unable to cope, sent his younger son away to a 'very tough' English boarding school only two weeks later. Lewis bottled up his emotions for many years as a consequence. In his twenties he took as a companion for over thirty years a woman old enough to be his mother. Wilson argues that a few years after Janie Moore's death in 1951 he found a second mother substitute in Joy Gresham, an American poet, novelist, and fan of his books.[8]

Lewis was a deeply complex man, who was both revered and disliked. He abandoned his father's Ulster Protestantism in the aftermath of his mother's death and his unhappy schooldays. After fighting in the Great War in 1917–18 he earned a first class honours degree at Oxford: in 1925 he commenced his thirty years as a Fellow in English language and literature at Magdalen College, Oxford. Following a mystical experience in 1929 he moved reluctantly from agnosticism to theism, and in the next two years became fully reconverted to Christianity. This 'released in him a literary flow which only ceased with death. From then, works of scholarship, fantasy, literary appreciation, and apologetics poured from his ever-fertile brain'.[9] Where his colleagues at Oxford seemed to be jealous of his fame, Cambridge offered him the Chair in English in 1954, at the age of 56.

As Wilson puts it, '[Lewis] was ready for marriage and [Joy] was there'. Joy Gresham was an attractive, uninhibited, and lively American writer, who charmed Lewis from their first meeting in 1952, though his academic friends perceived her as assertive and strident. Her marriage to an alcoholic American was virtually over when she met Lewis, who was able to express his feelings openly with Joy in a manner rare for him. After her divorce was finalized, she and her two boys moved to Oxford in 1955. Lewis entered into a civil marriage of convenience with Joy in 1956, intended initially as a formality allowing her to obtain an official permit to stay in England. But Lewis's feelings for Joy deepened and he also discovered in 1957 that she was suffering from terminal bone cancer. Their marriage was later solemnized with nuptial Mass in hospital. Joy enjoyed a seemingly miraculous prolonged remission in 1957, whilst Lewis appeared to take on her pain himself when he developed what he described as agonizing osteoporosis.[10]

Yet, as Lewis told Dorothy L. Sayers in June 1957, 'We soon learn to love what we know we must lose'. They could do no more for Joy in hospital so he brought her home, where 'we have much gaiety and even some happiness...My heart is breaking and I was never so happy before: at any rate there is more in life than I knew about'. To another friend he acknowledged that 'new beauty and new tragedy have entered my life'.[11] However a hospital check-up in October 1959 revealed that Joy's cancer had returned. She fought the increasing pain with courage in the remaining months, but died in hospital on 14 July 1960. Lewis wrote of her death to two friends, acknowledging that it was 'less dreadful' than he expected. He was alone with her at the end and she was unconscious much of the time; yet she was still able to say 'you have made me happy', and that she was at peace with God. Lewis was in a state of 'psychological paralysis' immediately afterwards, as if he had been hit by a shell.[12]

Lewis's book, *A Grief Observed*, was written in the months after his wife Joy died in 1960, and was published the following year. Like Geoffrey Bickersteth's account of his bereavement during the war, it demonstrates the complexities and trauma that a profound religious faith could add to the grieving experience. Lewis's book may well have had more influence as a popular guide to grief in the 1960s and even the 1970s than the works of psychiatric experts. Lewis's biographer, A. N. Wilson, considers it a book which consoled thousands of the bereaved: 'Lewis knew by instinct what is now a commonplace of bereavement counselling, that grief must be expressed and lived through'. As Wilson sees it, Lewis's life had been marred by his inability to express grief for his mother in 1908. The process of emotional healing was made possible by loving Joy, but it was 'in losing her that the essential work of healing mysteriously began'.[13]

Lewis's little book commenced life, soon after Joy's death, as an attempt to 'make a map of sorrow'—to describe his own experience of grief and 'get a little outside of it', even give it some cohesion. Lewis's letters to American friends late in 1960 explained that compiling the record was helpful 'as a defence against total collapse, a safety-valve'; but it failed to be a cohesive map of sorrow, because grief was like an ever-changing journey along an endless winding road, with a new landscape at every bend. It is significant that he felt more comfortable engaging in intimate exchanges with far-away Americans—as indeed he had with Joy herself— than with his Oxford and Cambridge companions. Lewis's book was divided into four sections of about fifteen pages each, approximating presumably to the passage of time, perhaps six weeks or so each. The four sections did not denote stages so much as changing features which involved substantial regression and repetition. Wilson sees the essay as having the quality of a good novel: 'in its shooting stabs of pain, its yelps of despair, its tears, its emotional zig-zagging...it was written from the heart'.[14]

Lewis opened the book with the memorable sentence, 'No one ever told me that grief felt so like fear...The same fluttering in the stomach, the same restlessness, the yawning'. At other times he felt as if he were concussed or inebriated, unable to concentrate or take in conversation. And yet the slightest effort seemed too much, except at his university work, where he seemed to operate automatically. Even in the early weeks Lewis experienced the conflict between the desire to escape from the horror of sorrow and the sense that he must deal with the grief as it came. He tried to reason with himself that love was only part of his life; he had other resources such as his scholarly work and would recover in time. But each such impulse was obliterated by 'a sudden jab of red-hot memory'.[15]

Lewis began his book because his need was desperate and little other emotional support seemed available, from colleagues or family, except for a few close friends and correspondents who had also suffered great loss. This reflected the cultural climate of the fifties and sixties. Lewis was perhaps also partly responsible, in that he had been emotionally inaccessible to his Oxford colleagues and friends, and had kept his personal life almost entirely to himself. The silence was compounded because his academic friends failed to share Lewis's bewitched view of Joy Gresham's intellectual capacity and personality. The early pages of Lewis's book noted his serious problem in communicating with others about his sorrow, which further discouraged him from expressing it:

An odd by-product of my loss is that I'm aware of being an embarrassment to everyone I meet. At work, at the club, in the street, I see people, as they approach me, trying to make up their minds whether they'll 'say something about it' or not. I hate it if they do, and if they don't. Some funk it altogether. R. has been avoiding me for a week...Perhaps the bereaved ought to be isolated in special settlements like lepers.[16]

This widespread embarrassment was noted in similar terms by Geoffrey Gorer only three years later. Joy's two boys were equally embarrassed: though they had lost a mother, they acted as if Lewis committed an indecency in trying to comfort them.

Throughout his grief Lewis was obsessed by memories of his past happiness with Joy, which were a double-edged sword, capable of hurting as they raised unwanted problems. He became increasingly aware that despite their happiness during Joy's terrible illness, they were essentially separate beings: 'I had my miseries, not hers'. While her death may have ended her own pain, it was 'the coming-of age of mine'. Moreover, he was consumed with fear that the insidious process of time and deterioration of memory would gradually change the real woman he had loved into a fading figment of his imagination.[17]

Such thoughts led inevitably to a more fundamental problem: 'Where is she now?' If she no longer inhabited a human body, she could never live in this world again. Well-wishers tried to reassure him that she was with God. This opened up an appalling struggle for Lewis as his grief profoundly affected his view of God and seemed to shatter the foundations of his personal and essentially conservative faith. If Joy was indeed with God, that made her equally 'incomprehensible and unimaginable'. That was no help at all, as he needed 'the old life, the jokes, the drinks, the arguments, the lovemaking'. Friends who recommended the consolations of religion did not understand that family reunions in heaven depicted in earthly terms had no scriptural foundation. He thought the spiritualists 'baited their hook' well with their inducements of earthly pleasures in heaven. But he had promised his wife to avoid the lures of the spiritualists: 'keep clear of Psychical Researchers'.[18]

In the course of the first two months or so Lewis took this agonizing meditation a stage further. He continued to believe in God, but his experience of loss was forcing him to question the evidence of God's goodness. Joy's suffering from cancer had been extreme, though she had dealt with appalling pain with great bravery. In his own anguish he feared that God was either cruel or unintelligible, and might hurt her as intolerably after death as before. Surely a God who had broken Joy's body on the wheel was a 'cosmic sadist'? God seemed to have slammed the door in Lewis's face: and yet he could not face the prospect that God did not exist at all.[19] He tortured himself with unanswerable questions and rebuked himself for presuming to criticize God. His contrition was several times followed by further anger and agonized questioning about the meaning of death and the nature of God. He worried that he would have been less shattered by Joy's death had his faith been stronger. Perhaps he had to accept that human beings must endure intense suffering and not seek for meaning.[20]

There is an echo here of Geoffrey Bickersteth's crisis of faith on the loss of his son.

But then, in the third month of his ordeal, Lewis unexpectedly woke up one morning to find 'my heart was lighter...I find I can now believe again'. He had an unusually good night's sleep and the sun was shining. Suddenly he had a mystical experience of his wife's presence: it was deeply intimate and yet not at all emotional, as if she survived as 'pure intelligence'. It was an instantaneous, convincing impression. Though Joy's bodily presence was withdrawn, he could still love her essence, as 'she seems to meet me everywhere'. He no longer worried that his memory of Joy would become false.[21]

Lewis began to wonder why no one had ever explained that grief was like this. The answer, of course, was that Lewis was experiencing bereavement during a period of extreme cultural reticence: social scientists were only just starting to draw the 'map of sorrow' which he sought, and his own account would be a guide to others. He was starting to come to terms with the wayward nature of bereavement as he again came face to face with its awful reality: 'Tonight all the hells of young grief have opened again; the mad words, the bitter resentment, the fluttering in the stomach, the nightmare unreality, the wallowed-in tears. For in grief nothing "stays put". One keeps on emerging from a phase, but it always recurs. Round and round'.[22]

And so the cycle continued, but when Lewis emerged from his latest descent into 'the hells of young grief', he started the final manuscript volume of his book. Now he described the process which Freud and Lindemann had earlier depicted as a fundamental conflict between a desire to return to the past life with the dead loved one, and the need to build a new life without her. Psychiatrist Colin Murray Parkes subsequently depicted it as gradually relinquishing one set of assumptions about the world and developing another.

Lewis tried to formulate practical ways to keep his marriage alive, whilst continuing with his earthly life without Joy by his side. He tired himself out with long walks and one day revisited his old bachelor haunts: 'every horizon, every stile or clump of trees, summoned me into a past kind of happiness, my pre- [Joy] happiness. But the invitation seemed to me horrible'. To return to such an insipid past would be the worst fate of all: his years of love and marriage would then appear no more than an unreal 'charming episode', and Joy would 'die to me a second time'.[23]

To escape the torment of sorrow seemed to involve a betrayal of Lewis's love for Joy, forcing him to abandon her for ever. This he was not willing to do. But perhaps it was not necessary to release himself from bondage to his lost loved one in order to recover, as the psychiatrists recommended. He sought instead to prolong the essence of their married love by conceptualizing the problem differently: for all lovers, the necessary pain of bereavement should be a universal part of married love, one of its phases rather than its termination. It would still hurt, but it would preserve his marriage: 'and the more joy there can be in the marriage between dead and living, the better'.[24] This was Lewis's personal Christian version of the concept of continuing bonds between the dead and the living.

The final pages of Lewis's book record the success of his search for personal meaning and continuity in 'the marriage between dead and living'. It involved a struggle to retrieve his own personal identity while remaining loyal to Joy and his marriage. It was a fundamental personal crisis. He had to find a way to retain a kind of happiness, and a meaningful existence while keeping faith with both Joy and God. At last he realized it was possible to sustain a relationship with both. 'Joy and all the dead are like God. In that respect loving her has become, in its measure, like loving Him'. Thus his relationship with his wife became part of his broader spiritual communion with God. Lewis's book ended with a reference back to the power of his mystical experience of his wife's presence: 'it was quite incredibly unemotional. Just the impression of her *mind* momentarily facing my own ... Not at all like a rapturous reunion of lovers ... No sense of joy or sorrow. No love even'. It was enough, and he believed that he would understand one day. And he would remember Joy's last words on her deathbed: 'I am at peace with God'.[25] Lewis survived his wife only by three years, dying in 1963, his faith intact. His final years at Cambridge seem to have been fairly contented, but in his last year he suffered badly from the pain of prostate cancer and died of a heart attack.

Joy's death inevitably caused Lewis to think more deeply about the meaning of death as well as grief, and to lament the decline of Christian leadership in these key areas of life. His voluminous correspondence to friends and fans around the world reveals that he had rarely mentioned death before Joy died. It is a reflection on the profound silence of the culture of death in the 1950s and 1960s that even C. S. Lewis, as a celebrated Christian writer, had seen no need before his own crisis to explain the meaning of death in his books, as he had interpreted the problem of pain. When Edward T. Dell, editor of the *Episcopalian*, in 1961 invited Lewis to write an article or book on 'Christian Death', he declined, with the comment that Christians had lost much of their rich heritage in relation to death: 'Death is either: 1. unmentionable and faced stoically or 2. a hideous enemy against whom we frantically pray and wage unreasonable medical battles'.[26]

Lewis reverted to this theme when he and his friend, Mary Willis Shelburne, an American poet, were both close to death in 1963. He continued to wonder 'why the doctors inflict such torture to delay what cannot in any case be very long delayed. Or why God does!' Lewis regretted the tedium of dying, the need for dozens of blood transfusions, and the inability to sleep properly. But in old age, natural death held no real terror for him, as death was the 'friend and deliverer' to those who had led a good Christian life. 'There are better things ahead than we leave behind'.[27]

In earlier years Lewis had also been reticent in answering his many readers' enquiries about the nature of heaven and hell. He would define hell only as 'the working out of the soul's evil' or what lost souls miss. He evaded definition of heaven by commenting that it could not be imagined from earth, though he admitted that 'Heaven is leisure...But I picture it pretty vigorous too'. But he attempted more detailed responses to the many questions from bereaved people about the presence of spirits of the dead hovering about the deceased. On the death of his friend Charles Williams in 1945 he confessed to Florence, Charles's widow, that Charles seemed 'in some undefinable way to be all around us now', causing his own faith in the afterlife to be strengthened. He acknowledged to another friend, ten years later, that the spirit of a dead person could remain active, especially in the early weeks or months after the death: and those spirits might even do more good for their loved ones from the afterlife. He confessed in 1959 to having twice known, after a death, 'a strange excited (but utterly un-spooky) sense of the person's presence all about me'—though he admitted it might be pure hallucination, and it usually disappeared after a few weeks.[28]

The first edition of Lewis's remarkable book on his grief was published anonymously and sold only 1,300 copies. But after his early death in 1963, aged only 65, it was published under his name and rapidly became a bestseller. Quintin Hogg, Baron Hailsham, was devastated by his wife's death in a riding accident in 1978. Years later he admitted that there was no consolation on the loss of a wife, but that Lewis's book described exactly what Hailsham felt. Kind people had written suggesting that his Christian faith must provide consolation; but Hailsham agreed with Lewis that religion was not an anaesthetic—it simply helped the universe make sense. He also shared Lewis's view that the bereaved cannot fight grief, just simply suffer it: the agony was not indefinite provided one did not try to keep a stiff upper lip.[29]

Colin Murray Parkes drew strongly on Lewis's eloquent narrative in his own work in the 1970s. He quoted Lewis's evocative prose to illustrate the symptoms of grief, such as searching and anger, to highlight themes in his BBC lectures on bereavement in 1976. In the early 1970s Parkes was at least acknowledging the continuing influence of religion in relation to death and grief.[30] He was also implicitly recognizing the enormous popular enthusiasm for Lewis's books on religious themes, including his *A Grief Observed*.

# The Contribution of Colin Murray Parkes to Bereavement Theory

Peter Marris's analysis of widows' responses to bereavement in the East End of London in the 1950s was largely confirmed, though modified and developed, by the eminent psychiatrists Colin Murray Parkes and John Bowlby. They produced some of their most important work in the 1960s and 1970s when the culture of death avoidance was still powerful. The psychiatrist Margaret Stroebe has described Parkes as a leading expert in the field of bereavement, to which he has made an outstanding contribution. His classic 1972 book, *Bereavement: Studies of Grief in Adult Life*, provided an analytical framework of the symptoms of grief, drawn from his own empirical research and clinical experience. It was a unique and pioneering account in 1972, when so little had been published: twenty-five years later Stroebe believed it had stood the test of time, with a continuing appeal to general as well as specialist readers.[31]

In two recent essays Margaret Stroebe has teased out the enmeshed contribution of Parkes and Bowlby to bereavement theory. Parkes's 'symptomatology framework' was deeply influenced by Bowlby's attachment theory, developed initially in the 1950s, which argued that young children who were deprived of good maternal care could become incapable of making bonds of affection in the future. There was no suggestion in Bowlby's early work that bereavement responses might also be affected. However, Parkes collaborated closely with Bowlby for years and was largely responsible for extending Bowlby's attachment theory into bereavement. A child deprived of affection might also delay in confronting the reality of loss after bereavement, which was the most extreme form of relationship deprivation. Bowlby's own publication of *Loss* in 1980 came eight years after Parkes's *Bereavement*, and acknowledged his debt as well as their collaboration. Stroebe argues that Bowlby's attachment theory rescued bereavement research from the dominance of Freud and the limitations of psychoanalysis for understanding normal grief.[32]

Parkes himself noted that the theories of the English pioneers—Bowlby, Marris, Gorer, and his own—complemented and reinforced each other, and built empirically upon the actual experience of bereaved people. His own early research included a study of the experience of twenty-two London widows who were interviewed five times during their first year of bereavement in the late 1960s. They were asked about physical and psychological symptoms. Various passive responses were oriented towards the dead husband and the past, including preoccupation with thoughts of reunion, alternated with painful pining. But a second type of response was more active and self-preoccupied, as the bereaved 'angrily turns to face a potentially hostile world'.[33] The results of this and other studies were used throughout Parkes's 1972 book, *Bereavement*, to illustrate the various symptoms of grief at length—including alarm, searching, anger, guilt, and 'gaining a new identity'.

Like Peter Marris a decade earlier, Parkes understood the need to educate the community about bereavement and he used the BBC *Horizon* programme to achieve this in September 1976. Parkes gave several lectures which distilled the chief features of his 1972 *Bereavement* text, and disseminated it to a wider audience. Interspersed with Parkes's commentary were interviews with bereaved people and powerful extracts from C. S. Lewis's book, *A Grief Observed*, to demonstrate the range of deep emotions and the physical and psychological symptoms of grief.[34]

Parkes's BBC lectures in 1976 are valuable in highlighting those aspects of his work he considered most important and helpful to an audience which was still woefully ignorant about bereavement. Parkes made several references to the challenges of grief in a society which tried to avoid dealing directly with death. There was still 'a certain stigma attached to bereavement', even a sense of the bereaved as 'untouchable'. In the 1970s people could reach late middle age without experiencing death: it was almost as if 'science had abolished death, and pushed it to the end of life'. Parkes spoke of families he knew where all members thought they should maintain a 'stiff upper lip' the whole time: if anyone started to cry they were told to cheer up and pull themselves together: 'We try to jolly a person along, get them out of it, distract them at all costs so that they don't have a chance to grieve'. He believed children and young people might need to be taught about death.[35]

Parkes also warned listeners of the potential damage caused by seeking to evade the pain or embarrassment of grief. He thought that avoidance of grief was probably responsible for much of the physical and psychological illness among bereaved people: 'People who show the least amount of grief, who keep a stiff upper lip, behave extremely well in social terms during the first few weeks of bereavement, are the ones who are most likely to break down [later]'. It helped to share grief with family and friends, who should allow the bereaved to grieve, supporting them and giving practical help.[36]

Parkes took his BBC audience in 1976 briefly through the various phases of grieving which, he emphasized, were not a neat progression of stages: they overlapped, jumped back and forth, and varied significantly between individuals. In this he was closer to C. S. Lewis's perspective than to the more rigid stage theory of grief. He also explained his central concept of 'psycho-social transitions' whereby the bereaved would need to slowly relinquish one set of assumptions about the world and develop another: 'grief is a painful process of change, by which someone gradually gives up one world, and enters another'. The first phase of grief usually involved shock, numbness, and disbelief, most obvious when death was sudden and unexpected. Parkes described the second phase as one of intense yearning for the lost loved one, marked by very painful physical and emotional pangs of grief. The third phase overlapped with the second, but depression and apathy were likely to increase, while yearning for the deceased was reduced. During this period the struggle between the world of the lost past and the necessary future was most pronounced. The speed of moving through to the fourth phase of life's reorganization depended on individual circumstances and personality. It was sometimes easier to move on when children were involved, or a new relationship or a good job offered motivation.[37]

The pioneering work of Parkes, Marris, and Gorer responded to an earlier historical period with a different cultural and emotional climate, when most people found it harder to express feelings and when society discouraged discussion of death and loss. The theories developed since the 1970s have responded to broader changes in the cultural, intellectual, and social climate which have inspired greater freedom of emotional expression. Such change was encouraged by the international popularity of Elisabeth Kubler-Ross's 1969 book, *On Death and Dying*. The charismatic American psychiatrist argued that it was beneficial to the dying and to the bereaved to express their feelings openly; and that the process of grieving was a normal part of a tough experience. It was Kubler-Ross, rather than the earlier psychiatrists, who developed the overly simplistic five-stage model of dying, which has since been influential in self-help manuals in extending the framework to bereavement.[38]

During the last twenty-five years a substantial theoretical literature on grief has been published by social scientists, in a field which has become far more complex and sophisticated: as Parkes correctly notes, 'the multiplicity of view points...may create a confusion'.[39] This theoretical literature is beyond the time frame of my book, but a few points may suffice here to relate it in general terms to the earlier period. Recent experts have tended to emphasize the flexibility and the diversity of individual responses to sorrow, and the possibility that men and women may grieve in different ways. In particular, they argue that the final stage of 'acceptance' of death had sometimes been interpreted too rigidly to mean 'closure' or detachment from the dead person. The psychiatrists Margaret and Wolfgang Stroebe and Henk Schut have suggested that a complex multidimensional approach to grief is needed since its manifestations vary in different cultures, between different individuals, and over time. Some bereaved people cope by clinging to memories of the deceased, whereas others need some distraction. By 1999 Margaret Stroebe and Henk Schut developed the useful 'dual process model' of coping with bereavement. They suggested that healthy adaptation required oscillation between dwelling on the loss, on the one hand, and dealing with its consequences on the other—such as coping with finances and making new relationships. A balance is needed.[40]

It is rare for sociologists or psychiatrists in England today to give much acknowledgement either to C. S. Lewis's work or to the role of religion in dealing with death and grief. Even in his 1976 BBC lectures Parkes admitted that 'most of us' have abandoned religion and its rituals of mourning which had earlier helped to give meaning to death and loss.[41] By 1986 Parkes's new introduction to the third edition of his book, *Bereavement*, noted: 'The systems of religious ritual and belief, which formerly provided guidance and explanation at times of death and bereavement, have lost credibility in a world which is changing so rapidly that all traditional ideas are suspect'. This stark observation had not been included in his 1972 edition. In recent years, psychiatrists and sociologists have usually explained that the increasing secularization of western society makes religious faith less relevant and less consoling in bereavement.[42] They are also more likely to comment that medicine and science, rather than religion, now help to provide the answers to fundamental questions about death and bereavement. Or, like Clive Seale, they suggest that psychological discourse now offers an alternative script about the meaning of death, equating the rituals of psychotherapy with those of the church.[43] However, historians and others have in recent years questioned such premature assumptions as we shall see in the Epilogue.

# Epilogue: Change and Continuity since the 1970s

In 1965 Geoffrey Gorer expressed concern that the cultural prescription of silent grief had been internalized by so many people since the Second World War, and was reinforced by the long-term decline in traditional death rituals. He might well have approved some developments from the late 1970s, such as the major contribution of palliative care, the revival of expressive grieving, and the green burial movement, though perhaps not roadside memorials. Sadly, there has been no successor to Gorer to update his pioneering study. My aim in this Epilogue is not to attempt a short history of death and loss in the decades after 1970, which is beyond the scope of my book, but to explore a few key themes of contemporary interest with resonances from my earlier history, reflecting change as well as continuity.

## Death and Dying: Ageing, Medicine, and Demography

The role of medicine in the twentieth-century history of death was increasingly significant, especially after the advent of the sulphonamide drugs from the 1930s. Death rates of infants, young children, and mothers in childbirth were dramatically reduced, as was mortality from infectious diseases. But once doctors increased their capacity to cure, the death of a patient could seem to represent medical failure. Moreover, terminal illness gradually moved from the care of female family members at home to the control of mainly male doctors in hospitals dedicated to saving lives rather than managing deaths. The medicalization and hospitalization of death reinforced the culture of death avoidance in the thirty years after the Second World War. In response, the hospice movement and the euthanasia campaign both championed the dying patient, but their proposals for change were very different.

Improved patterns of life expectancy and reductions in infectious diseases were major drivers of change in the experiences of death in the later twentieth century. Much of this change was positive. Life expectancy in the 1890s of 44 for men and 47 for women, rose to 75 and 80 respectively a hundred years later. Clive Seale explains that this concentrates contemporary experience of death among older people: 'in 1997 83% of deaths in the UK occurred to people aged over 65, compared to a figure of 24.5% in the years 1900–1902'. There was also a continuing decline in infectious diseases such as tuberculosis, influenza, and diphtheria which reduced the death rates of people aged under 65. But there was a negative side to this medical balance sheet. Infectious diseases were replaced by degenerative diseases as the major killers, notably cancer, heart disease, and stroke. Consequently death became largely the monopoly of the elderly, who more often died slowly at older ages from chronic and debilitating diseases. The growing numbers of frail elderly people meant that about one-fifth of the cost of hospital services was devoted to terminal care by 1986.[1]

In their 1996 book, *A Good Death,* Michael Young and Lesley Cullen lamented the increase in long-drawn-out deaths due to the rise in the number of frail people over 80 who suffered from chronic rather than acute illnesses. Highly technical and specialized modern medicine could now prolong people's lives in conditions of extreme pain: 'A stock nightmare of modern times is of doctors in possession of the power to keep us alive when our bodies are at least partly dead, trussed up with tubes'. Conditions for dying patients in National Health Service hospitals in the late twentieth century were usually much improved on those in the 1950s and 1960s, especially where palliative care principles were applied, but they could still be challenging. It was still common practice in the 1990s to isolate people to die alone in side wards. However, if public hospitals could still be unpleasant places to die, at least doctors were making more effort to communicate with patients. Up to about 1970 most doctors gave the real diagnosis to the family rather than to the patient, as we saw in the case of Geoffrey Gorer's brother. The conspiracy of silence around the patient mirrored the community's attitude to death and dying. A gradual change in attitude occurred in the 1970s and 1980s, influenced by the hospice movement and the campaigns of Cicely Saunders and Elisabeth Kubler-Ross for greater openness about dying.[2]

By the late 1980s about 60 per cent of all deaths in Britain took place in hospital, only 25 per cent at home, and just 3.5 per cent in hospices (the remainder in a variety of locations including nursing homes).[3] Looking more closely at cancer patients, Young and Cullen observe that in 1994 51 per cent died in National Health Service hospitals, 18 per cent in hospices, and 6 per cent in old people's homes and elsewhere: only 25 per cent died at home, though more than half would prefer to do so. Their investigation of twelve dying people from the East End of London, referred to them by St Joseph's hospice between 1988 and 1992, explained why only 25 per cent died at home. Even with the help of an excellent home care team, care of the dying at home was highly stressful for the family. Most carers were still women, but fewer were available given the decline in family size, its geographical dispersal, and women's need for employment in the work-force. Some dying patients, especially older widows, lived alone and did not have a domiciliary option. Moreover, home care was complicated by the uncertainty about the trajectory of the cancer and the likely time of death.[4]

For most frail old people who died in the later twentieth century, the experience of dying was generally far better than in the grim former workhouses described by Townsend in *The Last Refuge*.[5] As we have seen, the hospice and palliative care movement had since made a remarkable contribution to improving the care of the dying, aiming to deal effectively with suffering that was emotional and spiritual as well as physical. However, in England and Wales in 1987, deaths from cancer, the chief focus of palliative care, accounted for only 27 per cent of all deaths, compared with 41 per cent from diseases of the circulatory system, including strokes and heart attacks. There have been many advocates for the extension of specialist palliative care services to patients dying from other causes, especially chronic non-malignant conditions, where conventional care is inadequate. But there are several major obstacles, not least the need for a massive increase in government funding.[6]

If specialist palliative care is usually thought to give the best care of the dying since the 1970s, private nursing homes and community residential homes are sometimes seen as the worst. It was estimated in 1981 that a quarter of all people over 85 lived in such homes, where between a third and a quarter of residents were expected to die every year.[7] Since many deaths in England now take place in extreme old age, accompanied by debility and dementia, many die in nursing homes or hospitals because they have no family to care for them or because they need specialist nursing care. Efforts have been made to keep older people in their homes in the community but, as the population aged, the number of frail aged in residential care increased by over 40 per cent between 1975 and 1994. Nursing home provision rose as National Health Service hospital beds for the aged were reduced and as government subsidies for aged homes in the 1980s encouraged this shift.[8]

As Allan Kellehear observes, 'Dying from old age with an assortment of serious, disabling and chronic diseases seems to be a difficult affair across all cultures, and dying in hospital and nursing home settings is a formidable and desperate picture even today'.[9] Jennifer Hockey's chilling ethnographic account of *Experiences of Death,* published in 1990, described her nine months' fieldwork in a residential home for the elderly, most of whom were over 80. Within ten months of her arrival about 25 per cent had died: 'The residential home is therefore a dying space concerned primarily with the slow process of deterioration'. As one resident explained, no one mentioned dying—they were expected to deceive themselves and others by silence about death, ignoring the slow demise of people around them. Residents lived in an 'unchanging, depersonalised environment' cut off from the outside world. The only trained nurse was the matron, who managed the transition of failing residents from the main section of the home still dedicated to life, to the 'frail' corridor leading to the sick bays, death, and the morgue. The failing residents were isolated, to separate life from death and ensure that death was 'distanced and disguised'.[10] This is the converse of the hospice policy of bringing life and death together.

## Expressive and Gendered Grieving Since the 1970s

A major change since the 1970s has been the revival of expressive grieving, led principally by middle-class women. This is a striking reversal of the process over the previous fifty years whereby women tended to follow men's more constrained pattern of grieving. Callum Brown argues that

Christianity still pervaded English public culture up to the 1950s and women maintained the traditional values of piety, home, and family. But this was transformed by the sixties' counter-culture and the women's movement, which encouraged women to reject both the domestic ideology and the churches.[11] This change in English cultural norms began in the 1960s, sometimes called the 'counter-culture' or the 'expressive revolution'. Significant changes in the cultural, intellectual, and social climate encouraged more liberal attitudes and greater freedom of emotional expression, the latter affecting women more than men. A shift in ideas, attitudes, and modes of behaviour included a new receptiveness to more permissive ideas from the United States, including a culture of protest and freedom of self-expression. In the 1960s the traditional social structures were threatened by the legalization of abortion and homosexuality, combined with challenges from women's liberation, student rebellion, and a youth culture fuelled by popular music and drugs.

The counter-culture of the 1960s chiefly inspired a minority of radicals, but some of their values were incorporated into mainstream culture in the next two decades. This transformation was also stimulated by reforms in higher education in the 1960s, with many more young people entering the new universities and the upgraded technical colleges. Sociologist Bernice Martin argues that the middle-class expressive and caring professions in the arts, education, and the mass media were most strongly affected, and women more than men. While the process was most advanced within the 'expressive professions', it also influenced broader cultural assumptions and values. Some of the churches' former functions in pastoral care and education were taken over by secular caring professionals and psychiatrists. Bereavement therapy sometimes replaced the pastoral functions of the churches, with secular psychology displacing religion.[12]

Sociologist Tony Walter argues that men and women in English culture tend to grieve in different ways, with women more inclined to be emotionally expressive and men to contain their feelings. He suggests that the way people grieve may reflect their natural ways of coping with stress: women prefer social support and talking through their feelings, whereas men prefer to deal primarily with the practical problems. This may explain why so many bereavement counsellors and their clients are women, while the care they offer focuses on the expression of feelings. Expressive grieving became more common from the 1970s, encouraged by the expansion of the popular bereavement counselling movement. CRUSE counsellors for widows focus on the individual, working emotionally through the stages of grief in one-to-one sessions or in groups, and moving to resolution. By contrast, mutual help groups such as Compassionate Friends for bereaved parents see themselves as communities in which common experiences of loss can best be shared with others suffering in the same way.[13]

The oral testimony of Val Hazel offers an insight into such gendered differences in grieving, as she describes the support she found in a mutual help group after her 9-year-old son Jeff died from a rare brain tumour in 1976. After the funeral Val found that people outside the family tried to avoid her, because they didn't know what to say and were afraid they would make her cry. They seemed to think she should stay at home to grieve, and she had to approach them rather than the reverse: they looked at her oddly, not realizing that 'crying is a very healthy part of grief'. Val needed to talk about Jeff and she found the ideal outlet for her feelings in talking to other parents she had met at St Bartholomew's Hospital, whose children had also died. She was in touch with many such parents 'all in the same boat... And we just rang each other and we were talking about the children endlessly. And it wasn't all doom and gloom'. This informal mutual help group was invaluable because other people who had suffered in the same way could sometimes help more than family or friends. Val tended to show a brave face to the outside world, not revealing her real feelings. Her husband John found bereavement particularly challenging because he internalized his emotions: 'he's a very quiet person anyway who does hide his feelings. And I think he found it extremely difficult, not being able to let go of his feelings'. He didn't join her in talking to other parents at Barts Hospital, sharing the reluctance of many men to attend mutual help groups.[14]

Though many more people have expressed their sorrow openly in England since the 1970s, the influence and geographical spread of expressive grieving should not be overstated. Those affected are more likely to be educated middle-class people, particularly women, from the cities, large towns, and the south. Tony Walter suggests that the majority of the English seem still to be stoical and reserved, reluctant to express grief openly, especially in public, though they may be deeply affected by loss. He believes there is still, for many people, 'a culturally accepted norm for proper grief in (white mainstream) Britain. This is that you should feel deeply about your loss... but you should affirm the cultural value of stoicism and show consideration for others by not actually expressing your feelings in their presence'.[15]

Geoffrey Gorer's geographical map of ways of death in 1963 continues to have resonance in recent decades. White working-class families are more likely to have retained vestiges of their traditional ways of mourning, at least up to the early 1970s. They are more likely to live in the north, the Celtic fringe, and rural areas. The pace of working-class change since the 1970s depends on many variables, such as age, education, affluence, gender, religion, and personality, and we can be sure that diversity continues. Gorer would doubtless have approved the increased willingness to express sorrow openly, while regretting that there were still too few formal rituals to guide behaviour.

In the last twenty years more emphasis has been placed on diversity in grieving and far less on prescriptive stages and time limits. In 1993 psychiatrist Paul Rosenblatt observed that grief is shaped by its social context: 'cultures differ widely in defining death and in defining what is an appropriate expression of grief'.[16] A number of experts over the last two decades have suggested that people may naturally show their sorrow in a variety of ways, and that patterns of behaviour may change over time and across gender and different cultures. Margaret Stroebe and Henk Schut proposed in 1999 that grief is not a simple universal process with a succession of fixed stages. Instead healthy oscillation is needed, between dwelling on the death, the grief, and the emotions on the one hand, and dealing with the practical consequences on the other.[17] This may perhaps be seen as a natural development from Colin Murray Parkes's 'psycho-social transitions'.

## Continuities: Religion, Spirituality, and Continuing Bonds

Some sociologists have argued that the gradual secularization of society since the eighteenth century would cause an inevitable decline of religion in modern society under the combined impact of science, Enlightenment ideas, industrialization, and urbanization. Historians have resisted this hypothesis, not least because its link between modernity and religious decline was weak and over-simplified. It did not explain the strength of religion in nineteenth-century Britain during the Industrial Revolution, nor in the United States in the twentieth century. Moreover, secularization theory could not account for the robustness of religion in England up to the 1960s, and its survival thereafter, albeit in weakened form.

John Wolffe and Adrian Hastings have advanced a strong case for the survival of religion in England up to the 1960s, with a relatively high level of churchgoing, and Christianity as an integral part of community identity and public culture. Indeed there was a renewal of Protestant religious culture and support between the 1940s and early 1960s, with a revival among Catholics from the 1960s. Thereafter there was a sharp decline in both relative and absolute numbers of church members of the Methodist Churches and the Church of England, which were particularly challenged by the departure of many women, the core of their congregations. But there were several compensating forces. The Church of England, as the national church, retained cultural and emotional links with many who were not regular churchgoers, while the Catholic Church increased its numbers through immigration from Eastern Europe. The evangelical charismatic wing of the Church of England gained members through its appeal to youth and even more from the influx of committed Christians from Africa and the Caribbean. The Church of England also made efforts to change with the times by introducing the ordination of women.[18]

Since 1918 the Protestant churches in England have offered less comfort and spiritual leadership in the face of death than they did in the nineteenth century. There was inadequate church leadership or pastoral guidance on the Christian meaning of death outside the Catholic Church. There is some justification for the argument that the church allowed leadership on death and loss to shift to medicine and psychology.[19] Even C. S. Lewis, a prolific writer on Christian doctrine, had little to say about death and grief in his correspondence and his popular books, until forced to confront his wife's death in 1960. Individuals were increasingly obliged to worry about their own salvation and to find their own meanings in death and loss.

Nevertheless, the Christian churches have survived in England and continue to offer some comfort to the dying and the bereaved, particularly the Catholic Church. Politician Clare Short remembered her father's death in old age. Her parents were practising Catholics, but her own faith had lapsed. 'I broadly think that humanity's search for God and religion is a searching for goodness, for a moral order in life'. She was 'brought up as a Catholic' and found great comfort in its deeply familiar rituals, prayers, and hymns: 'so Heaven knows what happens to people like us who don't believe in God'. The whole family came for her father's wake, to talk about his life and drink some whisky. For the next few days they planned the details of a Catholic funeral, with intense debates about favourite prayers. The rituals were immensely important to them all, including the fact that all seven children carried their father's coffin. Clare Short shared Gorer's concern that unbelievers in society lacked such beautiful and helpful rituals.[20]

From the 1970s a multicultural society developed in England as mass immigration brought large numbers of Muslims, Hindus, Sikhs, and Buddhists to the country. The growth of Islam affected the north and midlands strongly: a town like Blackburn in Lancashire had twenty-six mosques. These immigrants brought with them their own distinctive rituals and ways of dealing with death and grief. Christianity within England was thus increasingly challenged by religious pluralism as well as by secularism. Younger New Age enthusiasts selected their beliefs and rituals from any religion which suited them, but they believed strongly in reincarnation and saw death as a significant spiritual transition. They insisted on the spiritual importance of the deathbed and the justification of a future life by a good life on earth, as in earlier Christianity. They also devised their own funeral rituals.[21]

John Wolffe shows that church membership statistics substantially underestimated Christian folk religion—the popular belief in God of many people who rarely attended church but still considered themselves Christian. Opinion polls conducted in 1947 and 1982 recorded that 84 per cent believed in some kind of god in 1947 and this had only fallen to 73 per cent by 1982. In 2000 many people with no regular connection with the churches and an informal set of beliefs could still identify as believers in God and as Christians. Older people might have attended Sunday school and still remember hymns and Bible passages. The rates of nominal identification with religion remained quite high: in 1974 41.6 per cent of an English sample still saw themselves as Church of England, and religious ceremonies still followed most deaths.[22]

Folk religion was likely to have survived for longer in rural areas and in isolated villages like Staithes in Yorkshire, as we saw earlier. In 1996 sociologists Michael Young and Lesley Cullen interviewed East Londoners with terminal cancer and their carers, who suggested another dimension to folk religion. Most interviewees considered themselves attached to a church, chiefly Anglican and Catholic, but with one or two Jews, Muslims, and agnostics. Most of them believed in an ill-defined afterlife, which was not drawn directly from the Bible or sanctioned by the teaching of their church: its prime feature was a reunion with their dead loved ones. Beliefs in ghosts and spirits of the dead were common and could bring considerable comfort, especially to the elderly, who had a sense of their dead as a real presence in their lives, seen vividly in familiar places.[23]

But there was nothing new in the late twentieth century about the belief in such continuing bonds with the dead. As I noted in *Death in the Victorian Family*, it was common for bereaved people in the nineteenth century to feel a powerful sense of their deceased loved ones close to them in a favourite spot, and the survivors felt free to comment on the phenomenon. During and after the Great War, spiritualism flourished and belief in the supernatural was pervasive: the spirits of the dead were reported as widely experienced in the trenches and elsewhere. In the course of this book I have mentioned many examples of such private experiences of the presence of the dead, usually noted in diaries and occasionally in private letters to close friends. This sense of contact with the dead was more often kept private from the 1940s in case it seemed absurd, even pathological, as containment of the emotions was increasingly considered the appropriate way to grieve. The social silences surrounding such 'hallucinations' were reinforced by the emphasis of some earlier psychiatrists on the need for the bereaved to detach themselves emotionally from the dead and move on to a new life.

In 1971 W. Dewi Rees interviewed 227 widows and sixty-six widowers in mid-Wales and found that nearly half experienced a sense of the presence of their dead spouse, mostly during the first ten years of widowhood. These experiences increased with the age of the bereaved and the length of marriage; it was unusual for them to be disclosed to family or friends. One in ten spoke to the dead spouse and a few had the sense of being touched by the deceased. They usually kept these occurrences secret because they feared they might upset relatives or attract ridicule. Most found the experiences helpful. Rees's findings were similar to those in Peter Marris's earlier 1958 study of seventy-two young widows in East London, where 50 per cent had such experiences, which Rees concluded were normal and common, unconnected with depression or illness.[24]

More recently, Glennys Howarth and Tony Walter have written at length on such 'continuing bonds'. They stress that people grieve differently, and that many people wish to preserve continuity in their lives by talking and thinking about their dead, rather than cutting emotional ties. Memories, anniversaries, photographs, music, dreams, and conversations are all meaningful ways to preserve the memory of the dead. Others visit the grave in the cemetery to talk with their dead loved ones, a traditional form of 'continuing bonds' with a long history. Thus many people now more overtly seek to keep their dead alive and to share their memories.[25]

Unbelievers over the centuries have developed a rather different way of remembering their dead, sometimes described as collective immortality. Agnostics and atheists had long placed an emphasis on the value of memory as a prime consolation in the absence of religious faith and the loss of personal immortality in an afterlife. Intellectuals and unbelievers redefined the meaning of immortality in the eighteenth century with the idea that the memory of the virtues and contribution of the dead might inspire future generations. These ideas were developed by Enlightenment thinkers in the eighteenth century and by Auguste Comte and the Positivists in nineteenth-century France. Such ideas won support in nineteenth century England from Frederic Harrison, who wrote with enthusiasm in 1877: 'The highest part of ourselves, the abiding part of us, passes into other lives and continues to live in other lives'.[26] This concept has appealed to many unbelievers and humanists, including George Eliot, whose famous poem has been read aloud at many humanist funerals, including her own:

> Oh! May I join the choir invisible
> Of those immortal dead who live again
> In minds made better by their presence
> In thoughts sublime that pierce the night like stars.

After her father's death Clare Short believed that in a sense he still lived: 'I do believe we're all immortal in the sense that every single human being who's ever lived on this planet has left reverberations behind in other people's memories'.[27]

## Death, Mourning Rituals, and Green Burials

In 1965 Geoffrey Gorer expressed the hope that English people would create meaningful secular rituals to guide their behaviour in grief and offer comfort. But Gorer's own failure to suggest appropriate rituals underscored the difficulty of the task, especially as it meant challenging older traditions and entrenched interests. Young and Cullen described an

East London working-class culture in 1996 still in many ways unfriendly to death and bereavement: 'Fear of death, the uncertainty of how to deal with it, and embarrassment about what to say, tells against the very sympathy which the bereaved need so badly . . . In an individualistic society, people are left to get on with their grief work largely on their own'. The wider community was still not supportive of the bereaved in East London in the 1990s, with some bereaved people still inclined to hide their sorrow to 'show the proper spirit'. People might make an effort as friends were dying and at the death, but after the funeral their support disappeared into 'an uneasy silence and awkward shuffling'. Moreover, Young and Cullen echoed Gorer's 1965 critique of the absence of recognized rituals after the funeral:

> The experience [of death and dying] is not recognised, not supported and not harnessed effectively to any sort of renewal of society by a supporting body of ritual and observance. In this distancing from notions of the afterlife and by the threadbareness of the ritual with which it surrounds death, modern society is very much the exception among the general run of societies, historically and even contemporaneously.[28]

Young and Cullen felt most churches failed in this respect, although they arguably should have excluded from this criticism the Catholic Church, orthodox Jews, and some of the faiths of recent immigrants. Most of the bereaved, in their view, were often left to deal with shock and sorrow alone and in private in the months following family deaths. However, they acknowledged that in the Celtic fringe and rural areas of England, and the north of Scotland, many of the older traditions around death survived into the later twentieth century, as in Staithes.[29]

As I noted in an earlier chapter, though cremation numbers exceeded burials by 1967 and cremation was likely to remain the choice of most people, it was still subject to criticism. It was not easy to meet Gorer's challenge to evolve helpful and appropriate secular rituals at cremations, particularly as they had to combine a spiritual ritual with an industrial furnace. Cremations often fail to meet the needs of both secular and religious mourners, and are sometimes experienced as factories with conveyor belts, offering little in the way of spiritual meaning.

In 1997 Bernard Smale criticized commercial funerals as tawdry, expensive, and lacking sensitivity to the practical and social needs of individual bereaved people. In his view they were often miserable affairs, lacking in dignity, comfort, or appropriate symbolism; funeral directors were more concerned to exploit a lucrative market for profits and prestige than to tailor funerals to individual needs and to celebrate the life of the deceased. Further, in earlier decades small family funeral firms had been increasingly taken over by large multinational companies with even more commercial focus. Such criticisms stimulated change. Michael Young and others established the National Funerals College in 1996 as a pressure group to encourage reforms. They created 'The Dead Citizens' Charter' to promote the rights of the individual consumer, provide information about funeral choice, and support local independent family businesses. The Natural Death Centre was also established in the 1990s in North London as an educational charity and pressure group to encourage do-it-yourself funerals, woodland burials, and secular ceremonies to celebrate the life of the deceased.[30] While the National Funeral College, do-it-yourself funerals, and funeral supermarkets offer change and choice, so far they involve only a small proportion of the population.

However, there is growing enthusiasm for celebrating the life of the deceased in a range of ways with particular meanings for the family, including music, and personal tributes by family and friends. For agnostics and atheists these are not novel developments—Sir Sydney Cockerell had campaigned to bring spirituality and dignity to early cremations. The funeral ceremony on 26 June 1987 for Dr Cyril Bibby, a scientist of Queens College, Cambridge, illustrates a post-1970s humanist funeral which Dr Bibby probably planned with the help of his family. A message from Dr Bibby was read by his son, expressing gratitude to all who contributed to his rich and happy life, and he asked that, though they might mourn, 'they should nevertheless seek some happiness in their memories of me'. Family members read out a poem on 'Constancy' written by Dr Bibby, while colleagues and friends offered loving appreciations of his life, followed by silent contemplation.[31] Many such ceremonies have taken place on the deaths of educated unbelievers throughout the twentieth century, with celebration of the life of the deceased as the focal point. Some features today are indeed new, such as funeral songs chosen by teenage children from iPod lists, coffins made of cardboard and painted in bright colours, and slide shows featuring the deceased. Public emotion is now more often allowed in a funeral ceremony which was once strictly constrained.

The natural woodland burial movement is regarded by many as one of the more significant recent innovations. The first green burial ground in

England was opened in 1993 at Carlisle in Cumbria as an extension to an old Victorian cemetery, where many old graves with crumbling headstones were no longer visited: maintenance was an increasing problem, as was vandalism. This initiative came from Kenneth West, who managed the cemeteries and crematoria for the Carlisle council and was also a committed humanist. He was proud of his involvement with over a hundred thousand funerals since 1961, but increasingly concerned about the future; with the decline of religious faith, he believed that most people 'don't think about death' and failed to prepare for it in advance. Ken West established the Woodlands Burial Scheme in 1993, also because of his deep environmental concern that the cremation process polluted the atmosphere and contributed to the increase of asthma. In the years that followed there were thirty-five green burials annually in Carlisle, and more were expected. They appealed to single people with no relatives to tend their graves, to people committed to improving the environment, and to those who objected to cremation. The corpse was buried (usually in an environmentally friendly cardboard coffin) in a lovely woodland site with a ceremony of the family's choice; a month later they returned to plant an oak tree on the site, where a permanent plaque was fixed as commemoration.[32]

By 2007 there were about two hundred such green burial sites across England, chiefly extensions to existing local authority cemeteries, though some were managed privately or by charitable trusts. Andrew Clayden and Katie Dixon consider that natural burial is a response to changing attitudes both to death and to the environment in an increasingly individualistic society, whereas traditional burial and cremation are seen as environmentally damaging. They see woodland burial as an expression of growing 'ecological consciousness' in the community, reinforced by the hope of 'ecological immortality'. The 'living' physical presence of the tree and its message about the changing seasons and cycles of nature made it a more powerful memorial than a headstone.[33]

However, the woodland burial movement since the 1990s may appear less innovative to the historian. There is some evidence of inspiration from the English and American rural cemeteries of the nineteenth century, with Kensal Green the first of the great London private-enterprise cemeteries, opened in 1832. The natural landscape dominated these cemeteries: the aesthetic value of the beauty of nature in a lovely park was thought to evoke appropriate emotional responses to death, perhaps acting as a source of moral instruction and a civilizing influence.

# Roadside Memorials: Public
# Displays of Private Grief

Geoffrey Gorer had called for enterprising new rituals of death but he might have been surprised by the extraordinary phenomenon of roadside memorials marking the sites of sudden deaths in car accidents, often of young victims. Wayside shrines have long been associated with the Catholic countries of Europe such as Ireland, France, and Spain, and also South America. In the United States wayside shrines marked spots where early Hispanic settlers set coffins down on the walk to the graveyard. A spiritual element lingers today with the use of crosses as roadside memorials, though these are more common in Australia and the United States than England. In recent years roadside memorials have become a global phenomenon, encouraged by mass communications, though the fashions in memorials vary from country to country. Indeed, for many people today their most frequent contact with death is through the sight of roadside memorials as they travel by car or bus on the roads which define modern communities.

Flowers are traditionally used at funerals and in memorials as symbols of sorrow, affection, and respect for the dead. Glennys Howarth has noted that rosemary was traditionally linked in England with death, and that flowers were often placed around corpses to disguise unpleasant odours. Flowers have also been widely used at funerals as expressions of grief and respect, arranged around the coffin in the house before the funeral, and also massed around the hearse, as my illustrations demonstrate. Poppies continue to be worn in England to commemorate soldiers killed in the two world wars. Flowers were also used as public displays of loss at sites of sudden death and disaster, as at the funerals of mining disaster victims in the north in the interwar years and later for Blitz victims.[34]

Wayside memorials are very public displays of individual private grief, and they frequently feature flowers. As Ken Inglis observes, they are 'private projects occupying public space': they are rituals devised with therapeutic intent because the bereaved need to express their pain. It was estimated in Australia in 2007 that one in five road fatalities was remembered in this way.[35] But people differ about this issue of expressing private grief in such a public form. As the *Independent* observed in 2005, through much of the twentieth century mourning was a private affair, and the bereaved were advised to seek closure and move on: 'Now remembering the dead is regarded as an important part of what it means to be a caring society... The outer trappings of grief seem to be coming back again'.[36]

Many people are opposed to such public displays of emotion at sites of personal tragedy. The BBC Tyne 'Inside Out' online commentary in February 2006 explored both sides of this public/private debate. One writer argued that 'grieving should be a private thing not brought to the general public's attention'. Several writers emphasized that flowers should be laid in the cemetery or churchyard which are more appropriate for 'quiet remembrance'. Another commented that, 'A bit of decent British reticence and sense of proportion, propriety and fittingness is called for, not a mountain of dead teddy bears'. On the opposite side of the debate, one writer considered roadside wreaths an 'important symbolic gesture of grief for those bereaved', which was also a 'notable social act, bringing attention... to the increasing openness and acceptability of grieving in public'.[37]

These differences of view about socially acceptable behaviour for grieving within the community are a continuing reflection of changing cultural boundaries. Is the public display of sorrow at the site of a tragedy permissible as part of the necessary grieving process? Do 'bad deaths' such as the sudden traumatic deaths of young people justify roadside memorials imposed on all? Tracey Potts asks how far the emotion evoked by these roadside floral tributes is false or genuine. Much is in the eye of the beholder, depending on their age and class. For Jack Santino these road-side shrines 'display death in the heart of social life'; thus Potts argues that they allow us to 'recognise our common humanity' in that we all face death and loss.[38] Some view roadside memorials almost as sacred sites, and floral crosses as examples of underlying spirituality, though they are alien to English Protestant culture.

Others see roadside floral tributes as intrusive and inappropriate. British TV presenter Muriel Gray considered the practice of leaving makeshift memorials of cheap cellophane-wrapped flowers on the roadside tasteless and repulsive. Some commentators see a culture of false sentimentality which manipulates the emotions.[39] Rose George concludes that 'One person's tatty bouquet is another's shrine. The boundaries have gone, and in this individualistic, atomised society, new rituals are stepping in'.[40] Geraldine Excell sees it as a 'bottom-up anti-establishment culture that has developed a code and culture of its own'. The bouquet of flowers on the lamp-post allows the bereaved to announce their loss to the community. Tony Walter argues that 'it's about who society accepts as the sacred dead, deserving of public reverence'. Few people objected to public commemoration of the dead of the Great War, but public mourning for private individuals 'is illegitimate because they're not the sacred dead'.[41] The public expression of private grief remains contested, deeply influenced by our cultural and social history, but always open to new forms of memorialization and emotional expression. The place of death and grieving in individual and social life will continue to change, and to challenge historians in the future.

# *Notes*

## INTRODUCTION

1. Julie Rugg, 'Lawn Cemeteries: The Emergence of a New Landscape of Death', *Urban History*, 33/2 (2006), 213–14; Tony Walter, *On Bereavement: The Culture of Grief* (Open University Press, Buckingham, 1999), 39.

2. Pat Jalland, *Death in the Victorian Family* (OUP, Oxford, 1996). The following three paragraphs are based on my book.

3. Julie-Marie Strange, *Death, Grief and Poverty in Britain, 1870–1914* (CUP, Cambridge, 2005), 195, 254–5, *passim*.

4. Leonard Huxley, *The Life and Letters of T. H. Huxley*, 2 vols (Macmillan, London, 1900), i. 81–3.

5. Jose Harris, *Private Lives, Public Spirit: A Social History of Britain 1870–1914* (OUP, Oxford, 1993), 253.

6. Boyd Hilton, *The Age of Atonement: The Influence of Evangelicalism on Social and Economic Thought 1795–1865* (OUP, Oxford, 1988), 335–6.

7. David Clark, *Between Pulpit and Pew: Folk Religion in a North Yorkshire Fishing Village* (CUP, Cambridge, 1982), 11–34, 111–12, 143–68; James Obelkevich, 'Religion', in F. M. L. Thompson (ed.), *The Cambridge Social History of Britain, 1750–1950*, iii (CUP, Cambridge, 1990), 347 ff.

8. N. L. Tranter, *British Population in the Twentieth Century* (Macmillan, London, 1996), ch. 3; E. A. Wrigley and R. S. Schofield, *The Population History of England 1541–1871: A Reconstruction* (Edward Arnold, London, 1981), 528–9.

9. Michael Anderson, 'British Population History, 1911–1991', in Anderson (ed.), *British Population History from the Black Death to the Present Day* (CUP, Cambridge, 1996), 362, 381–2.

10. Tranter, *British Population in the Twentieth Century*, 62–6; Rosalind Mitchison, *British Population Change Since 1860* (Macmillan, London, 1977), 39–57; Michael Anderson, 'The Social Implications of Demographic Change', in F. M. L. Thompson (ed.), *The Cambridge Social History of Britain 1750–1950*, ii (CUP, Cambridge, 1990), 15–16.

11. Thomas McKeown, *The Modern Rise of Population* (Edward Arnold, London, 1976); J. M. Winter, 'Unemployment Nutrition and Infant Mortality in Britain, 1920–1950', in Winter (ed.), *The Working Class in Modern British History* (CUP, Cambridge, 1983), 232–56.

12. Roy Porter, *The Greatest Benefit to Mankind: A Medical History of Humanity from Antiquity to the Present* (Harper Collins, London, 1997), 426–45; Tranter, *British Population in the Twentieth Century*, 70–9; Anderson, 'British Population History 1911–1991', 376–9.

13. Anne Hardy, *Health and Medicine in Britain Since 1860* (Palgrave, Basingstoke, 2001), 139–71.

14. Porter, *The Greatest Benefit to Mankind*, 458–60, 595.

15. Anderson, 'British Population History, 1911–1991', 374.

16. Clive Seale, 'Demographic Change and the Experience of Dying', in D. Dickenson et al. (eds.), *Death, Dying and Bereavement* (Open University, Sage, London, 2000), 36–7.

17. David Cannadine, 'War and Death, Grief and Mourning in Modern Britain', in Joachim Whaley (ed.), *Mirrors of Mortality* (Europa, London, 1981), 187–242.

18. Anderson, 'British Population History, 1911–1991', 375–6; Hardy, *Health and Medicine in Britain*, 170–2.

19. Ruth Richardson, 'Old People's Attitudes to Death in the Twentieth Century', *Society for the Social History of Medicine Bulletin*, 34 (1984), 48–51.

20. Tony Walter, *On Bereavement: The Culture of Grief* (Open University Press, Buckingham, 1999), 40.

21. George MacDonald Fraser, *Quartered Safe Out Here: A Recollection of the War in Burma* (Harper Collins, London, 1993), 76–90.

22. *Manchester Guardian*, 13 July 1945 (also later cited as *Guardian*).

23. Geoffrey Gorer, *Death, Grief and Mourning in Contemporary Britain* (Cresset Press, London, 1965), 69–71.

24. Ibid., *passim*.

25. Philip Toynbee, *Observer*, 2 May 1965; John Hinton, *Dying* (Penguin, Harmondsworth, 1967), 13–14; Norbert Elias, *The Loneliness of the Dying* (Blackwell, Oxford, 1982).

CHAPTER I

1. Beverley Raphael, 'Death and the Great Australian Disaster', in Kathy Charmaz, Glennys Howarth, and Allan Kellehear (eds.), *The Unknown Country: Death in Australia, Britain and the USA* (Macmillan, Basingstoke, 1997), 81; Beverley Raphael, *When Disaster Strikes: How Individuals and Communities Cope with Catastrophe* (Basic Books, New York, 1986).

2. J. M. Winter, *The Great War and the British People* (Macmillan, Basingstoke, 1987), 30–3.

3. See Peter Parker, *The Great War and the Public School Ethos* (Constable, London, 1986); David Newsome, *Godliness and Good Learning* (Cassell, London, 1986).

4. See n. 3, above.

5. Jeanne MacKenzie, *The Children of the Souls* (Chatto and Windus, London, 1986), 184–5.

6. J. M. Winter, *The Great War and the British People*, 70–97; Gary Sheffield, *Forgotten Victory: The First World War, Myths and Realities* (Review, London, 2002), 6.

7. Lord Moran, *Anatomy of Courage* (Constable, London, 1945); Denis Winter, *Death's Men: Soldiers of the Great War* (Penguin, London, 1979), 117–19.

8. *Guardian*, 20 Mar. 1915.

9. Ibid., 16 July 1915.

10. Joanna Bourke, *An Intimate History of Killing: Face-to-Face Killing in 20th Century Warfare* (Granta, London 1999).

11. Raphael, *When Disaster Strikes*.

12. John Ellis, *Eye-Deep in Hell: Trench Warfare in World War I* (Johns Hopkins University Press, Baltimore, 1976), 63–5.

13. J. C. Dunn, *The War the Infantry Knew 1914–1919* (1938; Abacus, London, 1994), 235.

14. H. G. Boorer, IWM, con shelf.

15. Ellis, *Eye-Deep in Hell*, 97–8, 106.

16. Lieut. R. G. Dixon, 'The Wheels of Darkness', unpublished TS memoir, 1970s, IWM 92/36/1.

17. W. Clarke, IWM 87/18/1.

18. Frederick Manning, *Her Privates We* (Murray, 1930), cited in Denis Winter, *Death's Men*, 132.

19. Dunn, *The War the Infantry Knew*, 313.

20. Ibid., 316.

21. H. C. L. Heywood, IWM 91/10/1.

22. Ross McKibbin, *Classes and Cultures: England 1918–1951* (OUP, Oxford, 2000), 273–5.

23. Adrian Hastings, *A History of English Christianity 1920–2000* (SCM Press, London, rev. edn., 2001), 42.

24. Alan Wilkinson, *The Church of England and the First World War* (SPCK, London, 1978), 7, 260.

25. Ibid., 160–1.

26. Ibid., 120, 233–4, 243–4; Adrian Gregory, *The Silence of Memory: Armistice Day 1919–1946* (Berg, Oxford, 1994), 186, 206.

27. Wilkinson, *The Church of England*, 133–4.

28. John Bickersteth (ed.), *The Bickersteth Diaries, 1914–1918* (Leo Cooper, Barnsley, 1995), 160–1.

29. J. M. Winter, *Sites of Memory, Sites of Mourning: The Great War in European Cultural History* (CUP, Cambridge, 1995), 69.

30. Horace to Mrs Brown, 30 Oct. 1918, J. K. Brown, IWM 94/46/1.

31. G. K. Nelson, *Spiritualism and Society* (Routledge and Kegan Paul, 1969), 155–65; David Cannadine, 'War and Death, Grief and Mourning in Modern Britain', in Joachim Whaley (ed.), *Mirrors of Mortality* (Europa, London, 1981), 228–9; Ruth Brandon, *The Spiritualists: The Passion for the Occult in the 19th and 20th Centuries* (Weidenfeld & Nicolson, London, 1983), 215–17.

32. J. M. Winter, 'Spiritualism', in *Sites of Memory*, 58–63. See also J. Hazelgrove, *Spiritualism and British Society Between the Wars* (Manchester University Press, Manchester, 2000), 18–24.

33. J. M. Winter, *Sites of Memory*, 76–7.

34. Joanna Bourke, *Dismembering the Male: Men's Bodies, Britain and the Great War* (Reaktion, London, 1996), 107–12.

35. Wilfred Owen, 'Mental Cases', *Poetry of the First World War* (Collector's Poetry Library, CRW Publishing, London, 2004), 80.

36. W. H. Bloor, IWM 99/22/1.

37. Charles Carrington [Charles Edmonds], *A Subaltern's War* (Peter Davies, London, 1929), 15–19, 113–14, 118, 126–7.

38. Ibid., 128–9, 133, 139–41, 161–3.

39. See e.g. N. L. Woodroffe, IWM 95/31/1.

40. Capt. H. J. C. Leland, IWM 96/51/1.

41. Ibid.

42. Ibid.

43. Ibid.

44. *Poetry of the First World War*, 80.

45. H. J. C. Leland, IWM 96/51/1.

46. Denis Winter, *Death's Men*, 140.

47. Raphael, *When Disaster Strikes*.

48. 'When you see millions of the mouthless dead', *Poetry of the First World War*, 141.

49. Gregory, *The Silence of Memory*, 19.

50. Carrington, *A Subaltern's War*, 'Epilogue', 192–212.

51. Paul Fussell, *The Great War and Modern Memory* (1975; OUP, Oxford, 1977).

52. Brian Bond, *The Unquiet Western Front: Britain's Role in Literature and History* (CUP, Cambridge, 2002), 1–22; Sheffield, *Forgotten Victory*, 48–50, 56–8, 101–4, 126–7.

53. R. G. Dixon, 'The Wheels of Darkness', IWM 92/36/1.

54. Alice Reid, 'The Effects of the 1918–1919 Influenza Pandemic on Infant and Child Health in Derbyshire', *Medical History*, 49/1, (Jan. 2005), 29–54.

55. K. David Patterson and Gerald F. Pyle, 'The Geography and Mortality of the 1918 Influenza Pandemic', *Bulletin of the History of Medicine*, 65/1 (Spring 1991), 4–21.

56. Ibid., 13.

57. Ibid., 4–13; Sandra M. Tomkins, 'The Failure of Expertise: Public Health Policy in Britain During the 1918–1919 Influenza Epidemic', *Social History of Medicine*, 5 (1992), 435–7.

58. Patterson and Pyle, '1918 Influenza Pandemic', 14.

59. J. M. Winter, *The Great War and the British People*, table 3.1, 68.

60. *Guardian*, 8 Nov. 1919.

61. Tomkins, 'The Failure of Expertise', 440; *Guardian*, 21 Dec. 1918.

62. *Guardian*, 27 Nov. 1918.

63. J. Whyte, IWM 85/22/1.

64. Katharine Garvin, *J. L. Garvin: A Memoir* (W. Heinemann, London, 1948), 84–5.


CHAPTER 2

1. Adrian Gregory, *The Silence of Memory: Armistice Day 1919–1946* (Berg, Oxford, 1994), 19.

2. J. M. Winter, *The Great War and the British People* (Macmillan, Basingstoke, 1987), 279–83.

3. *Barnsley Chronicle*, 15 July 1916; Jon Cooksey, *Barnsley Pals* (Leo Cooper, London, 1986), 153, 178, 223–5; Fenton file, IWM 87/13/1.

4. Winter, *The Great War and the British People*, 96–9.

5. J. B. Priestley, 'The Lost Generation', John Johnson Collection, 'The Great War', Box 24, Bodleian Library.

6. *The Diaries of Lady Cynthia Asquith, 1915–1918* (Century, London, 1984), 97, 317.

7. J. M. Winter, *Sites of Memory, Sites of Mourning: The Great War in European Cultural History* (CUP, Cambridge, 1995), 29–53.

8. Hugh Cecil, *ODNB* (2004); Kenneth Rose, *The Later Cecils* (Harper and Row, London, 1975).

9. Rudyard Kipling's letters to Alfred Milner, 3 and 8 Dec. 1914, MS Milner dep. 666, fos. 98, 101–2, Alfred Lord Milner's Papers, Bodleian Library, Oxford.

10. 'War Diary 1914' by Violet Cecil, VM box 56; Violet Cecil's notes of her search for George, 1914, VM box 56; undated letter, VM box 57, Violet Milner Papers, Bodleian Library [VM].

11. 'War Diary 1914', VM box 56; Violet Cecil's notes of her search for George, VM box 56.

12. Violet Cecil to Col. R. G. Gordon Gilmour, 1 Oct. 1914, VM box 14; Violet Cecil to Philip Ashworth, 25 Oct. 1914; Ashworth to Alfred Milner, 2 and 6 Nov. 1914, MS Milner, dep. 666.

13. Violet Cecil's notes of her search for George 1914, VM box 56.

14. See *Guardian*, 16 July 1915; 4 Jan. 1919, 22 Feb. 1922; ACRS Macnaghten, IWM, 96/2/1; Angus Macnaghton, *Missing: An Account of the Efforts Made to Find an Officer of the Black Watch* (Bala, Dragon Books, 1970).

15. Violet Cecil to Philip Ashworth, 25 Oct. 1914, MS Milner, dep. 666.

16. Violet Cecil to Alfred Milner, 20 Sept. 1914, ibid.

17. Violet Cecil to Olive Maxse, 9 Dec. 1914, VM box 17.

18. Robert Cecil to Violet Cecil, 23 Oct. 1914, 18 Nov. 1914, VM boxes 56–7; Lord Killanin's account of the search at Villers Cotterets, Nov. 1914, VM box 14.

19. Lord Killanin's account to Violet Cecil, Nov. 1914, VM box 14.

20. Ibid.

21. Lord Killanin's account to Violet Cecil, Nov. 1914, VM box 14.

22. Killanin to Violet Cecil, 22 Nov. 1914, VM box 57.

23. Constance Manners to Violet Cecil, 8 Oct. 1914, VM box 56.

24. Constance Manners to Violet Cecil, 23 Nov., 9 Dec. 1914, VM box 56; Tonie and Valmai Holt, *My Boy Jack: The Search for Kipling's Only Son* (Leo Cooper, Barnsley, 1998), 65–6.

25. Replies to Violet Cecil's letters to bereaved families of Villers Cotterets, 1914–15, VM box 58.

26. Ibid.

27. Ibid.

28. Denis Winter, *Death's Men: Soldiers of the Great War* (Penguin, London, 1979), 223–31, 255–7.

29. Pte A. Clayden, IWM 92/3/1.

30. Robert F. Wearmouth, *Pages from a Padre's Diary: A Story of Struggle and Triumph* (R. F. Wearmouth, North Shields, n.d. [c. 1960]), 93, 95–7, 99, 106–7, 115, 129.

31. Eleanor Cecil to Violet Cecil, 8 Sept. 1915, VM box 25.

32. Jane Abdy and Charlotte Gere, *The Souls* (Sidgwick & Jackson, London, 1984), 67–8; *The Diaries of Lady Cynthia Asquith*, 102–3.

33. *The Diaries of Lady Cynthia Asquith*, 21 Nov. 1915, 103.

34. Constance Manners to Violet Cecil, 22 Aug. 1915, VM box 46.

35. H. A. L. Fisher to Violet Cecil, 16 Nov. 1914, VM box 39.

36. General Frederick Maxse to Violet Cecil, July 1915, VM box 19.

37. T. and V. Holt, *My Boy Jack*, passim.

38. Carrie Kipling to Violet Cecil, 1915, VM box 44.

39. Ibid., 19 May, 1 Sept. 1916.

40. T. and V. Holt, *My Boy Jack*, pp. xviii–xix.

41. J. M. Winter, *Sites of Memory, Sites of Mourning*, 72–3.

42. *The Diaries of Lady Cynthia Asquith*, 236–7.

43. Rose, *The Later Cecils*, 304.

44. Lord Selborne to Violet Cecil, 19 Jan. 1916, VM box 26.

45. Florence Cecil to Violet Cecil, 20 July, 12 Aug. 1915; 25 Sept. 1918, VM box 25.

46. Rose, *The Later Cecils*, 119.

47. Ibid. 223.

48. Hugh Cecil to Violet Cecil, 26 Oct., 6 and 25 Nov. 1914, VM box 57.

49. Eleanor Cecil to Violet Cecil, 2 Feb. 1915, VM box 57.

50. Constance Manners to Violet Cecil, 14 Sept. [1915], VM box 46.

51. Ibid., 20 June n.d. [1916/1917].

52. Ibid., 5 Sept. [1916?].

53. See e.g. Constance Manners to Violet Cecil, 8 Oct. 1914, VM box 56; 25 Sept. 1919, VM box 46.

54. Constance Manners to Violet Cecil, 13 May, 19 Aug., 4 Sept. [1915], VM box 46.

55. Envelope, VM box 14.

56. Correspondence between Mme Mouflier and Violet Cecil [in French], VM box 47. Thanks to Laurie Dennett for the translation.

57. Fabian Ware to Alfred Milner, 6 Mar. 1922, 11 Apr. 1923; Milner's reply, 7 Mar. 1922, MS Milner dep. 666.

58. Violet Milner's diary, 1934, VM papers.

59. Geoffrey Bickersteth to mother Ella, Easter Day 1945, MS Eng. E. 3150, Bodleian.

60. Adrian Hastings, *A History of English Christianity, 1920–2000* (SCM Press, London, rev. edn., 2001), ch. 7.

61. David Stevenson, *1914–1918: The History of the First World War* (Penguin, London, 2005), 252–4.

62. Feilding of Newnham Paddox Correspondence, CR 2017/C618: Warwick Record Office.

63. Ibid., CR 2017/C618.

64. Ibid.

65. Ibid.

66. Stevenson, *1914–1918: The History of the First World War*, 335.

67. Feilding of Newnham Paddox Correspondence, CR 2017/C622.

68. Ibid.

69. Ibid., CR 2017/C594.

## CHAPTER 3

1. Ken Inglis, *Sacred Places: War Memorials in the Australian Landscape* (Melbourne University Press, 1998). See below, nn. 2, 3, 6, 10.

2. J. M. Winter, *Sites of Memory, Sites of Mourning* (CUP, Cambridge, 1995), 28.

3. Mark Connelly, *The Great War, Memory and Ritual: Commemoration in the City and East London 1916–1939* (Royal Historical Society, Boydell Press, Woodbridge, Suffolk, 2002), 142–3.

4. J. M. Winter, *Sites of Memory*, 102–4.

5. Lucy Masterman, *C. F. G. Masterman: A Biography* (Nicholson and Watson, London, 1939), 318.

6. Adrian Gregory, *The Silence of Memory: Armistice Day 1919–1946* (Berg, Oxford, 1994), ch. 6; *The Times*, 12 Nov. 1919.

7. Accounts by Fabian Ware, *Manchester Guardian*, 18 Feb. 1919; 6 Mar. 1924, 11 Nov. 1932.

8. Ibid., 6 Mar. 1924.

9. Ibid., 14 Apr. 1919, 19 Nov. 1918, 18 Dec. 1919, 5 May 1920; Philip Longworth, *The Unending Vigil: A History of the Commonwealth War Graves Commission, 1917–1967* (Constable, London, 1967), 296–315.

10. David Lloyd, *Battlefield Tourism: Pilgrimage and the Commemoration of the Great War in Britain, Australia and Canada 1919–1939* (OUP, Oxford, 1998).

11. The Bickersteth family papers are split between Churchill College Cambridge (CCC) and the Bodleian Library, Oxford.
12. John Bickersteth, *ODNB* (2004), entries for Julian and Burgon Bickersteth; John Bickersteth (ed.), *The Bickersteth Diaries, 1914–1918* (1995; Leo Cooper, Barnsley, 1998), pp. ix–xiv.
13. John Bickersteth (ed.), *Diaries*, 104.
14. Robin Prior and Trevor Wilson, *The Somme* (UNSW Press, Sydney, 2005), 73–4.
15. John Bickersteth (ed.), *Diaries*, 101, 109–10.
16. Ibid., 95–9; Prior and Wilson, *The Somme*, 74.
17. John Bickersteth (ed.), *Diaries*, 100–1; Revd Samuel Bickersteth, *Morris Bickersteth, 1891–1916* (CUP, Cambridge, 1931), 122–33, 137.
18. *Morris Bickersteth*, 139–41; John Bickersteth (ed.), *Diaries*, 126.
19. Ella Bickersteth's journal, pp. xi–xii, July–Aug. 1916, Apr. 1917, Bickersteth Family Papers, box 25, Bodleian.
20. Ibid.
21. Ibid., pp. xii–xiiii, Aug. 1916–June 1918.
22. 'Tour of the Battlefields, 28 June to 3 July 1919', by Ella and Samuel Bickersteth, Bickersteth diaries, BIC 1/10, CCC.
23. *Guardian*, 14 Apr. 1919, 19 Nov. 1918.
24. Ibid., 26 May 1919, 5 Feb. 1920.
25. Julian Bickersteth to parents, 28 Apr. 1919, Bickersteth Diaries, vol. x. 3299, BIC 1/10, CCC.
26. Ibid.
27. Lloyd, *Battlefield Tourism*, 24, 140–6.
28. 'Tour of the Battlefields 1919', by Ella and Samuel Bickersteth, Bickersteth Diaries, June–July 1919, vol. x, BIC 1/10, CCC.
29. Ibid.
30. Ibid.
31. Ibid.
32. Ibid.
33. Ibid.
34. Ibid.
35. Ibid.
36. Ibid.
37. Ibid.
38. Ibid.
39. 'Short Account of a Tour of the Battlefields by Monier, Kitty, Julian and Burgon', 29 June–2 July 1926, Bickersteth Diaries, vol x., BIC 1/10, CCC.
40. Ibid.
41. Ibid.
42. Ibid.; *Manchester Guardian*, 11 Mar. 1926.
43. Bickersteth Diaries, June–July 1926, vol. x, BIC 1/10, CCC.

44. Visit to Serre, 29 June–3 July 1931, Miscellaneous Personal Papers, MS Eng. C. 6418, fos. 114–53, Bodleian.
45. Ibid.
46. Ibid.
47. Ibid.

## CHAPTER 4

1. Julie-Marie Strange, *Death, Grief and Poverty in Britain, 1870–1914* (CUP, Cambridge, 2005).
2. John Stevenson, *British Society 1914–1945* (Penguin, London, 1984), 108–9, 134–8, 186–98.
3. Ross McKibbin, *Classes and Cultures, England 1918–1951* (OUP, Oxford, 2000), 161.
4. J. B. Priestley, *English Journey* (Penguin, London, 1934), 300–1.
5. Ibid., 302–8.
6. Ibid., 309–14. See also George Orwell, *The Road to Wigan Pier* (Secker and Warburg, London, 1959), ch. 3.
7. *Whitehaven News*, 6 Sept. 1922; *Guardian*, 3 Jan. 1928.
8. *Guardian*, 3 and 8 Oct. 1930.
9. Beverley Raphael, *When Disaster Strikes: How Individuals and Communities Cope with Catastrophe* (Basic Books, New York, 1986), 80–95; Raphael, 'Death and the Great Australian Disaster', in Kathy Charmaz, Glennys Howarth, and Allan Kellehear (eds.), *The Unknown Country: Death in Australia, Britain and the USA* (Macmillan, Basingstoke, 1997), 72–83.
10. See e.g. Charles Forman, *Industrial Town* (David and Charles, Newton Abbott, 1978), 49, 159.
11. *Whitehaven News*, 6 Sept. 1922.
12. Ibid.; *Guardian,* 6 Sept. 1922.
13. *Guardian*, 6 and 7 Sept. 1922; *The Times*, 6 Sept. 1922.
14. *Whitehaven News*, 6 Sept. 1922; *Guardian*, 6 and 7 Sept. 1922.
15. See e.g. *Guardian*, 15 Nov. 1932.
16. *The Times*, 9 Sept. 1922; *Guardian*, 9 Sept. 1922.
17. Forman, *Industrial Town*, 160.
18. *The Times*, 21 and 23 Nov. 1931; *Guardian*, 23 and 24 Nov. 1931.
19. *Guardian*, 23 Nov. 1931.
20. Ibid., 24 Nov. 1931.
21. *The Times*, 24 Nov. 1931; *Guardian*, 24 Nov. 1931.
22. *The Times*, 26 Nov. 1931; *Guardian*, 24 and 26 Nov. 1931.
23. Jonathan Gammond, 'The Real Price of Coal', BBC 2000, accessed 22 Jan. 2008, available from <http://www.bbc.co.uk/wales/northeast/sites/wrexham/papers/gresford>.

24. *The Times*, 15 Dec. 1934; *Guardian*, 6 Feb. 1937; Gammond, 'The Real Price of Coal'.
25. Karen Holmes [comment], in BBC–North East Wales, 'Gresford Mining Disaster', 29 May 2007, accessed 22 Jan. 2008, <http://www.bbc.co.uk/wales/northeast/sites/wrexham/pages/gresford>.
26. Ibid.
27. Ibid., from Alex, Samantha Lloyd, Thomas Gregg.
28. Ibid., from Andrea Wilson.
29. James Obelkevich, 'Religion', in F. M. L. Thompson (ed.), *The Cambridge Social History of Britain, 1750–1950*, iii (CUP, Cambridge, 1990), 347 ff.; P. F. Clarke, *Hope and Glory. Britain 1900–2000* (Penguin, London, 2004), 160–1.
30. Obelkevich, 'Religion', 311–56; Adrian Hastings, *A History of English Christianity 1920–2000* (SCM Press, London, 2001), 104–7, 266–72.
31. James Obelkevich, *Religion and Rural Society: South Lindsey 1825–1875* (OUP, Oxford, 1976); Ruth Richardson, *Death, Dissection and the Destitute* (Routledge and Kegan Paul, London, 1987); Strange, *Death, Grief and Poverty in Britain*, *passim*.
32. David Clark, *Between Pulpit and Pew: Folk Religion in a North Yorkshire Fishing Village* (CUP, Cambridge, 1982), 11–34, 111–12, 143–68.
33. Ibid.
34. Ibid., 110–12, 128.
35. Ibid., 129–30; see also *Guardian*, 24 Mar. 1965.
36. Clark, *Between Pulpit and Pew*, 131–3.
37. Ibid., 135–142.
38. Elizabeth Roberts, *A Woman's Place: An Oral History of Working Class Women, 1890–1940* (Blackwell, Oxford, 1984), *passim*.
39. Ibid.; Elizabeth Roberts, 'The Lancashire Way of Death', in Ralph Houlbrooke (ed.), *Death, Ritual and Bereavement* (Routledge, London, 1989), 188–207.
40. Ibid.
41. Christine Kenny, *A Northern Thanatology: A Comprehensive Review of Illness, Death and Dying in the North West of England* (Quay, Denton, 1998). See also Sheila Adams, 'A Gendered History of the Social Management of Death in Foleshill, Coventry, during the Interwar Years', *Sociological Review* (1993), 149–67.
42. Roberts, 'The Lancashire Way of Death', 188–207; Kenny, *A Northern Thanatology*, chs. 7, 8.
43. Roberts, 'The Lancashire Way of Death', 205–6.
44. Adams, 'A Gendered History of Death in Foleshill', 149–67.
45. Ibid., 164–5; Roberts, 'The Lancashire Way of Death'.
46. Geoffrey Gorer, *Death, Grief and Mourning in Contemporary Britain* (Cresset Press, London, 1965).
47. Interview with Nicholas Taylor, 1999, *Millenium Memory Bank*, C900/11592 C1, British Library.

## CHAPTER 5

1. Julian Litten, *The English Way of Death: The Common Funeral Since 1450* (Robert Hale, London, 1991), 171; C. E. Lawrence, 'The Abolition of Death', *Fortnightly Review* (Feb. 1917), 101, 326–31.

2. Henry Thompson, 'Cremation: A Reply to Critics', *Contemporary Review* (23 Mar. 1874), 553–71; John Morley, *Death, Heaven and the Victorians* (Studio Vista, London, 1971), ch. 8, pp. 91–101; J. Leaney, 'Ashes to Ashes: Cremation and the Celebration of Death in 19th Century Britain', in Ralph Houlbrooke (ed.), *Death, Ritual and Bereavement* (Routledge, London, 1989), 118–35.

3. Pat Jalland, *Death in the Victorian Family* (OUP, Oxford, 1996), 205–9.

4. *Guardian*, 6 Aug. 1936.

5. Peter Jupp, *From Dust to Ashes: The Replacement of Burial by Cremation in England 1840–1967* (Congregational Memorial Hall Trust, London, 1990), 1, 13–17; Peter Jupp, *From Dust to Ashes: Cremation and the British Way of Death* (Palgrave Macmillan, Basingstoke, 2006).

6. Joanna Bourke, *Dismembering the Male: Men's Bodies, Britain and the Great War* (Reaktion, London, 1996), 222–5.

7. Ibid.

8. Hilary J. Grainger, 'Golders Green Crematorium and the Architectural Expression of Cremation', *Mortality*, 5/1 (2000).

9. Douglas J. Davies, 'The Sacred Crematorium', *Mortality*, 1/1 (Mar. 1996), 85.

10. Jupp, *From Dust to Ashes: Cremation and the British Way of Death*, 18.

11. Peter Jupp, 'Cremation or Burial? Contemporary Choice in City and Village', in David Clark (ed.), *The Sociology of Death* (Blackwell, Oxford, 1993), 192; Peter Jupp, 'Why Was England the First Country to Popularize Cremation?', in Kathy Charmaz, Glennys Howarth, and Allan Kellehear (eds.), *The Unknown Country: Death in Australia, Britain and the USA* (Macmillan, Basingstoke, 1997), 146–8.

12. Cited in Jupp, 'The First Country to Popularize Cremation?', 148.

13. *Guardian*, 10 Jan., 12 Oct. 1944.

14. Ibid., 25 June 1936.

15. Adrian Hastings, *A History of English Christianity 1920–2000* (SCM Press, London, 2001), 221–5.

16. Wilfrid Scawen Blunt, 'Sir Sydney Carlyle Cockerell', *DNB, 1961–1970* (OUP, London, 1981); Wilfrid Scawen Blunt, *Sydney Carlyle Cockerell, Friend of Ruskin and William Morris and Director of the Fitzwilliam Museum, Cambridge* (Hamish Hamilton, London, 1964).

17. Blunt, *Cockerell Friend of Ruskin*, p. xvii.

18. Siegfried Sassoon to Cockerell, 5 Jan. 1956, Cockerell Papers, BL Add MS 52752.

19. Hugh Whitemore, *The Best of Friends* (Amber Lane Press, Oxford, 1988).

20. Blunt, 'Cockerell', *DNB*; Blunt, *Cockerell, Friend of Ruskin*; Alan Bell, 'Sir Sydney Carlyle Cockerell', *ODNB* (2004).

21. Blunt, 'Cockerell', *DNB*; Blunt, *Cockerell, Friend of Ruskin*, 135.
22. Bell, 'Cockerell', *ODNB*; Blunt, 'Cockerell', *DNB*; Blunt, *Cockerell, Friend of Ruskin*.
23. Blunt, 'Cockerell', *DNB*; Blunt, *Cockerell, Friend of Ruskin*, p. xvii.
24. Cockerell Diary, 30 Jan. 1919, BL Add MS 52656.
25. Ibid., 13 Dec. 1928, BL Add MS 52666.
26. Ibid., 3 Sept. 1938, BL Add MS 52676.
27. Ibid., 1 Jan. 1946, BL Add MS 52685.
28. Caroline Doughty to Cockerell, 26 Jan., 3 Feb. 1926, BL Add MS 52713, fos. 65, 67.
29. Cockerell Diary, 17 Apr. 1915, BL Add MS 52651.
30. Ibid., 20, 23 Apr. 1915.
31. C. H. St John Hornby to Cockerell, 18 May 1915, Cockerell Papers, BL Add MS 52724.
32. Cockerell Diary, 9–10 July 1915, BL Add MS 52651.
33. Ibid., 10 and 15 Dec. 1932, 22 July 1933, BL Add MS 52670.
34. Ibid., 16–19 Dec. 1932, BL Add MS 52670.
35. Ibid., 13 and 22–4 July 1933, BL Add MS 52670.
36. Ibid., 24–5 July 1933, BL Add MS 52670.
37. Ibid., 25 July, 24 Nov., 6 Sept., 4 Oct. 1933, BL Add MS 52670.
38. Ibid., 11–17 Sept. 1922, BL Add MS 52659.
39. Ibid., 10–12 Jan. 1928, BL Add MS 52666.
40. Ibid., 12–13 Jan 1928.
41. Ibid., 20 Jan.–4 Feb. 1928.
42. Ibid., 3 Oct. 1940, BL Add MS 52678.
43. Ibid., 18 June 1927, BL Add MS 52665.
44. Ibid., 24–8 Apr., 16 Oct. 1943, BL Add MS 52681.
45. Ibid., 31 Dec. 1943, 18–26 July 1944, BL Add MS 52681–2.
46. Cockerell to Dr Eric Miller, 26 Nov. 1947, Cockerell MS, BL Add MS 52737.
47. Neville Lytton to Cockerell, 22 Sept. 1949, Cockerell MS, BL Add MS 52733.
48. Cockerell Diary, 21 Aug.–18 Sept. 1949, BL Add MS 52689.
49. Ibid., 19–23 Sept. 1949, BL Add MS 52689.
50. Blunt, *Cockerell, Friend of Ruskin*, 374.
51. D. Felicitas Corrigan, *The Nun, the Infidel and the Superman* (John Murray, London, 1985), 216.
52. Blunt, *Cockerell, Friend of Ruskin*, 336, 327.
53. Jupp, 'The First Country to Popularise Cremation?', 149–51; Jupp, *From Dust to Ashes: Cremation and the British Way of Death*, 20–4.
54. Ibid., 22–5; *Guardian*, 7 and 9 July 1965, 2 Jan. 1960.
55. Alan Bennett, *Untold Stories* (Faber, London, 2005), 121–2.
56. James Stevens Curl, *The Victorian Celebration of Death* (David and Charles, Newton Abbot, 1972), 185–7; J. S. Curl, Review of P. C. Jupp, 'From Dust to Ashes', *Mortality*, 11/4 (Nov. 2006).

## CHAPTER 6

1. Adrian Gregory, *The Silence of Memory: Armistice Day 1919–1946* (Berg, Oxford, 1994), 212–13; Angus Calder, *The Myth of the Blitz* (Pimlico, London, 1991), 41–2; Calder, *The People's War: Britain 1939–1945* (Panther, London, 1971), 261; Mark Connelly, *We Can Take It! Britain and the Memory of the Second World War* (Pearson, Harlow, 2004).

2. Calder, *The Myth of the Blitz*, 43.

3. Calder, *The People's War*, 195.

4. Philip Ziegler, *London at War 1939–1945* (Mandarin, London, 1996), 163.

5. Quoted in Calder, *Myth of the Blitz*, 35.

6. Quoted in Ziegler, *London at War*, 124.

7. Connelly, *We Can Take It!*, ch. 4; Tom Harrison, *Living Through the Blitz* (Penguin, Harmondsworth, 1979), chs. 1–2.

8. *Guardian*, 21 and 22 Nov. 1940.

9. Ziegler, *London at War*, 114–15.

10. Misc 180 (2708), IWM.

11. Juliet Gardiner, *Wartime Britain 1939–1945* (Headline, London, 2004), 292.

12. Ibid., 299.

13. Ziegler, *London at War*, 199.

14. Miss M. E. Allan, IWM, con shelf 95/8/7.

15. Calder, *The People's War*, 234–7.

16. R. Peat, IWM 97/40/1. My thanks to Mac Boot for his contribution on Hull.

17. Julie Rugg, 'Managing "Civilian Deaths" in World War II', *Twentieth Century British History*, 15/2 (2004), 161–72.

18. R. Peat, IWM 97/40/1.

19. Frances Faviell, *A Chelsea Concerto* (Cassell, London, 1959), 115.

20. Miss M. E. Allan, IWM, con shelf 95/8/7.

21. Philippa Strachey to [?], n.d., Strachey Papers, BL Add MS 60728, fo. 273.

22. *Guardian*, 28 Jan 1943.

23. Norman Longmate, *Air Raid: The Bombing of Coventry, 1940* (Hutchinson, London, 1976), 223.

24. Gardiner, *Wartime Britain*, 304.

25. *Manchester Guardian*, 23 Nov 1940.

26. Rugg, 'Managing "Civilian Deaths"', 163.

27. *Manchester Guardian*, 23 Nov 1940.

28. Ibid., 5 May 1942.

29. Ibid., 14 May 1941.

30. Rugg, 'Managing "Civilian Deaths"', 152–72.

31. Ibid.

32. *Guardian*, 13 July 1945.

33. Harrison, *Living Through the Blitz*, 13–14, 97–9.

34. Harold Orlans, 'Some Attitudes Towards Death', *Diogenes*, 19 (1957), 73–91.

35. David Field, 'Older People's Attitudes Towards Death in England', *Mortality*, 5/3 (2000), 277–97.
36. Audrey Deacon (née Hawkins), 'Diary of a WREN, 1940–1945: The Second World War Diaries of Mrs A D Deacon', IWM, 89/17/1.
37. Ibid.
38. E. Hudson, IWM, 98/10/1.
39. Mrs B. M. Holbrook, 'No Medals for us', Unpublished TS memoir, IWM 95/27/1; Ziegler, *London at War*, 282–91.
40. Holbrook, IWM 95/27/1.
41. Ibid.
42. Ibid.
43. Ibid.
44. Ibid.
45. Ibid.
46. *Guardian*, 19 Feb. 1941; Ziegler, *London at War*, 170–1.
47. *Guardian*, 19 Sept. 1944.
48. IWM MISC 180 (2708).

## CHAPTER 7

1. Richard Overy, *Bomber Command, 1939–1945* (Harper Collins, London, 1997), 152. I am most grateful to Hank Nelson for his careful reading and valuable suggestions on this chapter. I draw on British statistics in this chapter as it is difficult to identify those for England alone.
2. Mark K. Wells, *Courage and Air Warfare: The Allied Aircrew Experience in the Second World War* (Frank Cass, London, 1995), 1.
3. John Nichol and Tony Rennell, *Tail-End Charlies: The Last Battles of the Bomber War 1944–1945* (Viking/Penguin, London, 2004), 13.
4. Overy, *Bomber Command*, 183.
5. Mark Connelly, *Reaching for the Stars: A New History of Bomber Command in World War II* (I. B. Tauris, London, 2001), 137–57.
6. Overy, *Bomber Command*, 195.
7. Nichol and Rennell, *Tail-End Charlies*, 406.
8. Ibid., 407.
9. Overy, *Bomber Command*, 183–95; Wells, *Courage and Air Warfare*, passim.
10. Connelly, *Reaching for the Stars*, 2, 118–19; Wells, *Courage and Air Warfare*, 1.
11. Nichol and Rennell, *Tail-End Charlies*, p. xx.
12. Overy, *Bomber Command*, 152.
13. Wells, *Courage and Air Warfare*, 61–74; Nichol and Rennell, *Tail-End Charlies*, 135–6.
14. M. A. Scott, IWM, 74/93/1.

15. Nichol and Rennell, *Tail-End Charlies*, 135.

16. Wells, *Courage and Air Warfare* esp. chs. 3,5; Connelly, *Reaching for the Stars*, 75–7; Hank Nelson, *Chased by the Sun: Courageous Australians in Bomber Command* (ABC Books, Sydney, 2002), 198.

17. Wells, *Courage and Air Warfare*, 35.

18. Nichol and Rennell, *Tail-End Charlies*, 49, 138.

19. Olive J. Noble, 'A Winged Interlude: A WAAF of the Second World War Tells All', IWM, 91/4/1.

20. Ibid.

21. G. H. Martin, IWM 93/48/1–2.

22. Ibid.

23. W. T. Hurst, 28 May 1944; Joan Taylor, 31 Jan. 1944, IWM, 93/48/1–2.

24. Irene Wellington, 14 June 1944; Betty Caldwell, n.d., Mrs J. Bulson, 15 Sept. 1944., IWM 93/48/1–2.

25. Mrs B. Baldwin, 24 May 1944, IWM, 93/48/1–2.

26. Irene Scotland, 28 Oct. 1944; Mrs K. Richardson, 20 Oct. 1944; Margaret Burnside, 13 June 1944, IWM, 93/48/1–2.

27. Joan Watson, 27 Feb. 1945, IWM 93/48/1–2.

28. N. Whitehouse, 28 Jan. 1944; Joyce W. Knight, 29 May 1944, IWM, 93/48/1–2.

29. [?], Herts, 27 Feb. 1945; Kathleen Green, 21 June 1944, IWM, 93/48/1–2.

30. Mrs R. Simmonds, 14 Dec. 1944, IWM, 93/48/1–2.

31. J. W. Starmonby, 23 May 1944, IWM, 93/48/1–2.

32. Henry Devlin, 20 June 1944; Mrs J. Hughes, 3 Feb. 1944; Mrs Goulding, 18 June 1944, IWM, 93/48/1–2.

33. Mrs N. Downs, n.d.; Mrs Rose Glossop, 21 Jan. 1944; Mrs A. Wadham, 8 Apr. 1945, IWM, 93/48/1–2.

34. Mrs J. Baker, n.d., late May 1944, IWM, 93/48/1–2.

35. J. Spencer, 13 May 1944; Mrs J. Watson, 29 June 1944, IWM, 93/48/1–2.

36. Mrs Dorothy Masters, 22 June 1944, IWM, 93/48/1–2.

37. Beatrice Brandwood, 19 June 1944; Violet Grant-Smart, 23 May 1944; Ruth Davis, 12 Feb. 1945, IWM, 93/48/1–2.

38. Mrs Rose Glossop, 21 Jan. 1944; Mrs C. Bolt, Apr. 1944, IWM, 93/48/1–2.

39. Ethel N. Hosgood, 5 Jan. 1945; L. Nathanson, 19 June 1944, IWM, 93/48/1–2.

40. Mr and Mrs Maddocks, 16 Jan., 3 Feb. 1945, IWM, 93/48/1–2.

41. Stephen J. Knight, 23, 29 May 1944, IWM, 93/48/1–2.

42. J. Spencer, 13 May 1944; G. Matthews, 13 May 1944; Gertrude Young, 12 May 1944, IWM, 93/48/1–2.

43. Nichol and Rennell, *Tail-End Charlies*, 282–3.

44. H. S. Clifford, 23 Nov. 1944; Mrs B. Baldwin, 24 May 1944, IWM, 93/48/1–2.

45. Eleven-page typescript memoir by Flt Lt C. Mitchell, IWM Misc. 215 (3115), 1994.

46. Ibid.

47. Eleven-page typescript memoir by Flt Lt C. Mitchell, IWM Misc. 215 (3115).
48. Nichol and Rennell, *Tail-End Charlies*, 405.


CHAPTER 8

1. T. W. Pitfield, IWM 96/19/1.
2. Geoffrey Bickersteth to brother Monier, 1 Mar. 1945; G. Bickersteth to mother Ella, 31 Dec. 1944, Bickersteth Papers, MS Eng. E. 3150, Bodleian.
3. Letter to G. H. Martin from Peggy M. Ryle, 6 May 1944 G. H. Martin, IWM, 93/48/1–2.
4. Judy Lockhart, n.d.; G. H. Martin, IWM, 93/48/1–2.
5. Peggy Ryle, *Missing in Action, May–September 1944* (W. H. Allen, London, 1979), 166 pp. See also IWM 79/2400.
6. Ibid., 9 May 1944.
7. Ibid., 9–19 May 1944.
8. Ibid.
9. Ibid., 10 May–1 June 1944.
10. Ibid., 14–20 May 1944.
11. Ibid., 20 May–1 June 1944.
12. Ibid., 4–16 June 1944.
13. Ibid., 17 June–1 July 1944.
14. Ibid., 7–14 July 1944.
15. Ibid., 14–27 July 1944.
16. Ibid., 30 July–28 Aug. 1944.
17. Ibid., 3–7 Sept. 1945.
18. Ibid., 7–27 Sept. 1945.
19. Geoffrey Bickersteth to mother Ella, 4 Feb. 1945, Bickersteth Papers, MS Eng. E. 3150, Bodleian.
20. Ibid., 14 Jan., 4 and 11 Feb 1945.
21. Ibid., 14 Jan., 4 and 25 Feb., 18 Mar., 13 May 1945.
22. Geoffrey Bickersteth to brother Monier, 1 Mar. 1945, ibid.
23. Geoffrey Bickersteth to Ella, 31 Dec. 1944, ibid.
24. John Keegan, *The Second World War* (Pimlico, London, 1997), 429.
25. Geoffrey Bickersteth to Ella, 10 and 14 Jan. 1945, ibid.
26. Ibid., 10 and 14 Jan 1945.
27. Ibid., 4, 11 and 18 Feb. 1945; Geoffrey Bickersteth to brother Monier, 1 Mar. 1945, MS Eng. E. 3183, Bodleian.
28. Geoffrey Bickersteth to Ella, 4 Feb., 11 Mar. 1945, MS Eng. E. 3150, Bodleian.
29. Ibid., Easter Day 1945, 15 and 22 Apr. 1945.
30. Ibid., 13 May 1945.
31. John Bickersteth to Ella, 5 Feb. 1945, BICK 2/6, CCC.
32. Telegram, 22 Aug. 1945, Bickersteth Diaries, BICK 2/6, CCC; Geoffrey Bickersteth to Ella, 30 Dec. 1945, MS Eng. E. 3150, Bodleian.

33. Burgon Bickersteth to Ella Bickersteth, 14 Jan. 1945, MS Eng. C 6414, Bodleian.

34. Geoffrey Bickersteth to Ella, 12 Mar. 1946, Bickersteth Diaries, BICK 2/6, CCC.

35. Geoffrey Bickersteth to Lady Milner, 9 Sept. 1948, VM box 33, Violet Milner papers, Bodleian.

36. Gary Sheffield, *Forgotten Victory: The First World War, Myths and Realities* (Review, London, 2002), 274–6.

37. John Ellis, 'Reflections on the "Sharp End" of War', in Paul Addison and Angus Calder (eds.), *Time to Kill: The Soldier's Experience of War in the West 1939–1945* (Pimlico, London, 1997), 12–18. See also Ellis, *World War II: The Sharp End* (Windrow & Greene, London, 1990).

38. J. S. Lucas, IWM PP/MCR/57.

39. Ibid.

40. George MacDonald Fraser, *Quartered Safe Out Here: A Recollection of the War in Burma* (Harper Collins, London, 1993), 76–90.

41. Ibid.

42. Ibid.

43. Ibid.

CHAPTER 9

1. Jay Winter, *Sites of Memory, Sites of Mourning: The Great War in European Cultural History* (CUP, Cambridge, 1995), 8, 9, 203, 228.

2. Tony Walter, *On Bereavement: The Culture of Grief* (Open University Press, Buckingham, 1999), 142; Ruth Richardson, 'Old People's Attitudes to Death in the Twentieth Century', *Society for the Social History of Medicine Bulletin*, 34 (1984), 48–51.

3. *Guardian*, 28 Apr. 1944, 4 Apr., 5 Sept., 5 Oct. 1945.

4. For useful accounts see e.g. Joanna Bourke, *The Second World War: A People's History* (OUP, Oxford, 2001), 175–89; R. A. C. Parker, *The Second World War: A Short History* (OUP, Oxford, 1989), 233–42.

5. Bertrand Russell, 'The Bomb and Civilisation', a hypertextual draft edition of a paper from the Russell Editorial Project, vol. xxii, McMaster University, available from <http://Russell.mcmaster.ca/brbomb.htm>.

6. Samuel Brittan, *Spectator*, 14 Apr. 2001.

7. Russell–Einstein Manifesto, July 1955.

8. Adrian Gregory, *The Silence of Memory: Armistice Day 1919–1946* (Berg, Oxford, 1994), 222.

9. Richard Hoggart, *New Society*, 29 Apr. 1965.

10. A. Alvarez, *The Savage God: A Study in Suicide* (Weidenfeld & Nicolson, London, 1971), 199–203.

11. Anne Hardy, *Health and Medicine in Britain Since 1860* (Palgrave, Basingstoke, 2001), 139 ff.; Roy Porter, *The Greatest Benefit to Mankind: A Medical History of Humanity from Antiquity to the Present* (Harper Collins, London, 1997), 458–60, 595.

12. Norbert Elias, *The Loneliness of the Dying* (Blackwell, Oxford, 1982).

13. Philippe Ariès, *The Hour of Our Death* (Penguin, London, 1981), 559–60, 570.

14. Peter Marris, *Widows and Their Families* (Routledge and Kegan Paul, London, 1958).

15. Philip Toynbee, Review of Geoffrey Gorer, 'Death, Grief and Mourning in Contemporary Britain', *Observer*, 'Weekend Review', 2 May 1965.

16. John Hinton, *Dying* (Penguin, Harmondsworth, 1967), 13–14.

17. Beverley Raphael, *Anatomy of Bereavement* (Unwin Hyman, London, 1984).

18. Ian Grant, 'Care of the Dying', *British Medical Journal* (28 Dec. 1957), 1539.

19. Virginia Berridge, *Health and Society in Britain Since 1939* (CUP, Cambridge, 1999), 27.

20. David Clark, 'Originating a Movement: Cicely Saunders and the Development of St Christopher's Hospice, 1957–1967', *Mortality*, 3/1 (1998), 43–63.

21. H. L. Glyn Hughes, *Peace at the Last*, report to the Calouste Gulbenkian Foundation (London, 1960).

22. Richard Lamerton, *Care of the Dying* (Penguin, London, 1980), 13, 93.

23. Clark, 'Originating a Movement', 45.

24. Hughes, *Peace at the Last*, *passim*.

25. Hinton, *Dying*; Lamerton, *Care of the Dying*.

26. 'Report on a National Survey Concerning Patients with Cancer Nursed at Home', Marie Curie Memorial Foundation, 1952.

27. Lamerton, *Care of the Dying*, 10–11.

28. Hinton, *Dying*, 157–8.

29. 'Care of the Dying', *BMJ* (6 Jan. 1973), 29–30.

30. Hinton, *Dying*, 158–61, quoting J. H. Sheldon.

31. Peter Townsend, *The Last Refuge: A Survey of Residential Institutions and Homes for the Aged in England and Wales* (Routledge and Kegan Paul, London, 1962), 415–18.

32. Ibid., 4–5, 95–6.

33. Ibid., 95–6.

34. Ibid., 115, 147–8, 433–4.

35. Ibid.

36. Hughes, *Peace at the Last*, 60, 24–8.

37. Ibid.

38. Hinton, *Dying*, 150–3; Hinton, 'The Physical and Mental Distress of the Dying', *Quarterly Journal of Medicine*, NS 32 (1954), 1–20; A. N. Exton-Smith, *Lancet* (5 Aug. 1961).

39. Lamerton, *Care of the Dying*, 16.

40. Winifred Wooster to Geoffrey Gorer, n.d. [1965], Gorer papers, GM6 file 1/A, University of Sussex.

41. Elisabeth Kubler-Ross, *On Death and Dying* (Macmillan, New York, 1969).

42. Ibid.; Dennis Klass, 'Elisabeth Kubler-Ross', in Glennys Howarth and Oliver Leaman (eds.,) *Encyclopedia of Death and Dying* (Routledge, London, 2001), 278–9.

43. Tony Walter, 'British Sociology and Death', in David Clark (ed.), *The Sociology of Death* (Blackwell, Oxford, 1993), 277.

44. Clark, 'Originating a Movement', 43–63; Clark, 'Cradled to the Grave? Terminal Care in the United Kingdom, 1948–1967', *Mortality*, 4/3 (1999), 225–47.

45. Cicely Saunders, 'Evolution of Palliative Care', *Journal of the Royal Society of Medicine*, 94 (2001), 430–2; Saunders, 'Into the Valley of the Shadow of Death: A Personal Therapeutic Journey', *British Medical Journal* (1996), 313.

46. Clark, 'Cradled to the Grave?', 237.

47. Saunders, 'Evolution of Palliative Care', 430–2; Saunders, 'Into the Valley of the Shadow of Death', 313; Clark, 'Originating a Movement', 43–63; Clark, 'Cradled to the Grave?', 225–47.

48. Clark, 'Originating a Movement', 43–63; Saunders, 'Into the Valley of the Shadow of Death', 313–17.

49. Ibid.

50. Ian Maddocks, 'Changing Concepts in Palliative Care', *Medical Journal of Australia* (21 May 1990).

51. N. D. A. Kemp, *Merciful Release: The History of the British Euthanasia Movement* (Manchester University Press, Manchester 2002), 83–97.

52. Ibid., 139; Pat Jalland, *Changing Ways of Death in 20th Century Australia* (UNSW Press, Sydney, 2006), 235–57.

53. Kemp, *Merciful Release*, 117–61; Ian Dowbiggin, 'A Prey on Normal People: C. Killock Milliard and the Euthanasia Movement in Great Britain, 1930–1955', *Journal of Contemporary History*, 36/1 (2001), 59–85.

54. Kemp, *Merciful Release*, 174–203.

55. Hinton, *Dying*, 139–48; *Lancet* (12 Aug. 1961).

56. Kemp, *Merciful Release*, 180–222. See also Michael Young and Lesley Cullen, *A Good Death* (Routledge, London, 1996), 128–45.

57. Porter, *The Greatest Benefit to Mankind*, 692, 699. See also Hinton, *Dying*, 140–3.

58. Ivan Illich, *Limits to Medicine: Medical Nemesis, The Expropriation of Health* (Penguin, London, 1972), 210, 106, 110.

59. C. Seale and A. Cartwright, *The Year Before Death* (Aldershot, Avebury, 1994).

60. David Clark, 'Between Hope and Acceptance: The Medicalisation of Dying', *British Medical Journal* (13 Apr. 2002), 324, 905–7.

CHAPTER 10

1. Audrey Deacon (née Hawkins), 'Diary of a WREN, 1940–1945: The Second World War Diaries of Mrs A D Deacon', IWM, 89/17/1.

2. Ibid.

3. Ibid.

4. Ibid.

5. *The World of the Widow*, BBC 1960, Bowlby Papers, PP/BOW/F5/1/box 41, Wellcome Institute.

6. Peter Marris, *Widows and Their Families* (Routledge and Kegan Paul, London, 1958).

7. Colin Murray Parkes, 'Grief as Illness', *New Society* (9 Apr. 1964); Geoffrey Gorer, *Death, Grief and Mourning in Contemporary Britain* (Cresset Press, London, 1965), 118–19.

8. John Bowlby's 'Introduction' to Marris, *Widows and Their Families*.

9. Marris, *Widows and Their Families*, 29–30; Sigmund Freud, 'Mourning and Melancholia', in *On Metapsychology*, ii (Pelican Freud Library, Pelican, London, 1984), 251–67; Gorer, *Death, Grief and Mourning*, app. 1, pp. 118–25.

10. Eric Lindemann, 'Symptomatology and Management of Acute Grief', *American Journal of Psychiatry*, 101 (1944), 141–8.

11. Marris, *Widows and Their Families*, 23–5.

12. Lindsay Prior, 'The Social Distribution of Sentiments', in D. Dickenson et al. (eds.), *Death, Dying and Bereavement* (Open University, Sage, London, 2000), 332–7.

13. Marris, *Widows and Their Families*, 1–5.

14. Ibid., 4–9.

15. Ibid., 10–20, and conclusion.

16. See e.g. Tony Walter, *On Bereavement: The Culture of Grief* (Open University Press, Buckingham, 1999), ch. 9.

17. Marris, *Widows and Their Families*, 11–12.

18. Ibid., 14–16.

19. See e.g. Glennys Howarth, 'Dismantling Boundaries Between Life and Death', *Mortality*, 5/2, (2000), 130–4; Walter, *On Bereavement*, 56–68.

20. Marris, *Widows and Their Families*, 16–17.

21. Ibid., 17–22.

22. Ibid., 42–53.

23. Ibid., 55–67.

24. Ibid., 86–123.

25. Celia Jane Hobson, 'Widows of Blacktown', *New Society* (24 Sept. 1964).

26. Ibid.

27. Ibid.

28. *The World of the Widow*, Interviews with Dr and Mrs Torrie at CRUSE Club, BBC 1960, Bowlby Papers, PP/BOW/F5/1, box 41, Wellcome Institute.

29. Ibid.

30. Ibid.

31. Ibid.; Walter, *On Bereavement*, 196–8.

32. Peter Townsend, *The Family Life of Old People: An Inquiry in East London* (Routledge and Kegan Paul, London, 1957), ch. XIII.

33. Colin Murray Parkes, *Bereavement: Studies of Grief in Adult Life* (Tavistock Press, London, 1972), 102, 125–7, 212–13; Beverley Raphael, *The Anatomy of Bereavement* (Unwin Hyman, London, 1984), 312–18.

34. Beverley E. Schueller, 'Phyllis Bottome', *ODNB* (2004).

35. Condolence letters on Phyllis Bottome's death, 1963, Phyllis Bottome Papers, BL Add MS 78867.

36. Oliver Calder to Ernan Forbes-Dennis, 28 Oct. 1963, and Ernan's reply, 28 Jan. 1964, ibid.

37. Ruth Aspinall to Ernan Forbes-Dennis, 29 Aug., 15 Oct. 1963, 28 Jan. 1964, Phyllis Bottome Papers, BL Add MS 78862.

38. Forbes-Dennis to Aspinall, 28 Jan. 1964, ibid., BL Add MS 78862.

39. Ibid., 20 Jan. 1964, 10 Feb. 1964; and Aspinall's replies, 28 Jan. 1964, BL Add MS 78862.

40. Anne Slemons to Forbes-Dennis, 1 Jan. 1964, and his reply, 21 Jan. 1964, BL Add MS 78867.

41. Forbes-Dennis to Oliver Calder, 28 Jan. 1964; and to Contessa Nora Balzani, 10 Jan. 1964; and to Lady Carden, 16 Jan. 1964; and to Ms Swinhoe-Phelan, 17 Jan. 1964, BL Add MS 78867.

42. Ibid.


CHAPTER 11

1. Raymond Mortimer, 'The Changing Rites of Britain', *Sunday Times* (2 May 1965).

2. Colin Murray Parkes's notes on Geoffrey Gorer's *Death, Grief and Mourning in Contemporary Britain* (1965), Bowlby Papers, PP/BOW/H39, Wellcome Institute.

3. Tony Walter, 'Classics Revisited: A Sociology of Grief', *Mortality*, 3/1 (1998).

4. Jeremy MacLancy, 'Geoffrey Gorer', *ODNB* (2004).

5. Geoffrey Gorer, *Death, Grief and Mourning in Contemporary Britain* (Cresset Press, London, 1965), 8–9; Gorer, 'The Pornography of Death', *Encounter* (Oct. 1955).

6. Gorer, *Death, Grief and Mourning*, 9–11; Margaret Mead to Gorer, 5 May 1961, Geoffrey Gorer Papers, box G91, University of Sussex.

7. Gorer, *Death, Grief and Mourning*, 13–14.

8. Ibid., 14–15.

9. Elizabeth Gorer to Geoffrey Gorer, 16 Nov. 1978, Gorer Papers, box G84.

10. M. Masud R. Khan to Gorer, 20 July 1961, Gorer Papers, box G87; Elizabeth MacKenzie to Gorer, 15 Feb. 1969, Gorer Papers, box G88.

11. Gorer, *Death, Grief and Mourning*, 16–17.

12. H. L. Glyn Hughes, *Peace at the Last*, report to the Calouste Gulbenkian Foundation (London, 1960); Richard Lamerton, *Care of the Dying* (Penguin, London, 1980), 13, 93.

13. Gorer, *Death, Grief and Mourning*, 16–19.

14. Ibid., 20–2.

15. Julie-Marie Strange, *Death, Grief and Poverty in Britain, 1870–1914* (CUP, Cambridge, 2005), 99–105.

16. Gorer, *Death, Grief and Mourning*, 30–5.

17. Ibid., 43–5, 48–9.

18. Ibid., 46–50.

19. Ibid., 46–7.

20. Peter Marris, *Widows and Their Families* (Routledge and Kegan Paul, London, 1958), 33–6.
21. Glennys Howarth, 'Professionalising the Funeral Industry in England 1700–1960', in P. C. Jupp and Glennys Howarth (eds.), *The Changing Face of Death: Historical Accounts of Death and Disposal* (Macmillan, Basingstoke, 1997), 120–34.
22. Gorer, *Death, Grief and Mourning*, 51–2.
23. Ibid., 58–62.
24. Ibid., 72, 76–7, 110–16.
25. Ibid., 114–15; Philip Toynbee, *Observer*, 'Weekend Review', 2 May 1965.
26. Gorer, *Death, Grief and Mourning*, 110–14.
27. Colin Murray Parkes, *Bereavement: Studies of Grief in Adult Life* (2nd edn., Tavistock Press, London, 1986), 124–7, 198; Parkes, 'Grief as Illness', *New Society* (9 Apr. 1964); Parkes, BBC Bereavement lectures, 1976, Bowlby Papers, PP/BOW/F516, Wellcome Institute. See also Margaret S. Stroebe, 'Paving the Way: From Early Attachment Theory to Contemporary Bereavement Research', *Mortality*, 7/2 (2002).
28. Gorer, *Death, Grief and Mourning*, 91–9.
29. Ibid., 69–71.
30. Ibid.
31. Ibid., 81–3.
32. Mary Zobel to Gorer, 16 Nov. 1964; Muriel Skeet to editor, *Sunday Times*, 16 Nov. 1964, Gorer Papers, GM6, 1/A.
33. Lady Addison, 'Looking Glass Land', BL Add MS 71686; Kenneth O. Morgan, 'Christopher Addison, Viscount', *ODNB* (2004); Kenneth O. and Janet Morgan, *Portrait of a Progressive* (Clarendon Press, Oxford, 1980).
34. 'Funeral of Viscount Addison', notes by Lady Addison, MS Addison, dep. C.249, Bodleian; Diaries of Lady Addison 1938–58, BL Add MS 71680.
35. Diaries of Lady Addison 1938–58, BL Add MS 71680–71681.
36. Ibid., BL Add MS 71681.
37. Ibid.
38. Ibid., BL Add MS 71681–2.
39. Ibid.
40. Ibid., BL Add MS 71683–5.
41. Parkes, 'Grief as Illness'; Ruth Malkinson and Eliezer Witztum, *Encyclopedia of Death* (Routledge, London, 2001), 219–20.
42. Richard Hoggart, *New Society* (29 Apr. 1965).
43. C. S. Lewis, *A Grief Observed* (Faber & Faber, London, 1964).

CHAPTER 12

1. Geoffrey Gorer, *Death, Grief and Mourning in Contemporary Britain* (Cresset Press, London, 1965), app., 131.
2. Philip Toynbee, 'The Great Unmentionable', *Observer* (2 May 1965).

3. Harold Orlans, 'Some Attitudes Towards Death', *Diogenes*, 19 (1957), 73–91.

4. Hugh Auden to Geoffrey Gorer, Gorer Papers, GM6, 1 Aug 1965.

5. A. N. Wilson, *C. S. Lewis, A Biography* (Harper Perennial, London, 2005), 286.

6. Adrian Hastings, *A History of English Christianity 1920–2000* (SCM Press, London, 2001), 388, 444–7, 493–5; Wilson, *C. S. Lewis*, 166, 181, 215, 218.

7. Paul Ford (ed.), *Yours Jack: The Inspirational Letters of C. S. Lewis* (Harper Collins, London, 2008), 228.

8. Wilson, *C. S. Lewis*, pp. xi, *passim*.

9. Ibid., 133.

10. Ibid., 249–77.

11. Lewis to Dorothy L. Sayers and Sister Penelope, June 1957, in Ford (ed.), *Yours Jack*, 303–5.

12. Lewis to Revd Peter Bide and Arthur Greeves, 14 July, 30 Aug. 1960, in Ford (ed.), *Yours Jack*, 331, 333.

13. Wilson, *C. S. Lewis*, 283.

14. C. S. Lewis, *A Grief Observed* (Faber & Faber, London, 1964), 47: Ford (ed.), *Yours Jack*, 282, 334–5.

15. Lewis, *A Grief Observed*, 7–11.

16. Ibid., 11–13.

17. Ibid., 11–12, 14–18.

18. Ibid., 11, 21–3; Lewis to Phyllis Sandeman, 31 Dec. 1953, in Ford (ed.), *Yours Jack*, 228.

19. Lewis, *A Grief Observed*, 23–7.

20. Ibid., 30–3.

21. Ibid., 37–8, 41–2.

22. Ibid., 37–9, 46.

23. Ibid., 48.

24. Ibid.

25. Ibid., 49–60.

26. C. S. Lewis to Edward T. Dell, 5 Mar. 1961, MS Eng. Lett. C. 220/4, fols 95–6, Bodleian.

27. Lewis to Mary Willis Shelburne, 1963, in Ford (ed.), *Yours Jack*, 365, 368–70, 373.

28. Ford (ed.), *Yours Jack*, 345–6, 112, 162, 254, 296.

29. Baron Hailsham of St Marylebone, 'Perspective for Living', BL H835/020: 39'40".

30. Colin Murray Parkes, *Bereavement: Studies of Grief in Adult Life* (Tavistock Press, London, 1972; 2nd edn., 1986); BBC Bereavement lectures, 1976, Bowlby Papers, PP/BOW/F5/6, Wellcome Institute.

31. Margaret S. Stroebe, 'Classics Revisited, Testament of Grief: C. M. Parkes, "Bereavement: Studies of Grief in Adult Life"', *Mortality*, 2/2 (1997), 163–6.

32. Margaret S. Stroebe, 'Paving the Way: From Early Attachment Theory to Contemporary Bereavement Research', *Mortality*, 7/2 (2002); 'Classics Revisited: C. M. Parkes'.

33. Parkes, *Bereavement*, London, 223–5.

34. BBC *Horizon* Programme on bereavement, Sept. 1976, Bowlby Papers, PP/ BOW/F 516, Wellcome Institute. See also Parkes, *Bereavement* (1972).

35. Ibid.

36. Ibid.

37. Ibid.

38. Elisabeth Kubler-Ross, *On Death and Dying* (Macmillan, New York, 1969).

39. C. M. Parkes, 'Bereavement', *Mortality* (2003), 1.

40. Margaret Stroebe and Henk Schut, 'The Dual Process Model of Coping with Bereavement', *Death Studies*, 23 (1994), 197–224.

41. BBC Bereavement lectures 1976, Bowlby Papers, PP/BOW/F5/6, Wellcome Institute.

42. Parkes, *Bereavement* (2nd edn. 1986), 18; Jane Littlewood, *Aspects of Grief: Bereavement in Adult Life* (Tavistock/Routledge, London, 1992), 37.

43. Clive Seale, *Constructing Death: The Sociology of Dying and Bereavement* (CUP, Cambridge, 1998), esp. 62.

### EPILOGUE: CHANGE AND CONTINUITY SINCE THE 1970S

1. Clive Seale, 'Demographic Change and the Experience of Dying', in D. Dickenson et al. (eds.), *Death, Dying and Bereavement* (Open University, Sage, London, 2000), 35–43.

2. Michael Young and Lesley Cullen, *A Good Death* (Routledge, London, 1996), 1–6, 10, 19, 63, 70, 97–127.

3. Christina R. Victor, 'Health Policy and Services for Dying People and Their Carers', in Dickenson et al. (eds.), *Death, Dying and Bereavement*, 45, 48–9.

4. Young and Cullen, *A Good Death*, 63, 85–95.

5. Peter Townsend, *The Last Refuge: A Survey of Residential Institutions and Homes for the Aged in England and Wales* (Routledge and Kegan Paul, London, 1962), esp. 95–6, 147–8, 415–18.

6. David Field and Julia Addington-Hall, 'Extending Specialist Palliative Care to All?', in Dickenson et al. (eds.), *Death, Dying and Bereavement*, 91–106.

7. R. Clough, *Old Age Homes* (Allen and Unwin, London, 1981).

8. M. Sidell, J. Samson Katz, and C. Komaromy, 'The Case for Palliative Care in Residential and Nursing Homes', in Dickenson et al. (eds.), *Death, Dying and Bereavement*, 107–21.

9. Allan Kellehear, *A Social History of Dying* (CUP, Cambridge, 2007), 207–11.

10. Jennifer Hockey, *Experiences of Death: An Anthropological Account* (Edinburgh University Press, Edinburgh, 1990), 81–106.

11. Callum Brown, *The Death of Christian Britain: Understanding Secularisation 1800–2000* (Routledge, London, 2001), 1–11, 172–80.

12. Bernice Martin, *The Sociology of Contemporary Cultural Change* (Blackwell, Oxford, 1981), chs. 1, 9, 10.

13. Tony Walter, *On Bereavement: The Culture of Grief* (Open University Press, Buckingham, 1999), 168–204.

14. Interview with Val Hazel, 1991, *Perspective for Living*, H913/04 2:32'12", BL.

15. Tony Walter, Jane Littlewood, and Michael Pickering, 'Death in the News: The Public Invigilation of Private Emotion', *Sociology*, 29/4 (Nov. 1995), 591.

16. Paul C. Rosenblatt, 'Grief: The Social Context of Private Feelings', in M. Stroebe, W. Stroebe, and R. O. Hansson (eds.), *Handbook of Bereavement: Theory, Research and Interventions* (CUP, Cambridge 1993), 102–11.

17. Margaret Stroebe and Henk Schut, 'The Dual Process Model of Coping with Bereavement', *Death Studies*, 23 (1999), 197–224.

18. Adrian Hastings, *A History of English Christianity, 1920–2000* (SCM Press, London, 2001), pp. xv–lxi; John Wolffe, 'Religion and "Secularization"', in Paul Johnson (ed.), *Twentieth Century Britain* (Longman, Harlow, 1994), 427–30.

19. See Bruce Rumbold, 'Pastoral Care of the Dying and Bereaved', in Allan Kellehear (ed.), *Death and Dying in Australia* (OUP, Melbourne, 2000), 284–97.

20. Interview with Clare Short, *Perspective for Living*, H892/020: 37'27", BL.

21. Tony Walter, 'Death in the New Age', *Religion*, 23 (1993), 127–45.

22. Wolffe, 'Religion and "Secularization"', 427–30, 439.

23. Young and Cullen, *A Good Death*, 163–74.

24. W. Dewi Rees, 'The Hallucinations of Widowhood', *British Medical Journal*, 4 (1971), 37–41; Dewi Rees, *Death and Bereavement* (Whurr, London, 1997), 183–204.

25. Glennys Howarth, 'Dismantling Boundaries Between Life and Death', *Mortality*, 5/2 (2000), 130–4; Walter, *On Bereavement*, 56–68.

26. John McManners, *Death and the Enlightenment* (OUP, Oxford, 1981), 167–72; Martha Garland, 'Victorian Unbelief and Bereavement', in Ralph Houlbrooke (ed.), *Death, Ritual and Bereavement* (Routledge, London, 1989), 151–70.

27. Clare Short, *Perspective for Living*, H892/020 37'27", BL.

28. Young and Cullen, *A Good Death*, 160–1, 183, 190.

29. Ibid., 184–5, 188–9.

30. Bernard Smale, 'The Social Construction of Funerals in Britain', in Kathy Charmaz, Glennys Howarth, and Allen Kellehear (eds.), *The Unknown Country: Death in Australia, Britain and the USA* (Macmillan, Basingstoke, 1997), 113–26. See also Young and Cullen, *A Good Death*, 226–7.

31. Order of ceremony for the funeral of Dr Cyril Bibby, 26 June 1987, Bibby Papers, Cambridge University Library.

32. Interview with Kenneth West, 1998, *Millenium Memory Bank*, C900/02569 C1, BL.

33. Andrew Clayden and Katie Dixon, 'Woodland Burial: Memorial Arboretum Versus Natural Native Woodland?', *Mortality*, 12/3 (Aug. 2007), 239–58.

34. Glennys Howarth, 'Flowers', in Howarth and Oliver Leaman (eds.), *Encyclopedia of Death and Dying* (Routledge, London, 2001), 194–6.

35. Ken Inglis, *Sacred Places: War Memorials in the Australian landscape* (Melbourne University Press, Melbourne, 2008), 539.
36. *Independent*, 16 Sept. 2005.
37. BBC Tyne, 'Roadside Memorials: A Good Way to Remember or a Danger to Traffic?', updated 28 Mar. 2006, accessed 20 July 2009, available from <http://www.bbc.uk/tyne/content/articles/2006/02/23/roadside memorials>.
38. Tracey Potts, 'Crying the Wrong Tears: Floral Tributes and Aesthetic Judgement', Nottinghan Modern Languages Publications Archive, 2007, accessed 30 Mar. 2010, available from <http://mlpa.nottingham.ac.uk/archive/00000072>; Jack Santino, 'Performative Commemoratives', in Santino (ed.), *Spontaneous Shrines and the Public Memorialization of Death* (Palgrave Macmillan, Basingstoke, 2006), 1–15.
39. Potts, 'Crying the Wrong Tears'.
40. Rose George, 'An Unpublished Essay about Death', Rose George Blog Archive, accessed 20 July 2009, available from <http://rosegeorge.com/site/an-unpublished-essay-about-death>.
41. Ibid.

# Select Bibliography

## ABBREVIATIONS

CUP     Cambridge University Press
IWM    Imperial War Museum, London
*ODNB*  *Oxford Dictionary of National Biography*
OUP    Oxford University Press

## ARCHIVAL AND UNPUBLISHED SOURCES

### Family and Personal Papers

Addison, Bodleian Library, Oxford, and British Library
Bibby, Cambridge University Library
Bickersteth, family papers, Bodleian Library
Bickersteth diaries, Churchill College, Cambridge
Bottome, Phyllis, British Library
Bowlby, Wellcome Institute
Cockerell, British Library
Feilding of Newnham Paddox, correspondence, Warwick Record Office
Gorer, Geoffrey, University of Sussex Library, Brighton
Hailsham, British Library
Lewis, C. S., Bodleian Library
Milner [Alfred Lord Milner], Bodleian Library
Milner [Violet Cecil/Milner], Bodleian Library
Strachey, British Library

### Imperial War Museum Sources

Allan, Miss M E, IWM con shelf 95/8/7.
Bloor, W H, IWM 99/22/1.
Boorer, H G, IWM con shelf.
Brown, J K, IWM 94/46/1.
Clarke, W, IWM 87/18/1.
Clayden, Pte A, IWM 92/3/1.
Deacon, Audrey (nee Hawkins), 'Diary of a WREN, 1940–1945: The Second World War Diaries of Mrs A D Deacon', IWM 89/17/1.
Dixon, Lieut. R G, 'The Wheels of Darkness', TS memoir, 1970s, IWM 92/36/1.

Heywood, H C L, IWM 91/10/1.
Holbrook, Mrs B M, IWM 95/27/1.
Hudson, W, IWM 98/10/1.
Leland, Capt. H J C, IWM 96/51/1.
Lucas, J S, IWM PP/MCR/57.
Martin, G H, IWM 93/48/1–2.
Mitchell, Fl Lieut. C, IWM Misc 215(3115), 1994.
Noble, Olive J, 'A Winged Interlude: A WAAF of the Second World War Tells
    All', IWM, 91/4/1.
Peat, R, IWM 97/40/1.
Pitfield, T W, IWM 96/19/1.
Ryle, Peggy, IWM 79/2400.
Scott, M A, IWM 74/93/1.
Whyte, J, IWM 85/22/1.
Woodroffe, N L, IWM 95/31/1.

### NEWSPAPERS, PERIODICALS, AND JOURNALS

*Barnsley Chronicle*; *British Medical Journal*; *Death Studies*; *Journal of Contemporary
History*; *Lancet*; *Manchester Guardian*; *Mortality*; *New Society*; *Observer*; *Social
History of Medicine*; *Spectator*; *Sunday Times*; *The Times*; *Twentieth Century British
History*; *Whitehaven News*

### ORAL SOURCES

Gammond, Jonathan, Wrexham Museum, 'The Real Price of Coal', BBC 2002,
    <http://www.bbc.co.uk/wales/northeast/sites/wrexham/papers/gresford>
Hazel, Val, interview in *Perspective for Living*, H913/04 2:32'12, British Library
Short, Clare, interview in *Perspective for Living*, H892/020. 37'27, British Library
Taylor, Nicholas, *Millenium Memory Bank*, C900/11592 C1, British Library
West, Kenneth, interview in *Millenium Memory Bank*, C900/02569 C1, British
    Library

### SELECTED SECONDARY WORKS

**Books**

Abdy, Jane, and Gere, Charlotte, *The Souls* (Sidgwick & Jackson, London,
    1984).
Alvarez, A., *The Savage God: A Study in Suicide* (Weidenfeld & Nicolson, London,
    1971).
Ariès, Philippe, *The Hour of Our Death* (Penguin, London, 1981).
Asquith, Cynthia, *The Diaries of Lady Cynthia Asquith, 1915–1918* (Century,
    London, 1984).

Bennett, Alan, *Untold Stories* (Faber, London, 2005).

Berridge, Virginia, *Health and Society in Britain Since 1939* (CUP, Cambridge, 1999).

Bickersteth, John (ed.), *The Bickersteth Diaries 1914–1918* (1995; Leo Cooper, Barnsley, 1998).

Bickersteth, Samuel, *Morris Bickersteth, 1891–1916* (CUP, Cambridge, 1931).

Blunt, Wilfrid Scawen, *Sydney Carlyle Cockerell, Friend of Ruskin and William Morris and Director of the Fitzwilliam Museum, Cambridge* (Hamish Hamilton, London, 1954).

Bond, Brian, *The Unquiet Western Front: Britain's Role in Literature and History* (CUP, Cambridge, 2002).

Bourke, Joanna, *An Intimate History of Killing: Face-to-Face Killing in 20th Century Warfare* (Granta, London, 1999).

——*Dismembering the Male: Men's Bodies, Britain and the Great War* (Reaktion, London, 1996).

——*The Second World War: A People's History* (OUP, Oxford, 2001).

Brandon, Ruth, *The Spiritualists: The Passion for the Occult in the 19th and 20th Centuries* (Weidenfeld & Nicolson, London, 1983).

Brown, Callum, *The Death of Christian Britain: Understanding Secularisation 1800–2000* (Routledge, London, 2001).

Calder, Angus, *The Myth of the Blitz* (Pimlico, London, 1991).

——*The People's War: Britain 1939–1945* (Panther, London, 1971).

Carrington, Charles [Charles Edmonds], *A Subaltern's War* (Peter Davies, London, 1929).

Clark, David, *Between Pulpit and Pew: Folk Religion in a North Yorkshire Fishing Village* (CUP, Cambridge, 1982).

Clarke, P. F., *Hope and Glory: Britain 1900–2000* (Penguin, London, 2004).

Connelly, Mark, *The Great War, Memory and Ritual: Commemoration in the City and East London 1916–1939* (Royal Historical Society, Boydell Press, Woodbridge, Suffolk, 2002).

——*We Can Take It! Britain and the Memory of the Second World War* (Pearson, Harlow, 2004).

Cooksey, Jon, *Barnsley Pals* (Leo Cooper, London, 1996).

Corrigan, D. Felicitas, *The Nun, the Infidel and the Superman* (John Murray, London, 1985).

Curl, James Stevens, *The Victorian Celebration of Death* (David and Charles, Newton Abbott, 1972).

Dickenson, Donna, Johnson, Malcolm, and Katz, Jeanne Samson (eds.), *Death, Dying and Bereavement* (Open University, Sage, London, 2000).

Dunn, J. C., *The War the Infantry Knew, 1914–1919* (1938; Abacus, London, 1994).

Elias, Norbert, *The Loneliness of the Dying* (Blackwell, Oxford, 1982).

Ellis, John, *Eye-Deep in Hell: Trench Warfare in World War I* (Johns Hopkins University Press, Baltimore, 1976).

Ellis, John, *World War II: The Sharp End* (Windrowe & Greene, London, 1990).

Faviell, Frances, *A Chelsea Concerto* (Cassell, London, 1959).

Ford, Paul (ed.), *Yours Jack: The Inspirational Letters of C. S. Lewis* (Harper Collins, London, 2008).

Forman, Charles, *Industrial Town* (David and Charles, Newton Abbott, 1978).

Fraser, George MacDonald, *Quartered Safe Out Here: A Recollection of the War in Burma* (Harper Collins, London, 1993).

Fussell, Paul, *The Great War and Modern Memory* (1975; OUP, Oxford, 1977).

Gardiner, Juliet, *Wartime Britain 1939–1945* (Headline, London, 2004).

Garvin, Katharine, *J. L. Garvin: A Memoir* (W. Heinemann, London, 1948).

Gorer, Geoffrey, *Death, Grief and Mourning in Contemporary Britain* (Cresset Press, London, 1965).

Gregory, Adrian, *The Silence of Memory: Armistice Day 1919–1946* (Berg, Oxford, 1994).

Hardy, Anne, *Health and Medicine in Britain Since 1860* (Palgrave, Basingstoke, 2001).

Harris, Jose, *Private Lives, Public Spirit: A Social History of Britain, 1870–1914* (OUP, Oxford, 1993).

Harrison, Tom, *Living Through the Blitz* (Penguin, Harmondsworth, 1979).

Hastings, Adrian, *A History of English Christianity 1920–2000* (SCM Press, London, rev. edn. 2001).

Hazelgrove, J., *Spiritualism and British Society Between the Wars* (Manchester University Press, Manchester, 2000).

Hilton, Boyd, *The Age of Atonement: The Influence of Evangelicalism on Social and Economic Thought, 1795–1865* (OUP, Oxford, 1988).

Hinton, John, *Dying* (Penguin, Harmondsworth, 1967).

Hockey, Jennifer, *Experiences of Death: An Anthropological Account* (Edinburgh University Press, Edinburgh, 1990).

Holt, Tonie and Valmai, *My Boy Jack: The Search for Kipling's Only Son* (Leo Cooper, Barnsley, 1998).

Hughes, H. L. Glyn, *Peace at the Last,* report to the Calouste Gulbenkian Foundation (London, 1960).

Huxley, Leonard, *The Life and Letters of T. H. Huxley* (Macmillan, London, 1900).

Illich, Ivan, *Limits to Medicine: Medical Nemesis, the Expropriation of Health* (Penguin, London, 1972).

Inglis, Ken, *Sacred Places: War Memorials in the Australian Landscape* (Melbourne University Press, Melbourne, 2008).

Jalland, Pat, *Australian Ways of Death: A Social and Cultural History 1840–1918* (OUP, Melbourne, 2002).

—— *Changing Ways of Death in 20th Century Australia* (UNSW Press, Sydney, 2006).

—— *Death in the Victorian Family* (OUP, Oxford, 1996).

Jupp, Peter, *From Dust to Ashes: The Replacement of Burial by Cremation in England 1840–1967* (Congregational Memorial Hall Trust, London, 1990).

——*From Dust to Ashes: Cremation and the British Way of Death* (Palgrave Macmillan, Basingstoke, 2006).

Keegan, John, *The Second World War* (Pimlico, London, 1997).

Kellehear, Allan, *A Social History of Dying* (CUP, Cambridge, 2007).

Kemp, N. D. A., *Merciful Release: The History of the British Euthanasia Movement* (Manchester University Press, Manchester, 2002).

Kenny, Christine, *A Northern Thanatology: A Comprehensive Review of Illness, Death and Dying in the North West of England* (Quay, Denton, 1998).

Kubler-Ross, Elisabeth, *On Death and Dying* (Macmillan, New York, 1969).

Lamerton, Richard, *Care of the Dying* (Penguin, London, 1980).

Lewis, Clive Staples, *A Grief Observed* (Faber & Faber, London, 1964).

Litten, Julian, *The English Way of Death: The Common Funeral Since 1450* (Robert Hale, London, 1991).

Littlewood, Jane, *Aspects of Grief: Bereavement in Adult Life* (Tavistock/Routledge, London, 1992).

Lloyd, David, *Battlefield Tourism: Pilgrimage and the Commemoration of the Great War in Britain, Australia and Canada 1919–1939* (OUP, Oxford, 1998).

Longmate, Norman, *Air Raid: The Bombing of Coventry, 1940* (Hutchinson, London, 1976).

Longworth, Philip, *The Unending Vigil: A History of the Commonwealth War Graves Commission, 1917–1967* (Constable, London, 1967).

MacKenzie, Jeanne, *The Children of the Souls* (Chatto and Windus, London, 1986).

McKeown, Thomas, *The Modern Rise of Population* (Edward Arnold, London, 1976).

McKibbin, Ross, *Classes and Cultures: England 1918–1951* (OUP, Oxford, 2000).

McManners, John, *Death and the Enlightenment* (OUP, Oxford, 1981).

Marris, Peter, *Widows and Their Families* (Routledge and Kegan Paul, London, 1958).

Martin, Bernice, *The Sociology of Contemporary Cultural Change* (Blackwell, Oxford, 1981).

Masterman, Lucy, *C. F. G. Masterman: A Biography* (Nicholson and Watson, London, 1939).

Mitchison, Rosalind, *British Population Change Since 1865* (Macmillan, London, 1997).

Lord Moran, *Anatomy of Courage* (Constable, London, 1945).

Morgan, Kenneth O. and Janet, *Portrait of a Progressive* (Clarendon Press, Oxford, 1980).

Morley, John, *Death, Heaven and the Victorians* (Studio Vista, London, 1971).

Nelson, G. K., *Spiritualism and Society* (Routledge and Kegan Paul, London, 1969).

Nelson, Hank, *Chased by the Sun: Courageous Australians in Bomber Command* (ABC Books, Sydney, 2002).

Newsome, David, *Godliness and Good Learning* (Cassell, London, 1986).

Nichol, John, and Rennell, Tony, *Tail-End Charlies: The Last Battles of the Bomber War 1944–1945* (Viking/Penguin, London, 2004).

Obelkevich, James, *Religion and Rural Society: South Lindsey 1825–1875* (OUP, Oxford, 1976).

Orwell, George, *The Road to Wigan Pier* (Secker and Warburg, London, 1959).

Overy, Richard, *Bomber Command, 1939–1945* (Harper Collins, London, 1997).

—— *A New History of Bomber Command in World War II* (I. B. Taurus, London, 2001).

Parker, Peter, *The Great War and the Public School Ethos* (Constable, London, 1986).

Parker, R. A. C., *The Second World War: A Short History* (OUP, Oxford, 1989).

Parkes, Colin Murray, *Bereavement: Studies of Grief in Adult Life* (Tavistock Press, London, 1972; 2nd edn. 1986; 3rd edn. Routledge, 1996).

Porter, Roy, *The Greatest Benefit to Mankind: A Medical History of Humanity from Antiquity to the Present* (Harper Collins, London, 1997).

Priestley, J. B., *English Journey* (Penguin, London, 1934).

Prior, Robin, and Wilson, Trevor, *The Somme* (UNSW Press, Sydney, 2005).

Raphael, Beverley, *Anatomy of Bereavement* (Unwin Hyman, London, 1984).

—— *When Disaster Strikes: How Individuals and Communities Cope with Catastrophe* (Basic Books, New York, 1986).

Rees, W. Dewi, *Death and Bereavement* (Whurr, London, 1997).

*Report on a National Survey Concerning Patients with Cancer Nursed at Home* (Marie Curie Memorial Foundation, 1952).

Richardson, Ruth, *Death, Dissection and the Destitute* (Routledge and Kegan Paul, London, 1987).

Roberts, Elizabeth, *A Woman's Place: An Oral History of Working Class Women, 1890–1940* (Blackwell, Oxford, 1984).

Rose, Kenneth, *The Later Cecils* (Harper and Row, London, 1975).

Ryle, Peggy, *Missing in Action, May–September 1944* (W. H. Allen, London, 1979).

Seale, Clive, *Constructing Death: The Sociology of Dying and Bereavement* (CUP, Cambridge, 1998).

—— and Cartwright, A., *The Year Before Death* (Aldershot, Avebury, 1994).

Sheffield, Gary, *Forgotten Victory: The First World War, Myths and Realities* (Review, London, 2002).

Stevenson, David, *1914–1918: The History of the First World War* (Penguin, London, 2005).

Stevenson, John, *British Society 1914–1945* (Penguin, London, 1984).

Strange, Julie-Marie, *Death, Grief and Poverty in Britain, 1870–1914* (CUP, Cambridge, 2005).

Townsend, Peter, *The Family Life of Old People: An Inquiry in East London* (Routledge and Kegan Paul, London, 1957).

—— *The Last Refuge: A Survey of Residential Institutions and Homes for the Aged in England and Wales* (Routledge and Kegan Paul, London, 1962).

Tranter, N. L., *British Population in the Twentieth Century* (Macmillan, London, 1996).

Walter, Tony, *On Bereavement: The Culture of Grief* (Open University Press, Buckingham, 1999).

Wearmouth, Robert F., *Pages from a Padre's Diary: A Story of Struggle and Triumph, of Sorrow and Sympathy* (R. F. Wearmouth, North Shields, n.d. [c.1960]).

Wells, Mark K., *Courage and Air Warfare: The Allied Aircrew Experience in the Second World War* (Frank Cass, London, 1995).

Whaley, Joachim (ed.), *Mirrors of Mortality* (Europa, London, 1981).

Whitemore, Hugh, *The Best of Friends* (Amber Lane Press, Oxford, 1988).

Wilkinson, Alan, *The Church of England and the First World War* (SPCK, London, 1978).

Wilson, A. N., *C. S. Lewis: A Biography* (Harper Perennial, London, 2005).

Winter, Denis, *Death's Men: Soldiers of the Great War* (Penguin, London, 1979).

Winter, J. M., *The Great War and the British People* (Macmillan, Basingstoke, 1987).

—— *Sites of Memory, Sites of Mourning: The Great War in European Cultural History* (CUP, Cambridge, 1995).

Wrigley, Edward Anthony and Schofield, Roger S., *The Population History of England, 1541–1871: A Reconstruction* (Edward Arnold, London, 1981).

Young, Michael, and Cullen, Lesley, *A Good Death: Conversations with East Londoners* (Routledge, London, 1996).

Ziegler, Philip, *London at War 1939–1945* (Mandarin, London, 1996).

## Articles, Book Chapters, Essays, and Online

Adams, Sheila, 'A Gendered History of the Social Management of Death in Foleshill, Coventry, During the Interwar Years', *Sociological Review* (1993).

Anderson, Michael, 'British Population History, 1911–1991', in M. Anderson (ed.), *British Population History from the Black Death to the Present Day* (CUP, Cambridge, 1996).

—— 'The Social Implications of Demographic Change', in F. M. L. Thompson (ed.), *The Cambridge Social History of Britain, 1750–1950*, ii (CUP, Cambridge, 1990).

BBC Tyne, 'Roadside Memorials' (Feb. 2006), <http://www.bbc.uk/tyne/content/articles/2006/02/23/roadside memorials>.

Bell, Alan, 'Sir Sydney Carlyle Cockerell', *ODNB* (2004).

Bickersteth, John, 'Julian Bickersteth', 'Burgon Bickersteth', *ODNB* (2004).

Blunt, Wilfrid Scawen, 'Sir Sydney Carlyle Cockerell', *DNB, 1961–1970* (OUP, London, 1981).

Cannadine, David, 'War, Death and Mourning in Modern Britain', in Whaley (ed.), *Mirrors of Mortality*.

Clark, David, 'Between Hope and Acceptance: The Medicalisation of Dying', *British Medical Journal* (13 Apr 2002).

——'Cradled to the Grave? Terminal Care in the United Kingdom, 1948–1967', *Mortality*, 4/3 (1999).

——'Originating a Movement: Cicely Saunders and the Development of St Christopher's Hospice, 1957–1967', *Mortality*, 3/1 (1998).

Clayden, Andrew, and Dixon, Katie, 'Woodland Burial: Memorial Arboretum Versus Natural Native Woodland', *Mortality*, 12/3 (Aug. 2007).

Curl, James Stevens, Review of P. C. Jupp, 'From Dust to Ashes', *Mortality*, 11/4 (Nov. 2006).

Davies, Douglas J., 'The Sacred Crematorium', *Mortality*, 1/1 (Mar. 1996).

Ellis, John, 'Reflections on the "Sharp End" of War', in Paul Addison and Angus Calder (eds.), *Time to Kill: The Soldier's Experience of War in the West 1939–1945* (Pimlico, London, 1997).

Dowbiggin, Ian, 'A Prey on Normal People: C. Killock Milliard and the Euthanasia Movement in Great Britain 1930–1955', *Journal of Contemporary History*, 36/1 (2001).

Field, David, 'Older People's Attitudes Towards Death in England', *Mortality*, 5/3 (2000).

——and Addington-Hall, Julia, 'Extending Specialist Palliative Care to All', in Dickenson et al. (eds.), *Death, Dying and Bereavement* (2008).

Freud, Sigmund, 'Mourning and Melancholia', in *On Metapsychology*, ii (Pelican Freud Library, Penguin, London, 1984).

Garland, Martha, 'Victorian Unbelief and Bereavement', in Ralph Houlbrooke (ed.), *Death, Ritual and Bereavement* (Routledge, London, 1989).

George, Rose, <http://rosegeorge.com/site/an-unpublished-essay-about-death>.

Grainger, Hilary J., 'Golders Green Crematorium and the Architectural Expression of Cremation', *Mortality*, 5/1 (2000).

Grant, Ian, 'Care of the Dying', *British Medical Journal* (28 Dec. 1957).

Gray, Muriel, 'In Memory of Solipsism', *Guardian* (15 Sept. 2005).

Hinton, John, 'The Physical and Mental Distress of the Dying', *Quarterly Journal of Medicine*, NS 32 (1954).

Hobson, Celia Jane, 'Widows of Blacktown', *New Society* (24 Sept. 1964).

Howarth, Glennys, 'Dismantling Boundaries Between Life and Death', *Mortality*, 5/2 (2000).

——'Flowers', in Glennys Howarth and Oliver Leaman (eds.), *Encyclopedia of Death and Dying* (Routledge, London, 2001).

——'Professionalising the Funeral Industry in England, 1700–1960', in P. C. Jupp and Glennys Howarth (eds.), *The Changing Face of Death: Historical Accounts of Death and Disposal* (Macmillan, Basingstoke, 1997).

Jalland, Pat, 'Victorian Death and Its Decline, 1850–1918', in P. C. Jupp and Clare Gittings (eds.), *Death in England: An Illustrated History* (Manchester University Press, Manchester, 1999).

Jupp, Peter, 'Cremation or Burial? Contemporary Choice in City and Village', in David Clark (ed.), *The Sociology of Death* (Blackwell, Oxford, 1993).

—— 'Why Was England the First Country to Popularize Cremation?', in Kathy Charmaz, Glennys Howarth, and Allan Kellehear (eds.), *The Unknown Country: Death in Australia, Britain and the USA* (Macmillan, Basingstoke, 1997).

Klass, Dennis, 'Elisabeth Kubler-Ross', in Glennys Howarth and Oliver Leaman (eds.), *Encyclopedia of Death and Dying* (Routledge, London, 2001).

Lawrence, C. E., 'The Abolition of Death', *Fortnightly Review* (Feb. 1917).

Leaney, J, 'Ashes to Ashes: Cremation and the Celebration of Death in 19th Century Britain', in Ralph Houlbrooke (ed.), *Death, Ritual and Bereavement* (Routledge, London, 1989).

Lindemann, Eric, 'Symptomatology and Management of Acute Grief', *American Journal of Psychiatry*, 101 (1944).

MacLancy, Jeremy, 'Geoffrey Gorer', *ODNB* (2004).

Maddocks, Ian, 'Changing Concepts in Palliative Care', *Medical Journal of Australia* (21 May 1990).

Morgan, Kenneth O., 'Christopher Addison, Viscount', *ODNB* (2004).

Obelkevich, James, 'Religion', in F. M. L. Thompson (ed.), *The Cambridge Social History of Britain, 1750–1950*, iii (CUP, Cambridge, 1990).

Orlans, Harold, 'Some Attitudes Towards Death', *Diogenes*, 19 (1957).

Parkes, Colin Murray, 'Bereavement', *Mortality*, virtual themed issue (2003).

—— 'Grief as Illness', *New Society* (9 Apr. 1964).

Patterson, K. David and Gerald F. Pyle, 'The Geography and Mortality of the 1918 Influenza Pandemic', *Bulletin of the History of Medicine*, 65/1 (Spring 1991).

Potts, Tracey, 'Crying the Wrong Tears: Floral Tributes and Aesthetic Judgement', University of Nottingham, <http://mlpa.nottingham.ac.uk/archive/00000072/01/NMLP_Potts_article_Crying_the_wrong_tears.pdf>.

Prior, Lindsay, 'The Social Distribution of Sentiments', in Dickenson et al., (eds), *Death, Dying and Bereavement*.

Raphael, Beverley, 'Death and the Great Australian Disaster', in Kathy Charmaz, Glennys Howarth, and Allan Kellehear (eds.), *The Unknown Country: Death in Australia, Britain and the USA* (Macmillan, Basingstoke, 1997).

Rees, W. Dewi, 'The Hallucinations of Widowhood', *British Medical Journal*, 4 (1971).

Reid, Alice, 'The Effects of the 1918–1919 Influenza Pandemic on Infant and Child Health in Derbyshire', *Medical History*, 49/1 (Jan. 2005).

Richardson, Ruth, 'Old People's Attitudes to Death in the Twentieth Century', *Society for the Social History of Medicine Bulletin*, 34 (1984).

Roberts, Elizabeth, 'The Lancashire Way of Death', in Ralph Houlbrooke (ed.), *Death, Ritual and Bereavement* (Routledge, London, 1989).

Rose, Kenneth, 'Hugh Cecil', *ODNB* (2004).

Rosenblatt, Paul C., 'Grief: The Social Context of Private Feelings', in M. S. Stroebe, W. Stroebe, and R. O Hansson (eds.), *Handbook of Bereavement: Theory, Research and Intervention* (CUP, Cambridge, 1993).

Rugg, Julie, 'Lawn Cemeteries: The Emergence of a New Landscape of Death', *Urban History*, 33/2, (2006).

—— 'Managing "Civilian Deaths" in World War II', *Twentieth Century British History*, 15/2 (2004).

Rumbold, Bruce, 'Pastoral Care of the Dying and Bereaved', in Allan Kellehear (ed.), *Death and Dying in Australia* (OUP, Melbourne, 2000).

Russell, Bertrand, 'The Bomb and Civilisation', a hypertextual draft edition of a paper from the Russell Editorial Project, vol. xxii, McMaster University, <http://Russell.mcmaster.ca/brbomb.htm>.

Santino, Jack, 'Performative Commemoratives', in Santino (ed.), *Spontaneous Shrines and the Public Memorialization of Death* (Palgrave Macmillan, Basingstoke, 2006).

Saunders, Cicely, 'Evolution of Palliative Care', *Journal of the Royal Society of Medicine*, 94 (2001).

—— 'Into the Valley of the Shadow of Death: A Personal Therapeutic Journey', *British Medical Journal* (1996).

Schueller, Beverley E., 'Phyllis Bottome', *ODNB* (2004).

Seale, Clive, 'Demographic Change and the Experience of Dying', in Dickenson et al. (eds.), *Death, Dying and Bereavement*.

Sidell, M., Katz, J. S., and Komaromy, C., 'The Case for Palliative Care in Residential and Nursing Homes', in Dickenson et al. (eds.), *Death, Dying and Bereavement*.

Smale, Bernard, 'The Social Construction of Funerals in Britain', in Kathy Charmaz, Glennys Howarth, and Allan Kellehear (eds.), *The Unknown Country: Death in Australia, Britain and the USA* (Macmillan, Basingstoke, 1997).

Stroebe, Margaret, 'Classics Revisited. Testament of Grief: C. M. Parkes, "Bereavement: Studies of Grief in Adult Life" ', *Mortality*, 2/2 (1997).

—— 'Paving the Way from Early Attachment Theory to Contemporary Bereavement Research', *Mortality*, 7/2 (2002).

—— and Schut, Henk, 'The Dual Process Model of Coping with Bereavement', *Death Studies*, 23 (1999).

Thompson, Henry, 'Cremation, A Reply to Critics', *Contemporary Review* (23 Mar. 1874).

Tomkins, Sandra M., 'The Failure of Expertise: Public Health Policy in Britain During the 1918–1919 Influenza Epidemic', *Social History of Medicine*, 5 (1992).

Toynbee, Philip, 'The Great Unmentionable', *Observer* (2 May 1965).

Victor, Christina R., 'Health Policy and Services for Dying People and Their Carers', in Dickenson et al. (eds.), *Death, Dying and Bereavement*.

Walter, Tony, 'British Sociology and Death', in David Clark (ed.), *The Sociology of Death* (Blackwell, Oxford, 1993).

——'Classics Revisited: A Sociology of Grief', *Mortality*, 3/1 (1998).

——'Death in the New Age', *Religion*, 23 (1993).

——Littlewood, Jane, and Pickering, Michael, 'Death in the News: The Public Invigilation of Private Emotion', *Sociology*, 29/4 (Nov. 1995).

Winter, J. M., 'Unemployment, Nutrition and Infant Mortality in Britain, 1920–1950', in Winter (ed.), *The Working Class in Modern British History* (CUP, Cambridge, 1983).

Wolffe, John, 'Religion and "Secularization"', in Paul Johnson (ed.), *Twentieth Century Britain* (Longman, Harlow, 1994).

# Index